# Rainbow
# Days

D1057802

2

Story and Art by
**Minami Mizuno**

## CONTENTS



## CHARACTERS

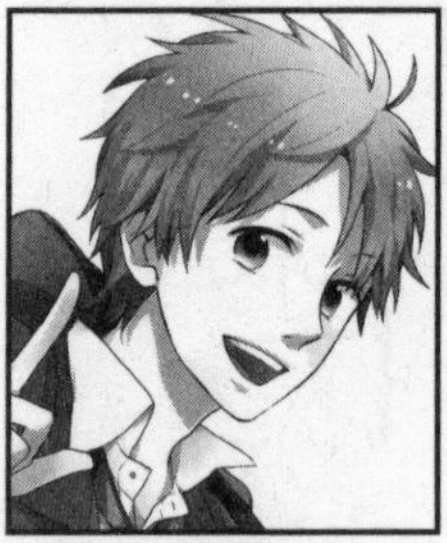

**NATSUKI HASHIBA**

A dreamer with a pure and romantic heart. Nickname: Natchan.

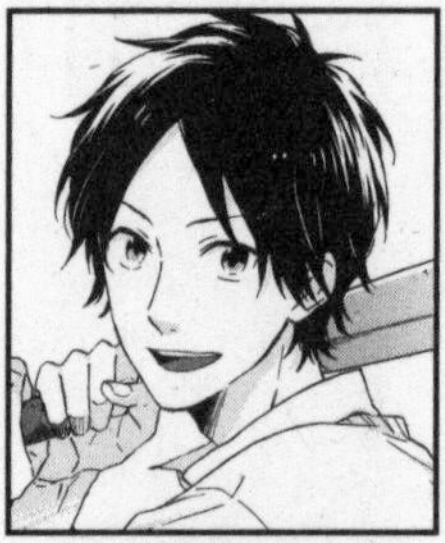

**KEIICHI KATAKURA**

Always smiling, but actually a sadist. Never without his whip. Nickname: Kei-chan.

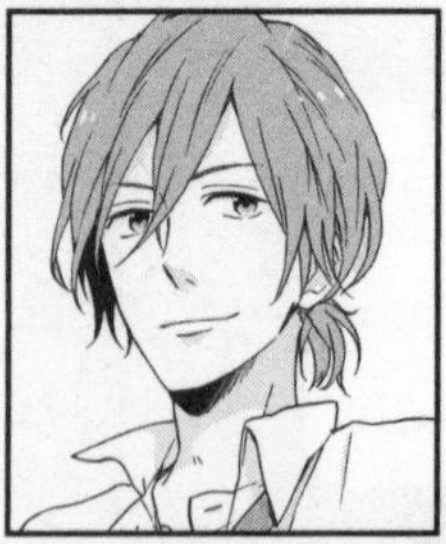

**TOMOYA MATSUNAGA**

A narcissist playboy who loves girls. Tends to involve himself in other people's problems. Nickname: Mattsun.

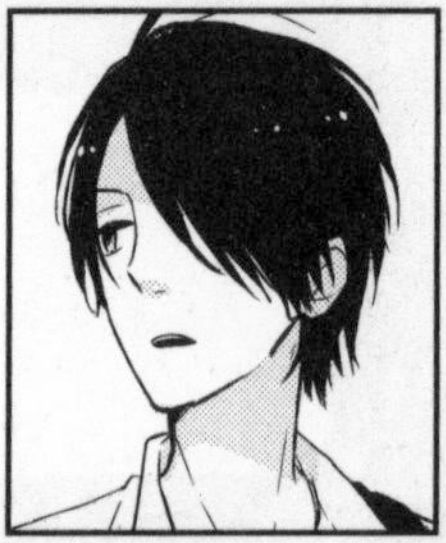

**TSUYOSHI NAOE**

An otaku. Cannot read the room, but gets great grades. Nickname: Tsuyopon.

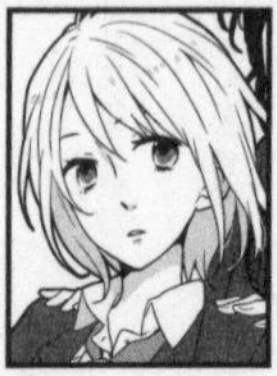

**ANNA KOBAYAKAWA**

The oblivious object of Natsuki's affections. Doesn't talk much. Does things at her own pace.

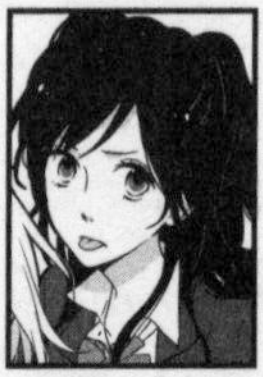

**MARI TSUTSUI**

A beautiful girl besotted with Anna. She and Mattsun loathe each other.

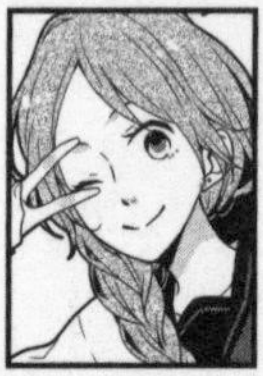

**YUKIKO ASAI**

Tsuyoshi's girlfriend. A cosplayer. Nickname: Yukirin.

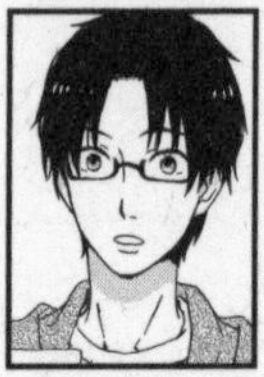

**MR. KATAKURA**

Kei-chan's big brother. Teaches math at their school.

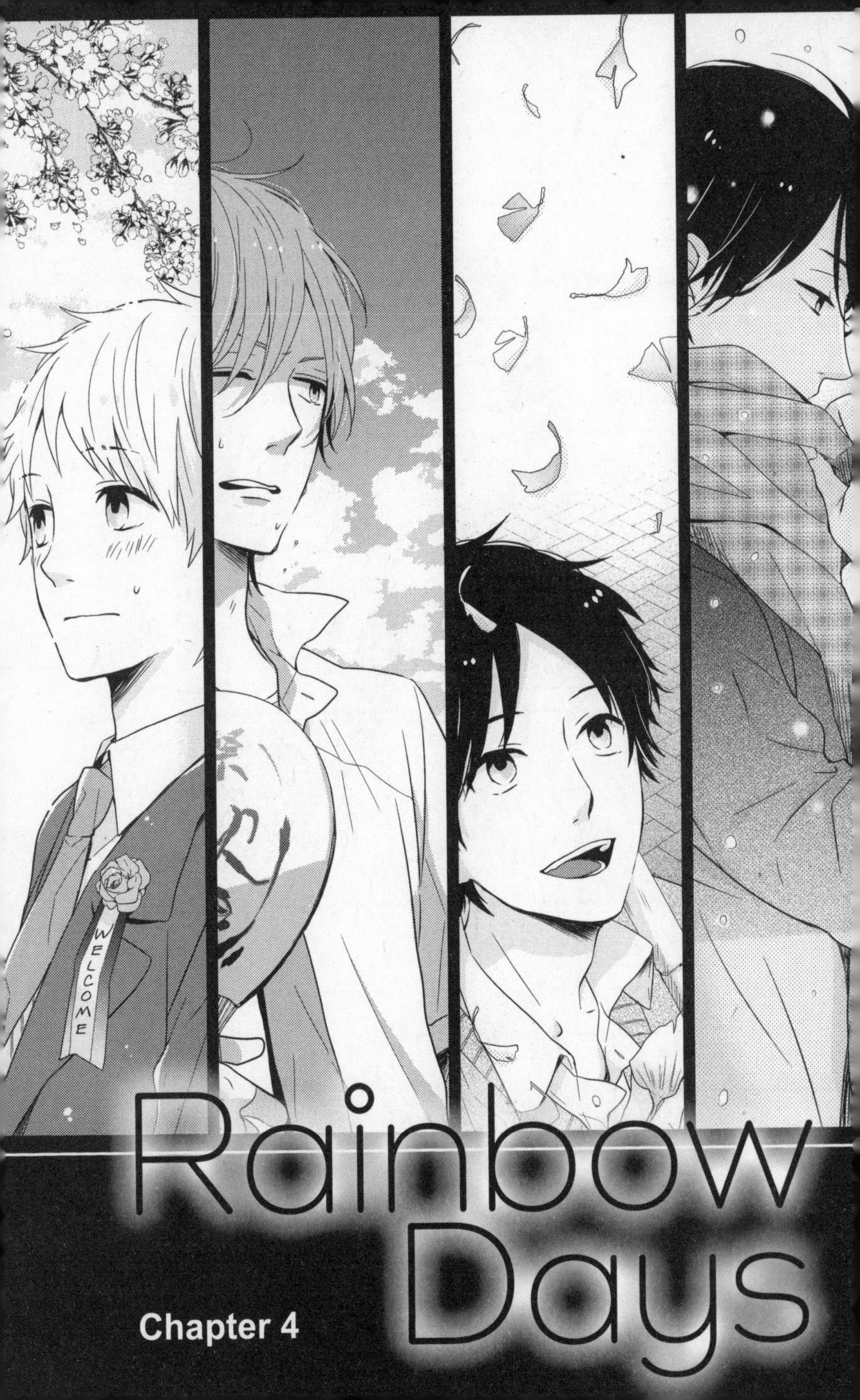
WELCOME
Rainbow Days
Chapter 4

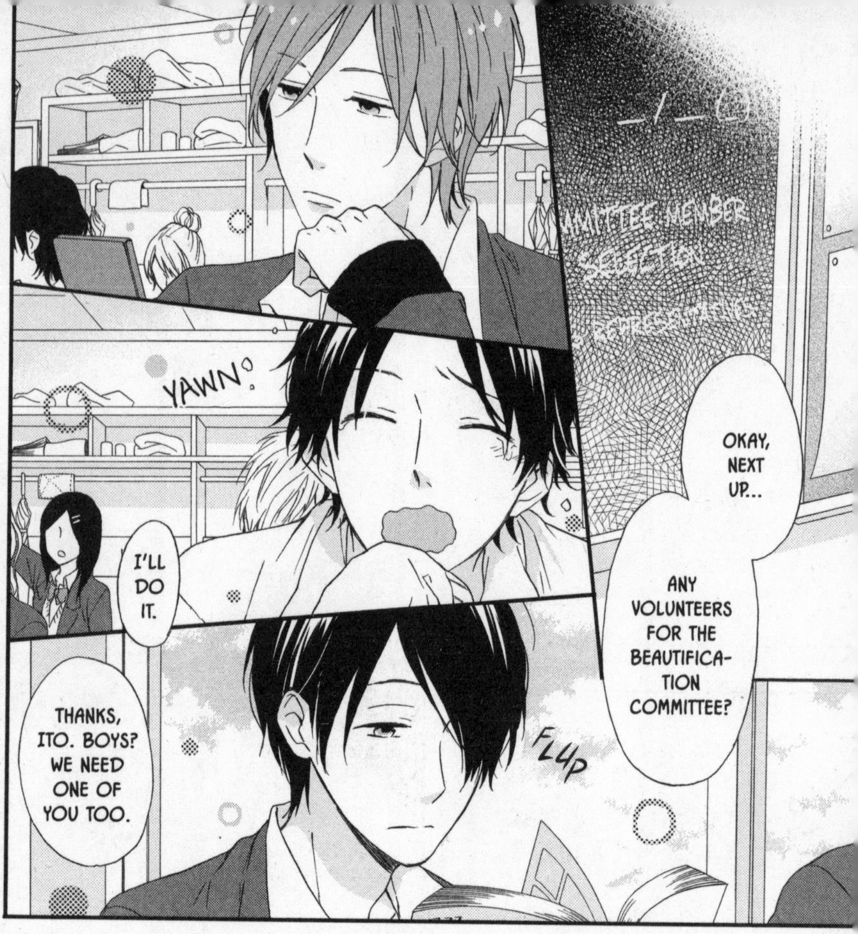
MMITTEE MEMBER
SELECTION
OKAY, NEXT UP...
ANY VOLUNTEERS FOR THE BEAUTIFICA-TION COMMITTEE?
YAWN
I'LL DO IT.
FLUP
THANKS, ITO. BOYS? WE NEED ONE OF YOU TOO.

*Rainbow Days* vol. 2 is underway!

I included a profile for Natchan in this volume, but I'm kind of wondering if there was any demand in the first place...

Should I do the other characters?

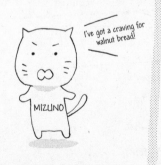

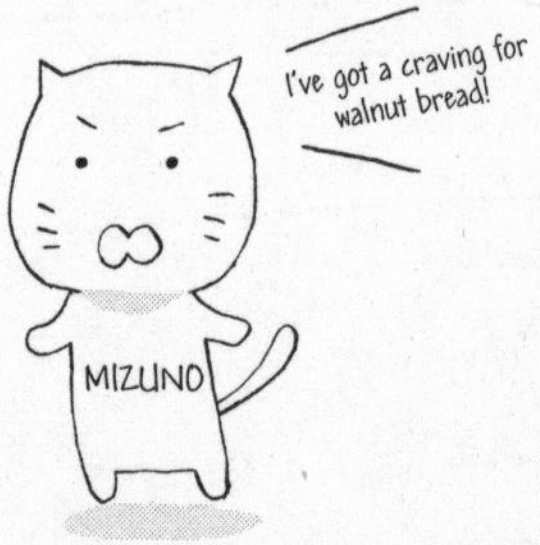
I've got a craving for walnut bread!
MIZUNO

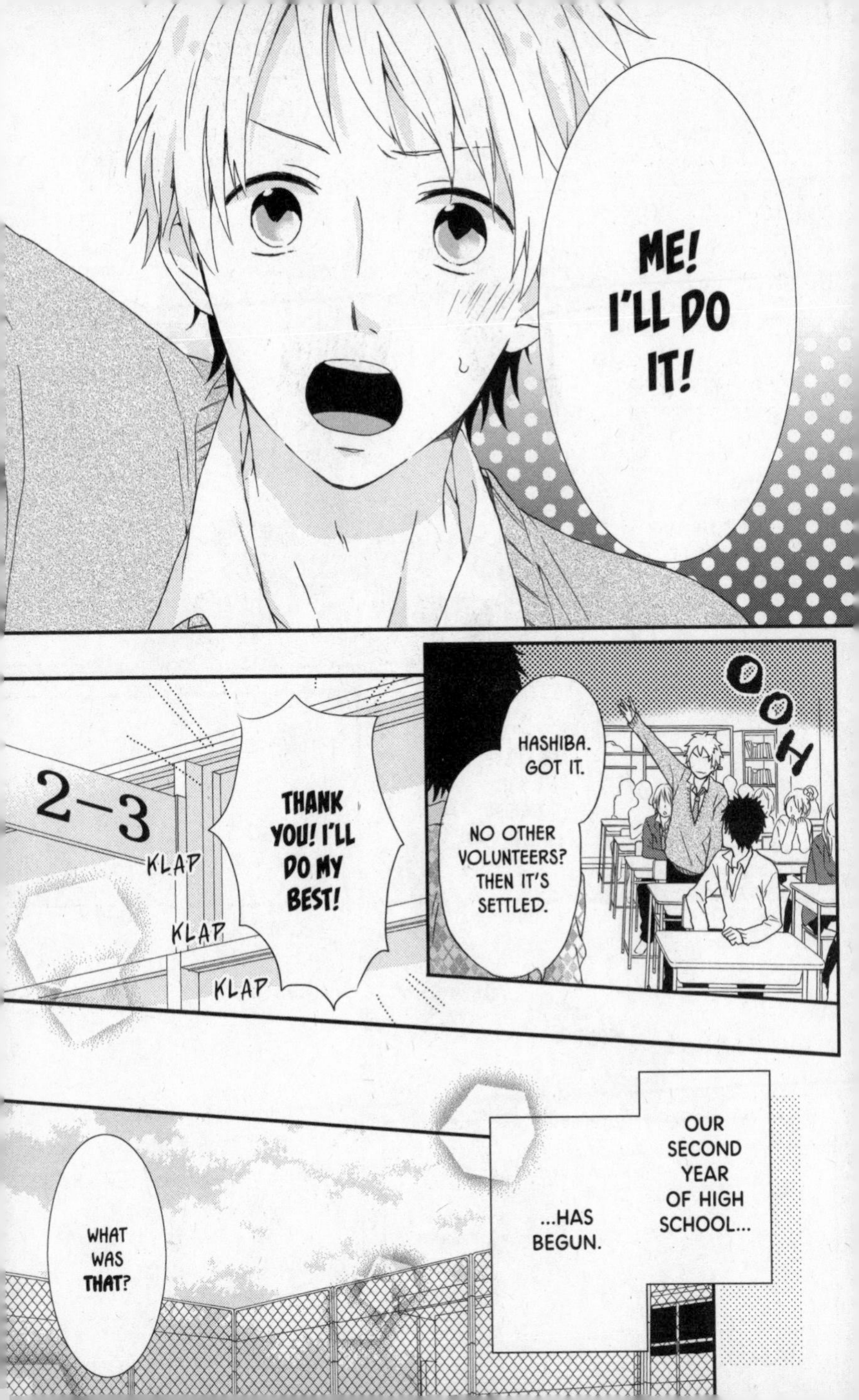
ME! I'LL DO IT!
OOOH
HASHIBA. GOT IT.
NO OTHER VOLUNTEERS? THEN IT'S SETTLED.
2-3
THANK YOU! I'LL DO MY BEST!
KLAP
KLAP
KLAP
OUR SECOND YEAR OF HIGH SCHOOL...
...HAS BEGUN.
WHAT WAS THAT?

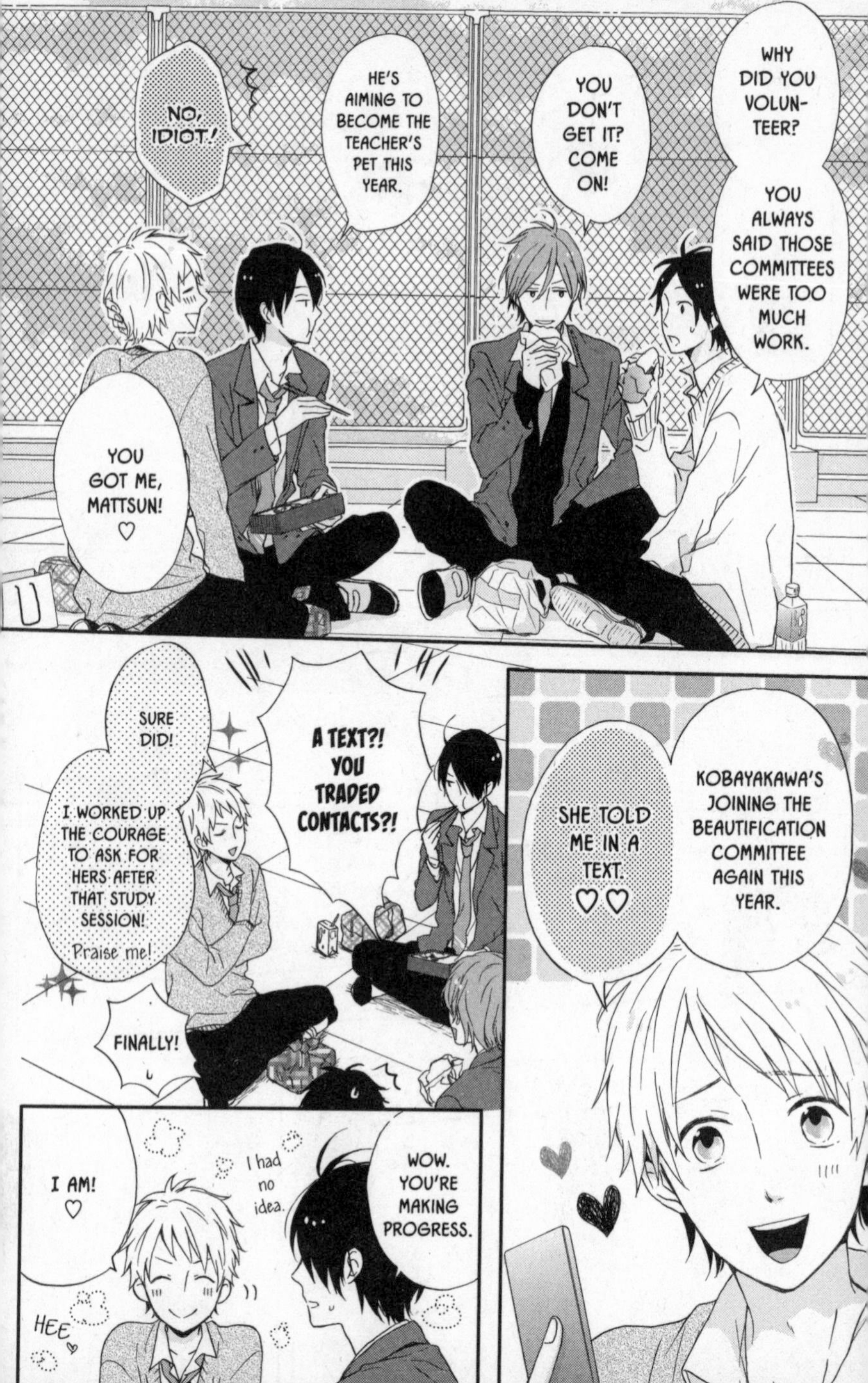
WHY DID YOU VOLUNTEER?
YOU ALWAYS SAID THOSE COMMITTEES WERE TOO MUCH WORK.
YOU DON'T GET IT? COME ON!
HE'S AIMING TO BECOME THE TEACHER'S PET THIS YEAR.
NO, IDIOT!
YOU GOT ME, MATTSUN! ♡
KOBAYAKAWA'S JOINING THE BEAUTIFICATION COMMITTEE AGAIN THIS YEAR.
SHE TOLD ME IN A TEXT. ♡♡
A TEXT?! YOU TRADED CONTACTS?!
SURE DID!
I WORKED UP THE COURAGE TO ASK FOR HERS AFTER THAT STUDY SESSION!
Praise me!
FINALLY!
WOW. YOU'RE MAKING PROGRESS.
I had no idea.
I AM! ♡
HEE

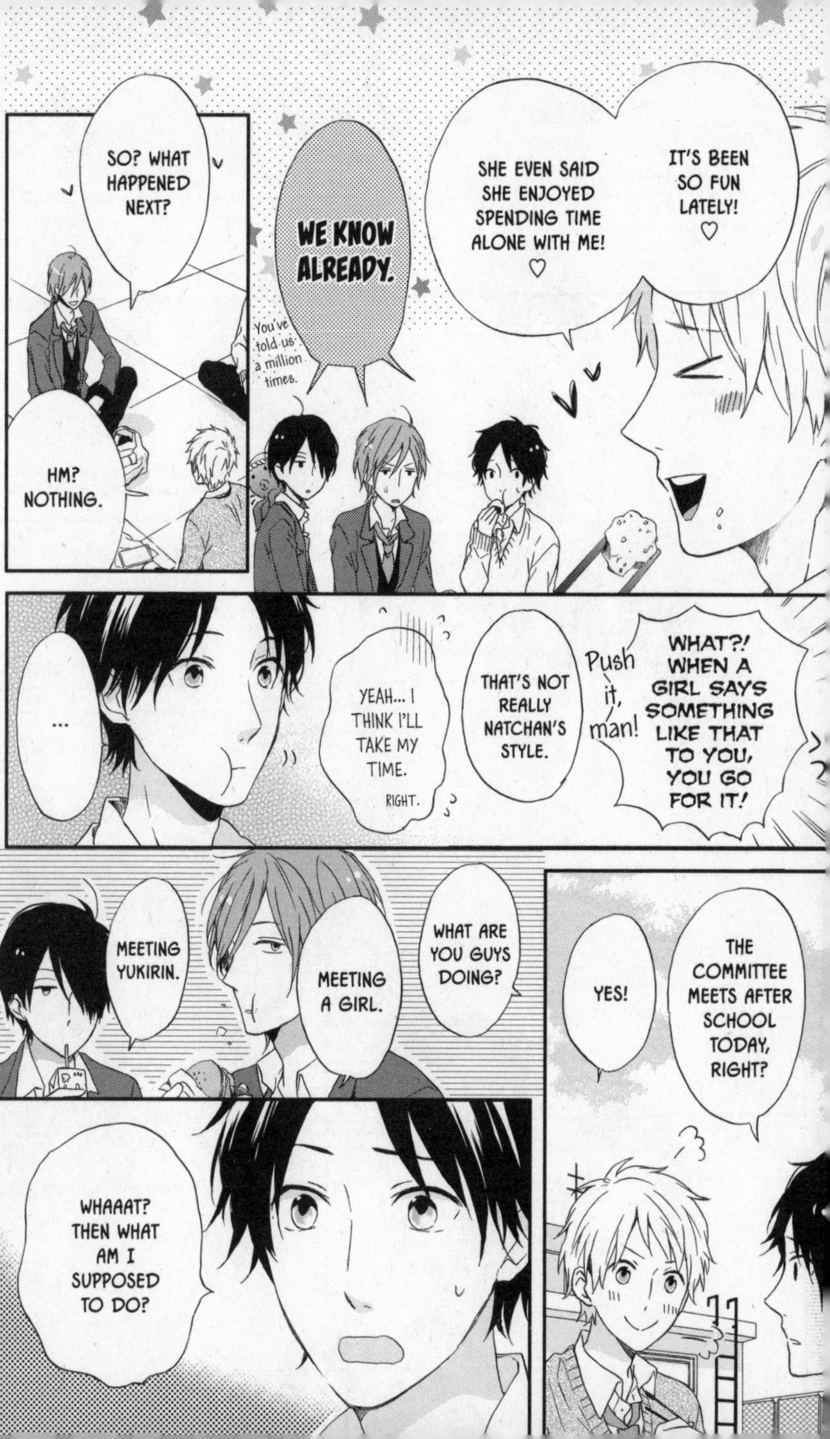
IT'S BEEN SO FUN LATELY! ♡
SHE EVEN SAID SHE ENJOYED SPENDING TIME ALONE WITH ME! ♡
WE KNOW ALREADY.
You've told us a million times.
SO? WHAT HAPPENED NEXT?
HM? NOTHING.
WHAT?! WHEN A GIRL SAYS SOMETHING LIKE THAT TO YOU, YOU GO FOR IT!
Push it, man!
THAT'S NOT REALLY NATCHAN'S STYLE.
YEAH... I THINK I'LL TAKE MY TIME.
RIGHT.
...
THE COMMITTEE MEETS AFTER SCHOOL TODAY, RIGHT?
YES!
WHAT ARE YOU GUYS DOING?
MEETING A GIRL.
MEETING YUKIRIN.
WHAAAT? THEN WHAT AM I SUPPOSED TO DO?

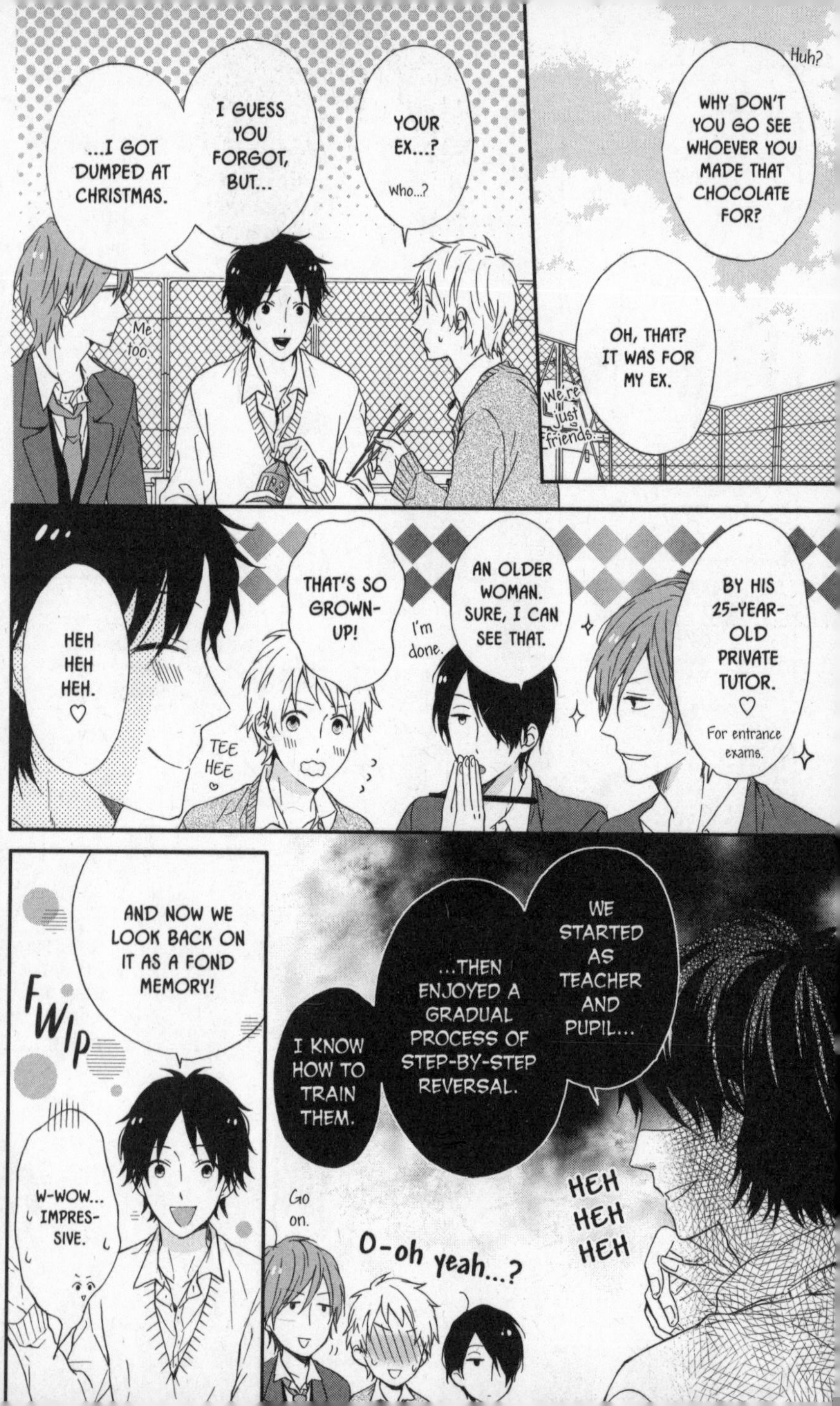
Huh?
WHY DON'T YOU GO SEE WHOEVER YOU MADE THAT CHOCOLATE FOR?
OH, THAT? IT WAS FOR MY EX.
We're just friends.
YOUR EX...?
Who...?
I GUESS YOU FORGOT, BUT...
...I GOT DUMPED AT CHRISTMAS.
Me too.
BY HIS 25-YEAR-OLD PRIVATE TUTOR. ♡
For entrance exams.
AN OLDER WOMAN. SURE, I CAN SEE THAT.
I'm done.
THAT'S SO GROWN-UP!
TEE HEE ♡
HEH HEH HEH. ♡
WE STARTED AS TEACHER AND PUPIL...
...THEN ENJOYED A GRADUAL PROCESS OF STEP-BY-STEP REVERSAL.
I KNOW HOW TO TRAIN THEM.
HEH HEH HEH
O-oh yeah...?
Go on.
AND NOW WE LOOK BACK ON IT AS A FOND MEMORY!
FWIP
W-WOW... IMPRESSIVE.

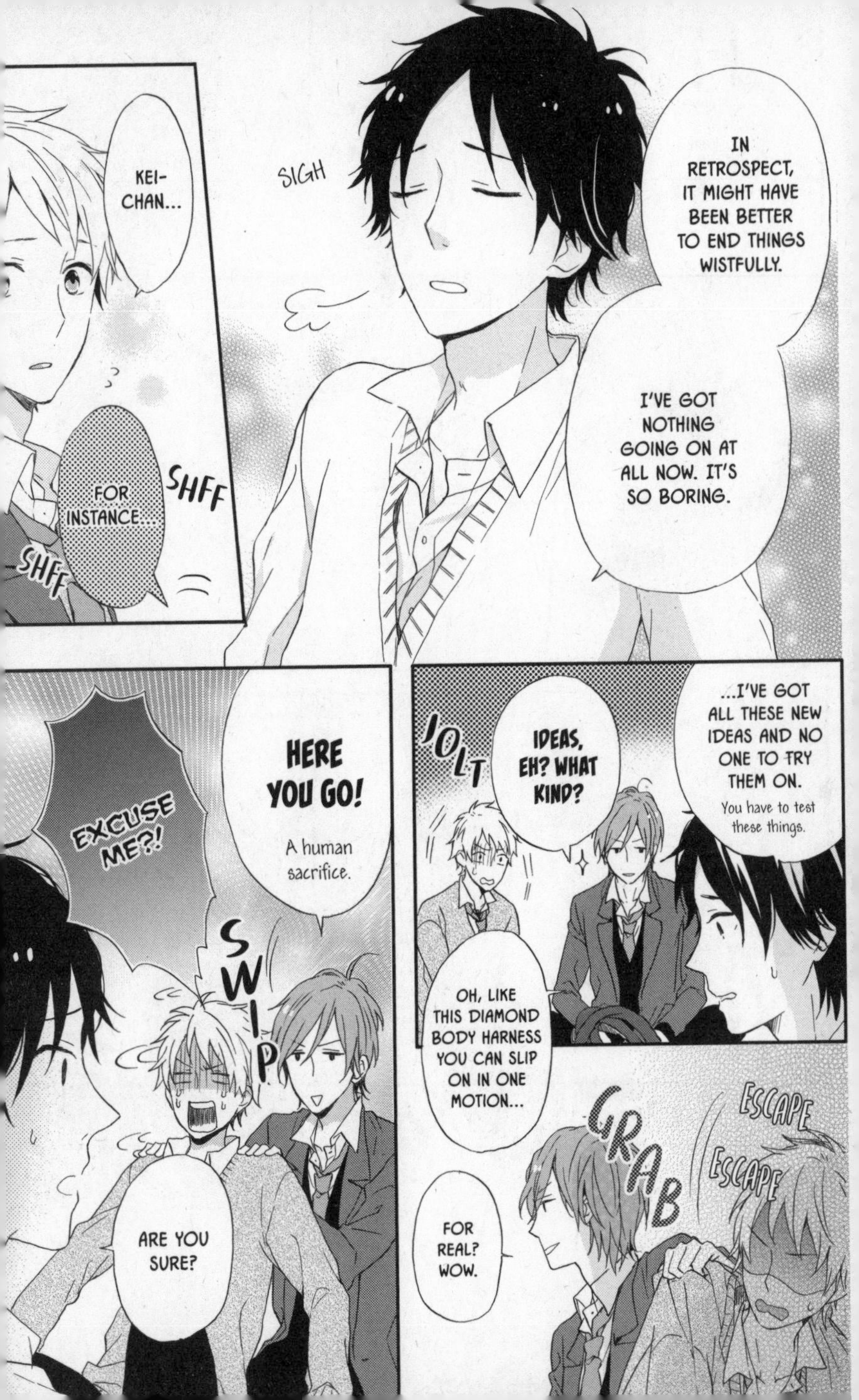
IN RETROSPECT, IT MIGHT HAVE BEEN BETTER TO END THINGS WISTFULLY.
SIGH
I'VE GOT NOTHING GOING ON AT ALL NOW. IT'S SO BORING.
KEI-CHAN...
SHFF
SHFF
FOR INSTANCE...
...I'VE GOT ALL THESE NEW IDEAS AND NO ONE TO TRY THEM ON.
You have to test these things.
JOLT
IDEAS, EH? WHAT KIND?
OH, LIKE THIS DIAMOND BODY HARNESS YOU CAN SLIP ON IN ONE MOTION...
ESCAPE
ESCAPE
GRAB
FOR REAL? WOW.
HERE YOU GO!
A human sacrifice.
SWIP
EXCUSE ME?!
ARE YOU SURE?

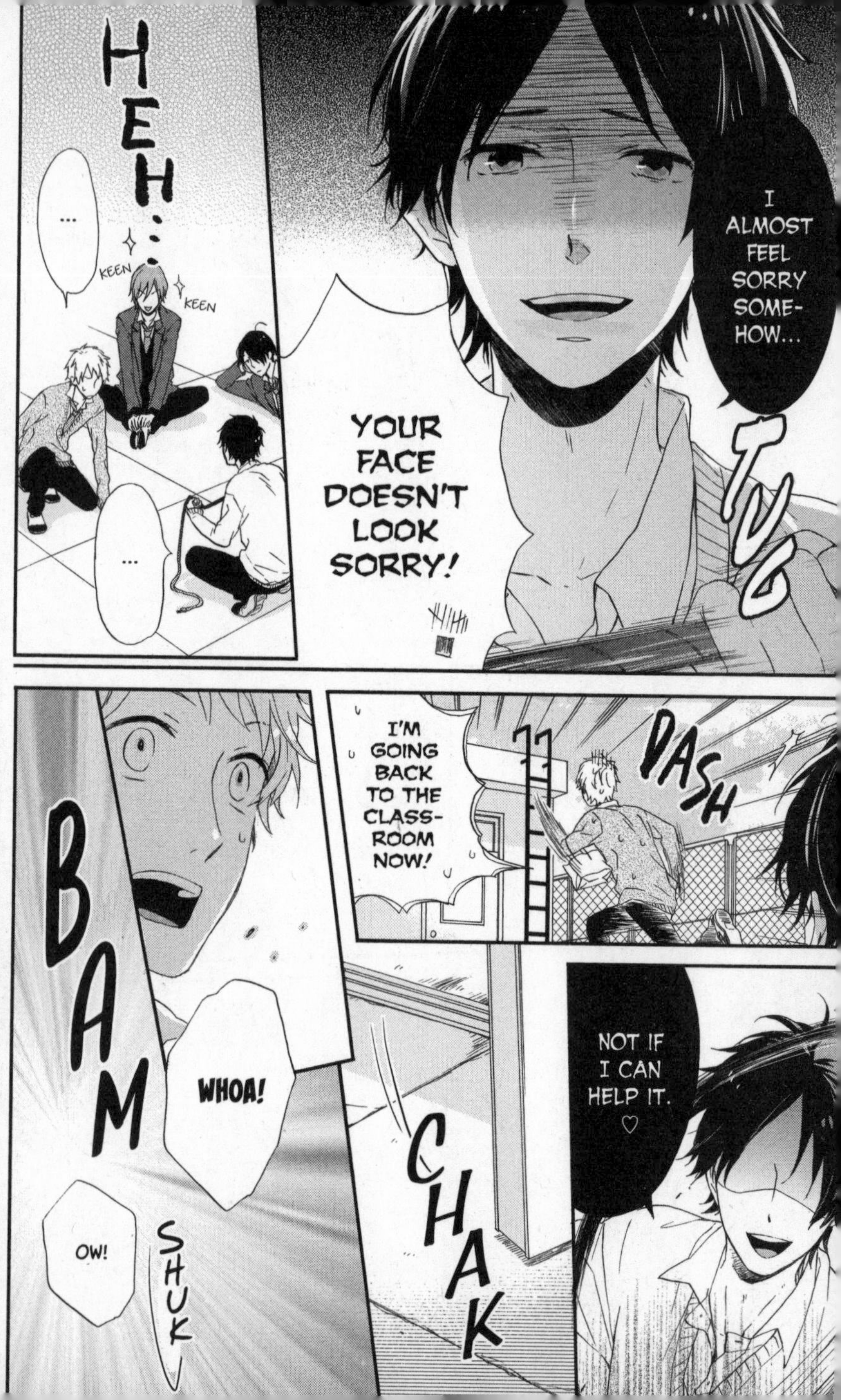
I ALMOST FEEL SORRY SOMEHOW...
TUG
YOUR FACE DOESN'T LOOK SORRY!
HEH...
KEEN
KEEN
...
...
DASH
I'M GOING BACK TO THE CLASSROOM NOW!
NOT IF I CAN HELP IT. ♡
CHAK
BAM
WHOA!
OW!
SHUK

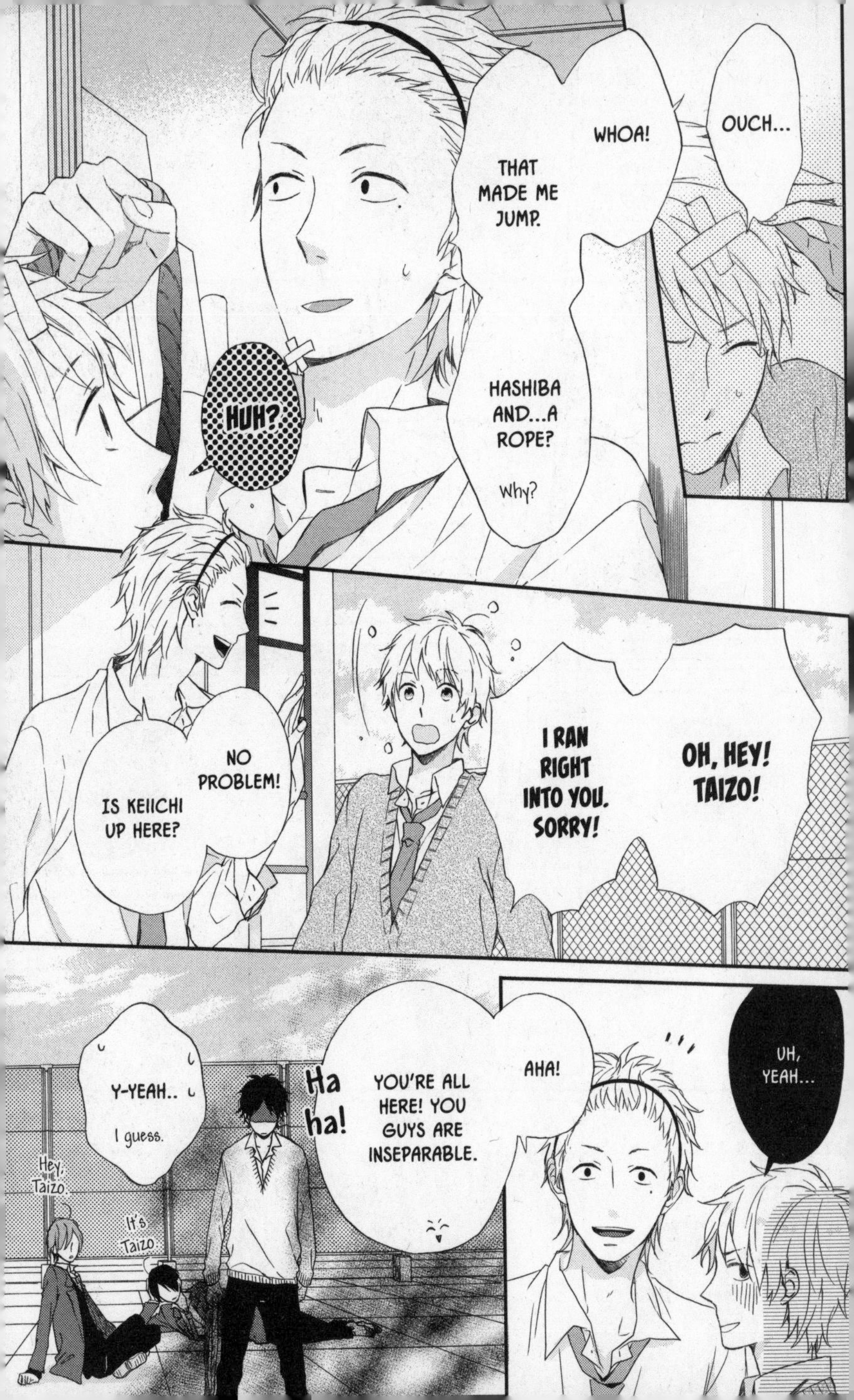
OUCH...
WHOA!
THAT MADE ME JUMP.
HASHIBA AND...A ROPE?
Why?
HUH?
OH, HEY! TAIZO!
I RAN RIGHT INTO YOU. SORRY!
NO PROBLEM!
IS KEIICHI UP HERE?
UH, YEAH...
AHA!
YOU'RE ALL HERE! YOU GUYS ARE INSEPARABLE.
Ha ha!
Y-YEAH..
I guess.
Hey, Taizo.
It's Taizo.

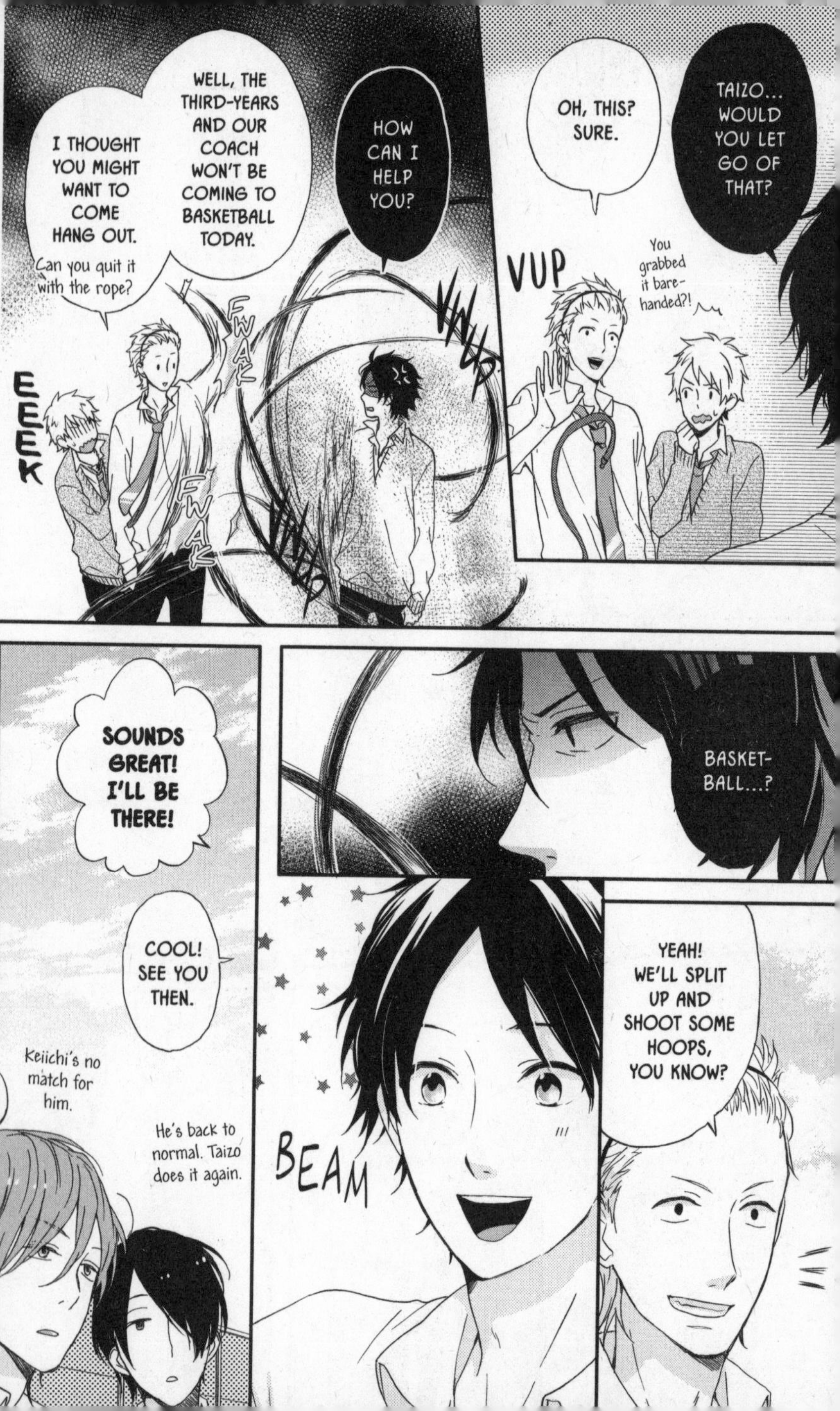

TAIZO... WOULD YOU LET GO OF THAT?
OH, THIS? SURE.
VUP
You grabbed it bare-handed?!
HOW CAN I HELP YOU?
WELL, THE THIRD-YEARS AND OUR COACH WON'T BE COMING TO BASKETBALL TODAY.
I THOUGHT YOU MIGHT WANT TO COME HANG OUT.
Can you quit it with the rope?
FWAK
FWAK
EEEK
BASKET-BALL...?
YEAH! WE'LL SPLIT UP AND SHOOT SOME HOOPS, YOU KNOW?
BEAM
SOUNDS GREAT! I'LL BE THERE!
COOL! SEE YOU THEN.
Keiichi's no match for him.
He's back to normal. Taizo does it again.

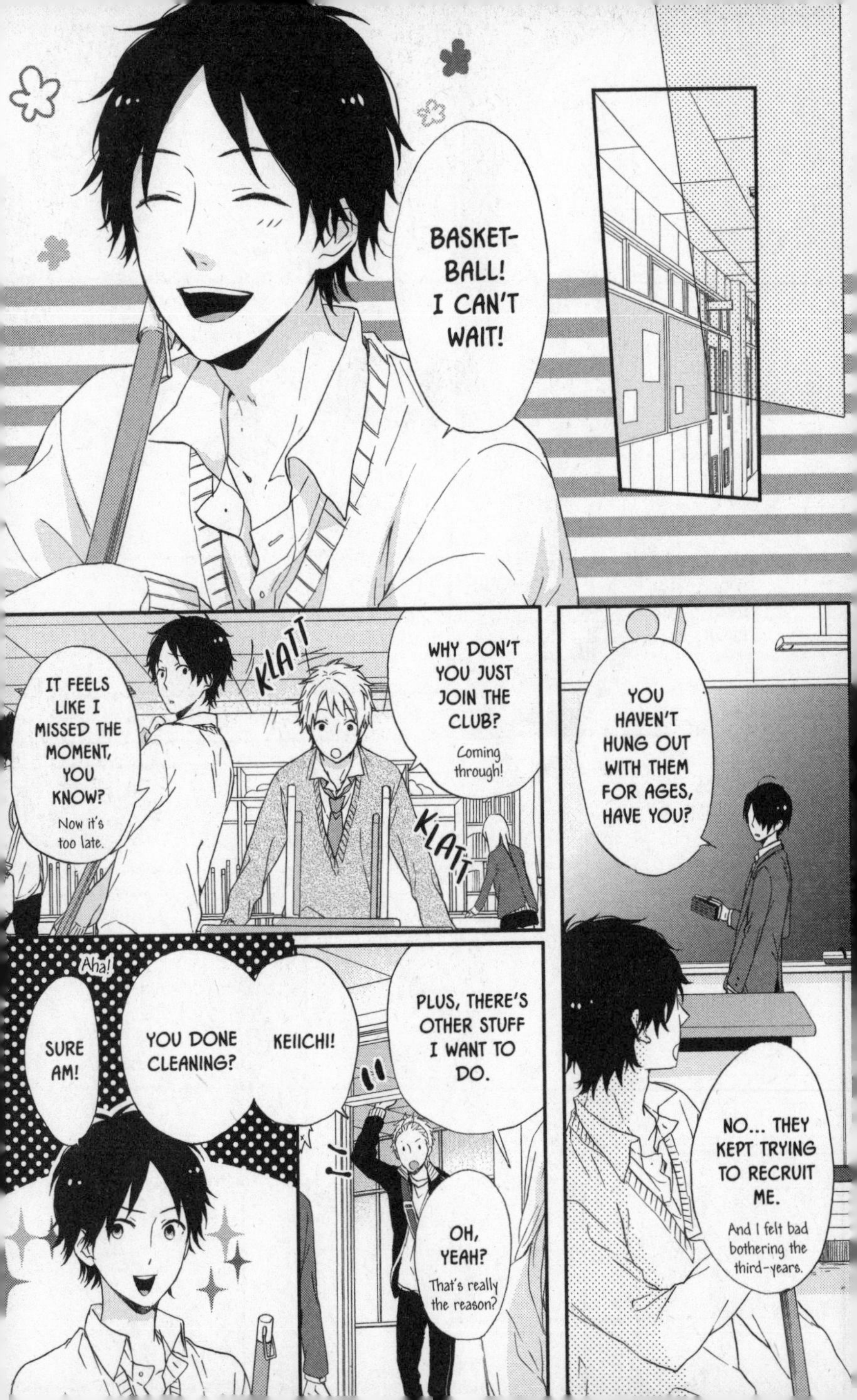
BASKET-BALL! I CAN'T WAIT!
YOU HAVEN'T HUNG OUT WITH THEM FOR AGES, HAVE YOU?
NO... THEY KEPT TRYING TO RECRUIT ME.
And I felt bad bothering the third-years.
KLATT
WHY DON'T YOU JUST JOIN THE CLUB?
Coming through!
KLATT
IT FEELS LIKE I MISSED THE MOMENT, YOU KNOW?
Now it's too late.
PLUS, THERE'S OTHER STUFF I WANT TO DO.
OH, YEAH?
That's really the reason?
KEIICHI!
YOU DONE CLEANING?
Aha!
SURE AM!

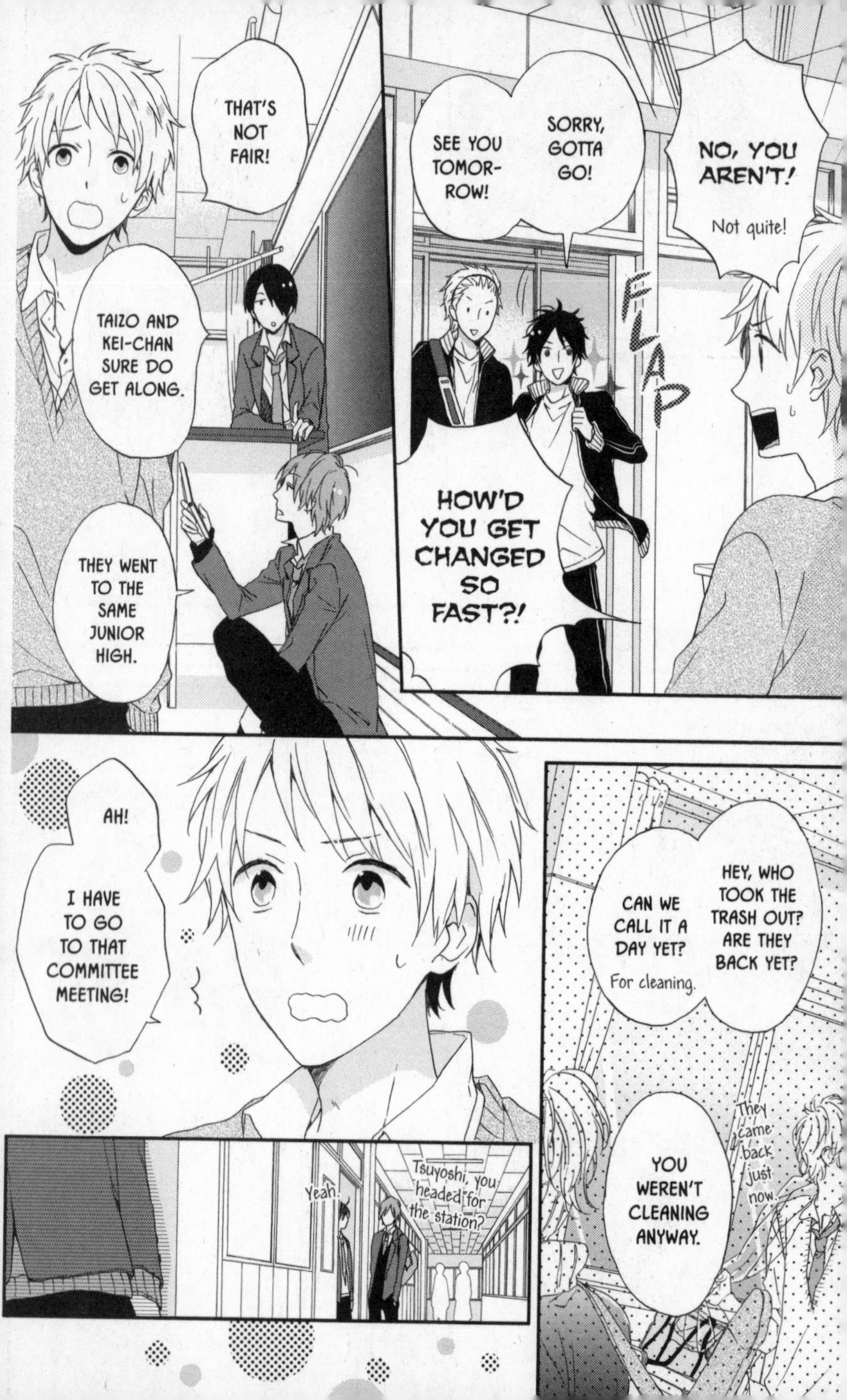
NO, YOU AREN'T!
Not quite!
FLAP
SORRY, GOTTA GO!
SEE YOU TOMORROW!
HOW'D YOU GET CHANGED SO FAST?!
THAT'S NOT FAIR!
TAIZO AND KEI-CHAN SURE DO GET ALONG.
THEY WENT TO THE SAME JUNIOR HIGH.
HEY, WHO TOOK THE TRASH OUT? ARE THEY BACK YET?
CAN WE CALL IT A DAY YET?
For cleaning.
YOU WEREN'T CLEANING ANYWAY.
They came back just now.
AH!
I HAVE TO GO TO THAT COMMITTEE MEETING!
Tsuyoshi, you headed for the station?
Yeah!

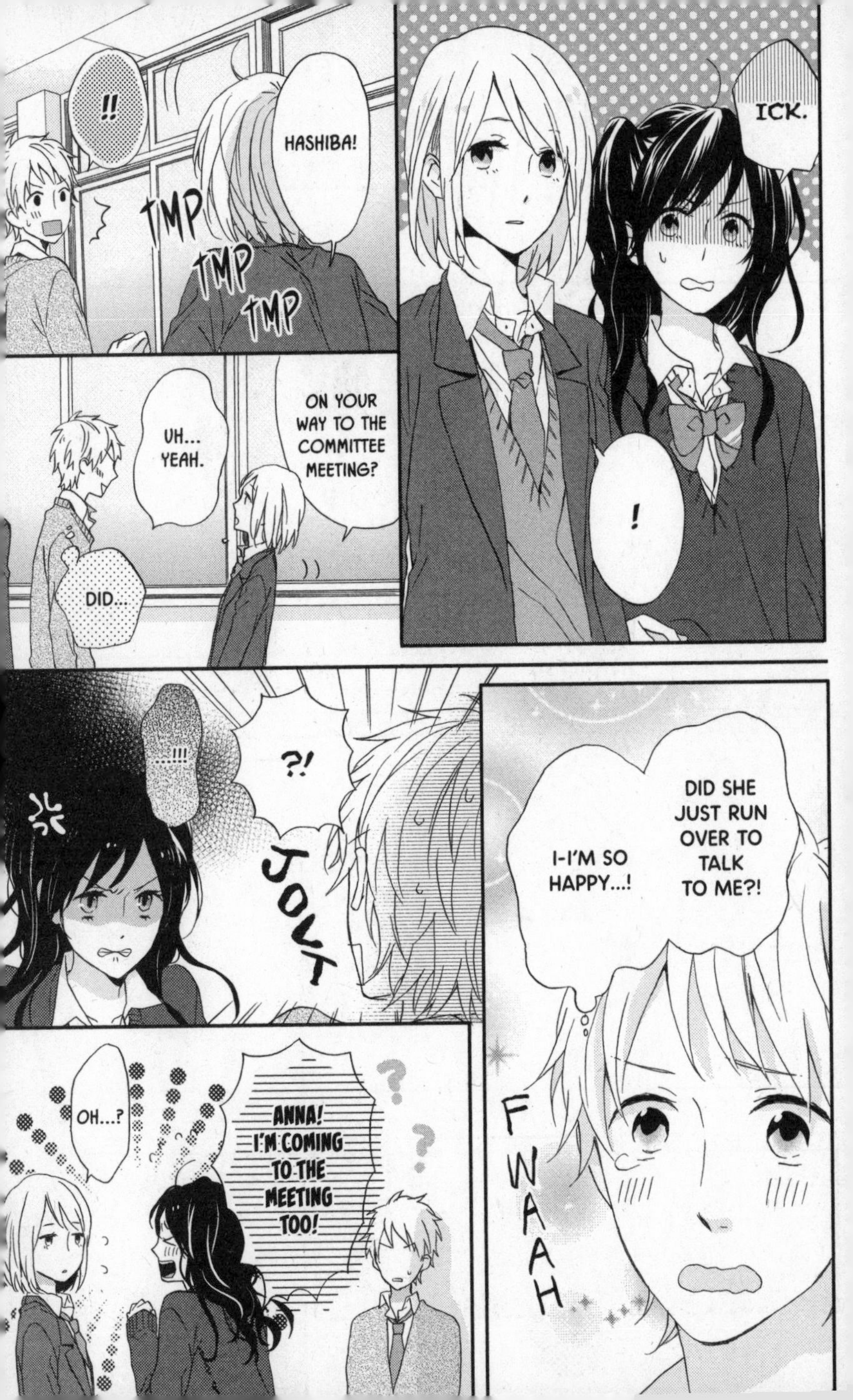
ICK.
!
HASHIBA!
!!
TMP
TMP
TMP
ON YOUR WAY TO THE COMMITTEE MEETING?
UH... YEAH.
DID...
DID SHE JUST RUN OVER TO TALK TO ME?!
I-I'M SO HAPPY...!
FWAAH
?!
...!!!
JOLT
ANNA! I'M COMING TO THE MEETING TOO!
OH...?

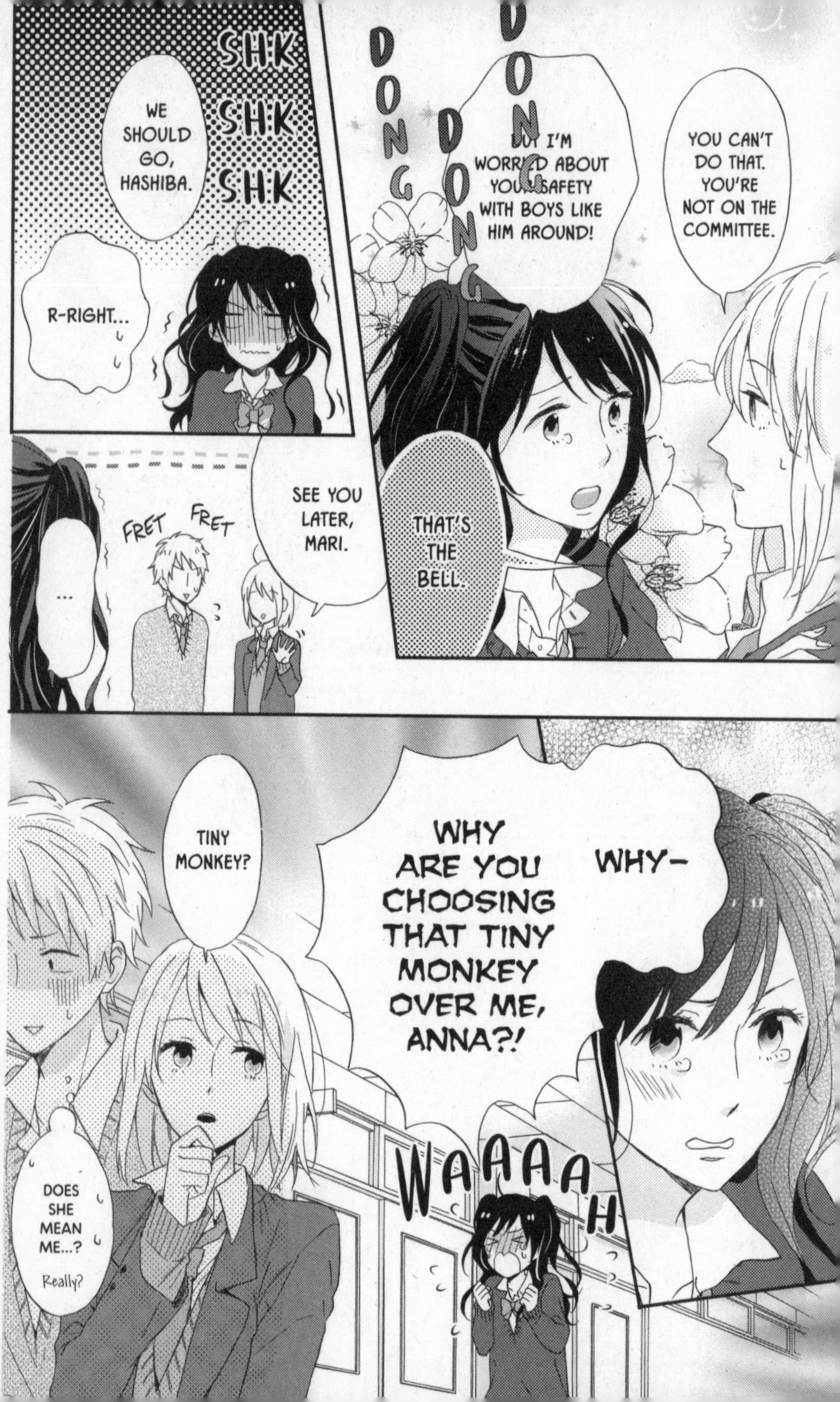
YOU CAN'T DO THAT. YOU'RE NOT ON THE COMMITTEE.
BUT I'M WORRIED ABOUT YOUR SAFETY WITH BOYS LIKE HIM AROUND!
DONG DONG DONG DONG
THAT'S THE BELL.
SHK SHK SHK
WE SHOULD GO, HASHIBA.
R-RIGHT...
SEE YOU LATER, MARI.
FRET FRET
...
WHY-
WHY ARE YOU CHOOSING THAT TINY MONKEY OVER ME, ANNA?!
WAAAAAH
TINY MONKEY?
DOES SHE MEAN ME...?
Really?

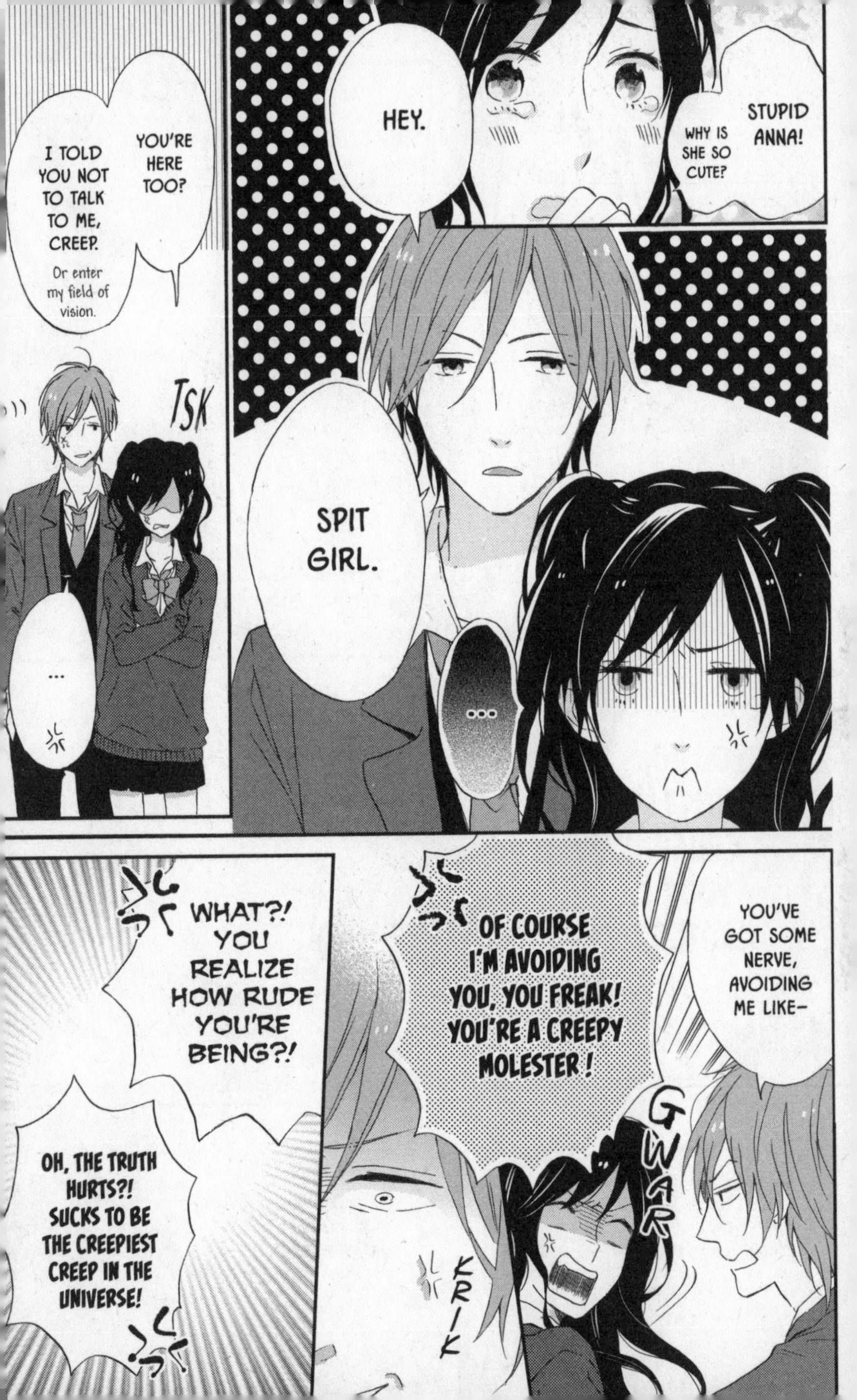
STUPID ANNA!
WHY IS SHE SO CUTE?
HEY.
SPIT GIRL.
...
YOU'RE HERE TOO?
I TOLD YOU NOT TO TALK TO ME, CREEP.
Or enter my field of vision.
TSK
...
YOU'VE GOT SOME NERVE, AVOIDING ME LIKE–
OF COURSE I'M AVOIDING YOU, YOU FREAK! YOU'RE A CREEPY MOLESTER!
GWAR
KRIK
WHAT?! YOU REALIZE HOW RUDE YOU'RE BEING?!
OH, THE TRUTH HURTS?! SUCKS TO BE THE CREEPIEST CREEP IN THE UNIVERSE!

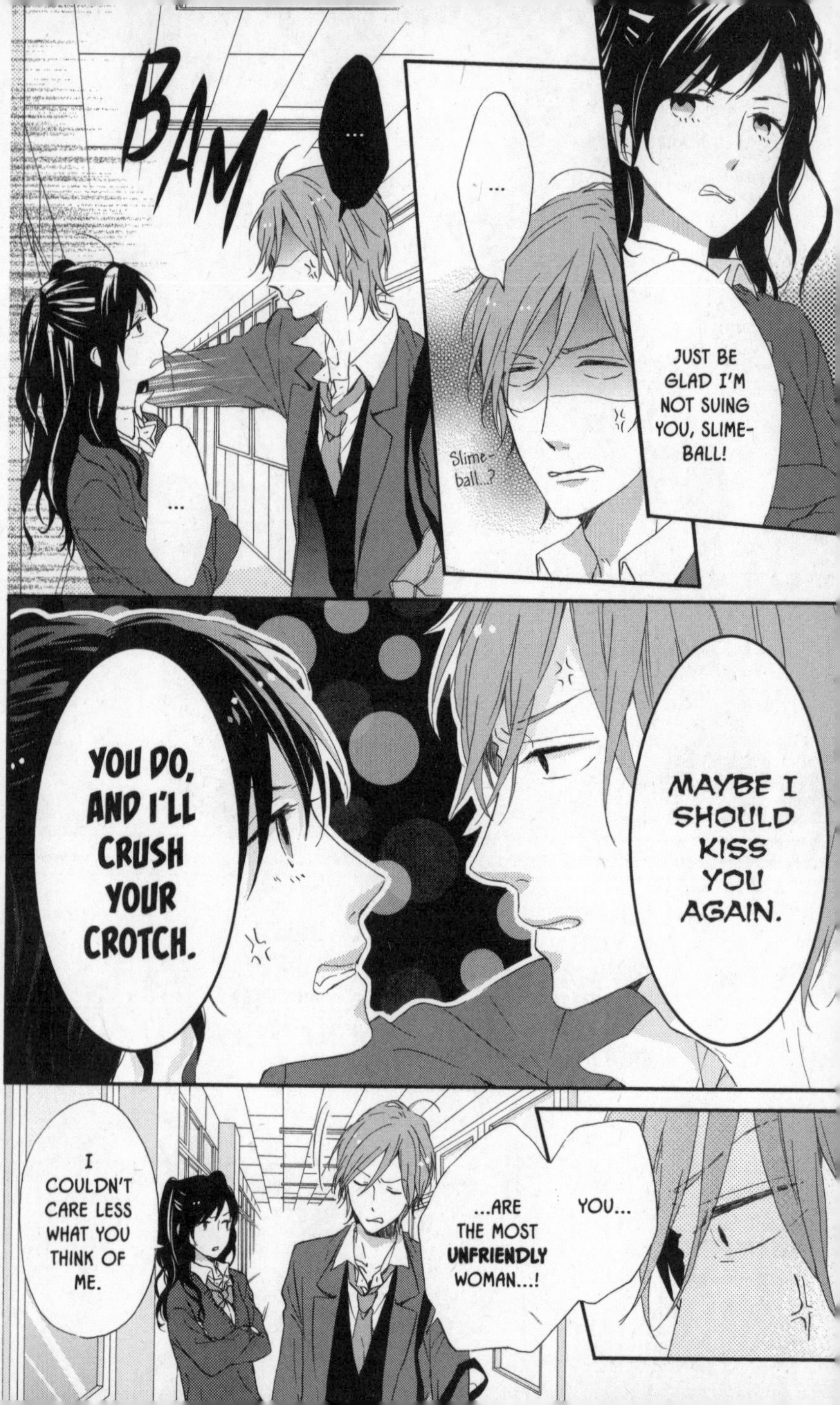
JUST BE GLAD I'M NOT SUING YOU, SLIME-BALL!
...
Slime-ball...?
BAM
...
...
MAYBE I SHOULD KISS YOU AGAIN.
YOU DO, AND I'LL CRUSH YOUR CROTCH.
YOU...
...ARE THE MOST UNFRIENDLY WOMAN...!
I COULDN'T CARE LESS WHAT YOU THINK OF ME.

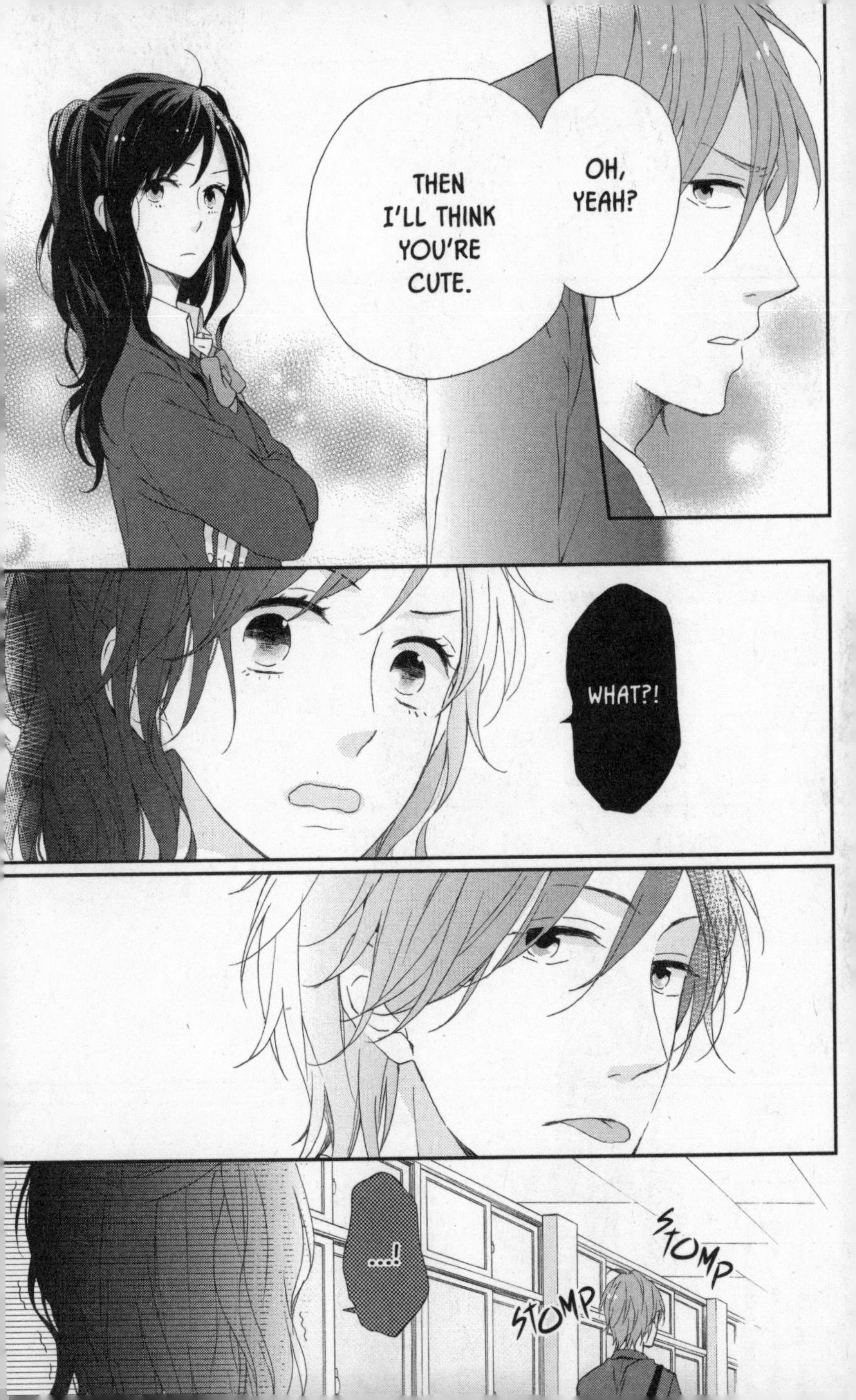
OH, YEAH?
THEN I'LL THINK YOU'RE CUTE.
WHAT?!
...!
STOMP
STOMP

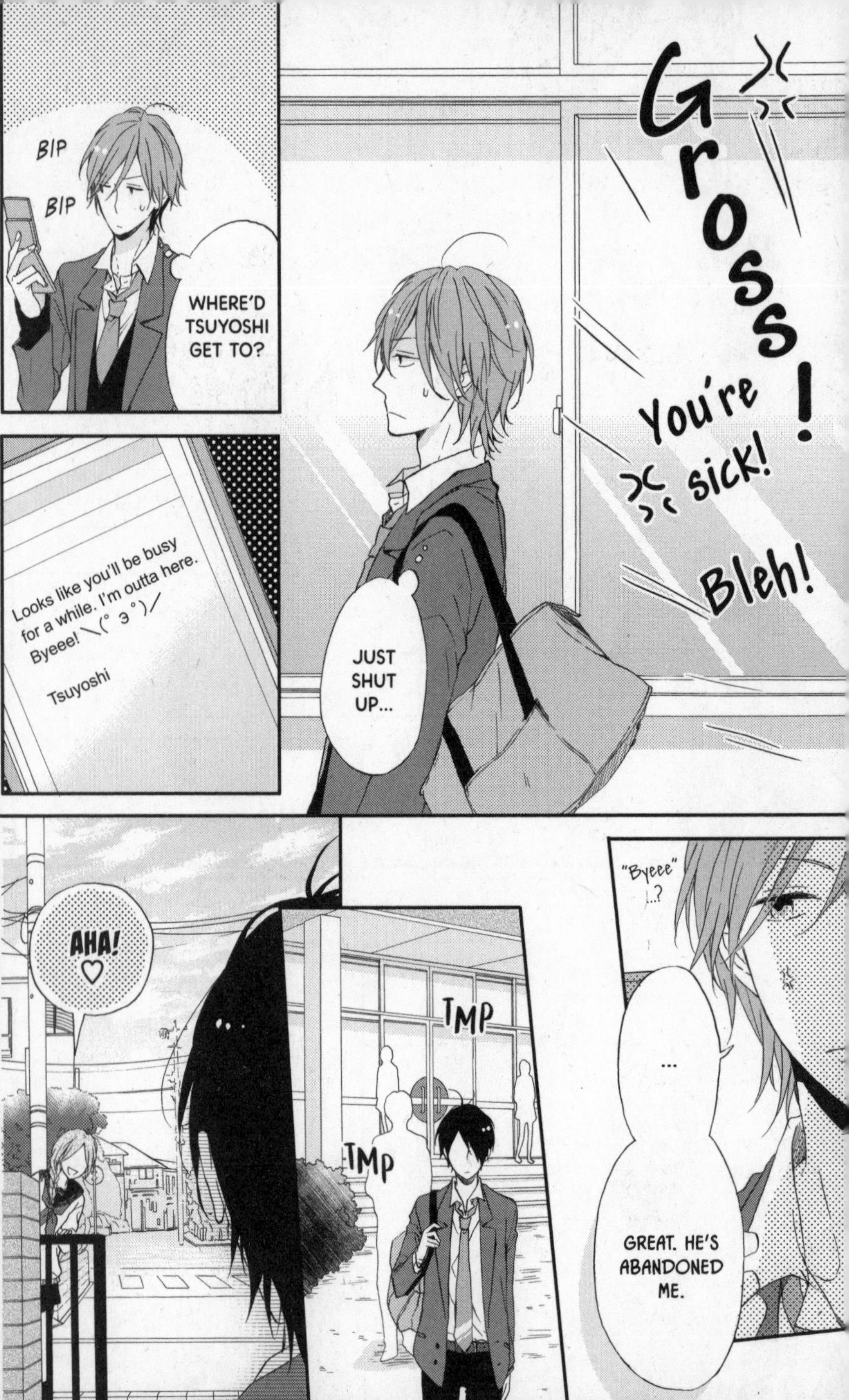
Gross!
You're sick!
Bleh!
JUST SHUT UP...
BIP
BIP
WHERE'D TSUYOSHI GET TO?
Looks like you'll be busy for a while. I'm outta here. Byeee! ＼(° з °)／
Tsuyoshi
"Byeee"...?
...
GREAT. HE'S ABANDONED ME.
TMP
TMP
AHA! ♡

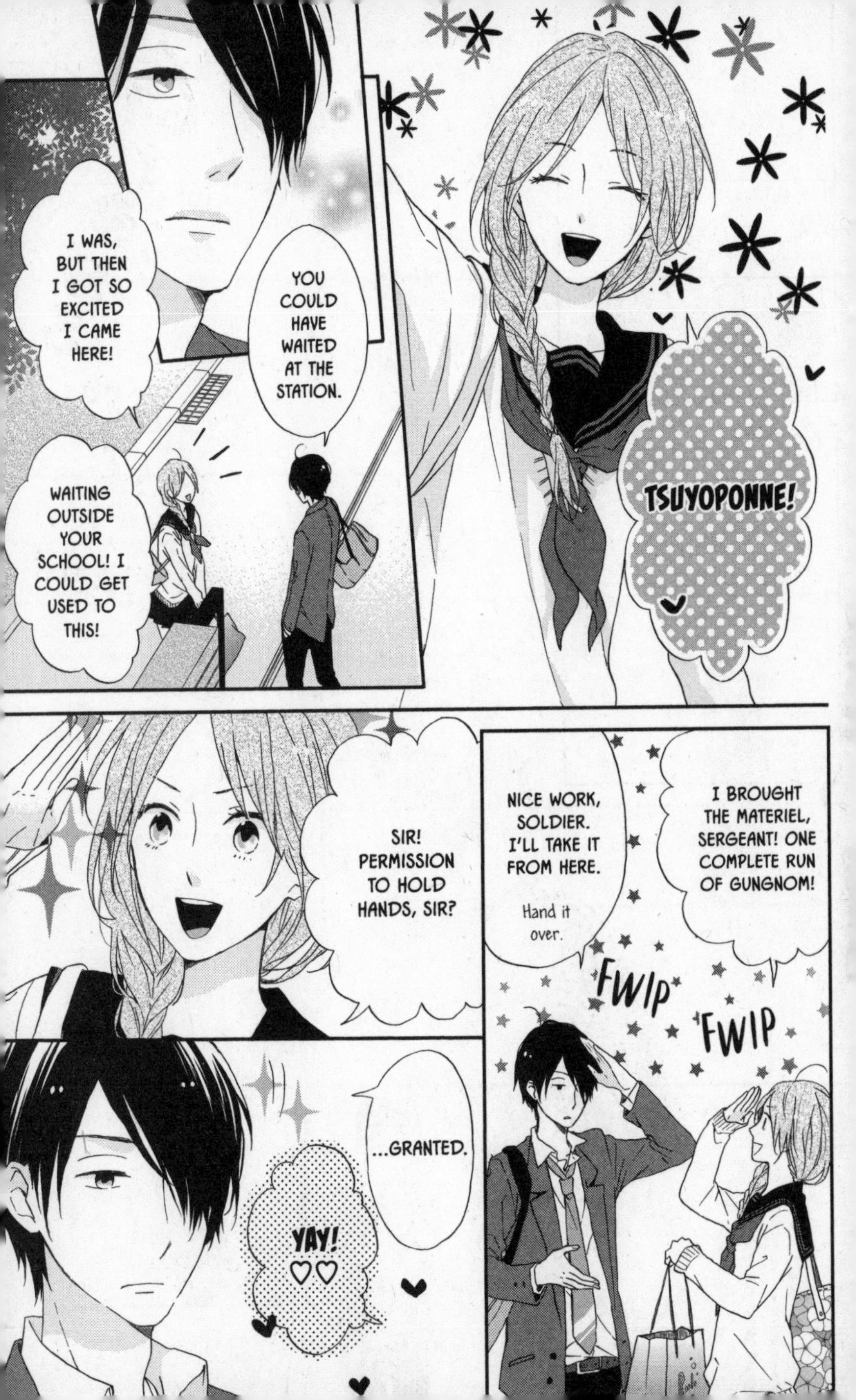

TSUYOPONNE!
YOU COULD HAVE WAITED AT THE STATION.
I WAS, BUT THEN I GOT SO EXCITED I CAME HERE!
WAITING OUTSIDE YOUR SCHOOL! I COULD GET USED TO THIS!
I BROUGHT THE MATERIEL, SERGEANT! ONE COMPLETE RUN OF GUNGNOM!
NICE WORK, SOLDIER. I'LL TAKE IT FROM HERE.
Hand it over.
FWIP
FWIP
SIR! PERMISSION TO HOLD HANDS, SIR?
...GRANTED.
YAY! ♡♡

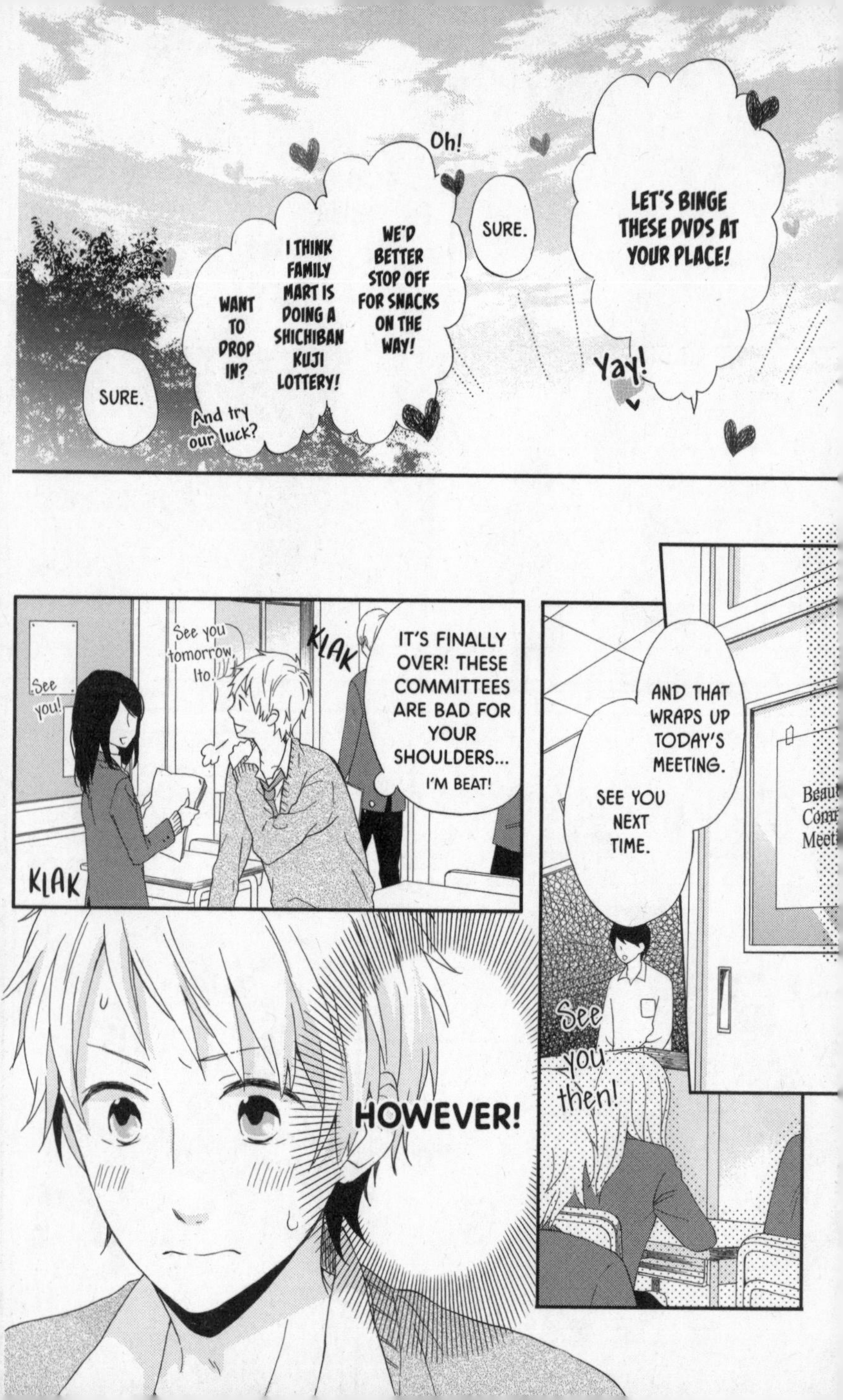
LET'S BINGE THESE DVDS AT YOUR PLACE!
Yay!
SURE.
Oh!
WE'D BETTER STOP OFF FOR SNACKS ON THE WAY!
I THINK FAMILY MART IS DOING A SHICHIBAN KUJI LOTTERY!
WANT TO DROP IN?
And try our luck?
SURE.
AND THAT WRAPS UP TODAY'S MEETING.
SEE YOU NEXT TIME.
See you then!
IT'S FINALLY OVER! THESE COMMITTEES ARE BAD FOR YOUR SHOULDERS...
I'M BEAT!
KLAK
See you tomorrow, Ito.
See you!
KLAK
HOWEVER!

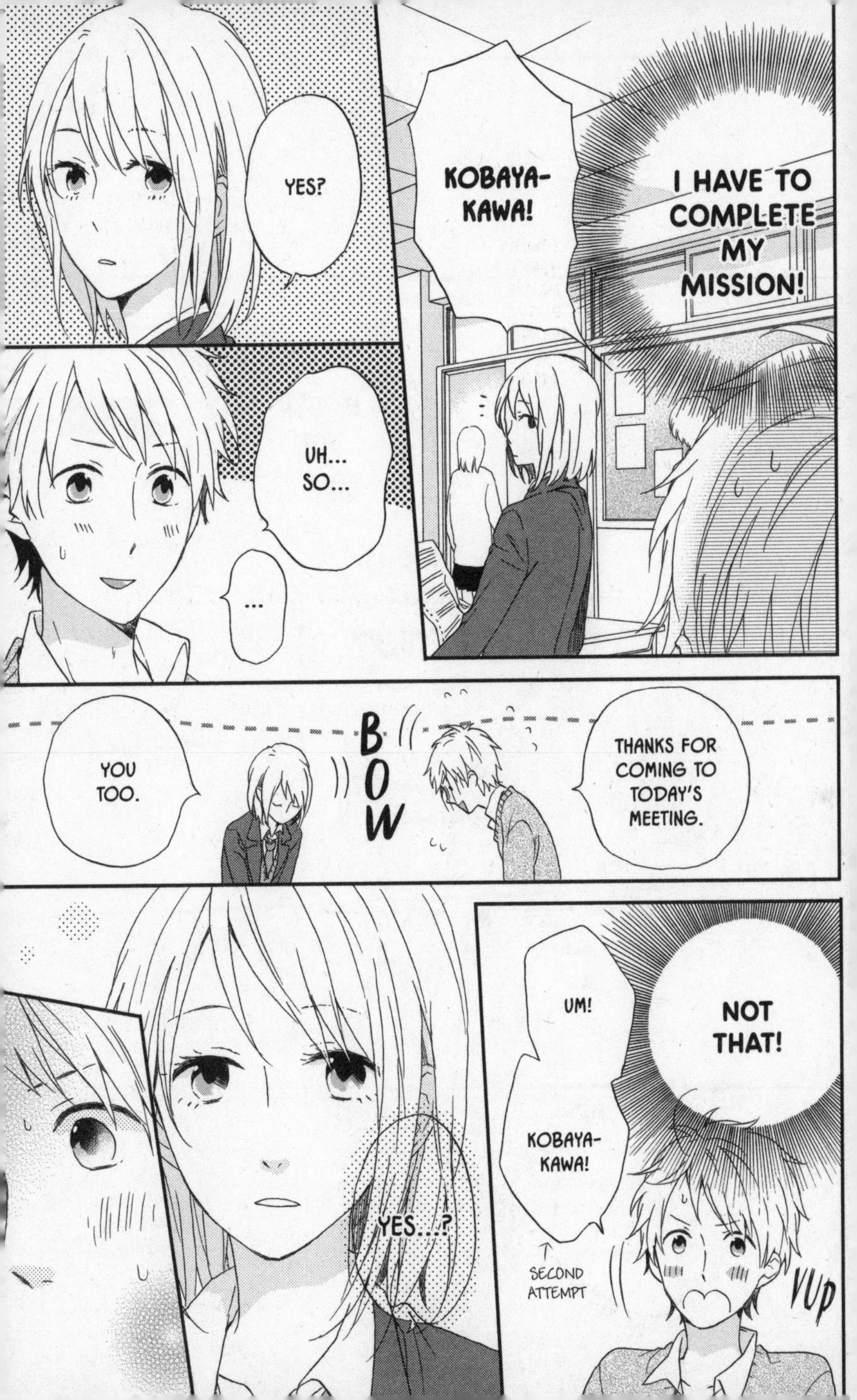
I HAVE TO COMPLETE MY MISSION!
KOBAYA-KAWA!
YES?
UH... SO...
...
THANKS FOR COMING TO TODAY'S MEETING.
BOW
YOU TOO.
NOT THAT!
UM!
KOBAYA-KAWA!
SECOND ATTEMPT
VUP
YES...?

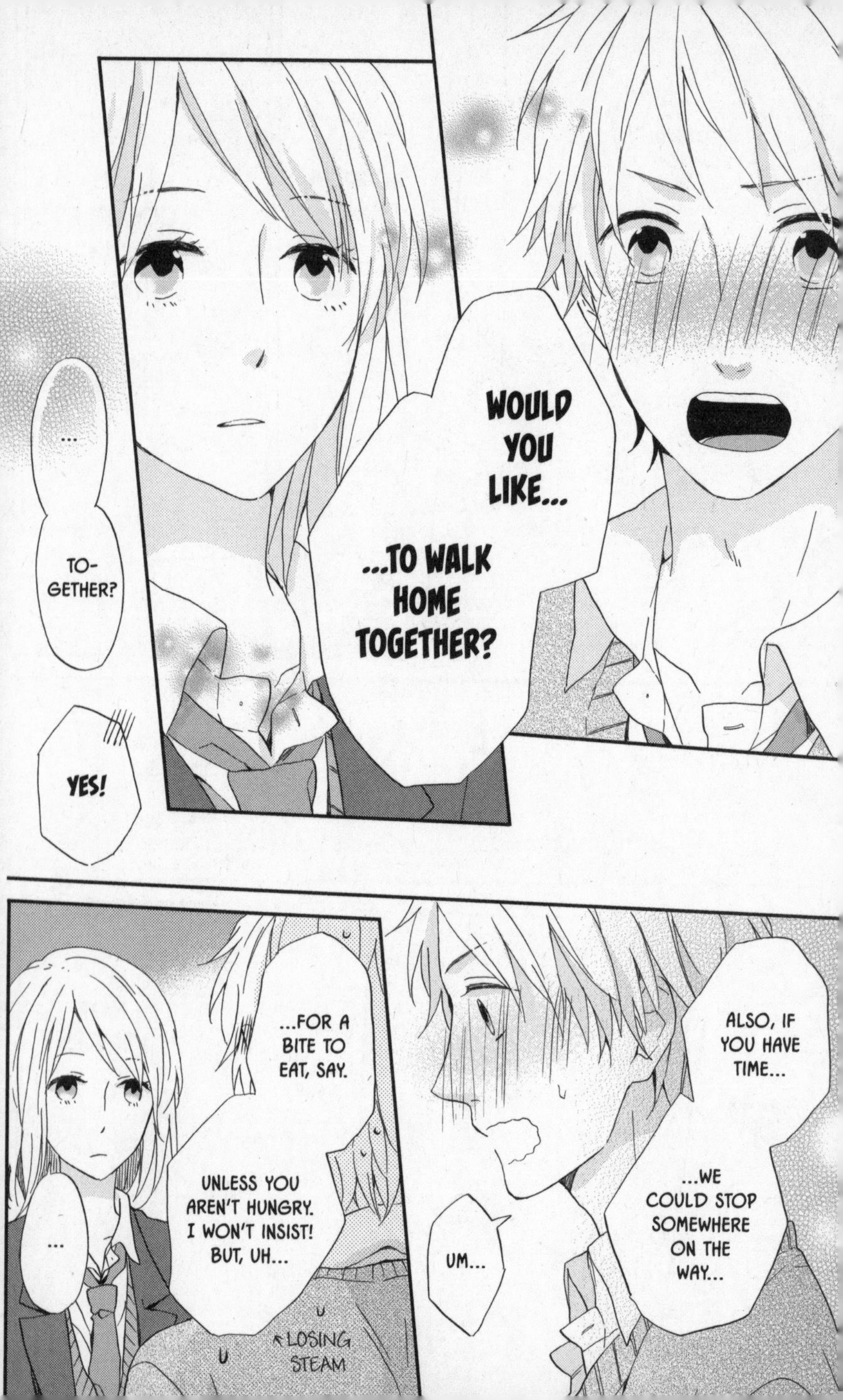
WOULD YOU LIKE...
...TO WALK HOME TOGETHER?
...
TO-GETHER?
YES!
ALSO, IF YOU HAVE TIME...
...WE COULD STOP SOMEWHERE ON THE WAY...
UM...
...FOR A BITE TO EAT, SAY.
UNLESS YOU AREN'T HUNGRY. I WON'T INSIST! BUT, UH...
LOSING STEAM
...

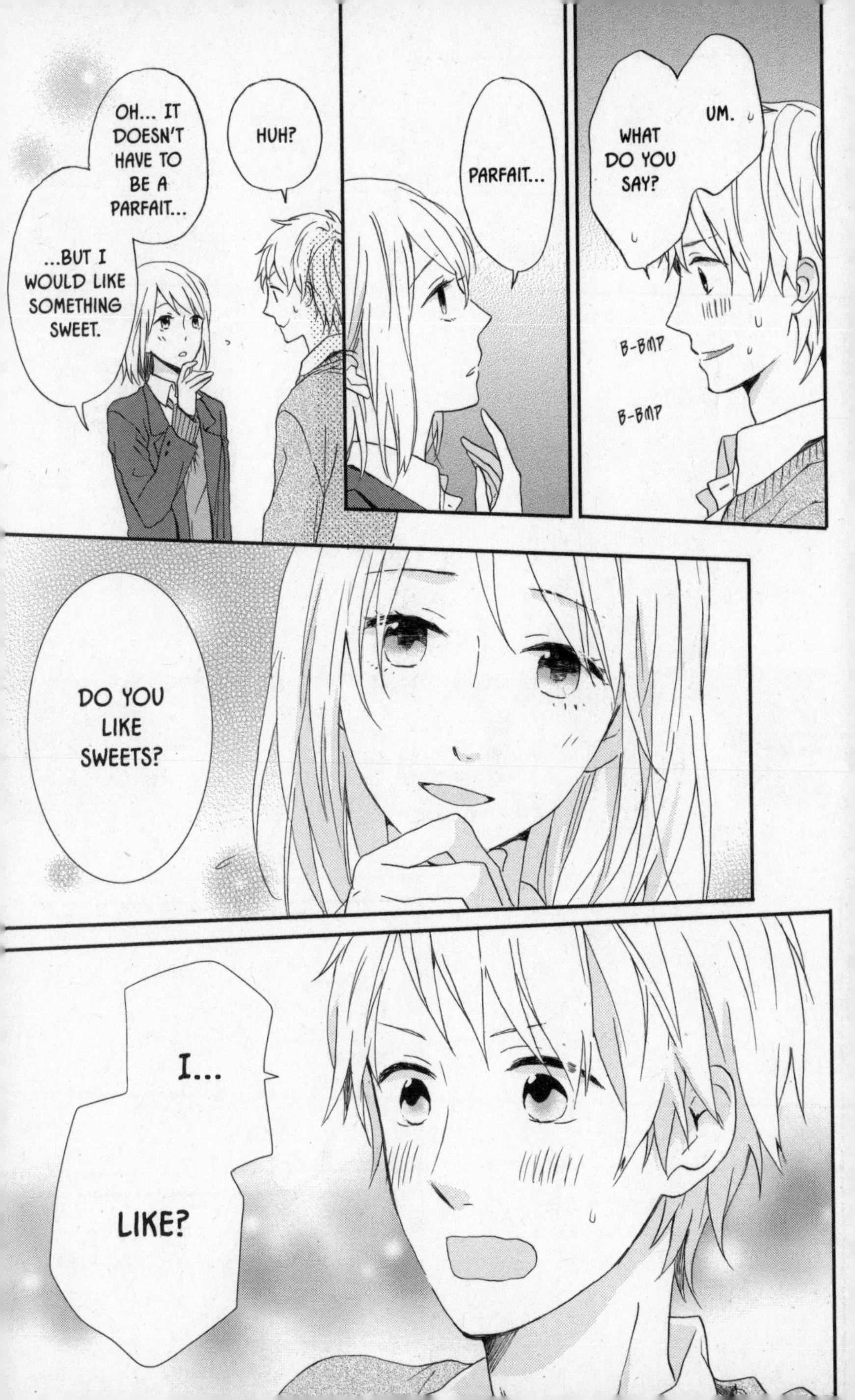
UM.
WHAT DO YOU SAY?
B-BMP
B-BMP
PARFAIT...
HUH?
OH... IT DOESN'T HAVE TO BE A PARFAIT...
...BUT I WOULD LIKE SOMETHING SWEET.
DO YOU LIKE SWEETS?
I...
LIKE?

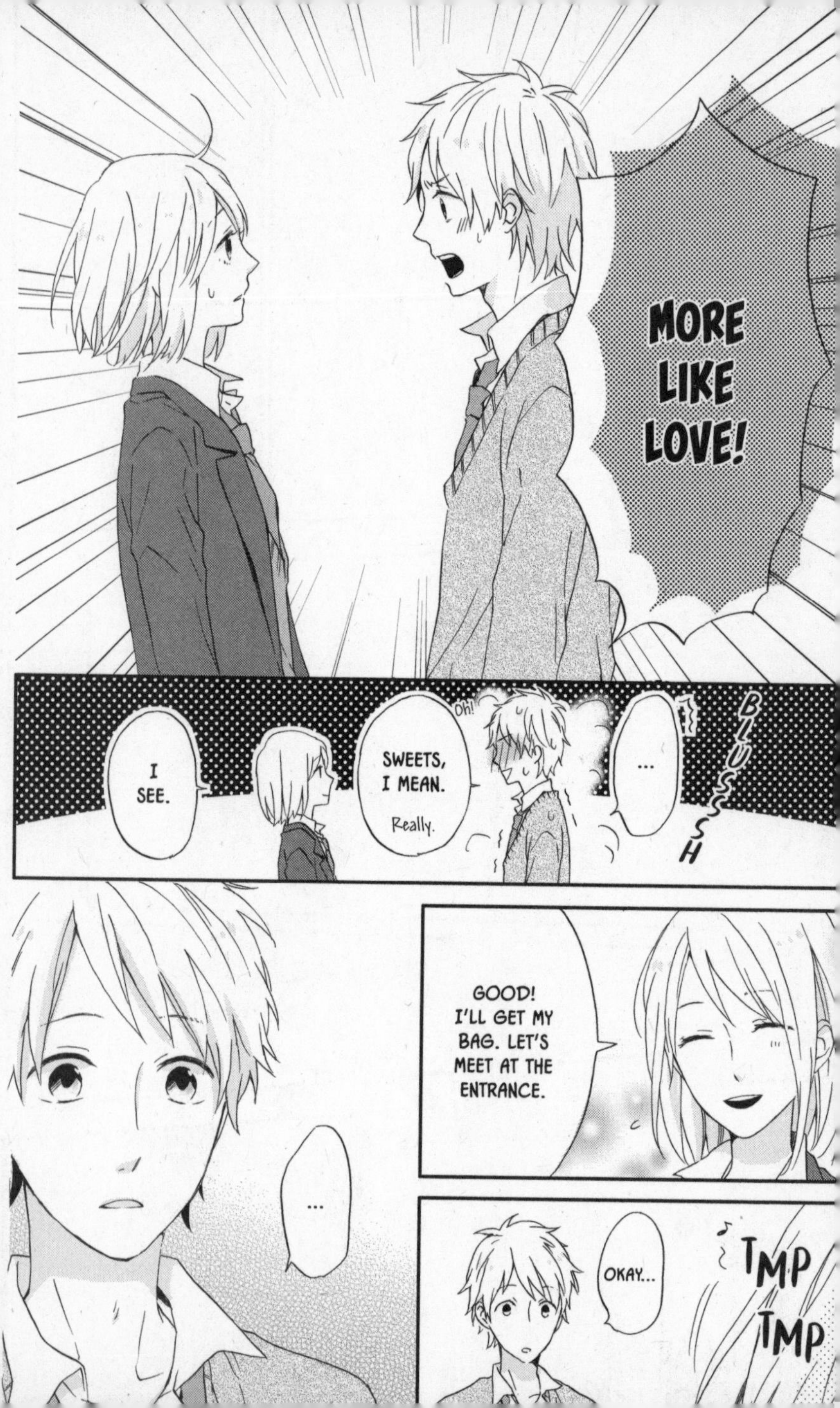
MORE LIKE LOVE!
BLUSSSH
...
Oh!
SWEETS, I MEAN.
Really.
I SEE.
GOOD! I'LL GET MY BAG. LET'S MEET AT THE ENTRANCE.
TMP TMP
OKAY...
...

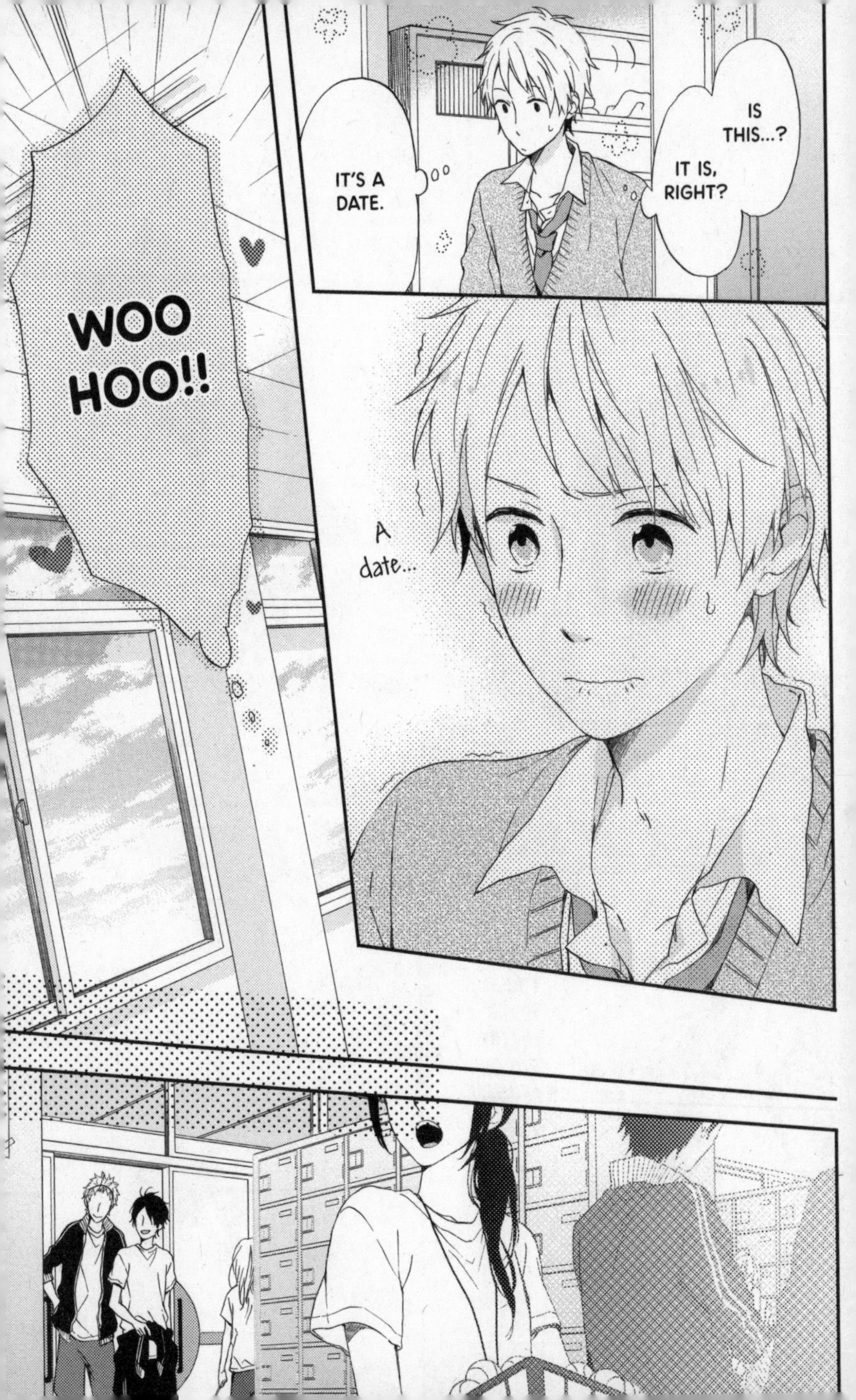
IS THIS...?
IT IS, RIGHT?
IT'S A DATE.
A date...
WOO HOO!!

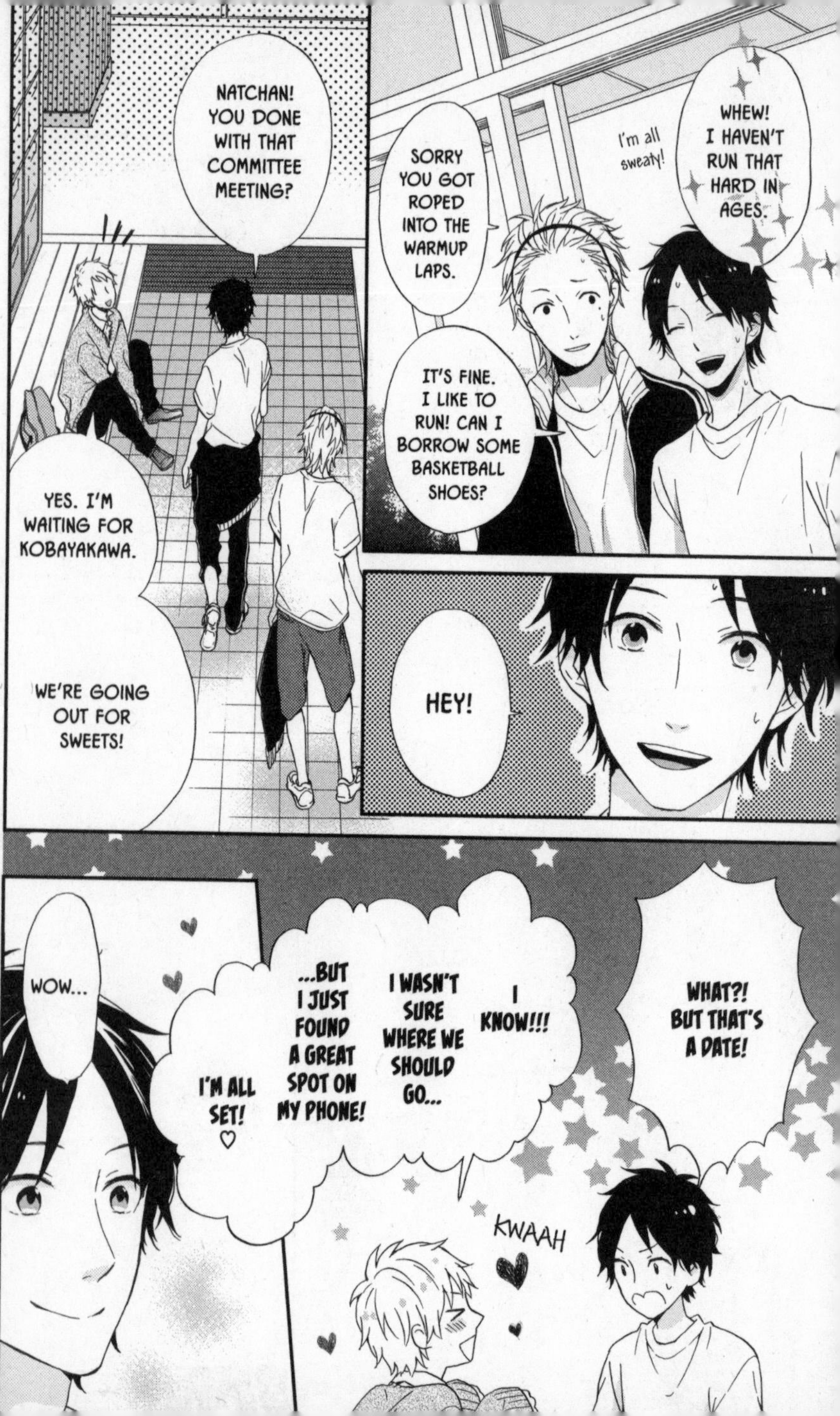

WHEW! I HAVEN'T RUN THAT HARD IN AGES.
I'm all sweaty!
SORRY YOU GOT ROPED INTO THE WARMUP LAPS.
IT'S FINE. I LIKE TO RUN! CAN I BORROW SOME BASKETBALL SHOES?
HEY!
NATCHAN! YOU DONE WITH THAT COMMITTEE MEETING?
YES. I'M WAITING FOR KOBAYAKAWA.
WE'RE GOING OUT FOR SWEETS!
WHAT?! BUT THAT'S A DATE!
I KNOW!!!
I WASN'T SURE WHERE WE SHOULD GO...
...BUT I JUST FOUND A GREAT SPOT ON MY PHONE!
I'M ALL SET! ♡
KWAAH
WOW...

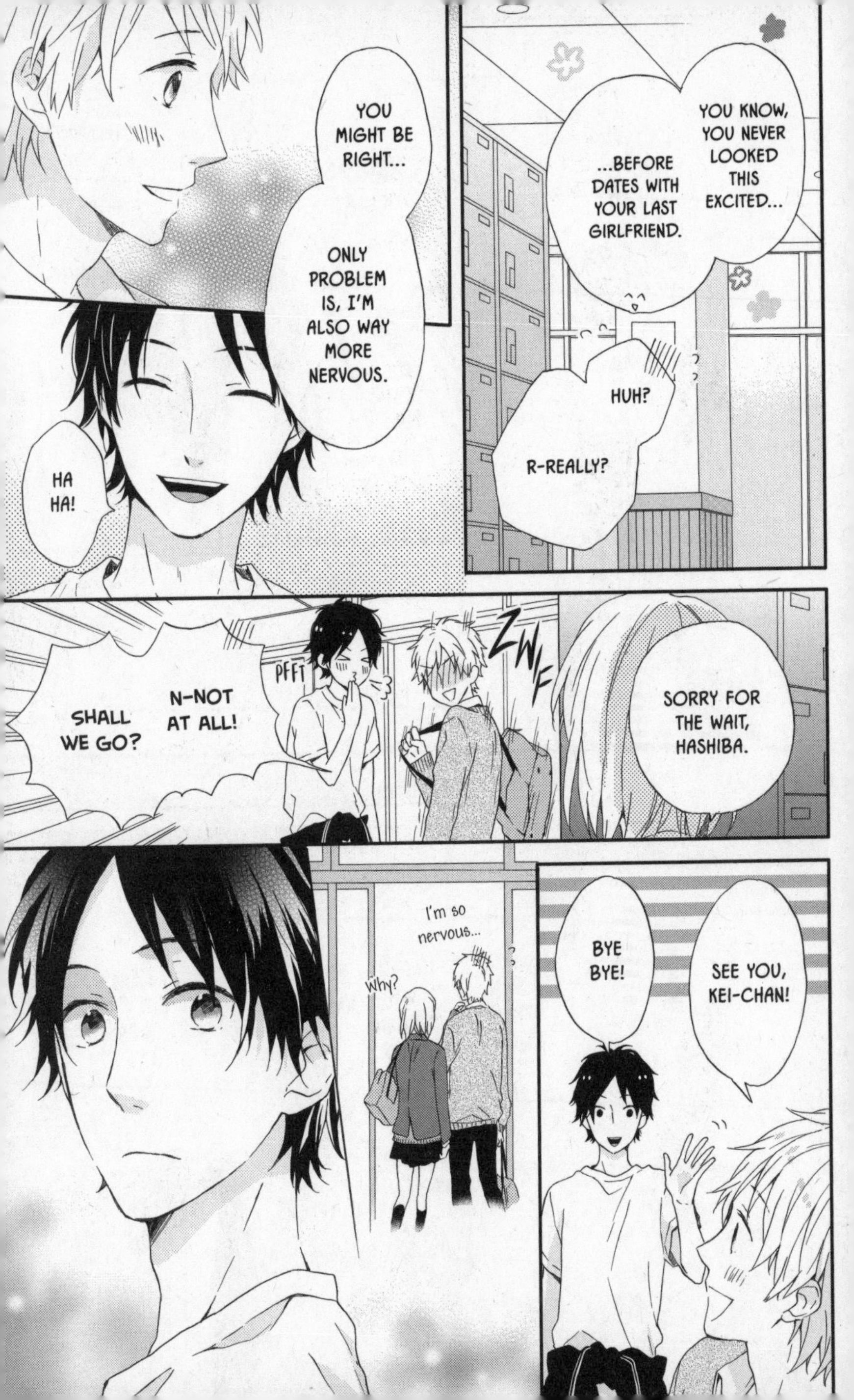

YOU KNOW, YOU NEVER LOOKED THIS EXCITED...
...BEFORE DATES WITH YOUR LAST GIRLFRIEND.
HUH?
R-REALLY?
YOU MIGHT BE RIGHT...
ONLY PROBLEM IS, I'M ALSO WAY MORE NERVOUS.
HA HA!
SORRY FOR THE WAIT, HASHIBA.
ZWIF
PFFT
N-NOT AT ALL!
SHALL WE GO?
SEE YOU, KEI-CHAN!
BYE BYE!
I'm so nervous...
Why?

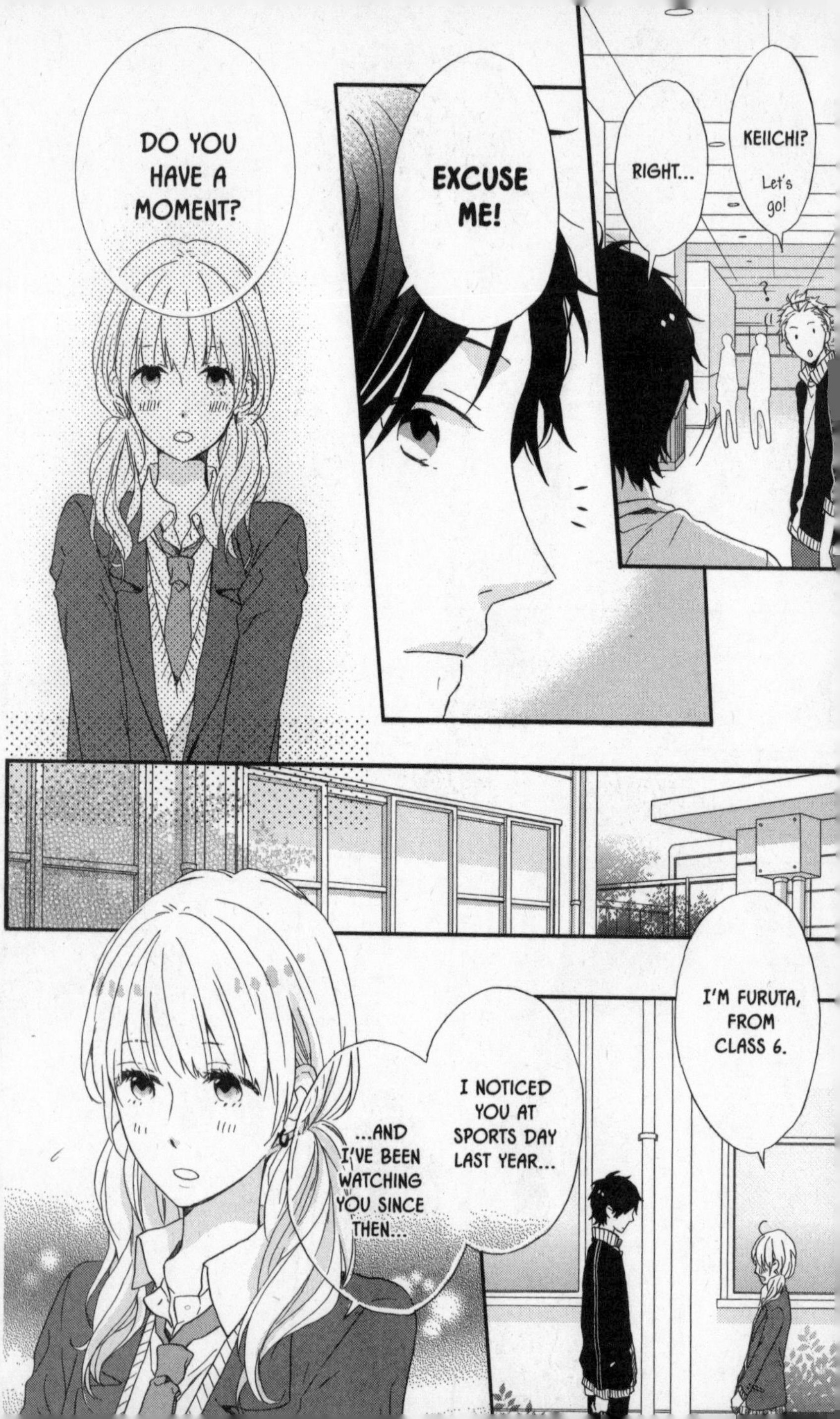
KEIICHI?
Let's go!
RIGHT...
EXCUSE ME!
DO YOU HAVE A MOMENT?
I'M FURUTA, FROM CLASS 6.
I NOTICED YOU AT SPORTS DAY LAST YEAR...
...AND I'VE BEEN WATCHING YOU SINCE THEN...

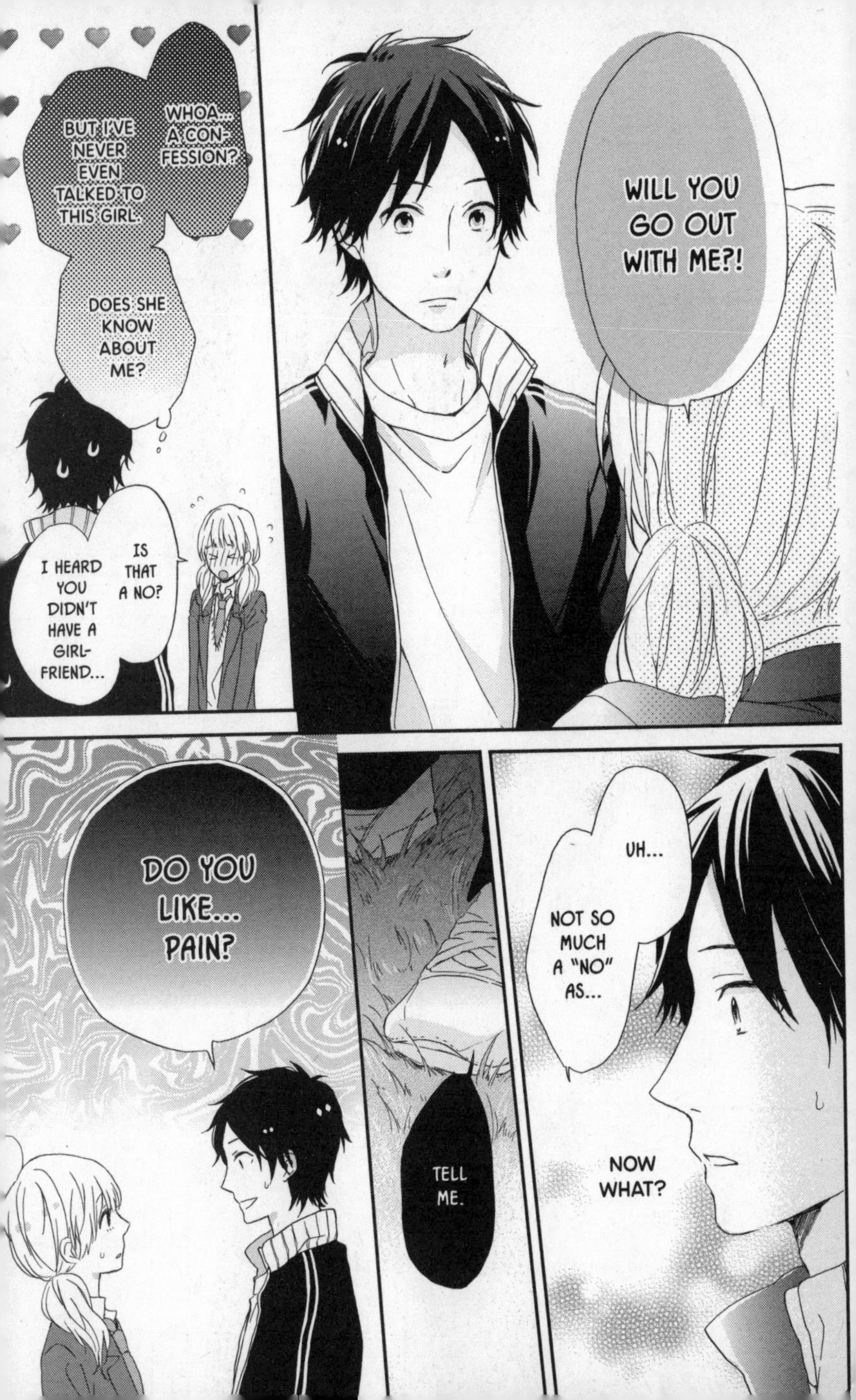
WILL YOU GO OUT WITH ME?!
WHOA... A CON-FESSION?
BUT I'VE NEVER EVEN TALKED TO THIS GIRL.
DOES SHE KNOW ABOUT ME?
IS THAT A NO?
I HEARD YOU DIDN'T HAVE A GIRL-FRIEND...
UH...
NOT SO MUCH A "NO" AS...
NOW WHAT?
TELL ME.
DO YOU LIKE... PAIN?

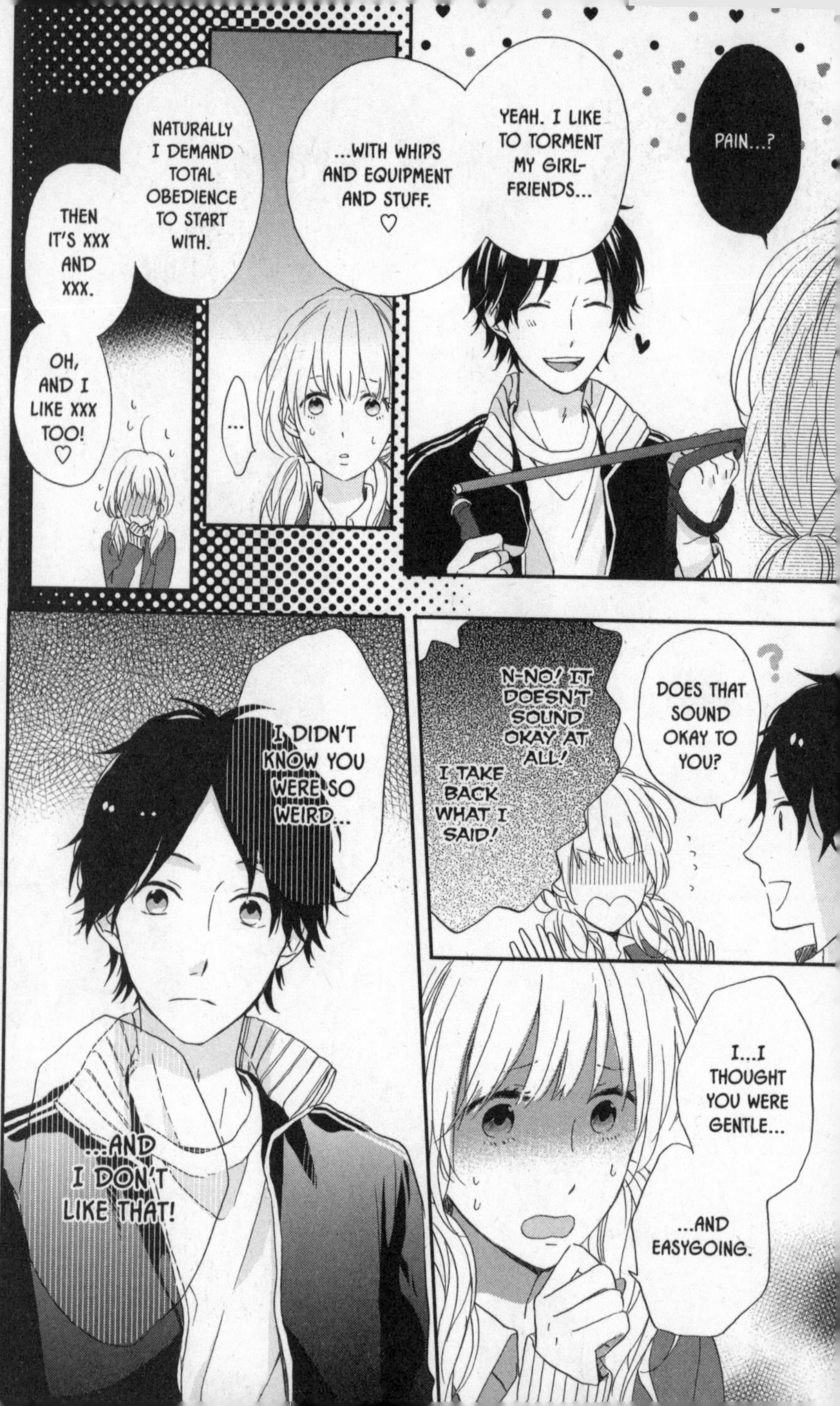
PAIN...?
YEAH. I LIKE TO TORMENT MY GIRL-FRIENDS...
...WITH WHIPS AND EQUIPMENT AND STUFF. ♡
...
NATURALLY I DEMAND TOTAL OBEDIENCE TO START WITH.
THEN IT'S XXX AND XXX.
OH, AND I LIKE XXX TOO! ♡
DOES THAT SOUND OKAY TO YOU?
N-NO! IT DOESN'T SOUND OKAY AT ALL!
I TAKE BACK WHAT I SAID!
I...I THOUGHT YOU WERE GENTLE...
...AND EASYGOING.
I DIDN'T KNOW YOU WERE SO WEIRD...
...AND I DON'T LIKE THAT!

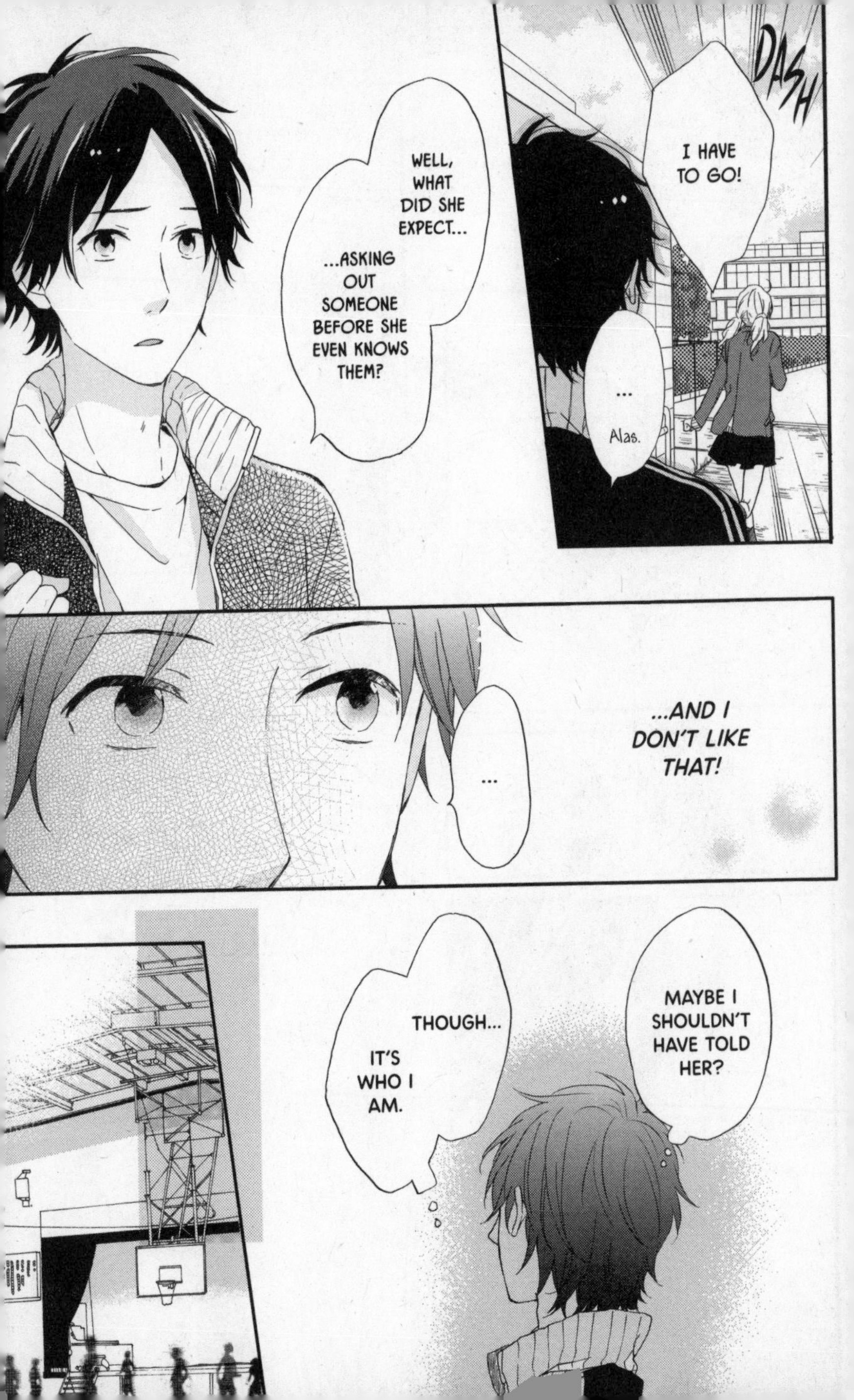
DASH
I HAVE TO GO!
... Alas.
WELL, WHAT DID SHE EXPECT...
...ASKING OUT SOMEONE BEFORE SHE EVEN KNOWS THEM?
...AND I DON'T LIKE THAT!
...
MAYBE I SHOULDN'T HAVE TOLD HER?
THOUGH...
IT'S WHO I AM.

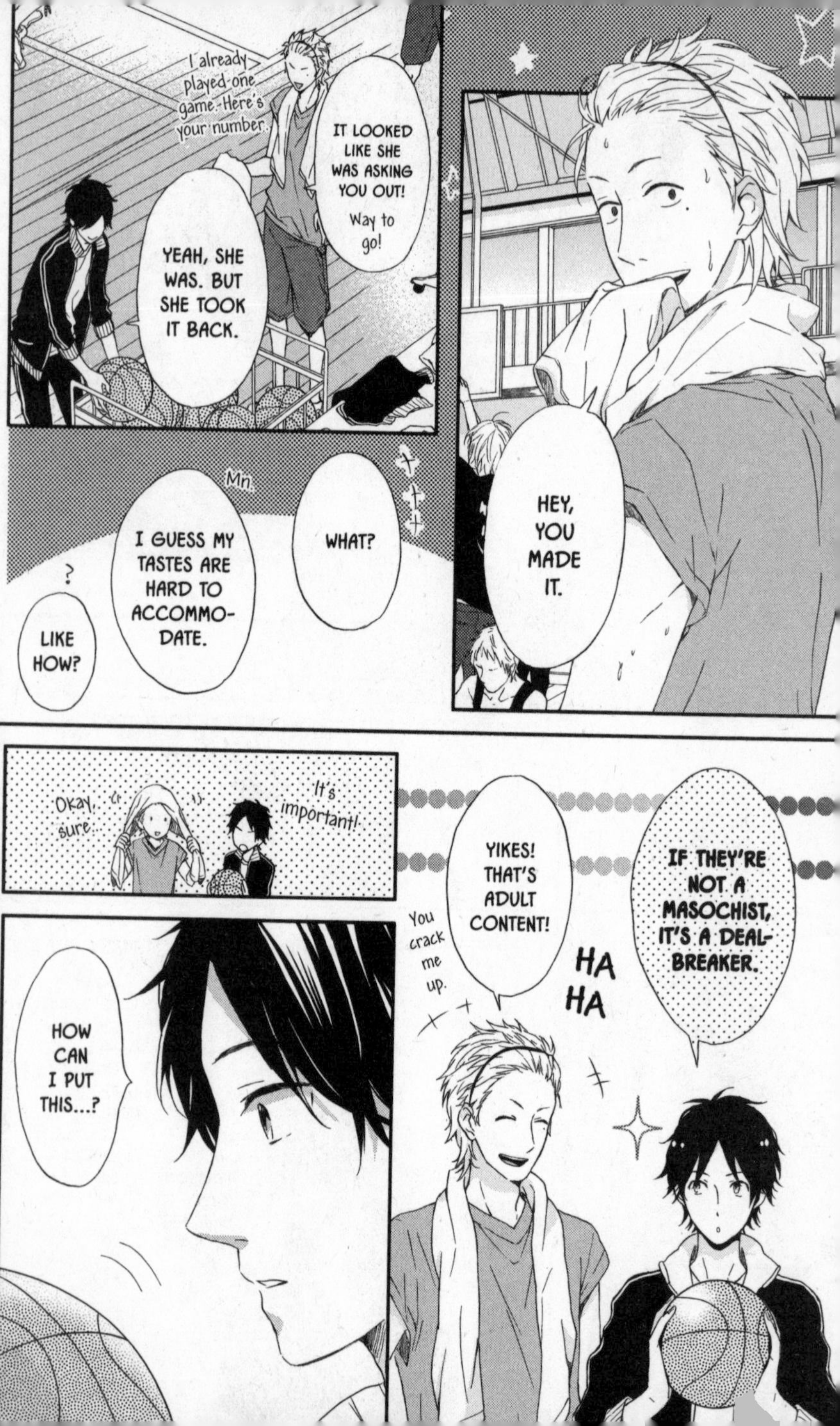
HEY, YOU MADE IT.
I already played one game. Here's your number.
IT LOOKED LIKE SHE WAS ASKING YOU OUT!
Way to go!
YEAH, SHE WAS. BUT SHE TOOK IT BACK.
WHAT?
Mn.
I GUESS MY TASTES ARE HARD TO ACCOMMODATE.
?
LIKE HOW?
IF THEY'RE NOT A MASOCHIST, IT'S A DEAL-BREAKER.
HA HA
YIKES! THAT'S ADULT CONTENT!
You crack me up.
It's important!
Okay, sure.
HOW CAN I PUT THIS...?

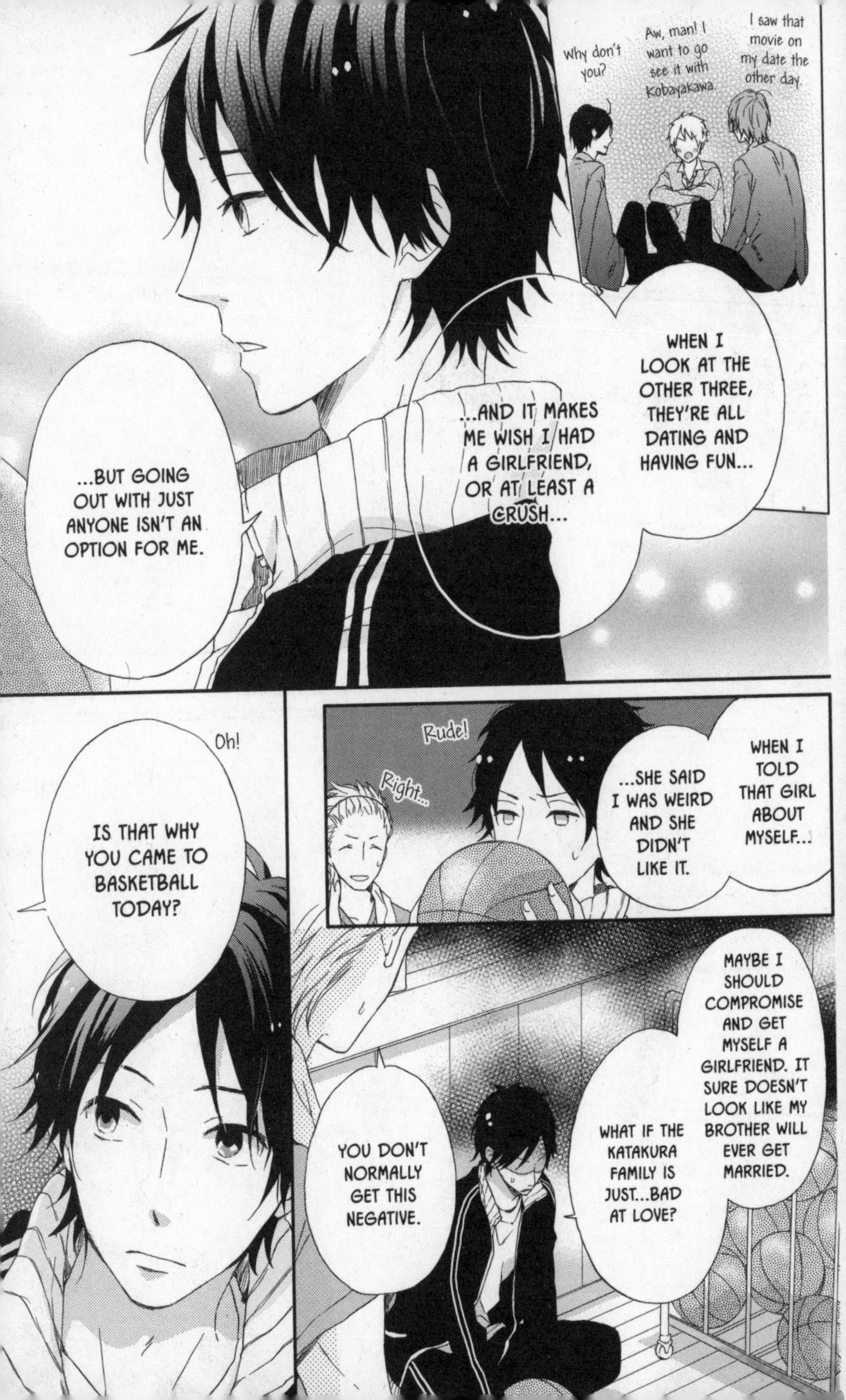
I saw that movie on my date the other day.
Aw, man! I want to go see it with Kobayakawa.
Why don't you?
WHEN I LOOK AT THE OTHER THREE, THEY'RE ALL DATING AND HAVING FUN...
...AND IT MAKES ME WISH I HAD A GIRLFRIEND, OR AT LEAST A CRUSH...
...BUT GOING OUT WITH JUST ANYONE ISN'T AN OPTION FOR ME.
WHEN I TOLD THAT GIRL ABOUT MYSELF...
...SHE SAID I WAS WEIRD AND SHE DIDN'T LIKE IT.
Rude!
Right...
MAYBE I SHOULD COMPROMISE AND GET MYSELF A GIRLFRIEND. IT SURE DOESN'T LOOK LIKE MY BROTHER WILL EVER GET MARRIED.
WHAT IF THE KATAKURA FAMILY IS JUST...BAD AT LOVE?
YOU DON'T NORMALLY GET THIS NEGATIVE.
Oh!
IS THAT WHY YOU CAME TO BASKETBALL TODAY?

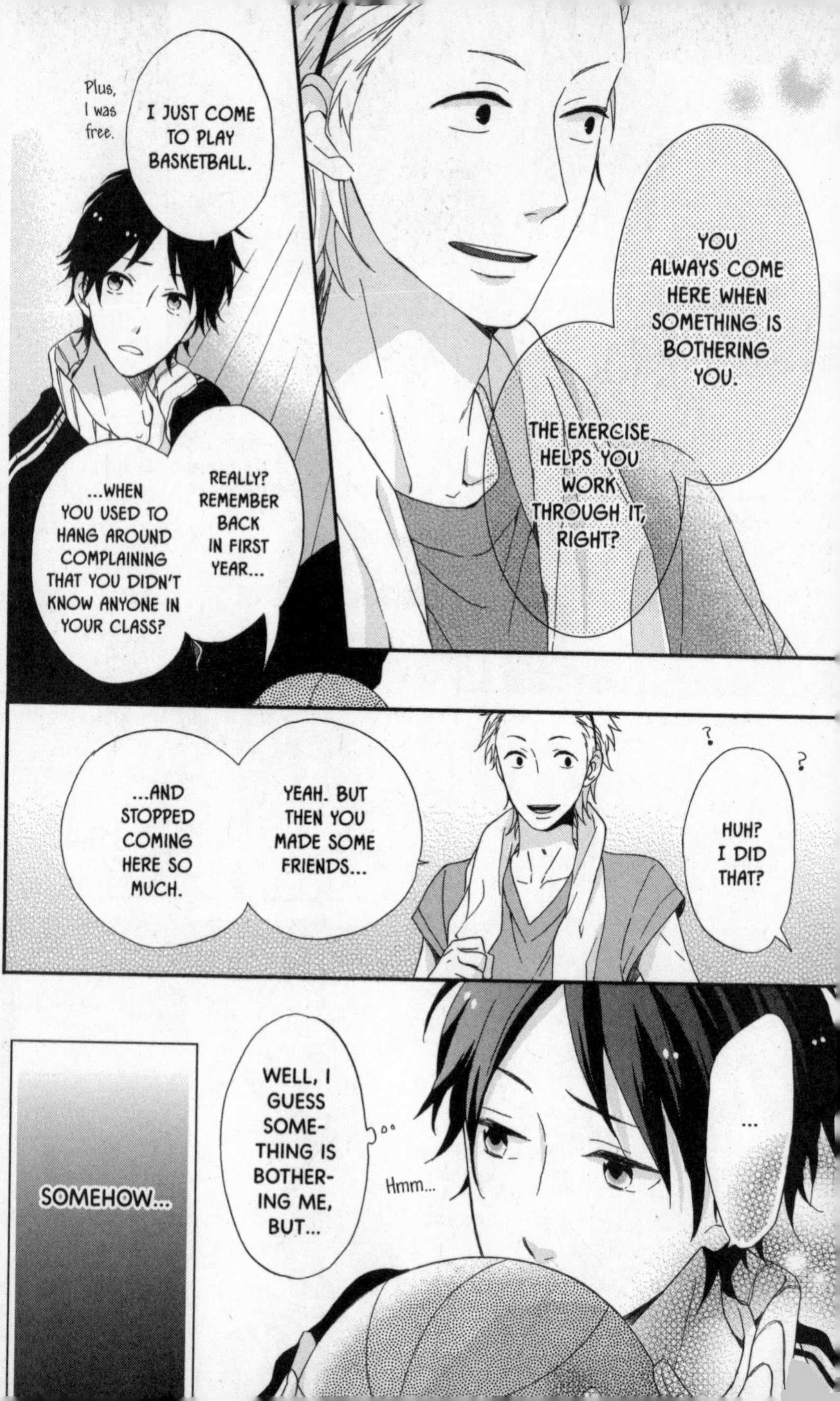
YOU ALWAYS COME HERE WHEN SOMETHING IS BOTHERING YOU.
THE EXERCISE HELPS YOU WORK THROUGH IT, RIGHT?
I JUST COME TO PLAY BASKETBALL.
Plus, I was free.
REALLY? REMEMBER BACK IN FIRST YEAR...
...WHEN YOU USED TO HANG AROUND COMPLAINING THAT YOU DIDN'T KNOW ANYONE IN YOUR CLASS?
? ?
HUH? I DID THAT?
YEAH. BUT THEN YOU MADE SOME FRIENDS...
...AND STOPPED COMING HERE SO MUCH.
...
Hmm...
WELL, I GUESS SOME-THING IS BOTHER-ING ME, BUT...
SOMEHOW...

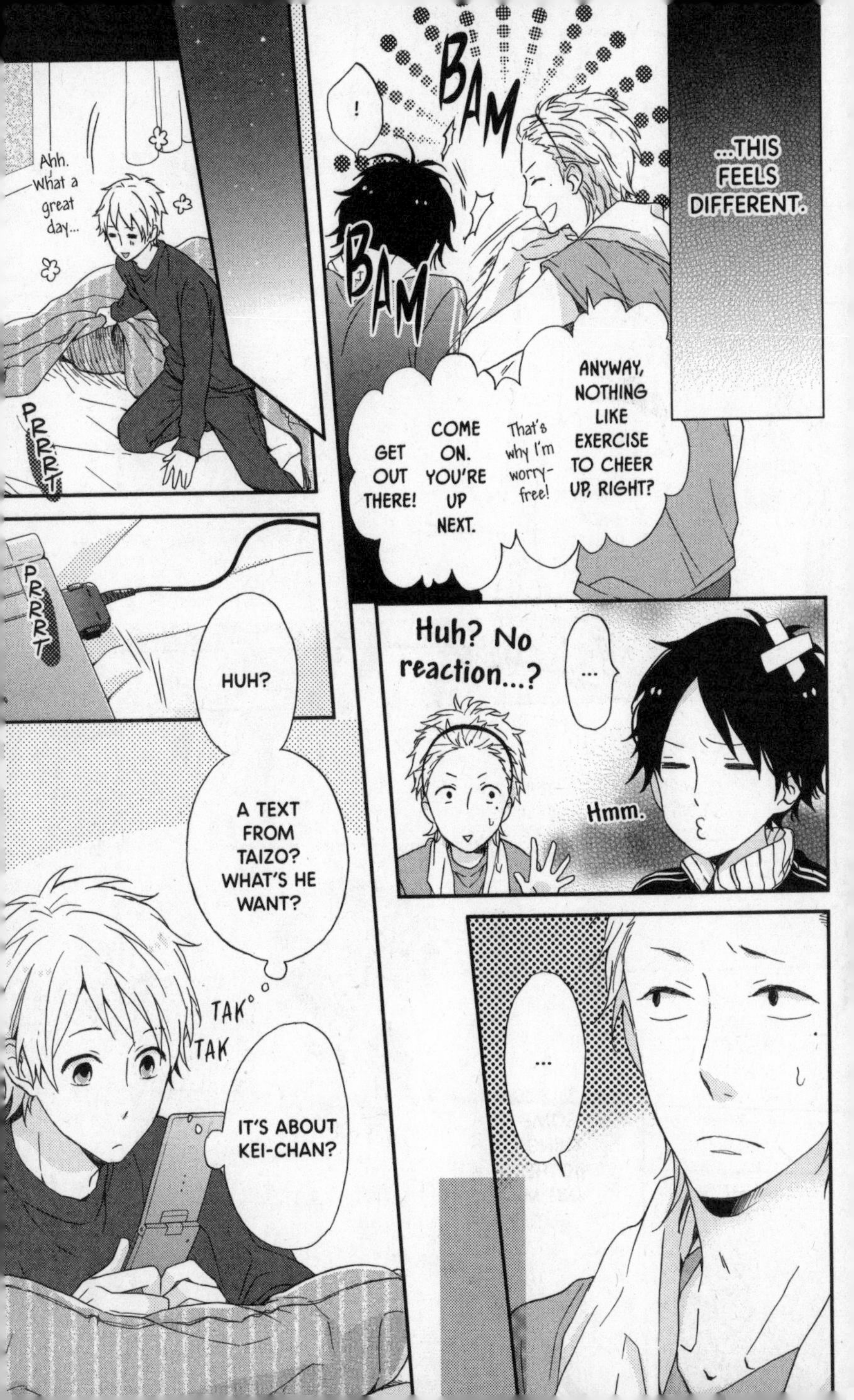
...THIS FEELS DIFFERENT.
BAM
BAM
ANYWAY, NOTHING LIKE EXERCISE TO CHEER UP, RIGHT?
That's why I'm worry-free!
COME ON. YOU'RE UP NEXT.
GET OUT THERE!
!
Huh? No reaction...?
...
Hmm.
...
Ahh. What a great day...
PRRRT
PRRRT
HUH?
A TEXT FROM TAIZO? WHAT'S HE WANT?
TAK
TAK
IT'S ABOUT KEI-CHAN?

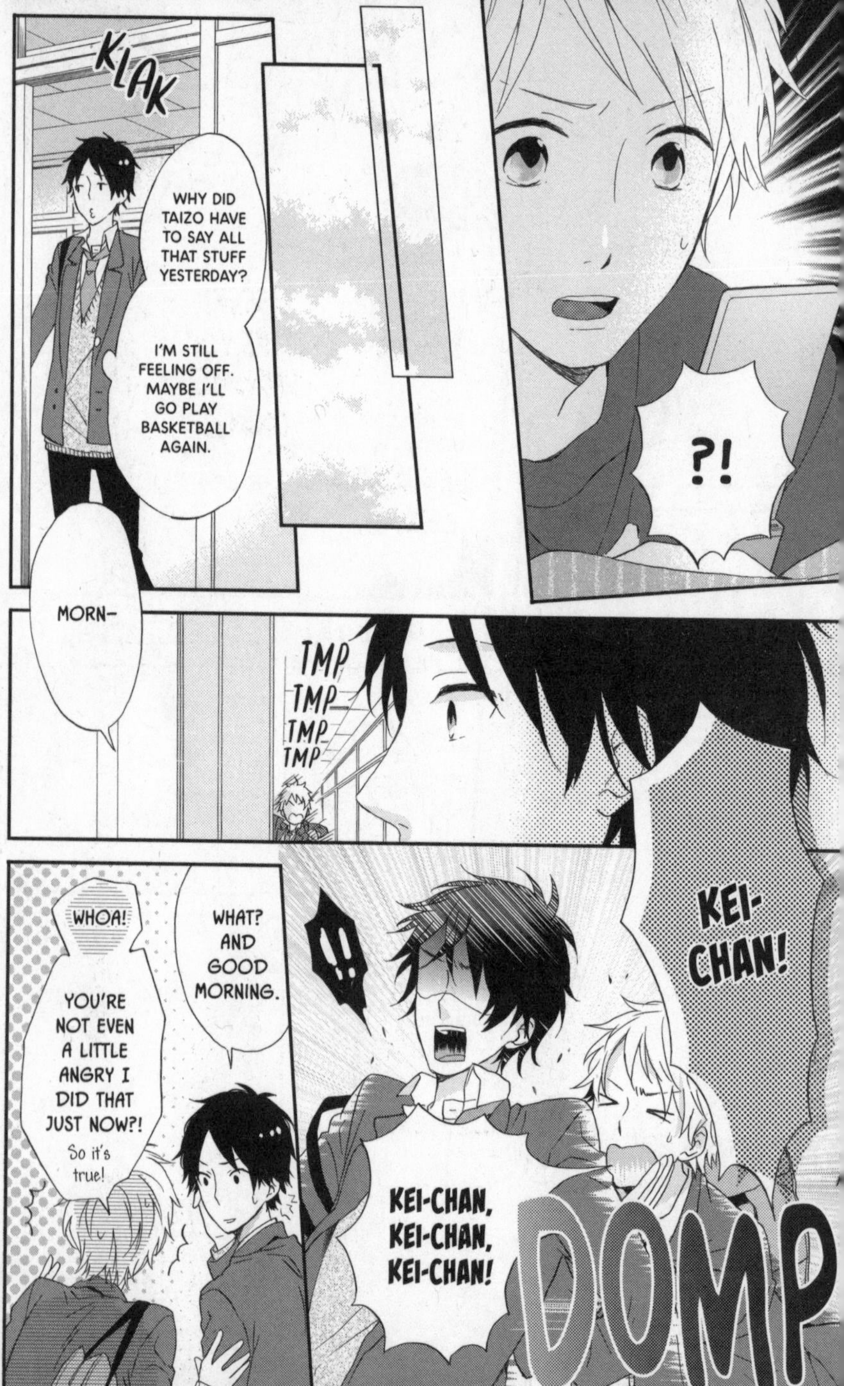
?!
KLAK
WHY DID TAIZO HAVE TO SAY ALL THAT STUFF YESTERDAY?
I'M STILL FEELING OFF. MAYBE I'LL GO PLAY BASKETBALL AGAIN.
MORN-
TMP TMP TMP TMP
KEI-CHAN!
KEI-CHAN, KEI-CHAN, KEI-CHAN!
DOMP
!!
WHAT? AND GOOD MORNING.
WHOA!
YOU'RE NOT EVEN A LITTLE ANGRY I DID THAT JUST NOW?!
So it's true!

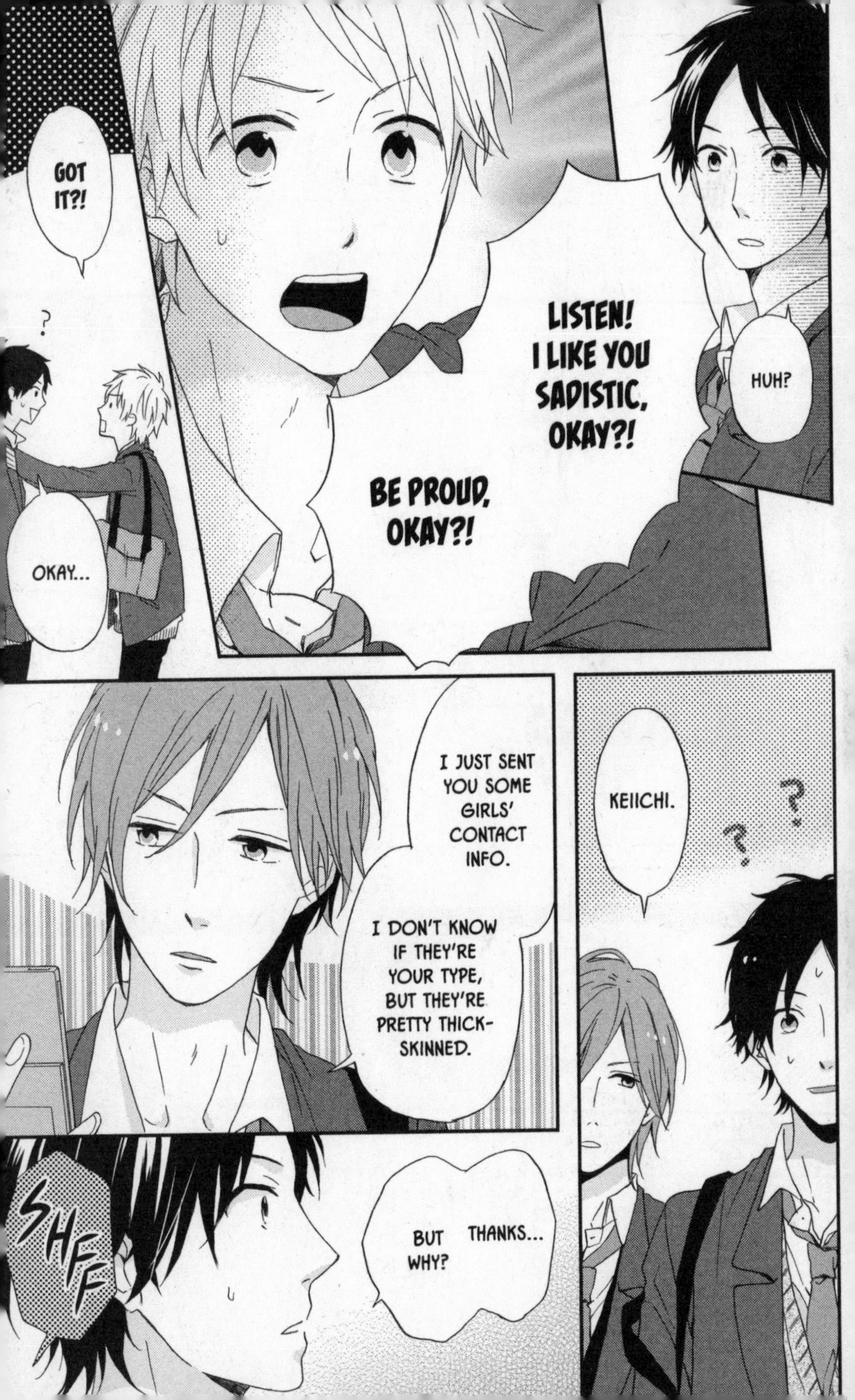
HUH?
LISTEN! I LIKE YOU SADISTIC, OKAY?!
BE PROUD, OKAY?!
GOT IT?!
?
OKAY...
KEIICHI.
? ?
I JUST SENT YOU SOME GIRLS' CONTACT INFO.
I DON'T KNOW IF THEY'RE YOUR TYPE, BUT THEY'RE PRETTY THICK-SKINNED.
SHFF
THANKS... BUT WHY?

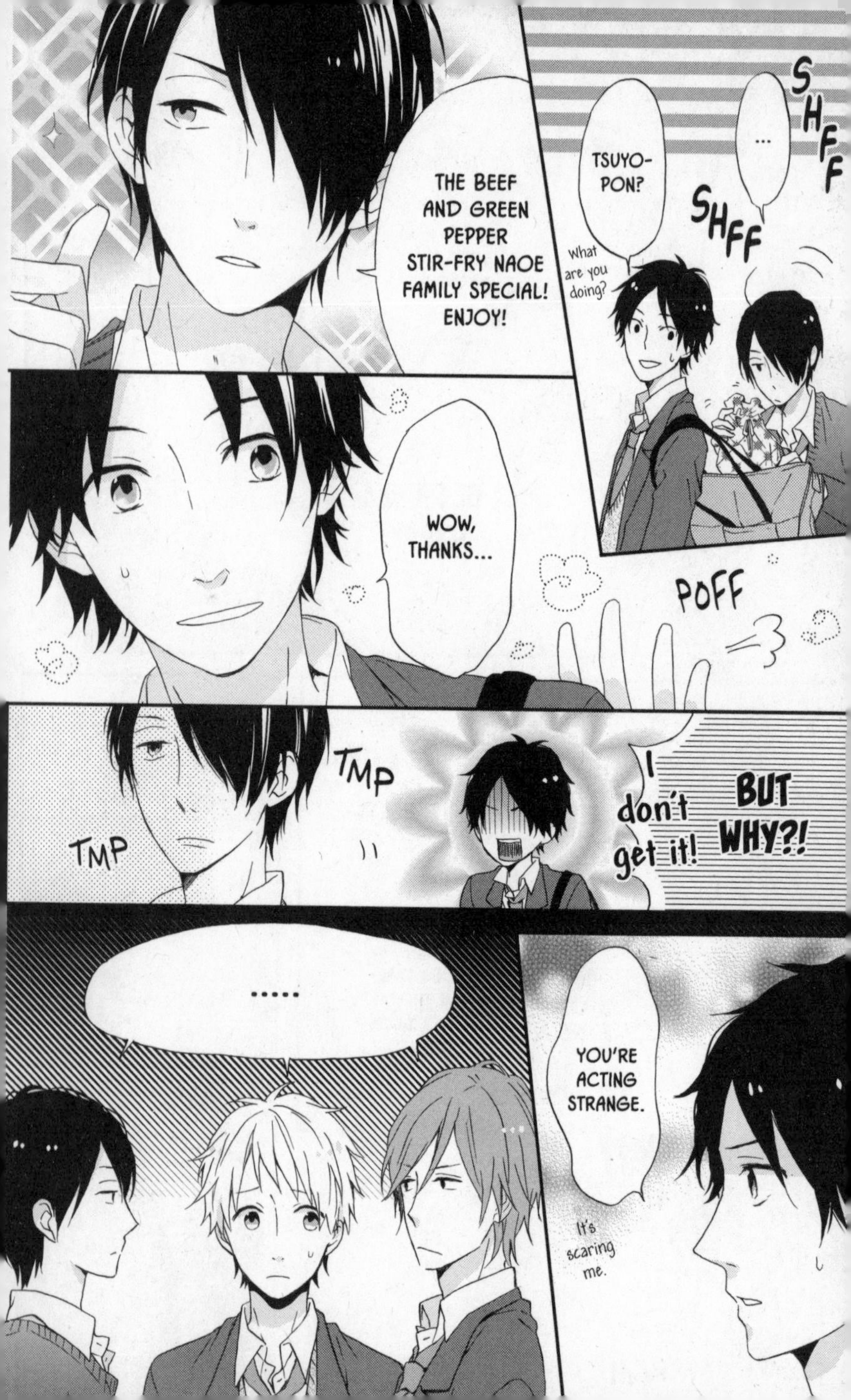
SHFF
...
SHFF
TSUYO-PON?
What are you doing?
THE BEEF AND GREEN PEPPER STIR-FRY NAOE FAMILY SPECIAL! ENJOY!
WOW, THANKS...
POFF
BUT WHY?!
I don't get it!
TMP
TMP
YOU'RE ACTING STRANGE.
It's scaring me.
.....

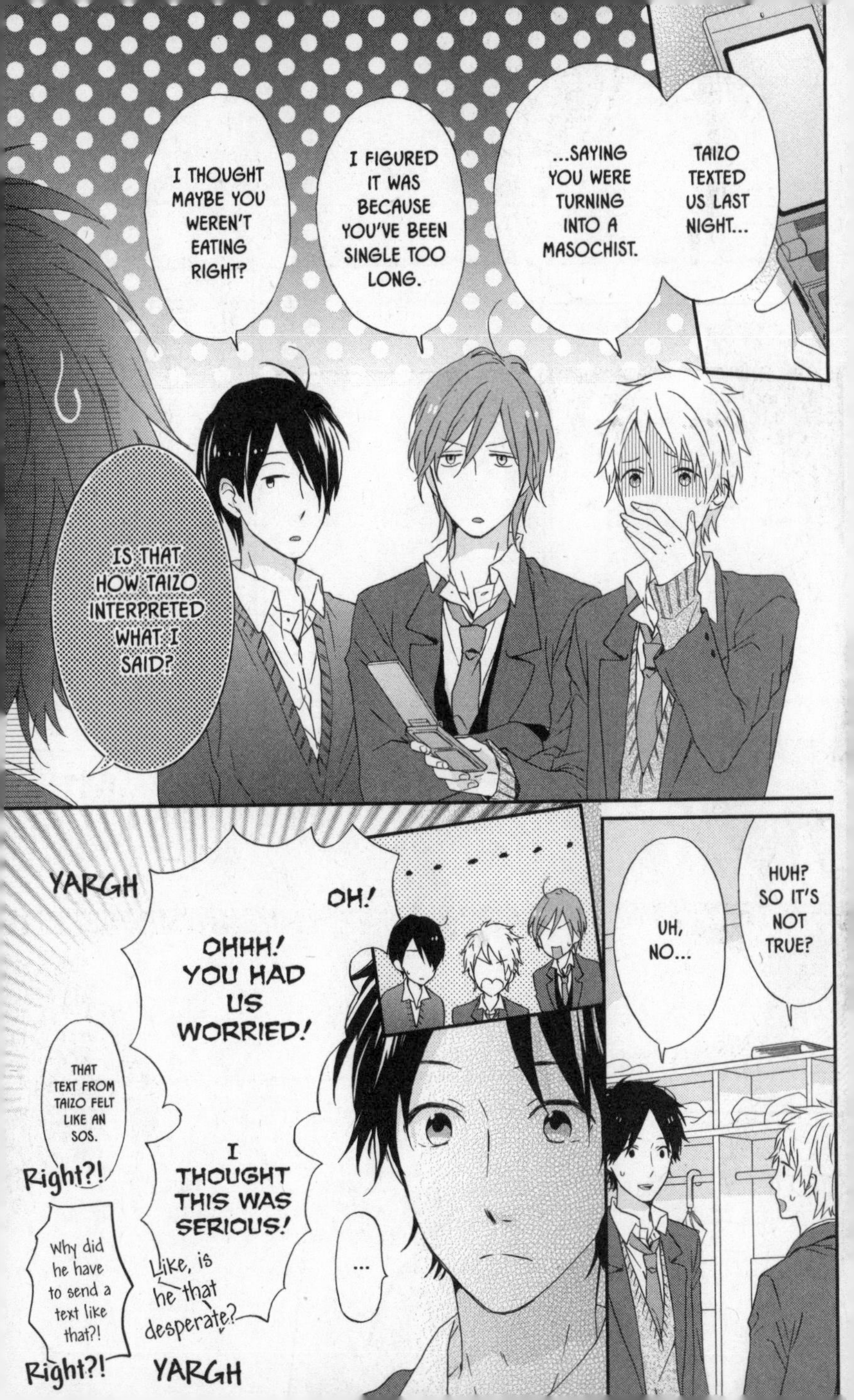

TAIZO TEXTED US LAST NIGHT...
...SAYING YOU WERE TURNING INTO A MASOCHIST.
I FIGURED IT WAS BECAUSE YOU'VE BEEN SINGLE TOO LONG.
I THOUGHT MAYBE YOU WEREN'T EATING RIGHT?
IS THAT HOW TAIZO INTERPRETED WHAT I SAID?
HUH? SO IT'S NOT TRUE?
UH, NO...
. . . . .
OH!
OHHH! YOU HAD US WORRIED!
YARGH
...
I THOUGHT THIS WAS SERIOUS!
THAT TEXT FROM TAIZO FELT LIKE AN SOS.
Right?!
Like, is he that desperate?
Why did he have to send a text like that?!
Right?!
YARGH

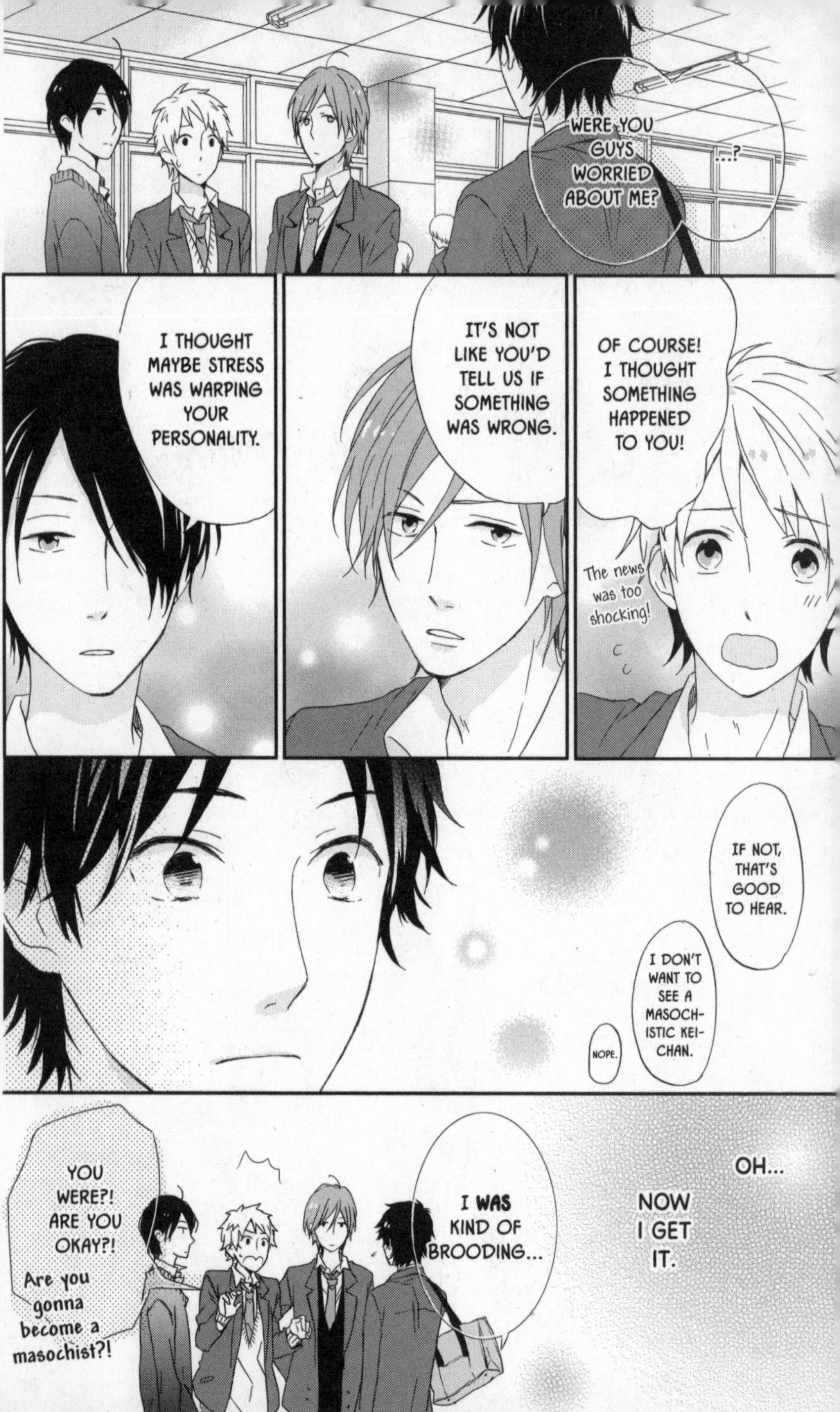
WERE YOU GUYS WORRIED ABOUT ME?
...?
OF COURSE! I THOUGHT SOMETHING HAPPENED TO YOU!
The news was too shocking!
IT'S NOT LIKE YOU'D TELL US IF SOMETHING WAS WRONG.
I THOUGHT MAYBE STRESS WAS WARPING YOUR PERSONALITY.
IF NOT, THAT'S GOOD TO HEAR.
I DON'T WANT TO SEE A MASOCH-ISTIC KEI-CHAN.
NOPE.
OH...
NOW I GET IT.
I WAS KIND OF BROODING...
YOU WERE?! ARE YOU OKAY?!
Are you gonna become a masochist?!

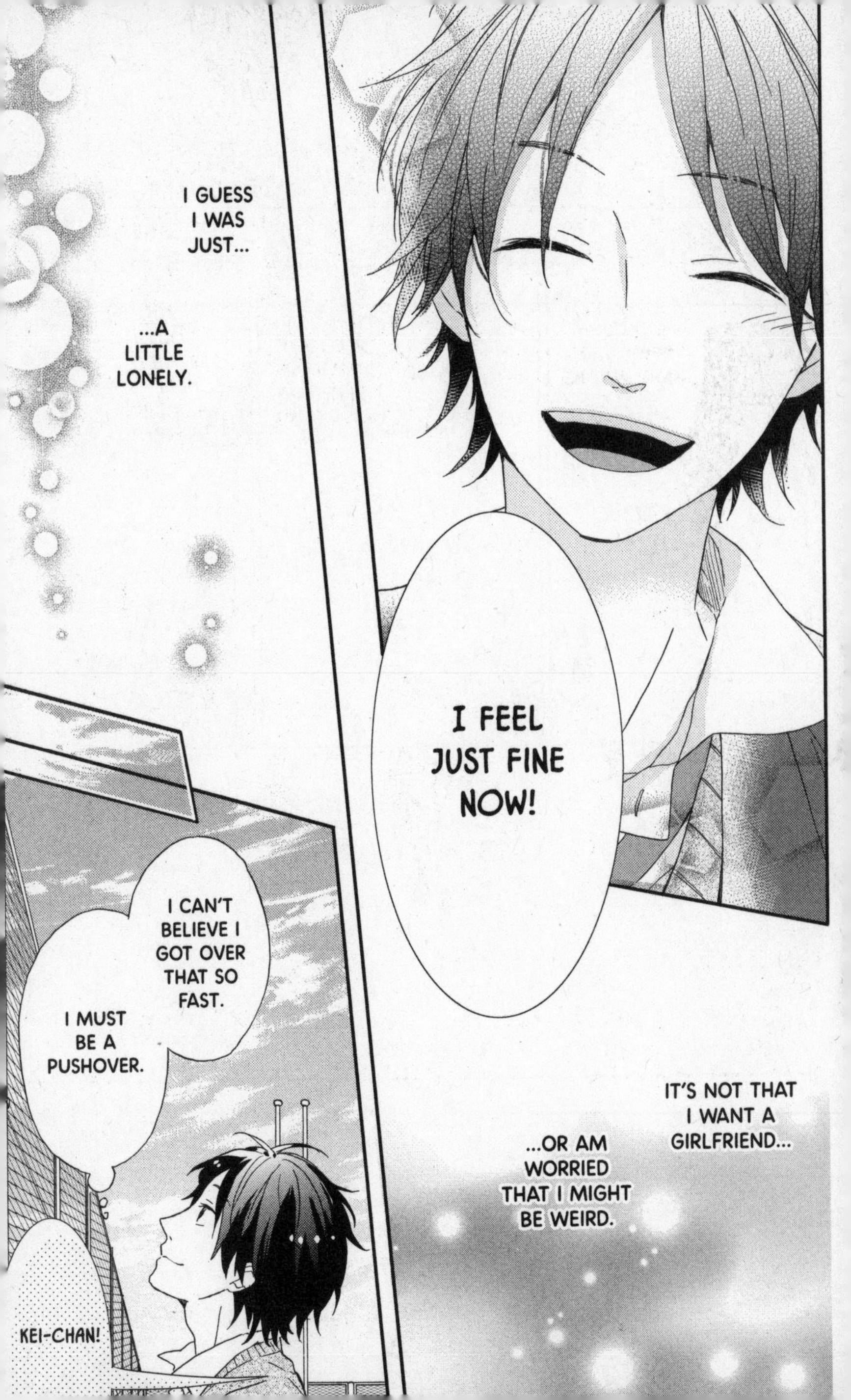
I FEEL JUST FINE NOW!
I GUESS I WAS JUST...
...A LITTLE LONELY.
IT'S NOT THAT I WANT A GIRLFRIEND...
...OR AM WORRIED THAT I MIGHT BE WEIRD.
I CAN'T BELIEVE I GOT OVER THAT SO FAST.
I MUST BE A PUSHOVER.
KEI-CHAN!

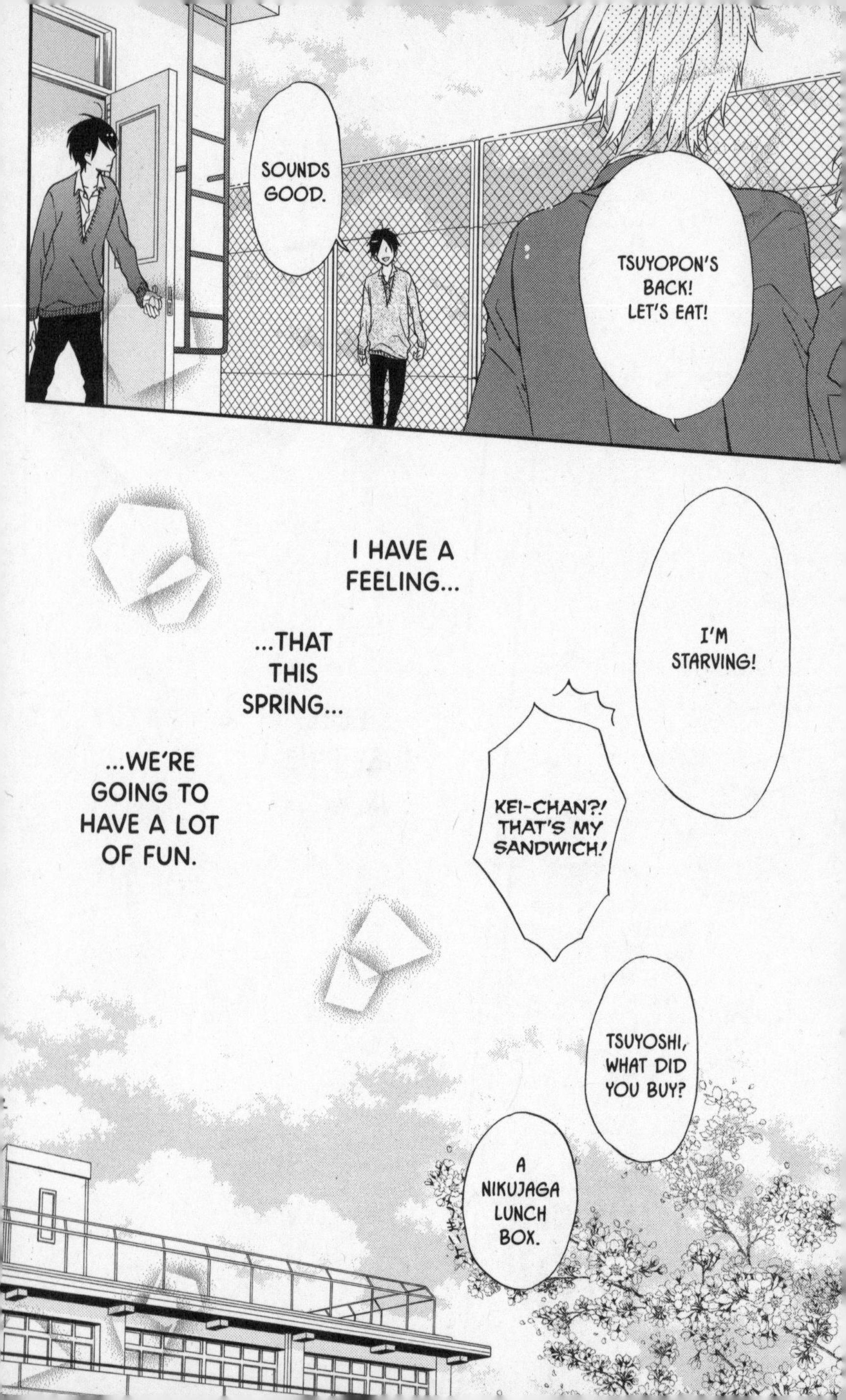
TSUYOPON'S BACK! LET'S EAT!
SOUNDS GOOD.
I'M STARVING!
KEI-CHAN?! THAT'S MY SANDWICH!
I HAVE A FEELING...
...THAT THIS SPRING...
...WE'RE GOING TO HAVE A LOT OF FUN.
TSUYOSHI, WHAT DID YOU BUY?
A NIKUJAGA LUNCH BOX.

# Rainbow
## Days

POINTLESS RAINBOW TRIVIA

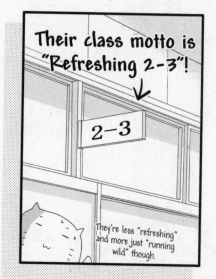

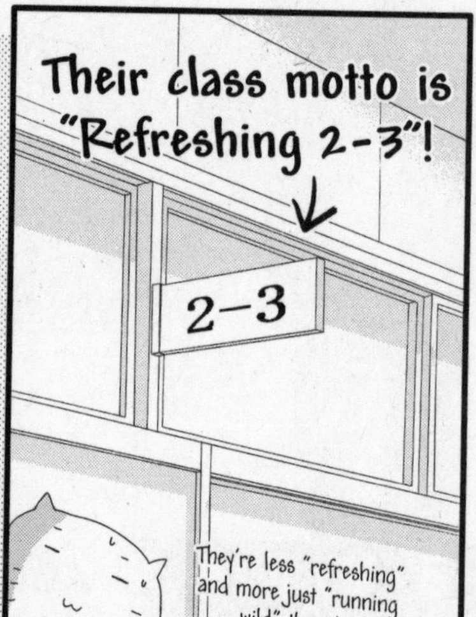
Their class motto is "Refreshing 2-3"!
2-3
They're less "refreshing" and more just "running wild" though.

# Rainbow Weather

## *Rainbow Days* Side Story

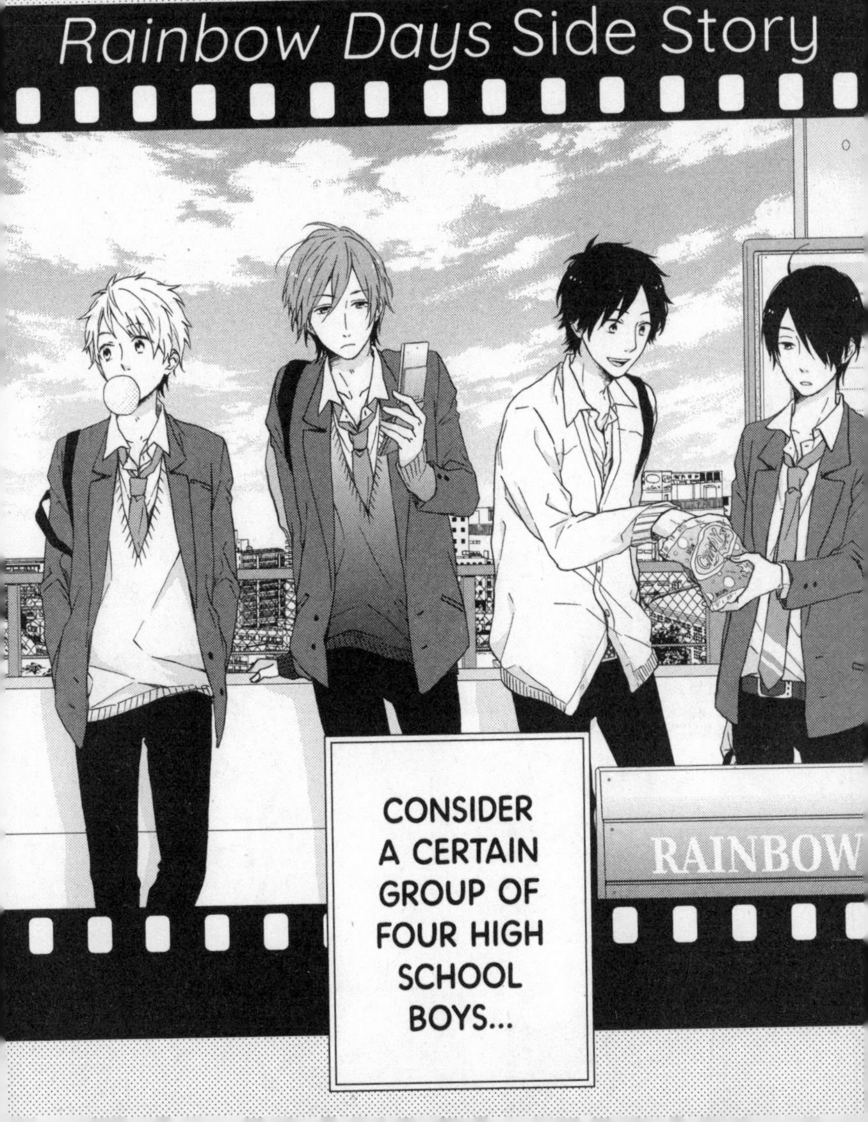
CONSIDER A CERTAIN GROUP OF FOUR HIGH SCHOOL BOYS...
RAINBOW

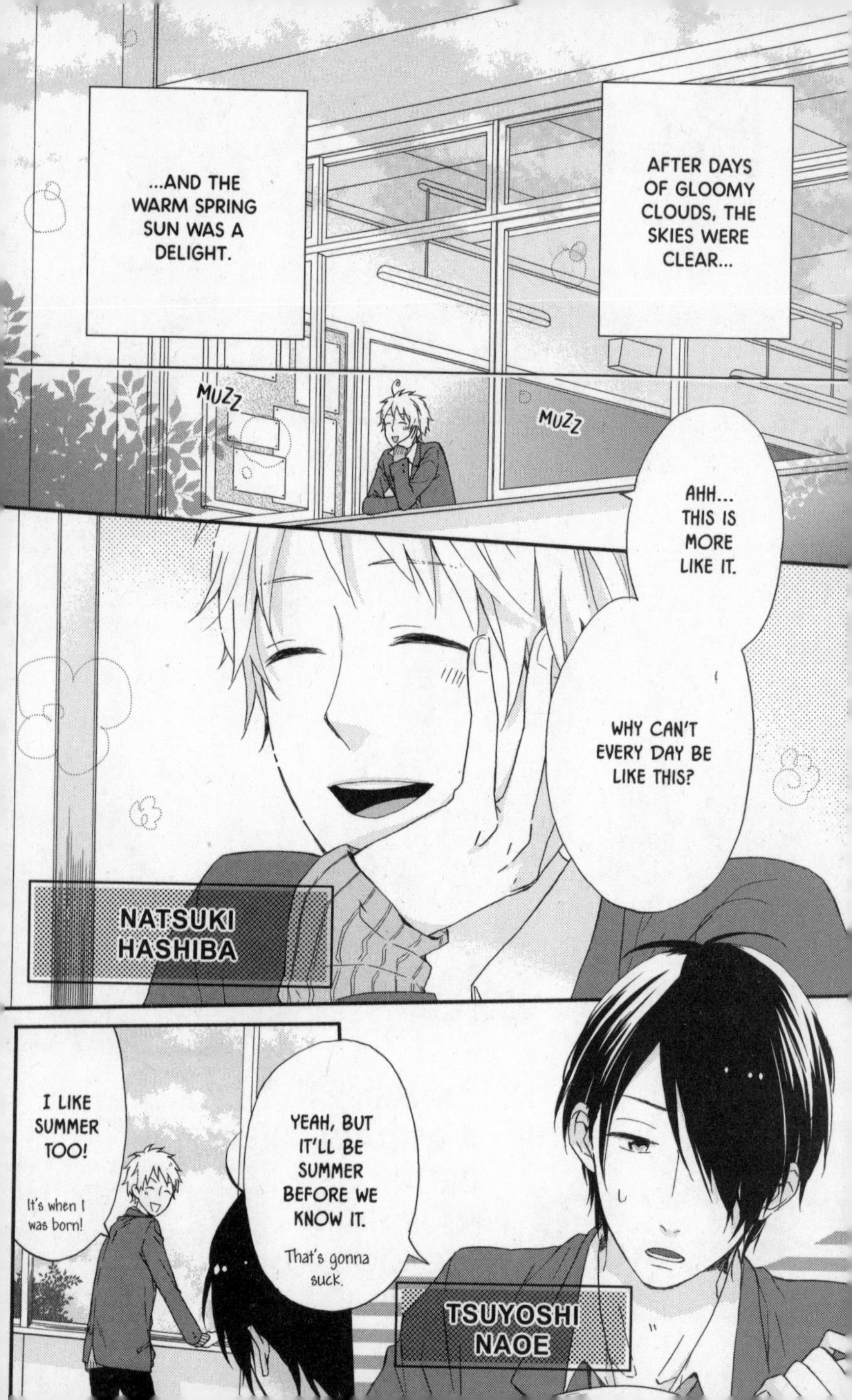
AFTER DAYS OF GLOOMY CLOUDS, THE SKIES WERE CLEAR...
...AND THE WARM SPRING SUN WAS A DELIGHT.
MUZZ
MUZZ
AHH... THIS IS MORE LIKE IT.
WHY CAN'T EVERY DAY BE LIKE THIS?
NATSUKI HASHIBA
TSUYOSHI NAOE
YEAH, BUT IT'LL BE SUMMER BEFORE WE KNOW IT.
That's gonna suck.
I LIKE SUMMER TOO!
It's when I was born!

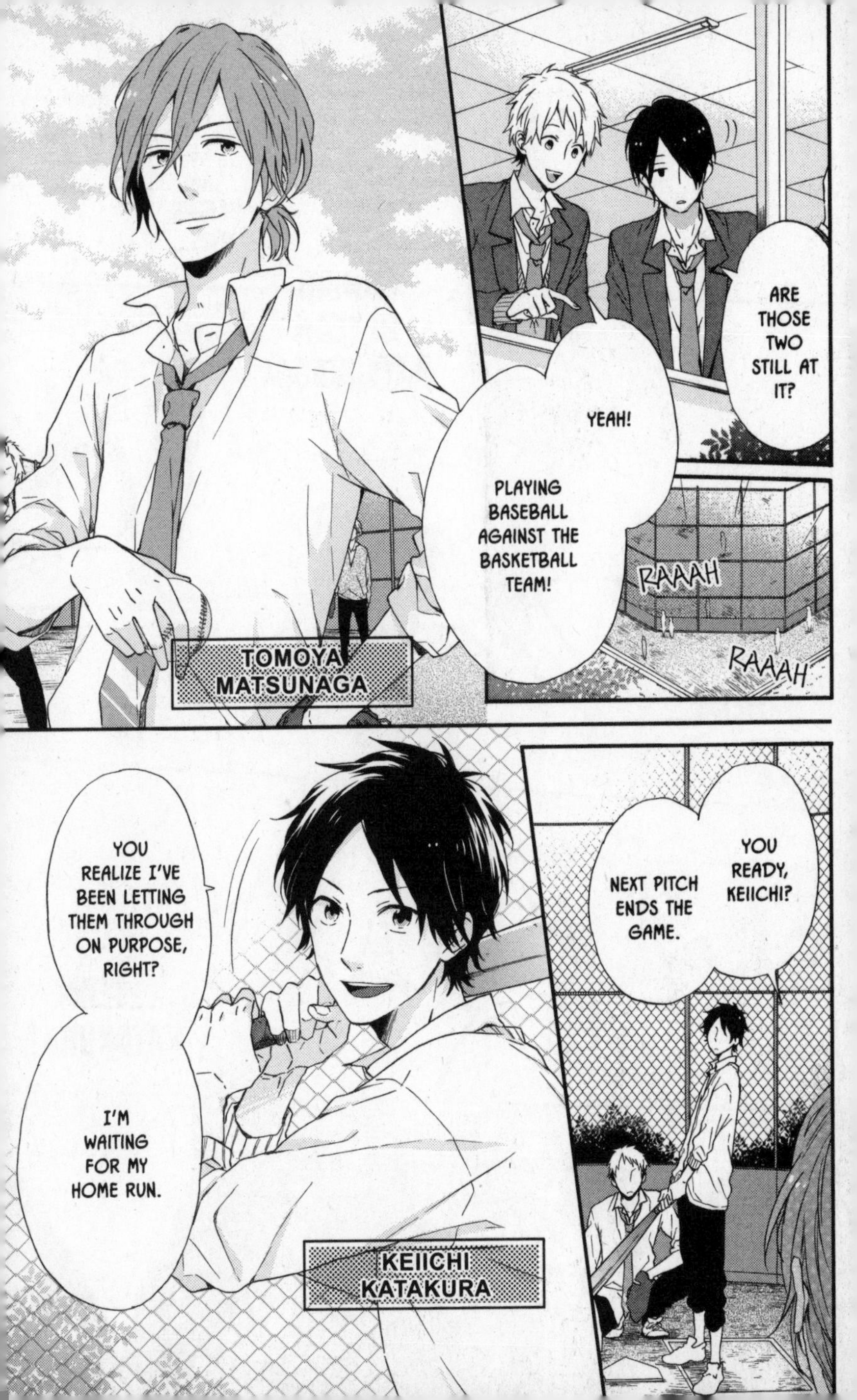
ARE THOSE TWO STILL AT IT?
YEAH!
PLAYING BASEBALL AGAINST THE BASKETBALL TEAM!
RAAAH
RAAAH
TOMOYA MATSUNAGA
YOU READY, KEIICHI?
NEXT PITCH ENDS THE GAME.
YOU REALIZE I'VE BEEN LETTING THEM THROUGH ON PURPOSE, RIGHT?
I'M WAITING FOR MY HOME RUN.
KEIICHI KATAKURA

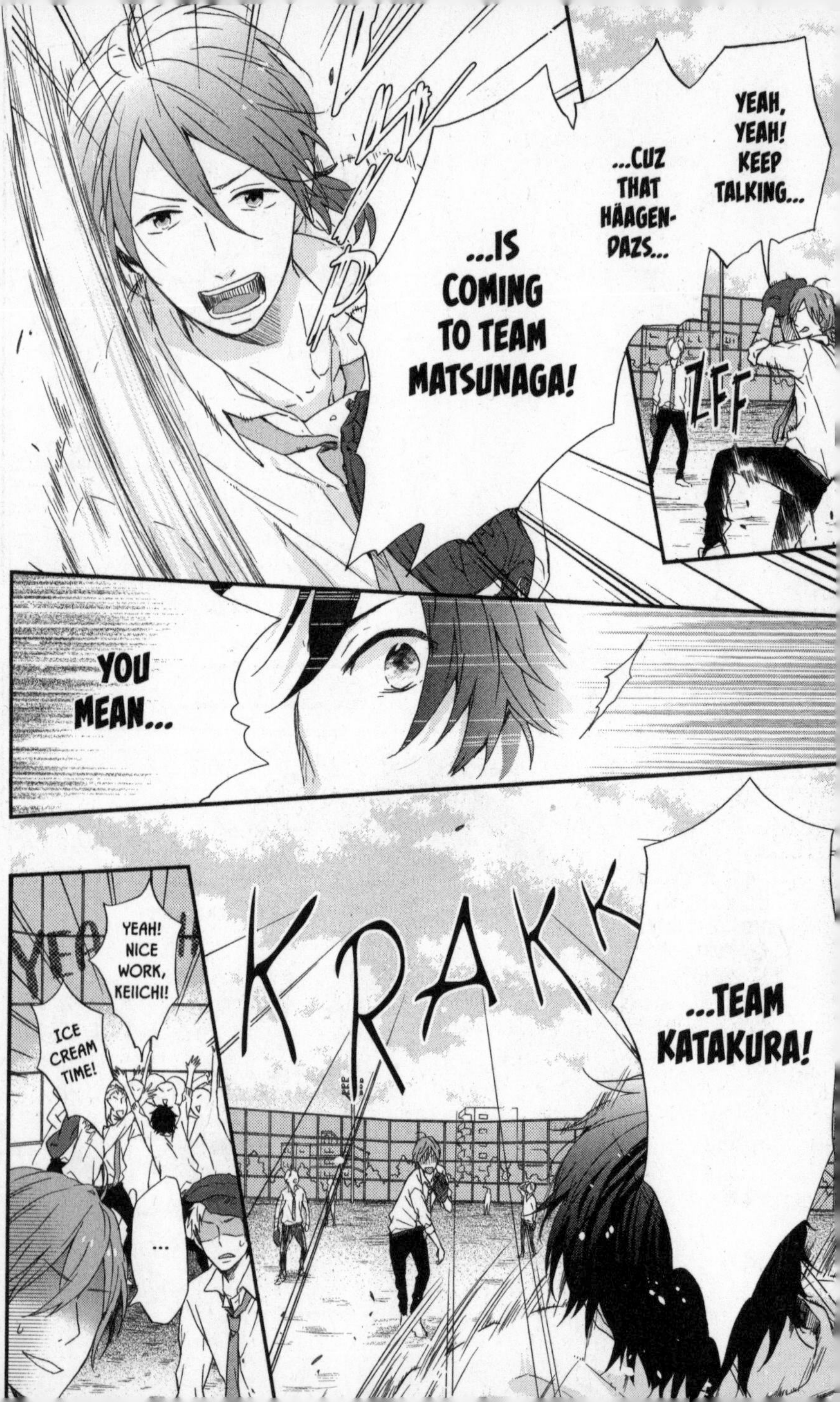
YEAH, YEAH! KEEP TALKING...
...CUZ THAT HÄAGEN-DAZS...
ZFF
...IS COMING TO TEAM MATSUNAGA!
YOU MEAN...
...TEAM KATAKURA!
KRAKK
YEAH! NICE WORK, KEIICHI!
ICE CREAM TIME!
...

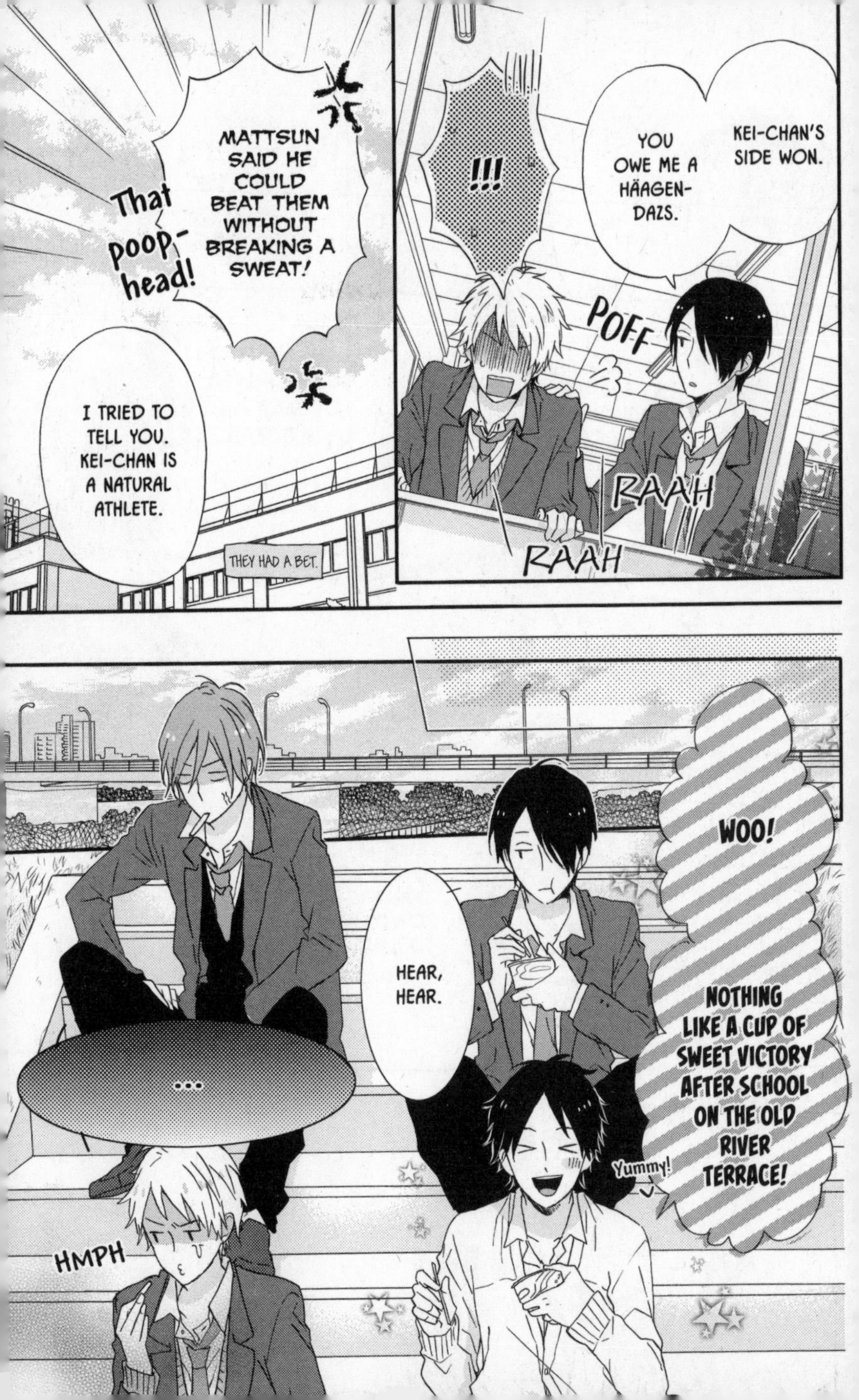
KEI-CHAN'S SIDE WON.
YOU OWE ME A HÄAGEN-DAZS.
!!!
POFF
RAAH
RAAH
MATTSUN SAID HE COULD BEAT THEM WITHOUT BREAKING A SWEAT!
That poop-head!
I TRIED TO TELL YOU. KEI-CHAN IS A NATURAL ATHLETE.
THEY HAD A BET.
WOO!
NOTHING LIKE A CUP OF SWEET VICTORY AFTER SCHOOL ON THE OLD RIVER TERRACE!
Yummy!
HEAR, HEAR.
...
HMPH

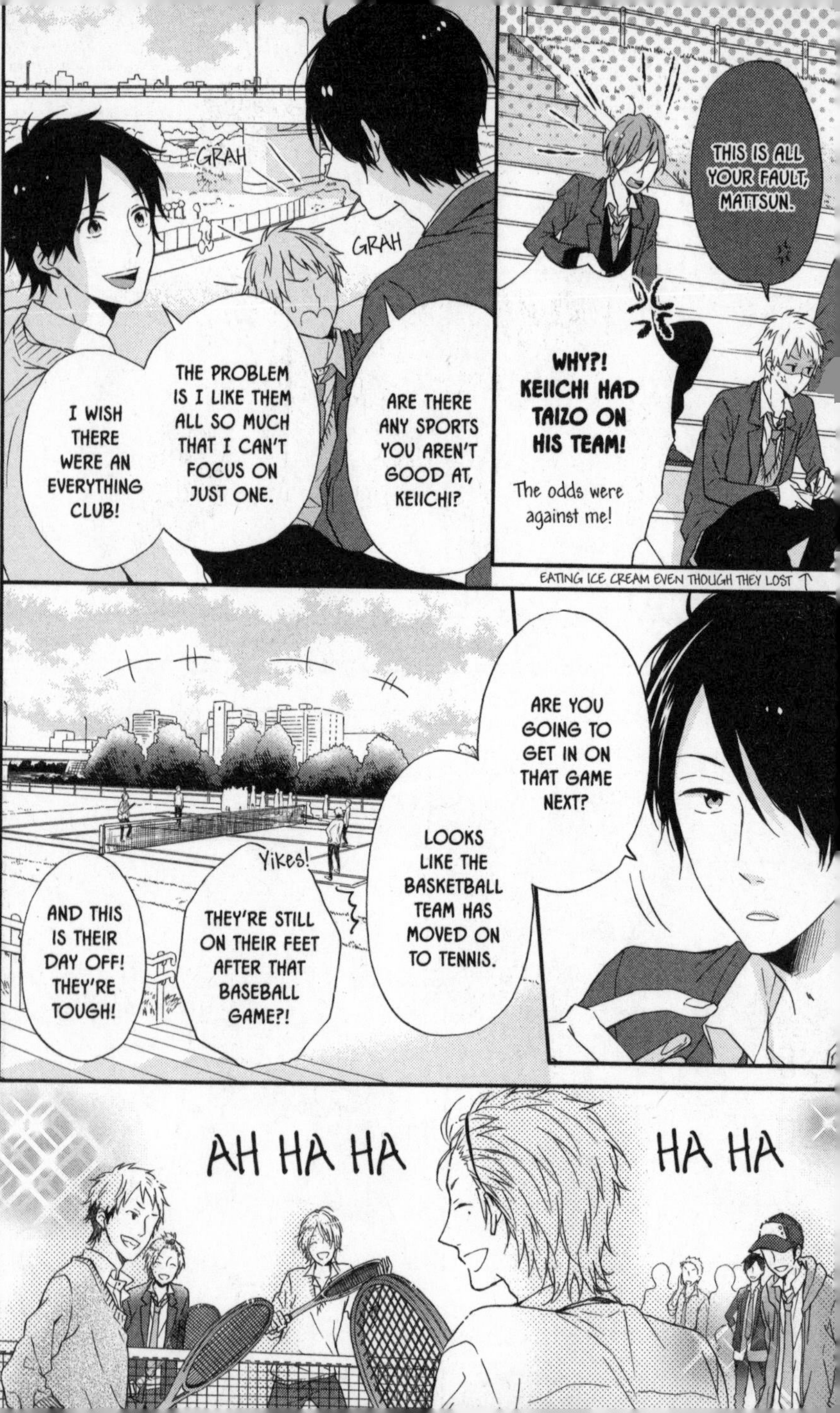
THIS IS ALL YOUR FAULT, MATTSUN.
WHY?! KEIICHI HAD TAIZO ON HIS TEAM!
The odds were against me!
EATING ICE CREAM EVEN THOUGH THEY LOST
GRAH
GRAH
ARE THERE ANY SPORTS YOU AREN'T GOOD AT, KEIICHI?
THE PROBLEM IS I LIKE THEM ALL SO MUCH THAT I CAN'T FOCUS ON JUST ONE.
I WISH THERE WERE AN EVERYTHING CLUB!
ARE YOU GOING TO GET IN ON THAT GAME NEXT?
LOOKS LIKE THE BASKETBALL TEAM HAS MOVED ON TO TENNIS.
Yikes!
THEY'RE STILL ON THEIR FEET AFTER THAT BASEBALL GAME?!
AND THIS IS THEIR DAY OFF! THEY'RE TOUGH!
HA HA
AH HA HA

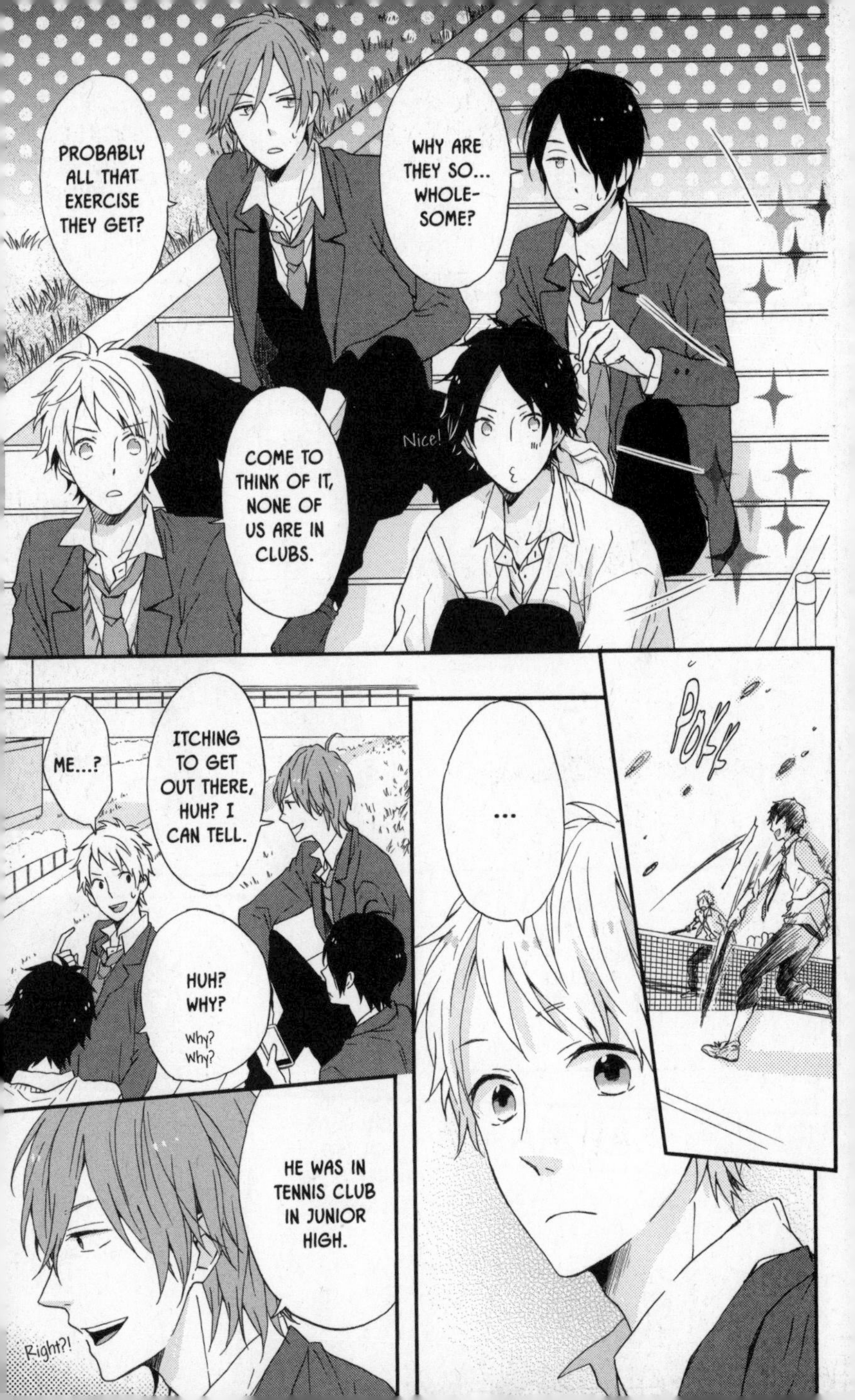
WHY ARE THEY SO... WHOLE-SOME?
PROBABLY ALL THAT EXERCISE THEY GET?
Nice!
COME TO THINK OF IT, NONE OF US ARE IN CLUBS.
POK
...
ITCHING TO GET OUT THERE, HUH? I CAN TELL.
ME...?
HUH? WHY?
Why? Why?
HE WAS IN TENNIS CLUB IN JUNIOR HIGH.
Right?!

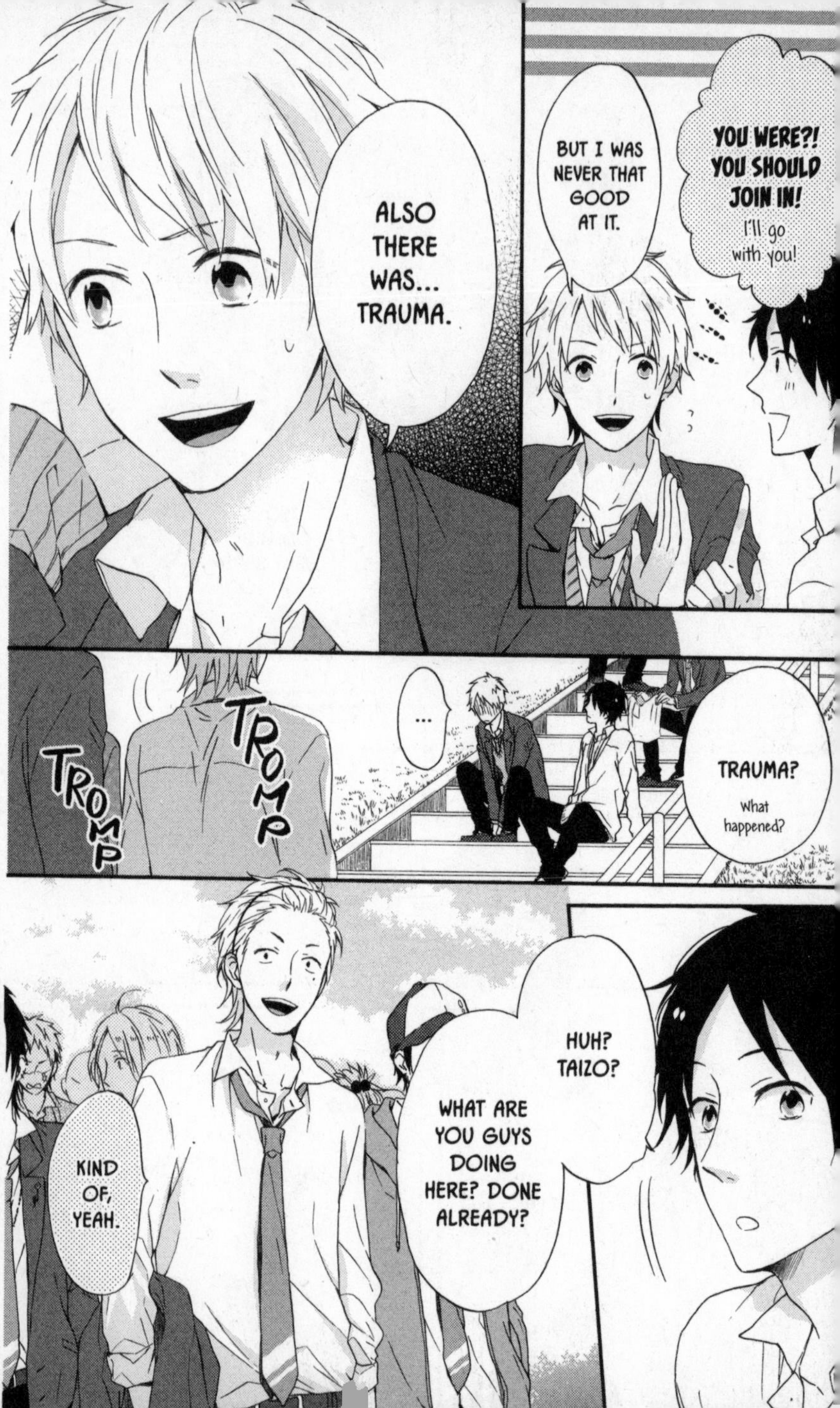
YOU WERE?! YOU SHOULD JOIN IN! I'll go with you!
BUT I WAS NEVER THAT GOOD AT IT.
ALSO THERE WAS... TRAUMA.
TRAUMA? What happened?
...
TROMP
TROMP
HUH? TAIZO?
WHAT ARE YOU GUYS DOING HERE? DONE ALREADY?
KIND OF, YEAH.

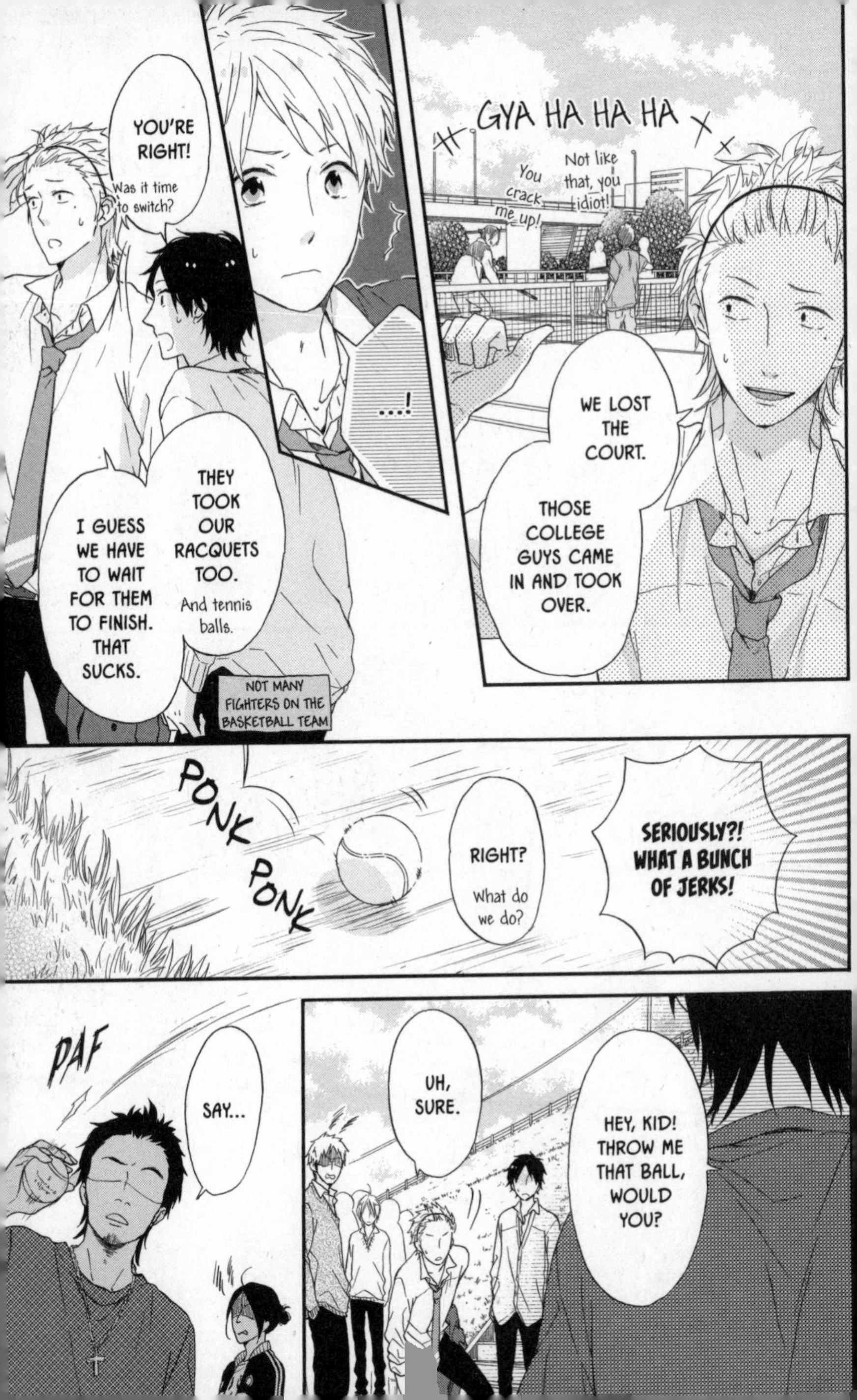
GYA HA HA HA
Not like that, you idiot!
You crack me up!
WE LOST THE COURT.
THOSE COLLEGE GUYS CAME IN AND TOOK OVER.
...!
YOU'RE RIGHT! Was it time to switch?
THEY TOOK OUR RACQUETS TOO. And tennis balls.
I GUESS WE HAVE TO WAIT FOR THEM TO FINISH. THAT SUCKS.
NOT MANY FIGHTERS ON THE BASKETBALL TEAM
SERIOUSLY?! WHAT A BUNCH OF JERKS!
RIGHT? What do we do?
PONK PONK
HEY, KID! THROW ME THAT BALL, WOULD YOU?
UH, SURE.
SAY...
PAF

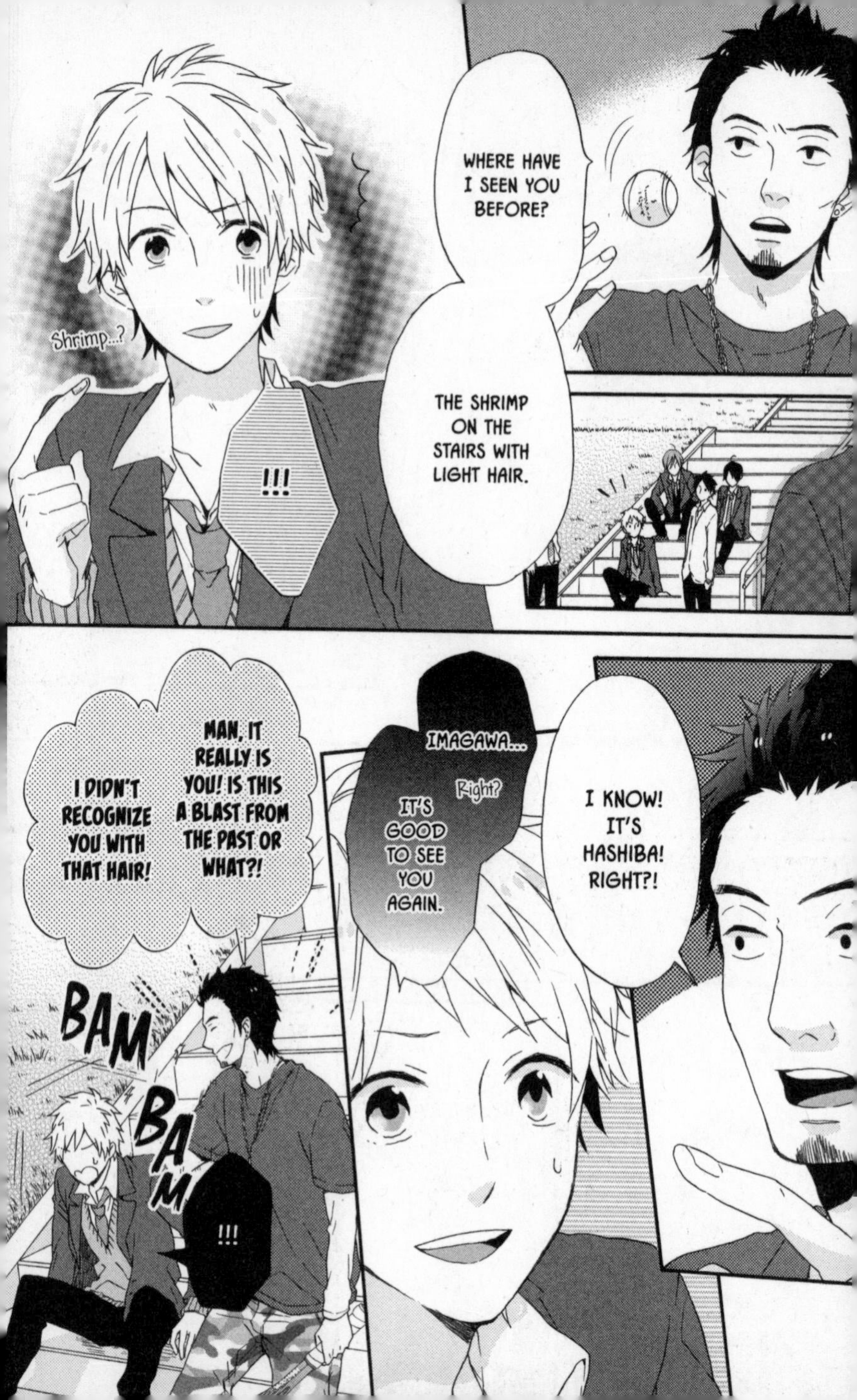
WHERE HAVE I SEEN YOU BEFORE?
THE SHRIMP ON THE STAIRS WITH LIGHT HAIR.
!!!
Shrimp...?
I KNOW! IT'S HASHIBA! RIGHT?!
IMAGAWA...
Right?
IT'S GOOD TO SEE YOU AGAIN.
MAN, IT REALLY IS YOU! IS THIS A BLAST FROM THE PAST OR WHAT?!
I DIDN'T RECOGNIZE YOU WITH THAT HAIR!
BAM
BAM
!!!

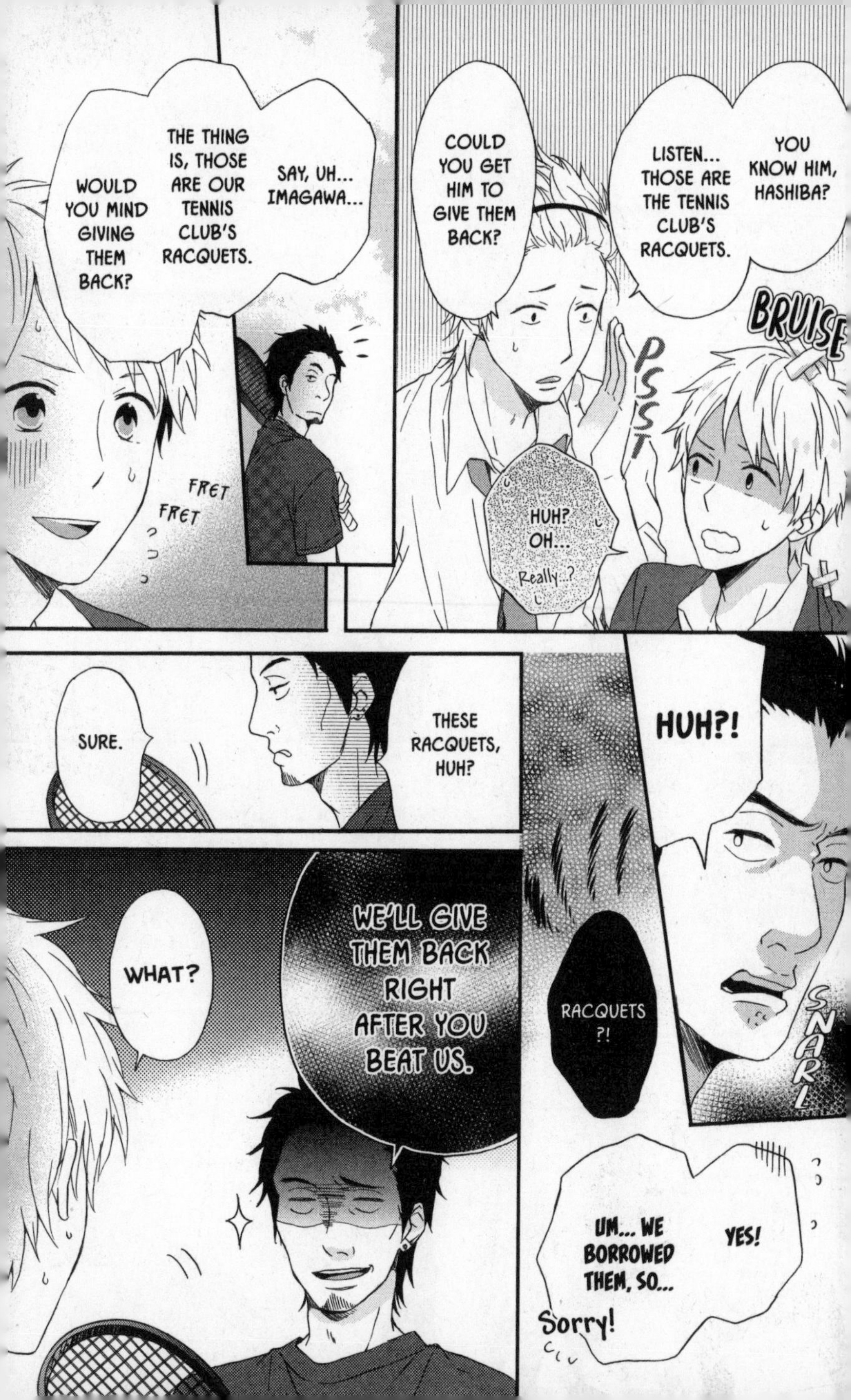
YOU KNOW HIM, HASHIBA?
LISTEN... THOSE ARE THE TENNIS CLUB'S RACQUETS.
BRUISE
PSST
COULD YOU GET HIM TO GIVE THEM BACK?
HUH? OH... Really...?
SAY, UH... IMAGAWA...
THE THING IS, THOSE ARE OUR TENNIS CLUB'S RACQUETS.
WOULD YOU MIND GIVING THEM BACK?
FRET
FRET
HUH?!
RACQUETS ?!
SNARL
YES!
UM... WE BORROWED THEM, SO...
Sorry!
THESE RACQUETS, HUH?
SURE.
WE'LL GIVE THEM BACK RIGHT AFTER YOU BEAT US.
WHAT?

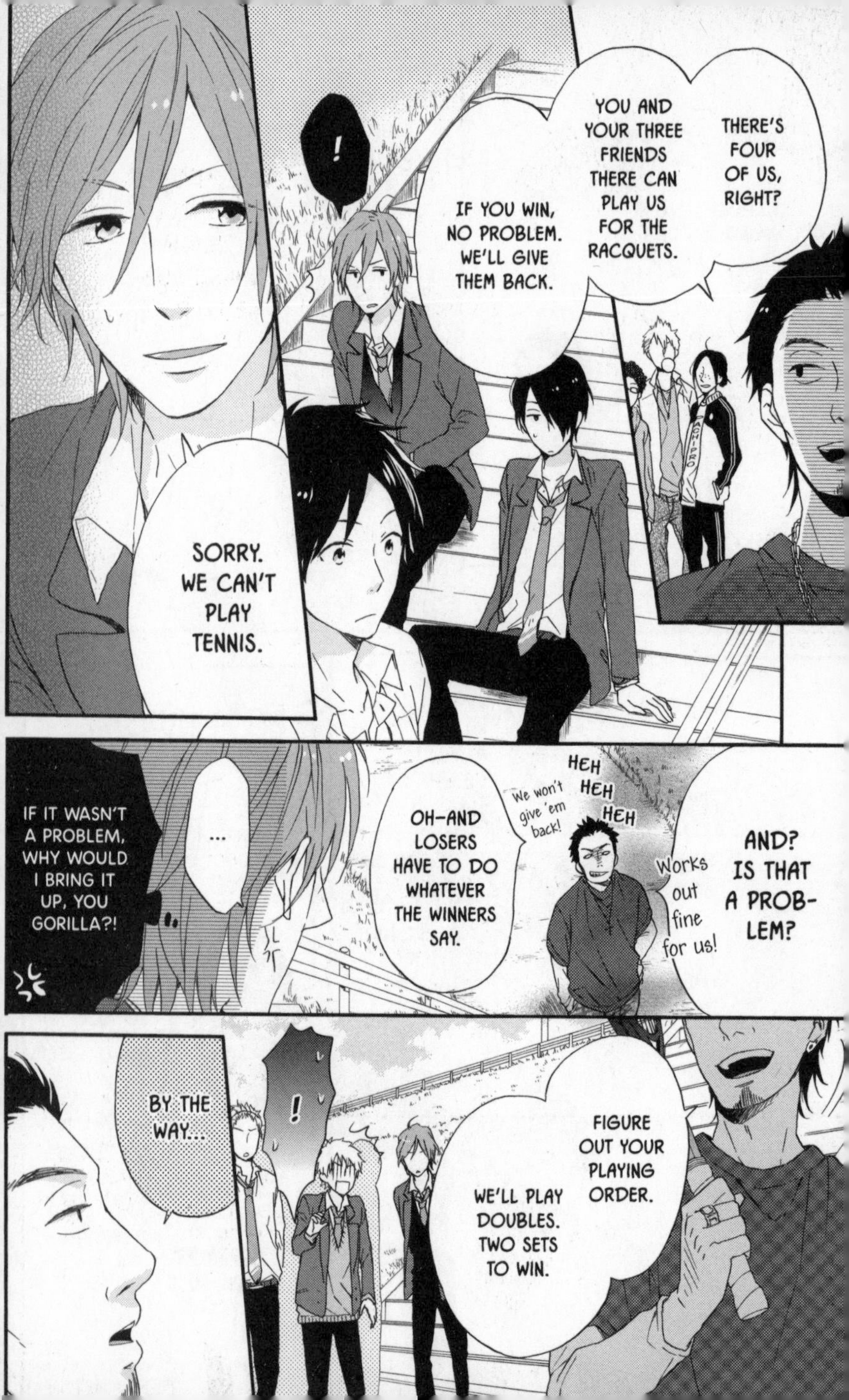
THERE'S FOUR OF US, RIGHT?
YOU AND YOUR THREE FRIENDS THERE CAN PLAY US FOR THE RACQUETS.
IF YOU WIN, NO PROBLEM. WE'LL GIVE THEM BACK.
!
SORRY. WE CAN'T PLAY TENNIS.
AND? IS THAT A PROB-LEM?
Works out fine for us!
HEH HEH HEH
We won't give 'em back!
OH—AND LOSERS HAVE TO DO WHATEVER THE WINNERS SAY.
...
IF IT WASN'T A PROBLEM, WHY WOULD I BRING IT UP, YOU GORILLA?!
FIGURE OUT YOUR PLAYING ORDER.
WE'LL PLAY DOUBLES. TWO SETS TO WIN.
!
BY THE WAY...

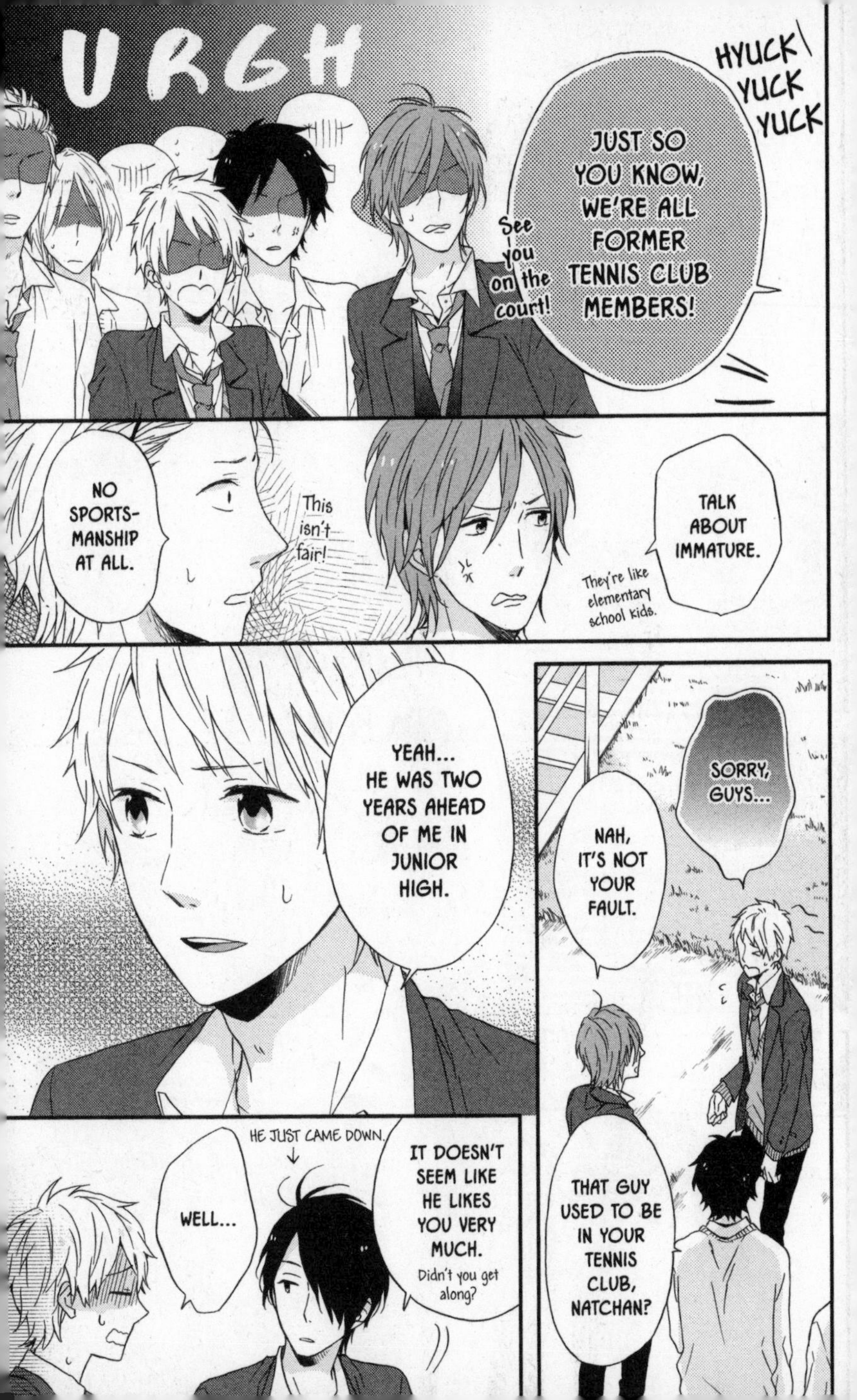
HYUCK YUCK YUCK
JUST SO YOU KNOW, WE'RE ALL FORMER TENNIS CLUB MEMBERS!
See you on the court!
URGH
TALK ABOUT IMMATURE.
They're like elementary school kids.
This isn't fair!
NO SPORTSMANSHIP AT ALL.
SORRY, GUYS...
NAH, IT'S NOT YOUR FAULT.
THAT GUY USED TO BE IN YOUR TENNIS CLUB, NATCHAN?
YEAH... HE WAS TWO YEARS AHEAD OF ME IN JUNIOR HIGH.
IT DOESN'T SEEM LIKE HE LIKES YOU VERY MUCH.
Didn't you get along?
HE JUST CAME DOWN.
WELL...

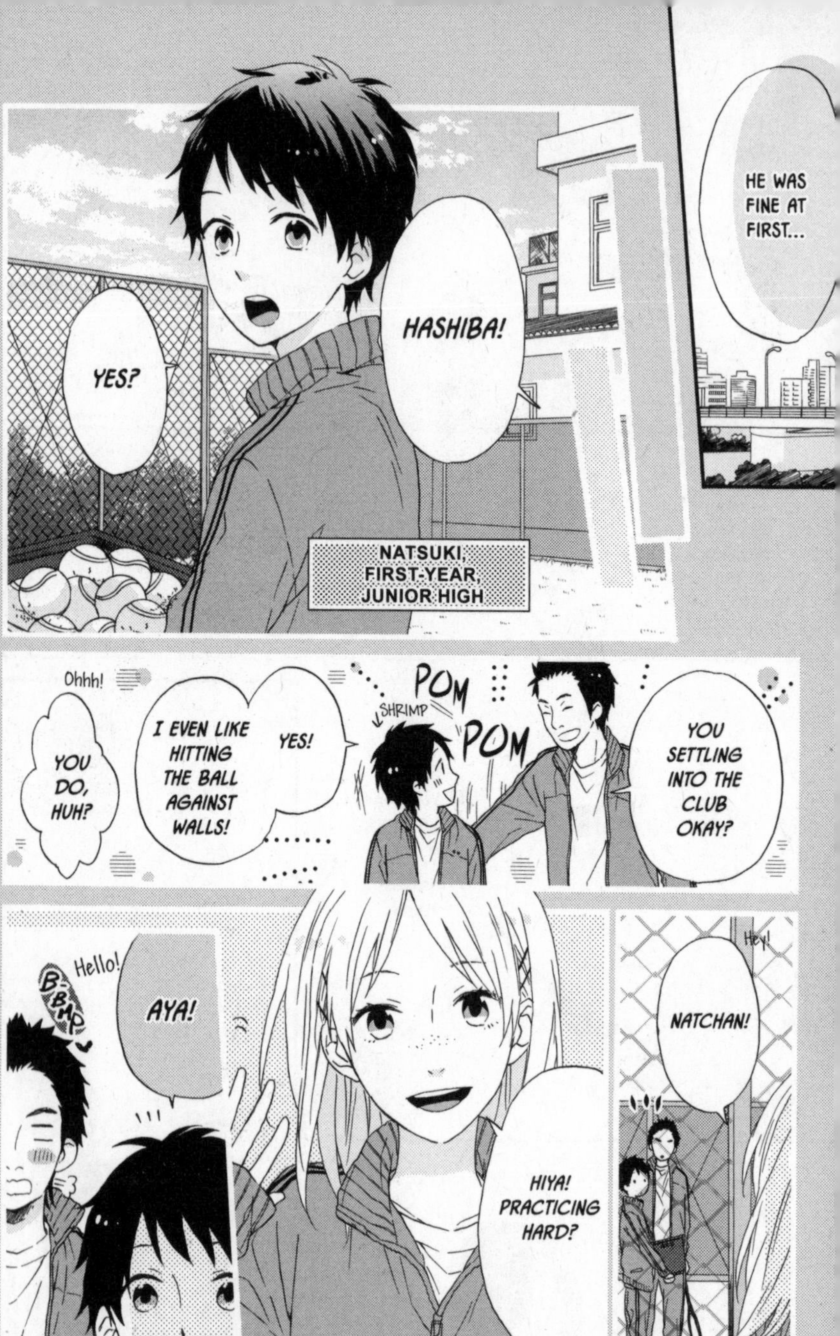
HE WAS FINE AT FIRST...
HASHIBA!
YES?
NATSUKI, FIRST-YEAR, JUNIOR HIGH
YOU SETTLING INTO THE CLUB OKAY?
POM
POM
SHRIMP
YES!
I EVEN LIKE HITTING THE BALL AGAINST WALLS!
Ohhh!
YOU DO, HUH?
Hey!
NATCHAN!
HIYA! PRACTICING HARD?
AYA!
Hello!
B-BMP

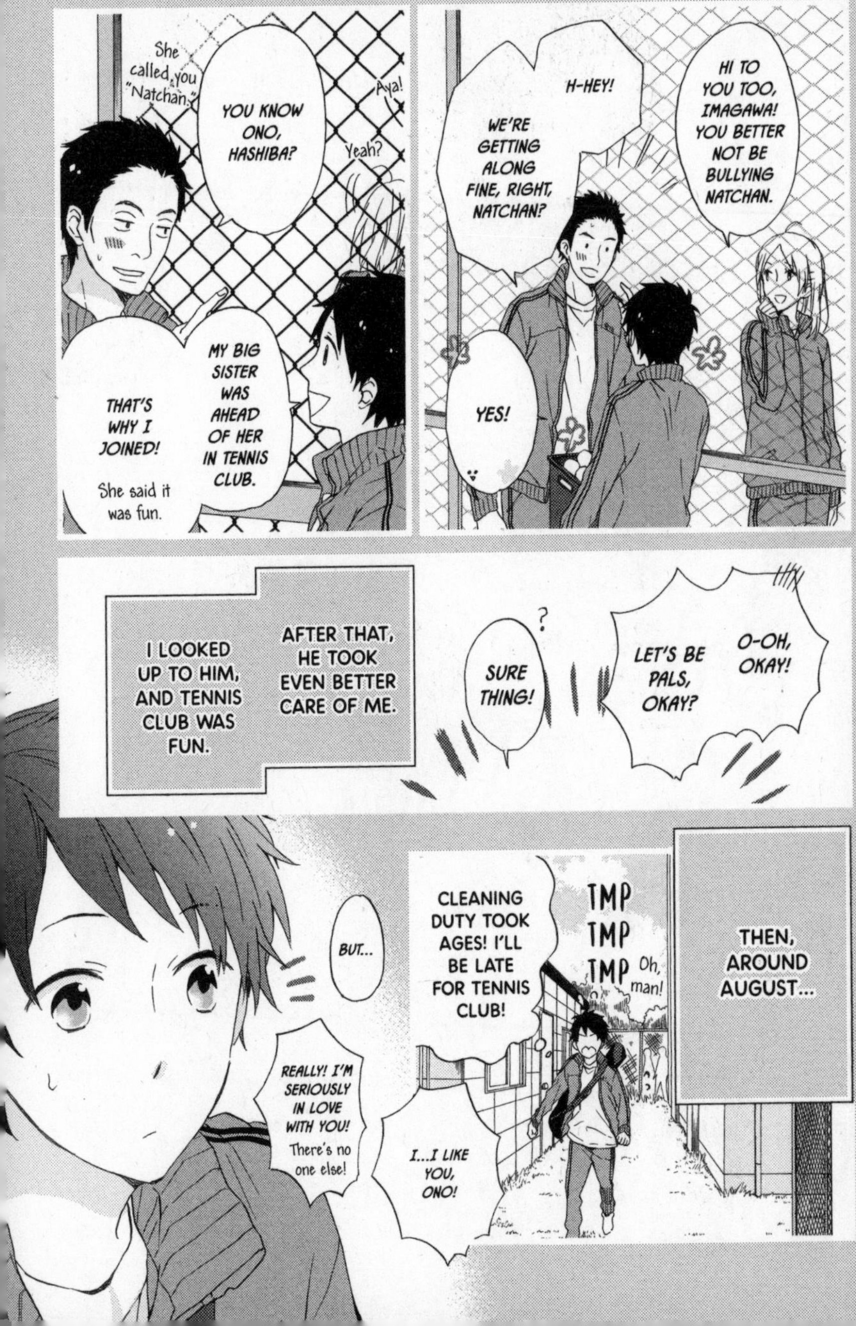
HI TO YOU TOO, IMAGAWA! YOU BETTER NOT BE BULLYING NATCHAN.
H-HEY!
WE'RE GETTING ALONG FINE, RIGHT, NATCHAN?
YES!
Aya!
Yeah?
YOU KNOW ONO, HASHIBA?
She called you "Natchan."
MY BIG SISTER WAS AHEAD OF HER IN TENNIS CLUB.
THAT'S WHY I JOINED!
She said it was fun.
O-OH, OKAY!
LET'S BE PALS, OKAY?
?
SURE THING!
AFTER THAT, HE TOOK EVEN BETTER CARE OF ME.
I LOOKED UP TO HIM, AND TENNIS CLUB WAS FUN.
THEN, AROUND AUGUST...
TMP TMP TMP
Oh, man!
CLEANING DUTY TOOK AGES! I'LL BE LATE FOR TENNIS CLUB!
I...I LIKE YOU, ONO!
REALLY! I'M SERIOUSLY IN LOVE WITH YOU! There's no one else!
BUT...

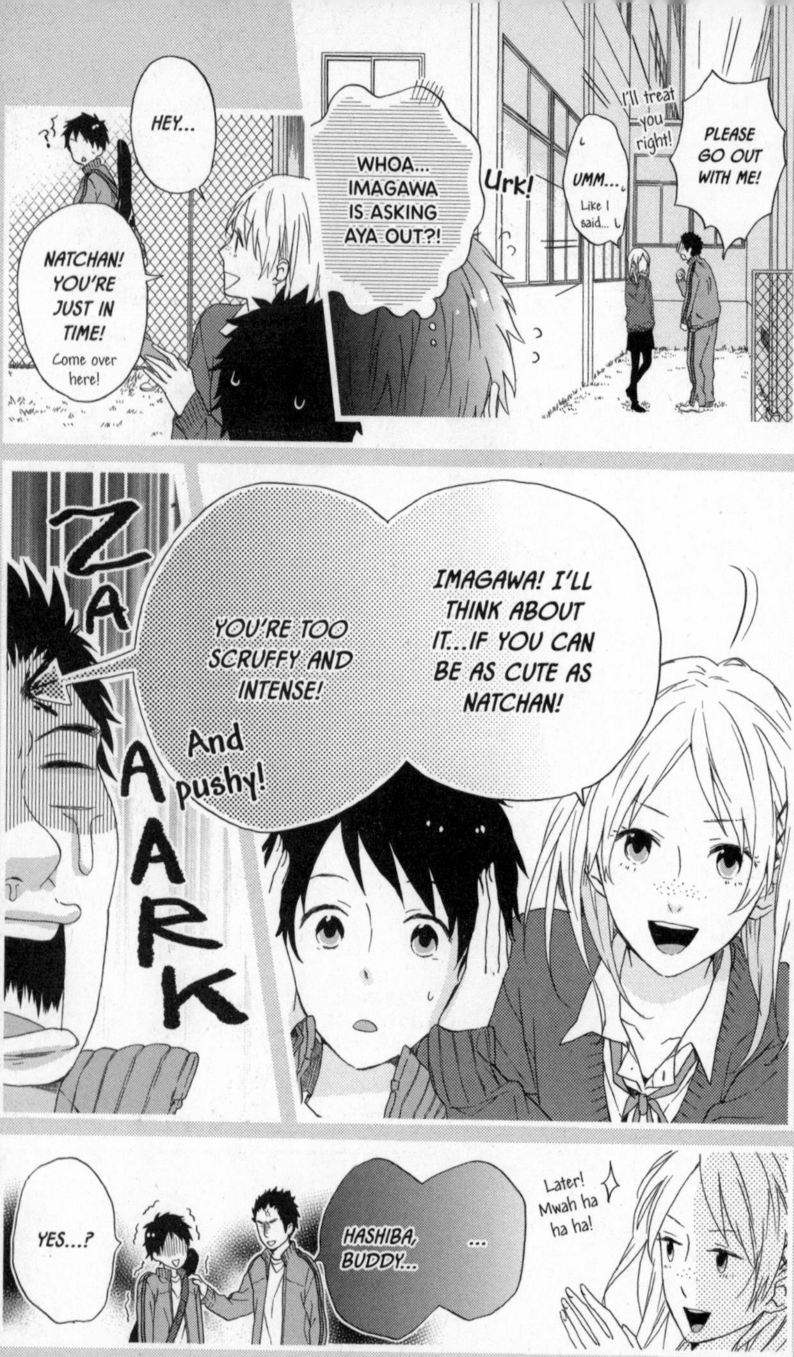
PLEASE GO OUT WITH ME!
I'll treat you right!
UMM... Like I said...
Urk!
WHOA... IMAGAWA IS ASKING AYA OUT?!
HEY...
NATCHAN! YOU'RE JUST IN TIME! Come over here!
IMAGAWA! I'LL THINK ABOUT IT...IF YOU CAN BE AS CUTE AS NATCHAN!
YOU'RE TOO SCRUFFY AND INTENSE!
And pushy!
ZAARK
Later! Mwah ha ha ha!
HASHIBA, BUDDY...
...
YES...?

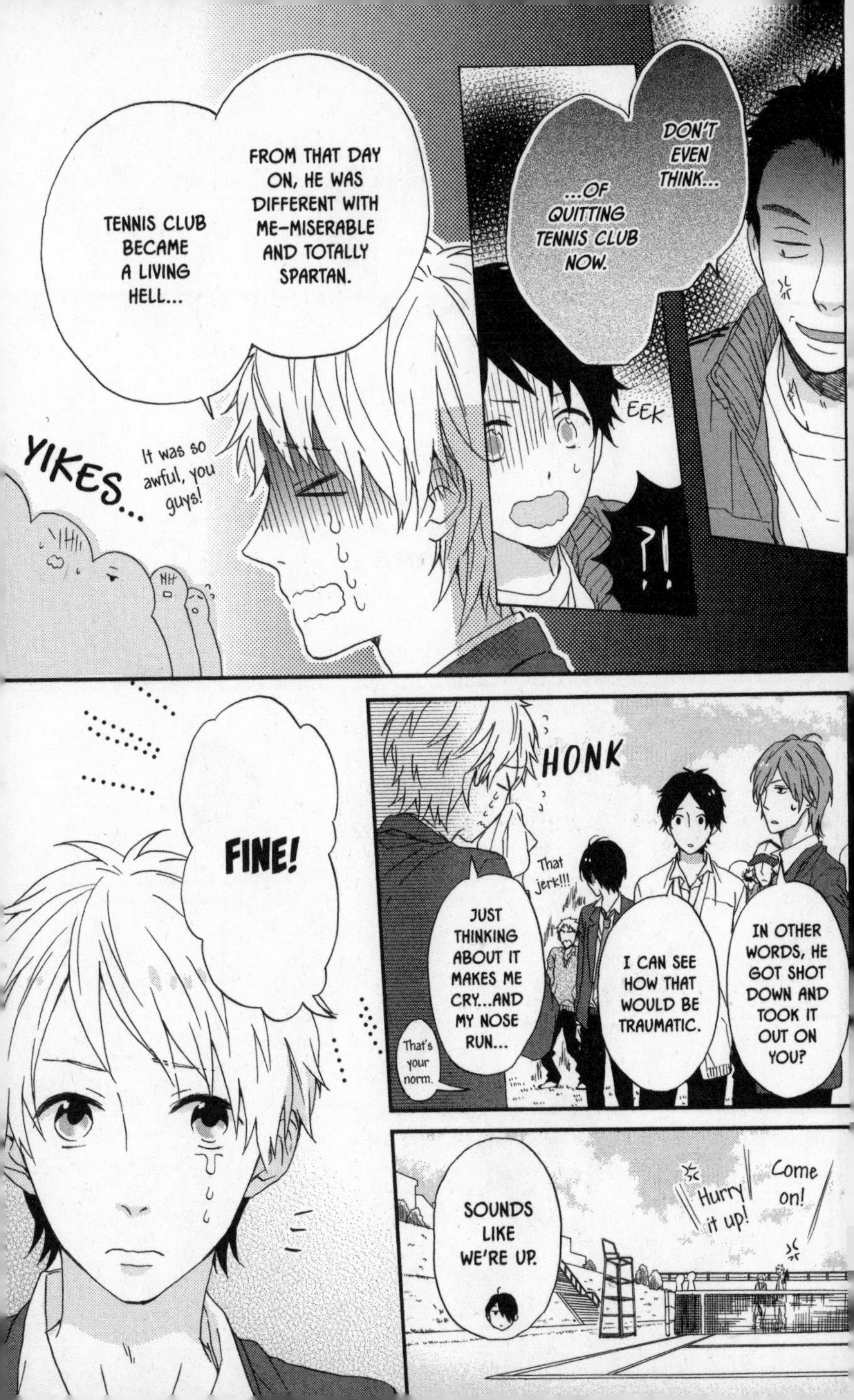
DON'T EVEN THINK...
...OF QUITTING TENNIS CLUB NOW.
EEK
?!
FROM THAT DAY ON, HE WAS DIFFERENT WITH ME—MISERABLE AND TOTALLY SPARTAN.
TENNIS CLUB BECAME A LIVING HELL...
It was so awful, you guys!
YIKES...
IN OTHER WORDS, HE GOT SHOT DOWN AND TOOK IT OUT ON YOU?
I CAN SEE HOW THAT WOULD BE TRAUMATIC.
HONK
That jerk!!!
JUST THINKING ABOUT IT MAKES ME CRY...AND MY NOSE RUN...
That's your norm.
Come on!
Hurry it up!
SOUNDS LIKE WE'RE UP.
FINE!

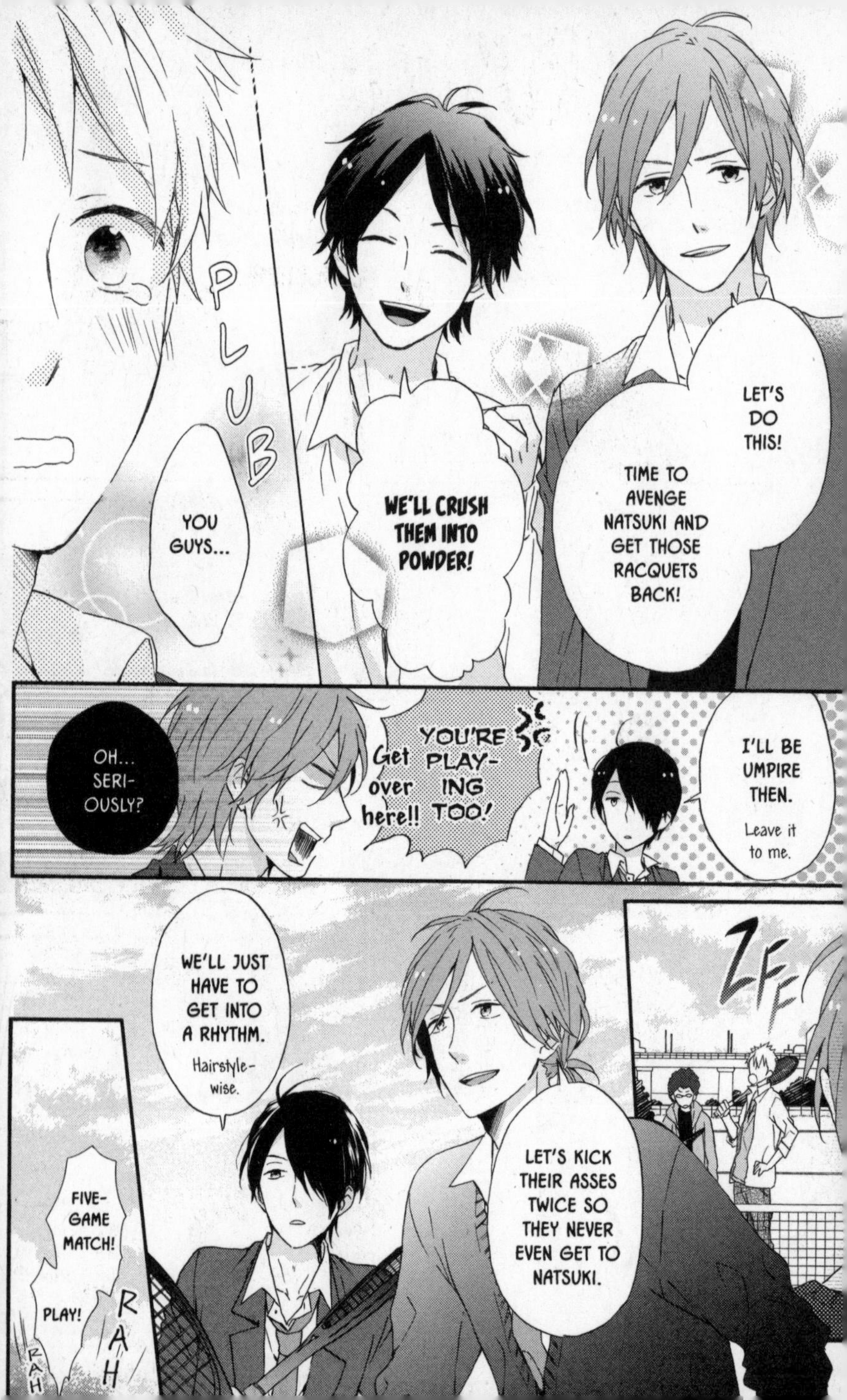
LET'S DO THIS!
TIME TO AVENGE NATSUKI AND GET THOSE RACQUETS BACK!
WE'LL CRUSH THEM INTO POWDER!
PLUB
YOU GUYS...
I'LL BE UMPIRE THEN.
Leave it to me.
YOU'RE PLAY-ING TOO!
Get over here!!
OH... SERI-OUSLY?
ZFF
LET'S KICK THEIR ASSES TWICE SO THEY NEVER EVEN GET TO NATSUKI.
WE'LL JUST HAVE TO GET INTO A RHYTHM.
Hairstyle-wise.
FIVE-GAME MATCH!
PLAY!
RAH
RAH

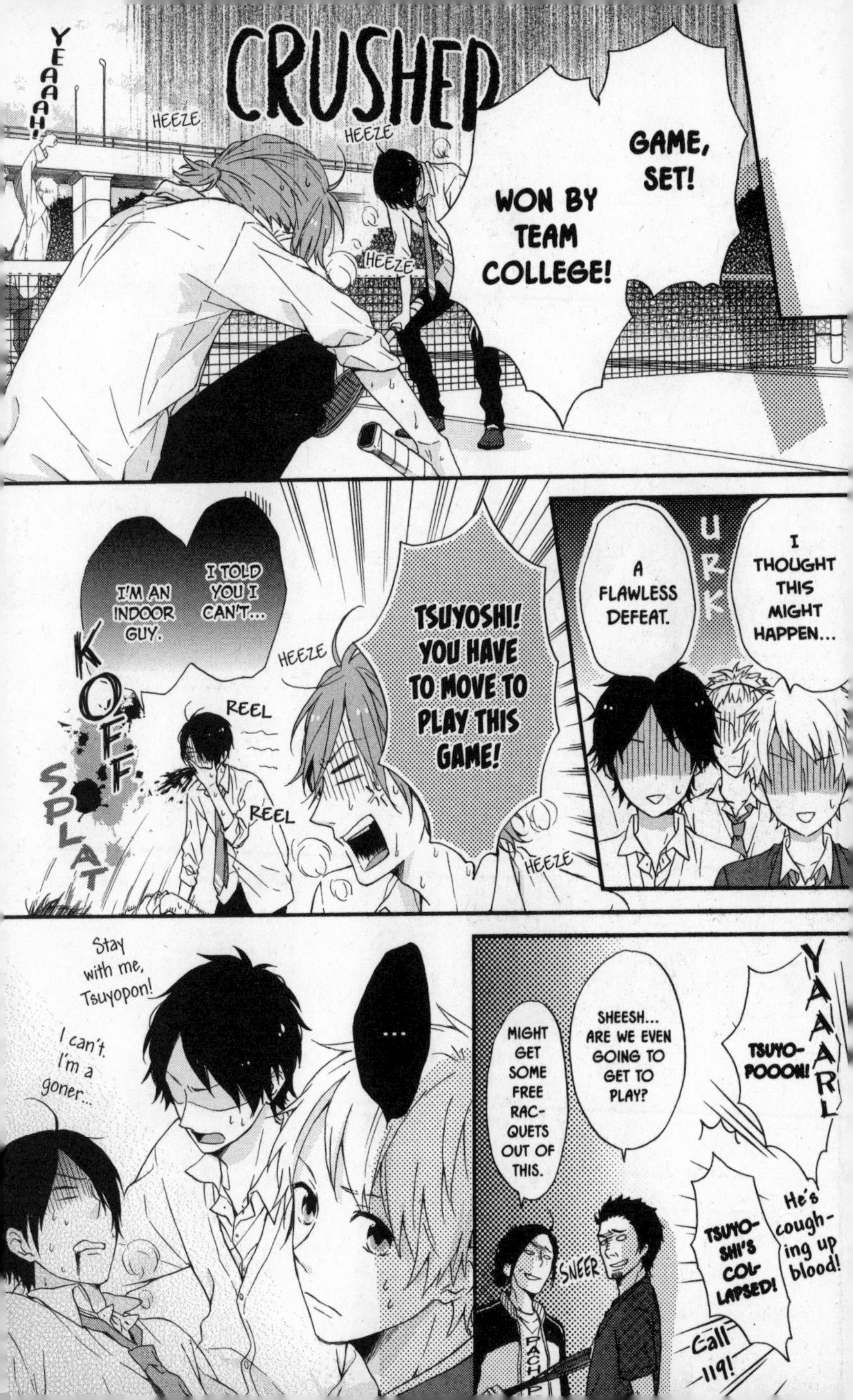
GAME, SET!
WON BY TEAM COLLEGE!
CRUSHED
HEEZE
HEEZE
HEEZE
HEEZE
YEAAAAH!
I THOUGHT THIS MIGHT HAPPEN...
URK
A FLAWLESS DEFEAT.
TSUYOSHI! YOU HAVE TO MOVE TO PLAY THIS GAME!
HEEZE
HEEZE
I TOLD YOU I CAN'T...
I'M AN INDOOR GUY.
KOFF
REEL
REEL
SPLAT
YAAARL
TSUYO-POOON!
SHEESH... ARE WE EVEN GOING TO GET TO PLAY?
MIGHT GET SOME FREE RAC-QUETS OUT OF THIS.
He's cough-ing up blood!
TSUYO-SHI'S COL-LAPSED!
SNEER
Call 119!
...
Stay with me, Tsuyopon!
I can't. I'm a goner...

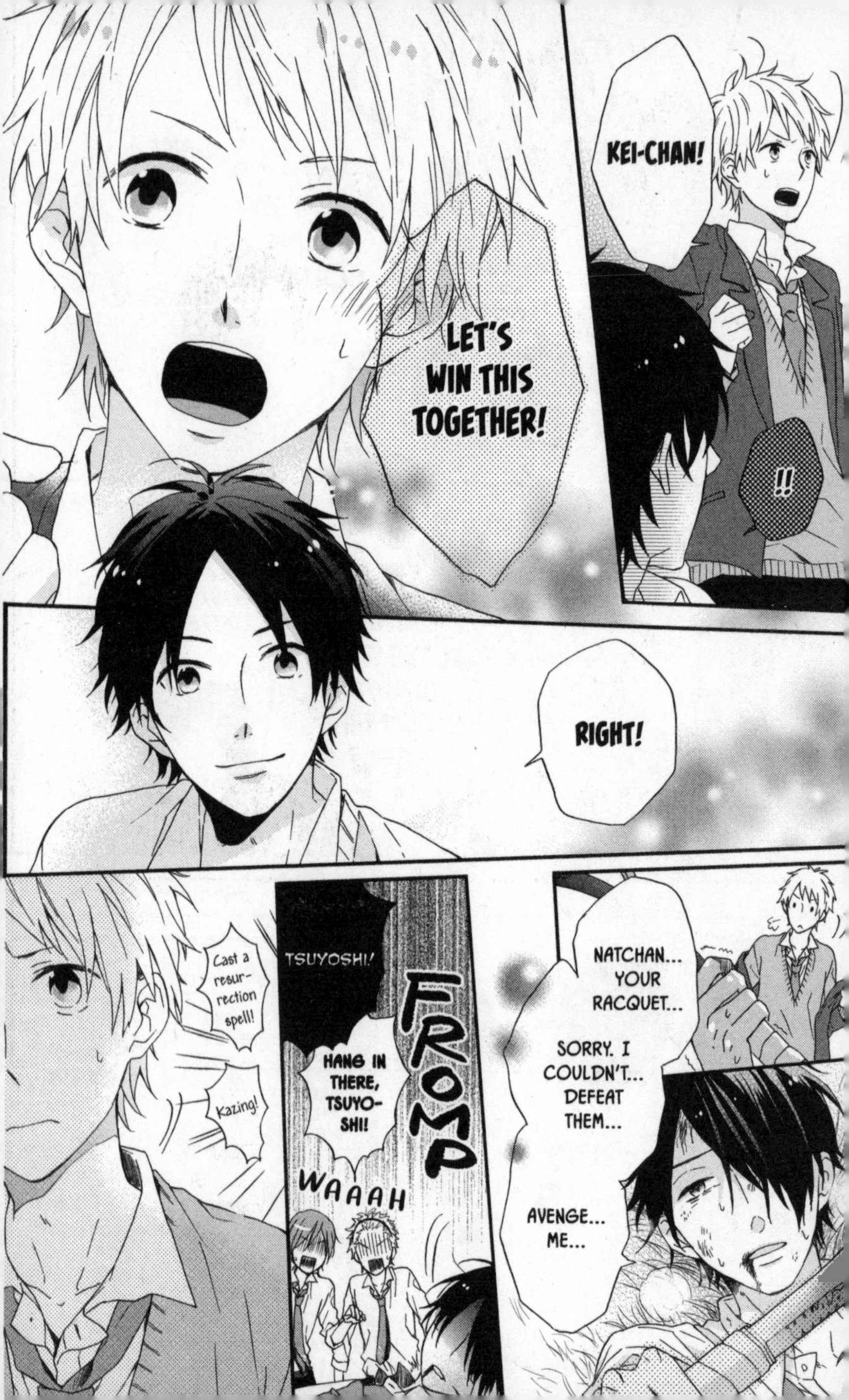
KEI-CHAN!
!!
LET'S WIN THIS TOGETHER!
RIGHT!
NATCHAN... YOUR RACQUET...
SORRY. I COULDN'T... DEFEAT THEM...
AVENGE... ME...
TSUYOSHI!
FROMP
HANG IN THERE, TSUYO-SHI!
WAAAH
Cast a resur-rection spell!
Kazing!

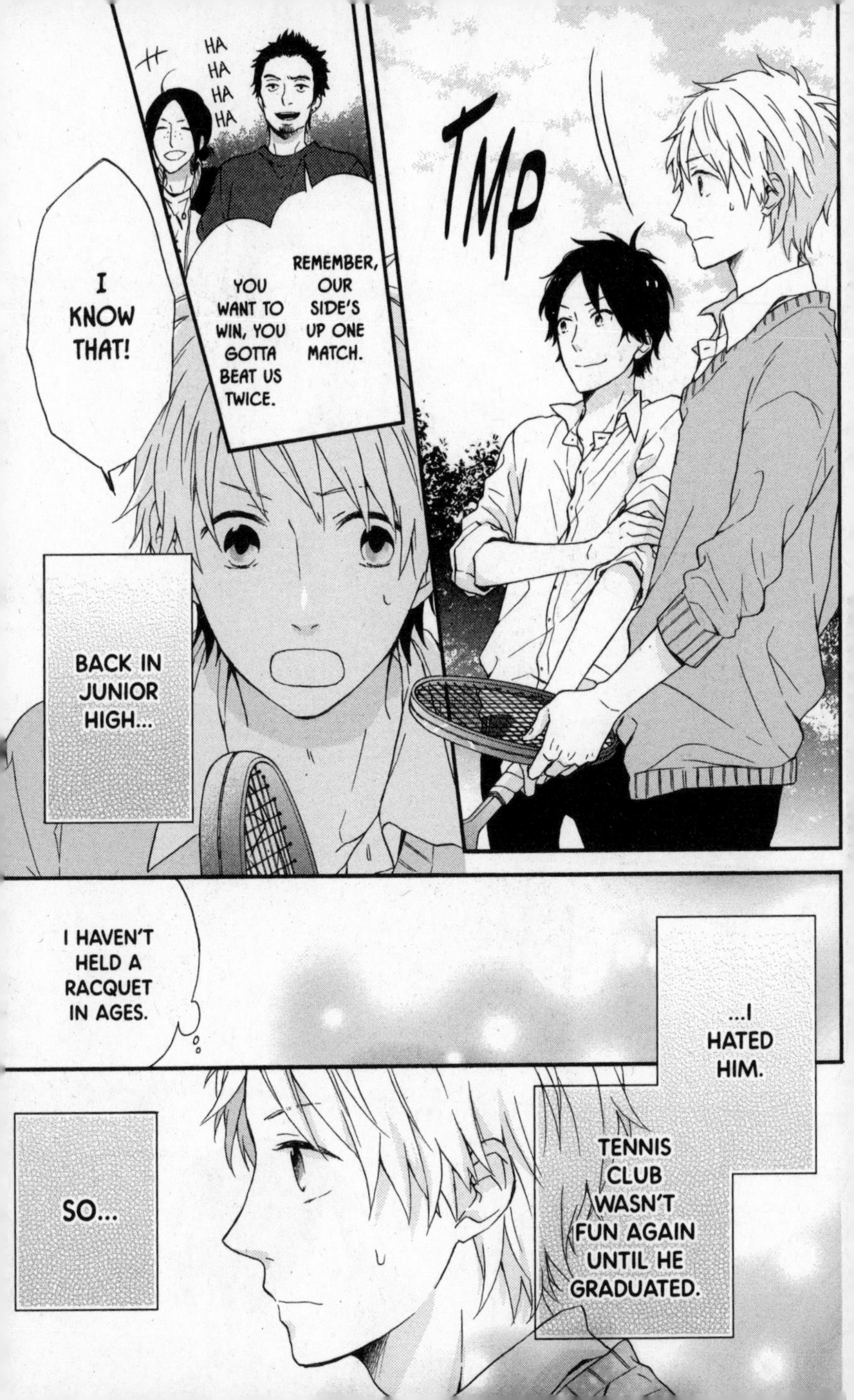
TMP
HA HA HA HA
REMEMBER, OUR SIDE'S UP ONE MATCH.
YOU WANT TO WIN, YOU GOTTA BEAT US TWICE.
I KNOW THAT!
BACK IN JUNIOR HIGH...
...I HATED HIM.
I HAVEN'T HELD A RACQUET IN AGES.
TENNIS CLUB WASN'T FUN AGAIN UNTIL HE GRADUATED.
SO...

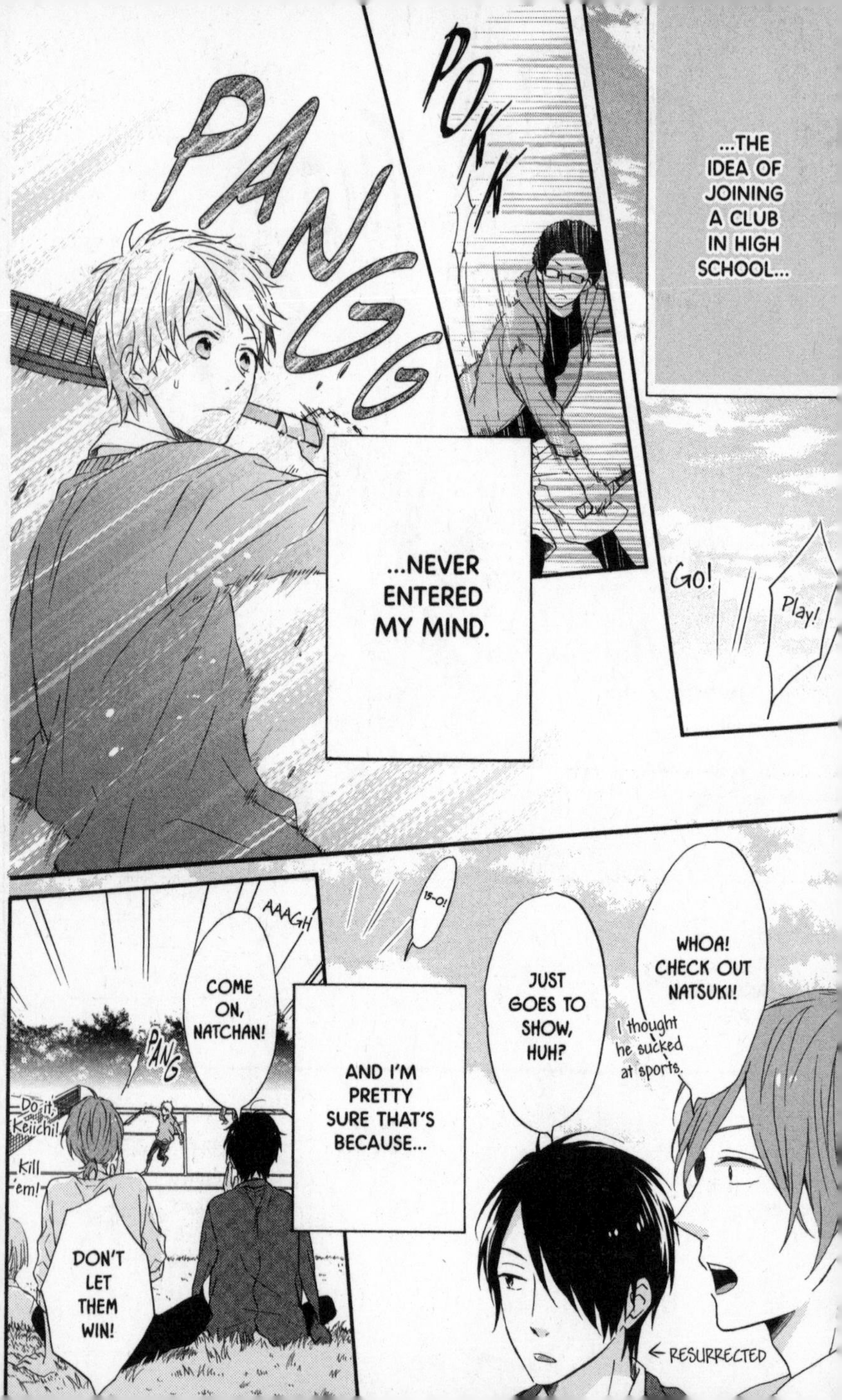
...THE IDEA OF JOINING A CLUB IN HIGH SCHOOL...
Play!
Go!
POKK
PANGG
...NEVER ENTERED MY MIND.
WHOA! CHECK OUT NATSUKI!
I thought he sucked at sports.
JUST GOES TO SHOW, HUH?
← RESURRECTED
15–0!
AND I'M PRETTY SURE THAT'S BECAUSE...
AAAGH
COME ON, NATCHAN!
PANG
Do it, Keiichi!
Kill 'em!
DON'T LET THEM WIN!

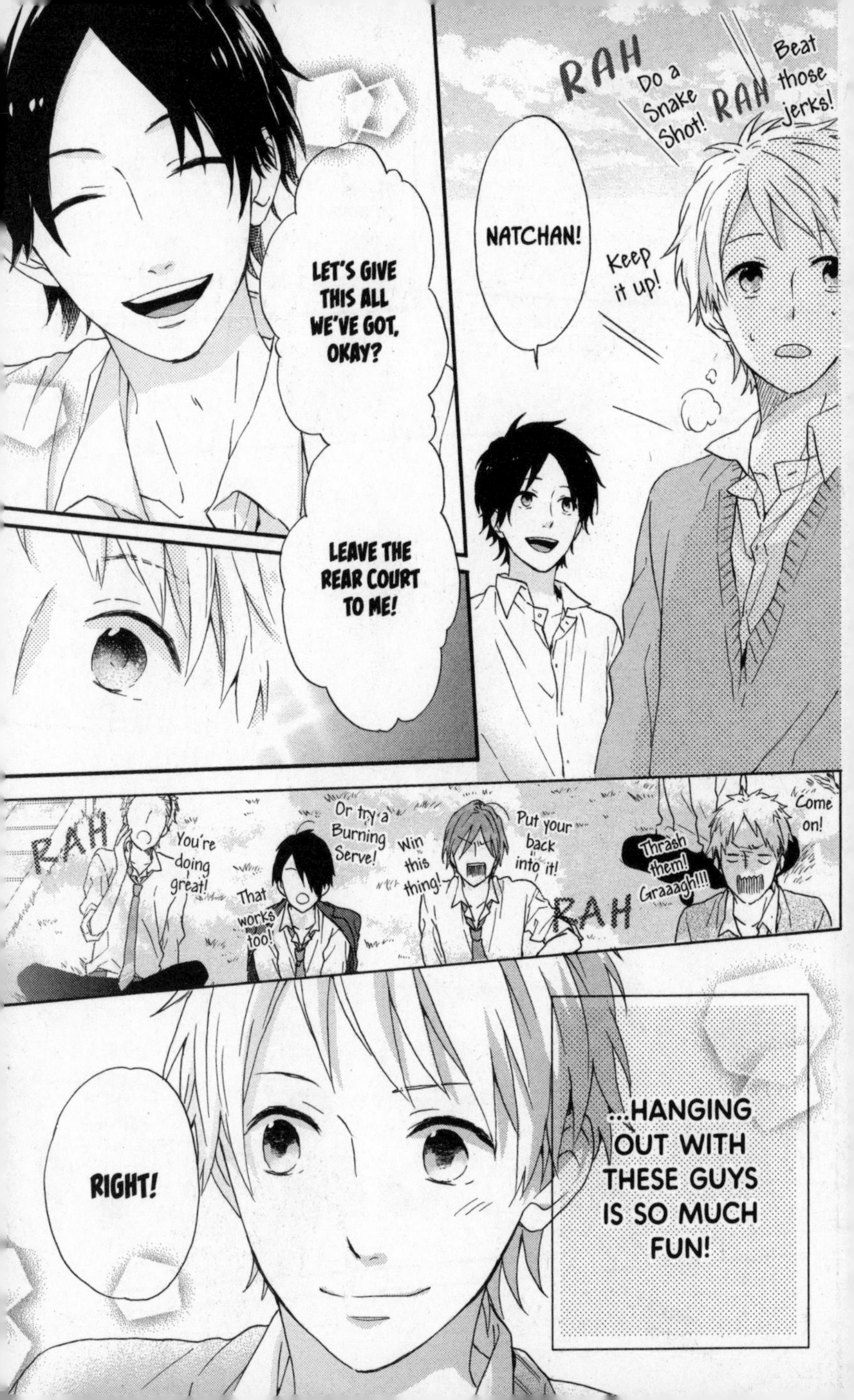
RAH
Beat those jerks!
Do a Snake Shot!
RAH
NATCHAN!
Keep it up!
LET'S GIVE THIS ALL WE'VE GOT, OKAY?
LEAVE THE REAR COURT TO ME!
Come on!
Thrash them! Graaagh!!!
RAH
Put your back into it!
Win this thing!
Or try a Burning Serve!
That works too!
You're doing great!
RAH
...HANGING OUT WITH THESE GUYS IS SO MUCH FUN!
RIGHT!

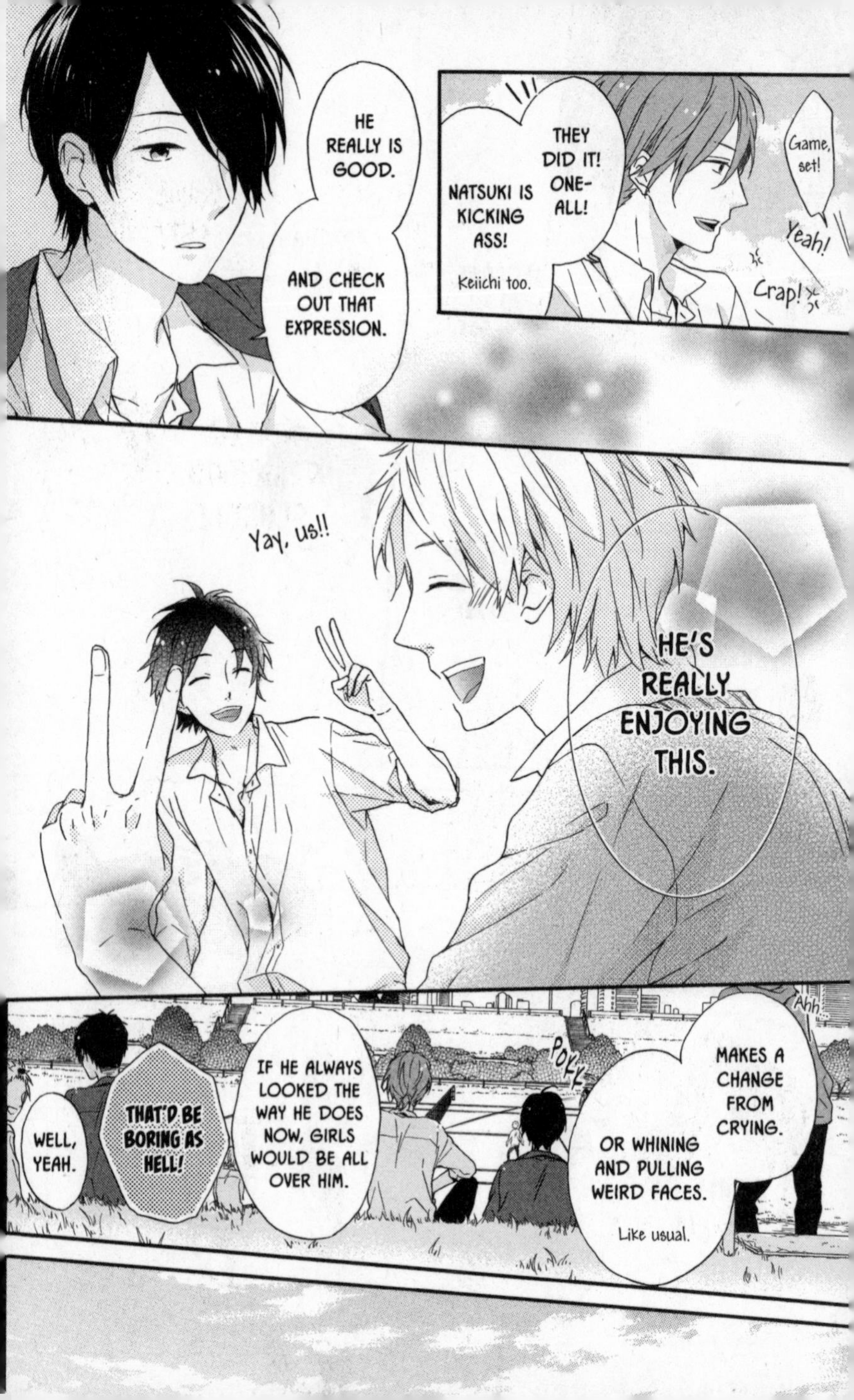

Game, set!
Yeah!
Crap!
THEY DID IT! ONE-ALL!
NATSUKI IS KICKING ASS!
Keiichi too.
HE REALLY IS GOOD.
AND CHECK OUT THAT EXPRESSION.
HE'S REALLY ENJOYING THIS.
Yay, us!!
Ahh...
MAKES A CHANGE FROM CRYING.
OR WHINING AND PULLING WEIRD FACES.
Like usual.
POKE
IF HE ALWAYS LOOKED THE WAY HE DOES NOW, GIRLS WOULD BE ALL OVER HIM.
THAT'D BE BORING AS HELL!
WELL, YEAH.

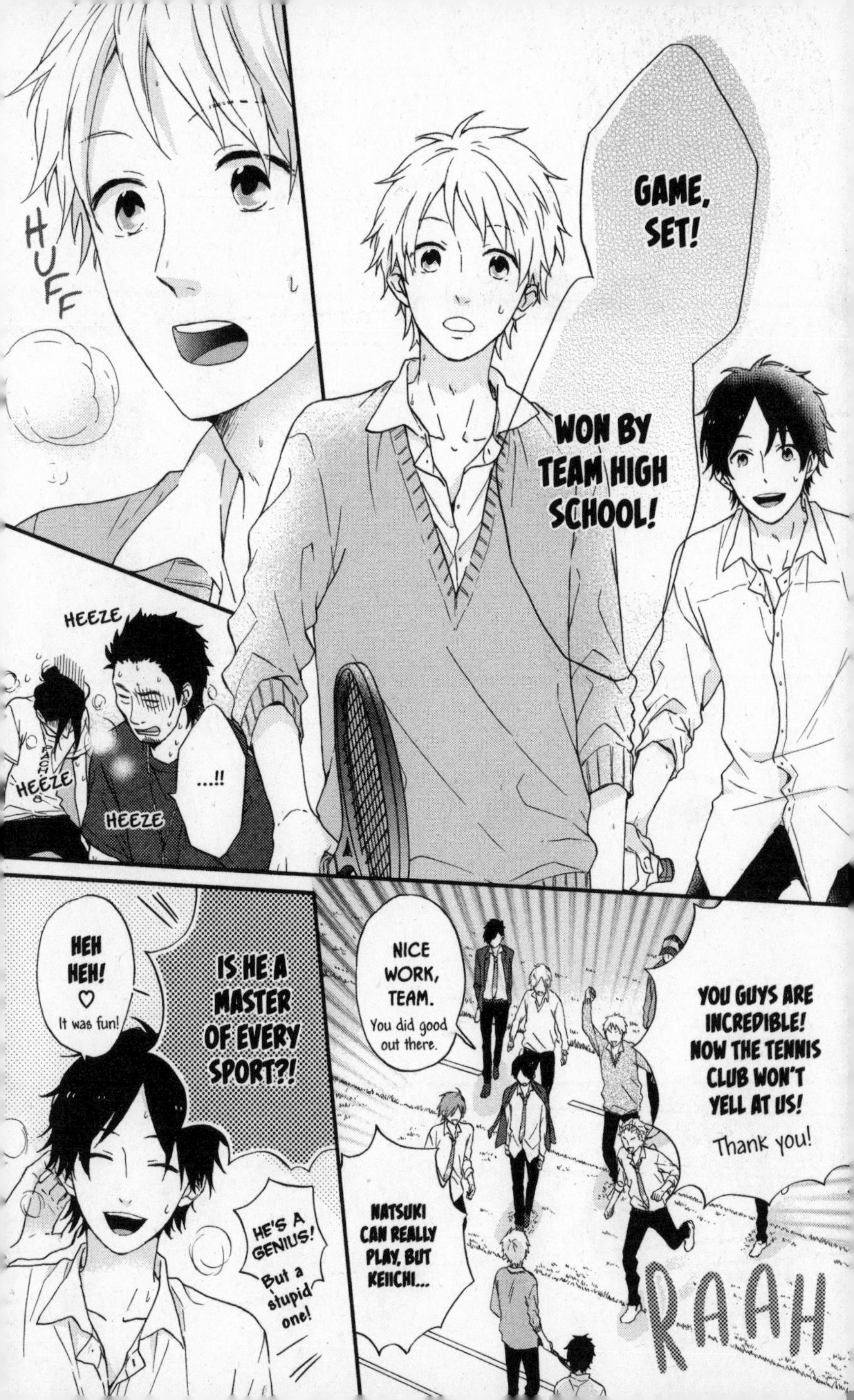
GAME, SET!
WON BY TEAM HIGH SCHOOL!
HUFF
HEEZE
HEEZE
...!!
HEEZE
YOU GUYS ARE INCREDIBLE! NOW THE TENNIS CLUB WON'T YELL AT US!
Thank you!
RAAH
NICE WORK, TEAM. You did good out there.
NATSUKI CAN REALLY PLAY, BUT KEIICHI...
HEH HEH! ♡ It was fun!
IS HE A MASTER OF EVERY SPORT?!
HE'S A GENIUS! But a stupid one!

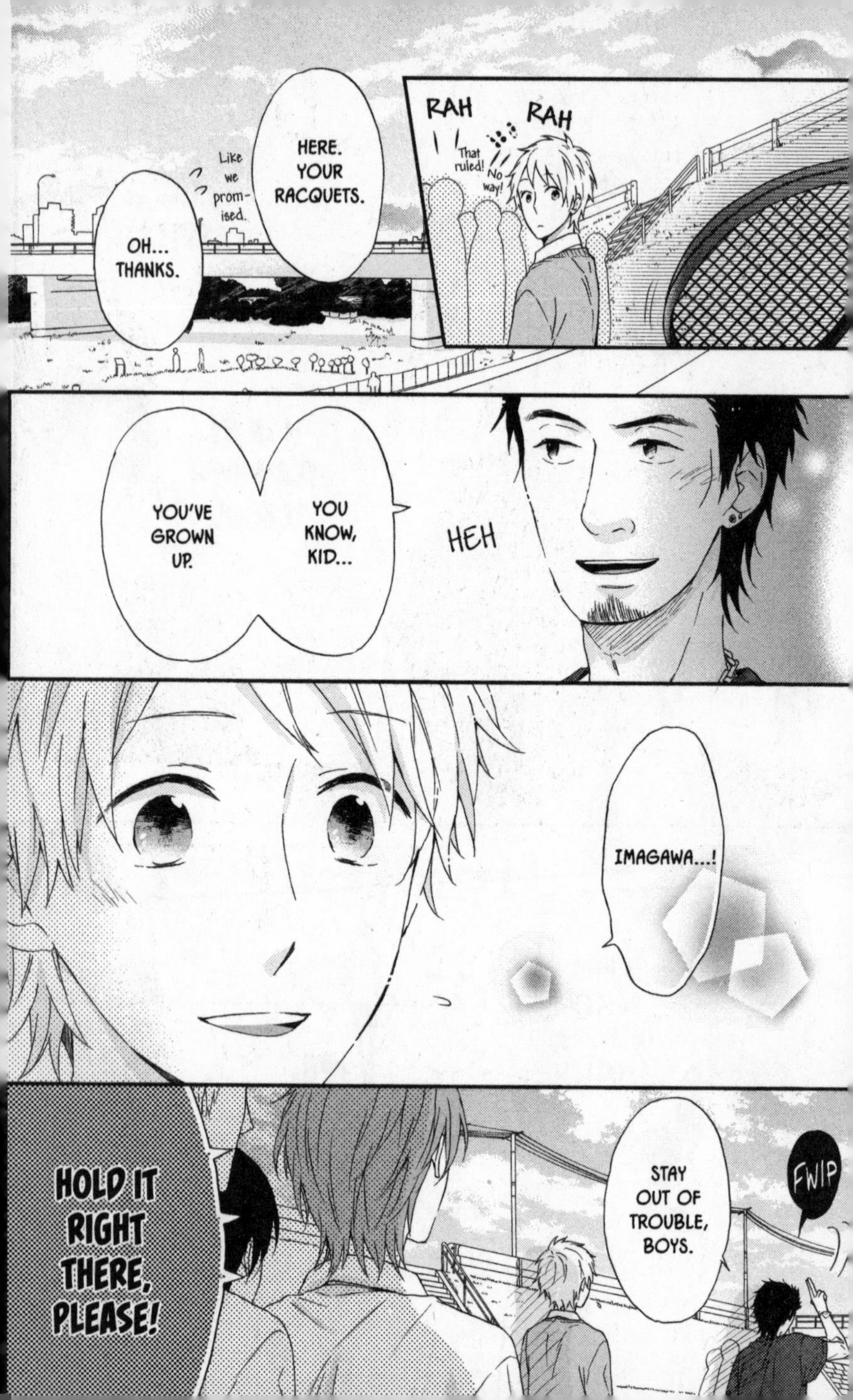
RAH RAH
That ruled!
No way!
HERE. YOUR RACQUETS.
Like we promised.
OH... THANKS.
HEH
YOU KNOW, KID...
YOU'VE GROWN UP.
IMAGAWA...!
FWIP
STAY OUT OF TROUBLE, BOYS.
HOLD IT RIGHT THERE, PLEASE!

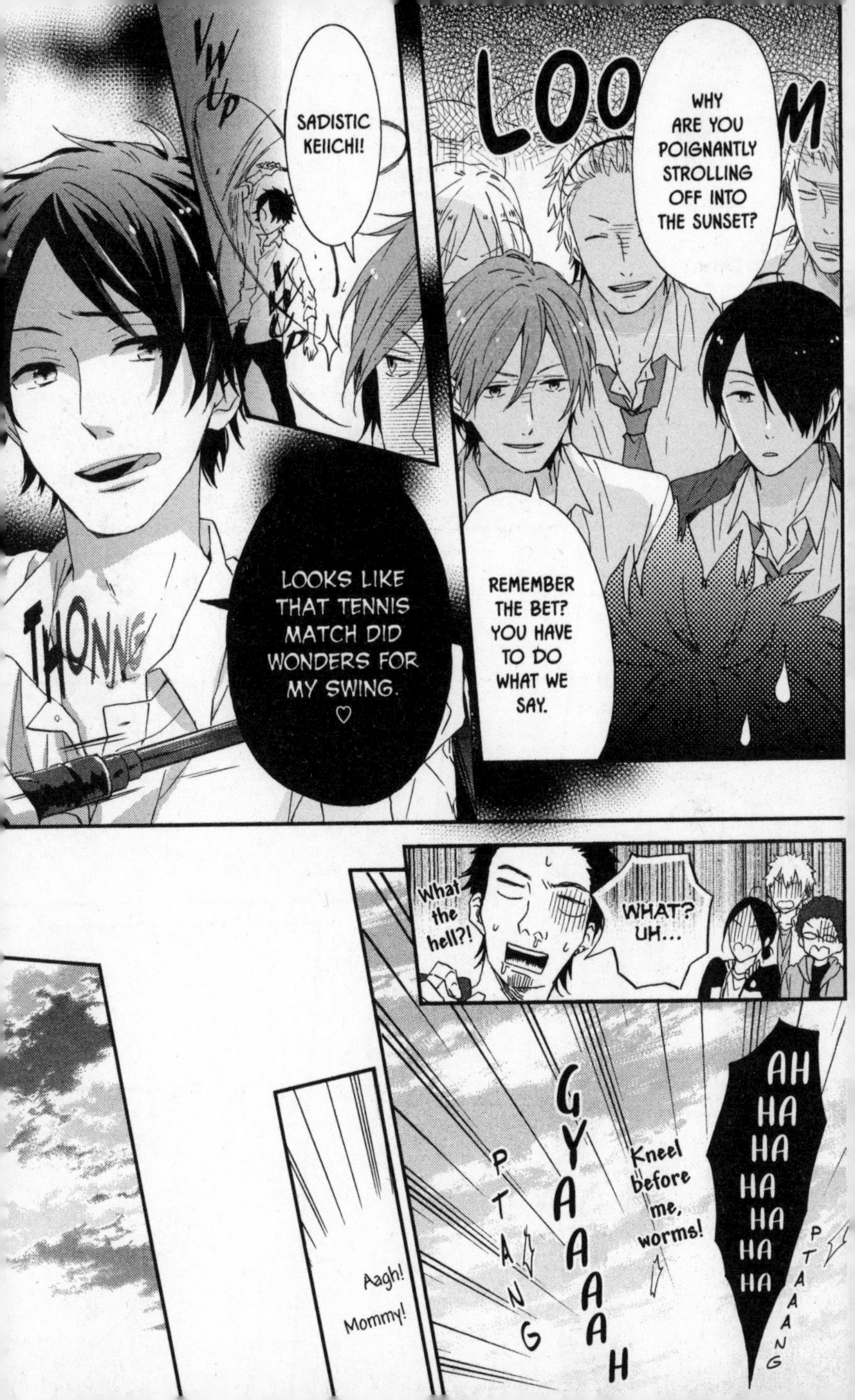
LOOOM
WHY ARE YOU POIGNANTLY STROLLING OFF INTO THE SUNSET?
REMEMBER THE BET? YOU HAVE TO DO WHAT WE SAY.
VWUP
SADISTIC KEIICHI!
VWUP
LOOKS LIKE THAT TENNIS MATCH DID WONDERS FOR MY SWING. ♡
THONNG
WHAT? UH...
What the hell?!
AH HA HA HA HA HA HA
PTAAAANG
Kneel before me, worms!
GYAAAAAAH
PTANG
Aagh!
Mommy!

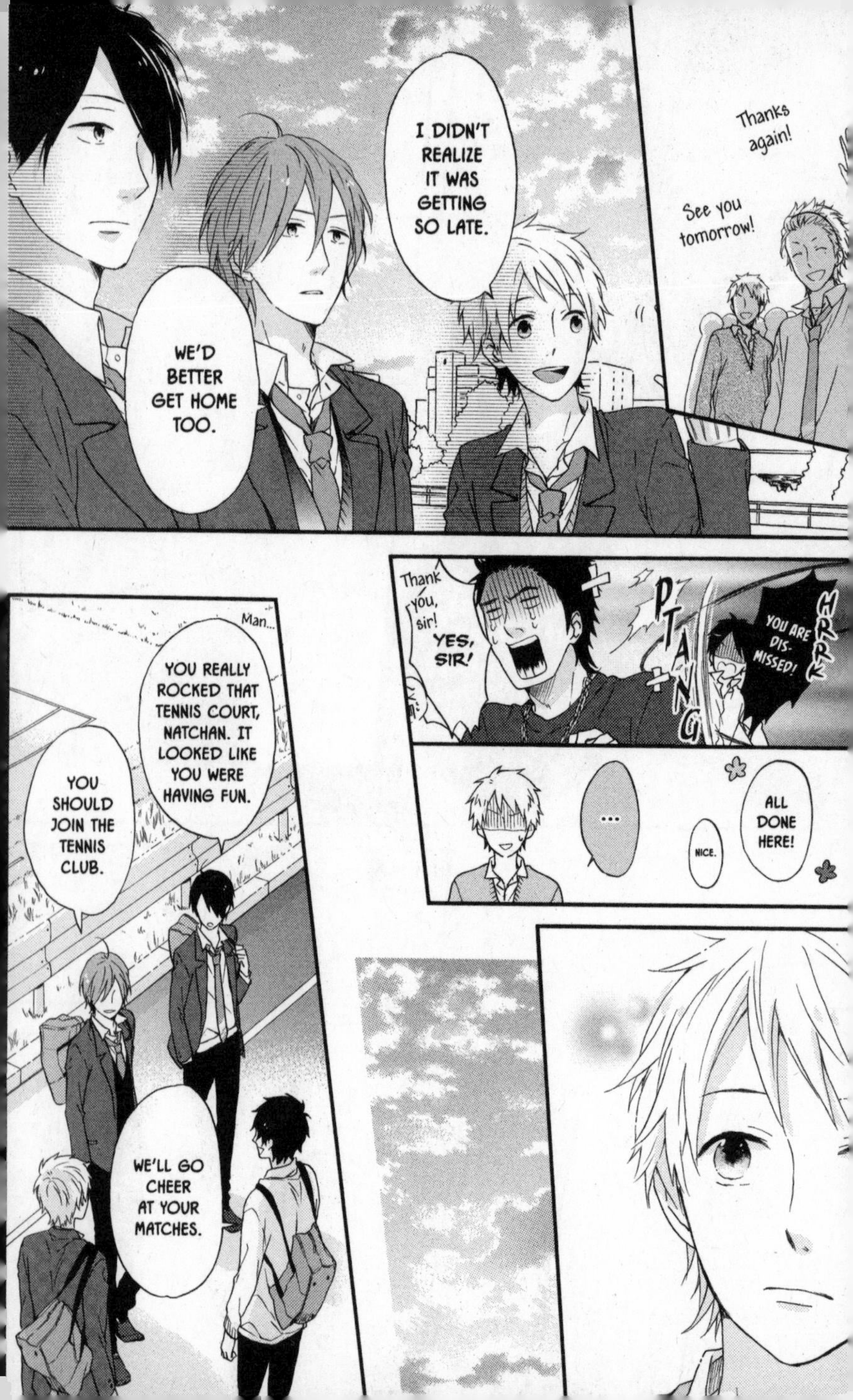

Thanks again!
See you tomorrow!
I DIDN'T REALIZE IT WAS GETTING SO LATE.
WE'D BETTER GET HOME TOO.
HRRK
YOU ARE DIS-MISSED!
PTANG
YES, SIR!
Thank you, sir!
ALL DONE HERE!
NICE.
...
Man...
YOU REALLY ROCKED THAT TENNIS COURT, NATCHAN. IT LOOKED LIKE YOU WERE HAVING FUN.
YOU SHOULD JOIN THE TENNIS CLUB.
WE'LL GO CHEER AT YOUR MATCHES.

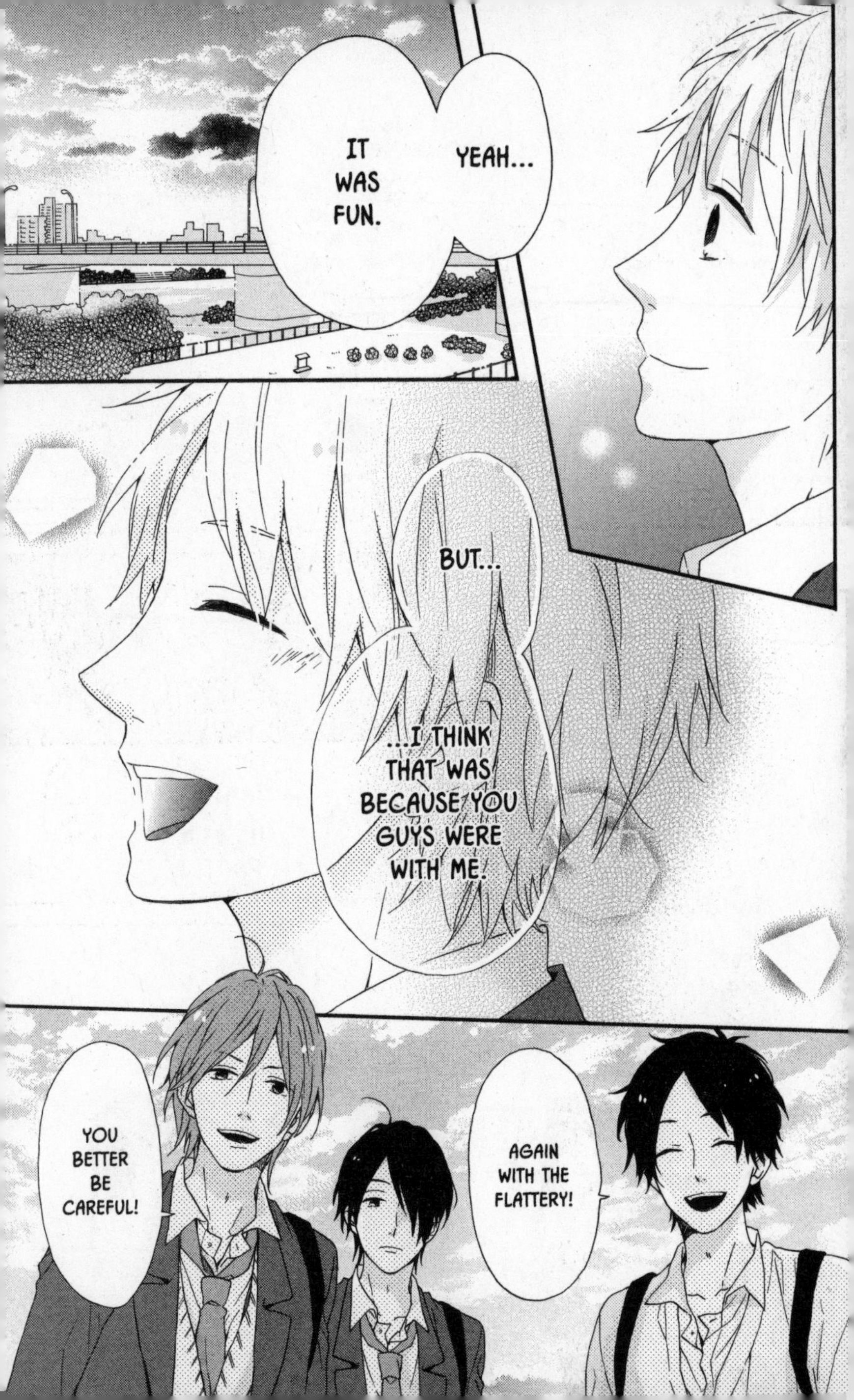
YEAH...
IT WAS FUN.
BUT...
...I THINK THAT WAS BECAUSE YOU GUYS WERE WITH ME.
AGAIN WITH THE FLATTERY!
YOU BETTER BE CAREFUL!

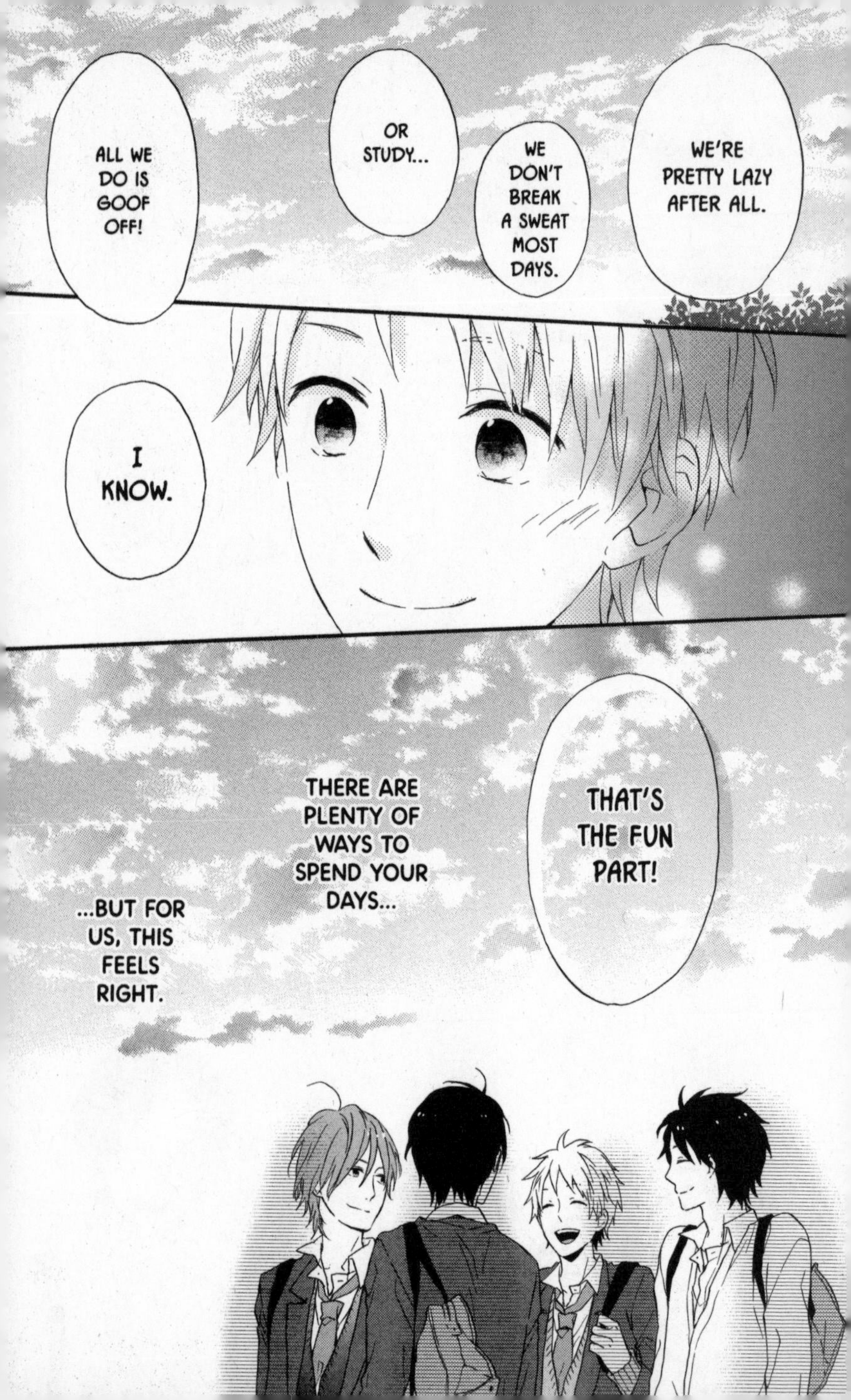
WE'RE PRETTY LAZY AFTER ALL.
WE DON'T BREAK A SWEAT MOST DAYS.
OR STUDY...
ALL WE DO IS GOOF OFF!
I KNOW.
THAT'S THE FUN PART!
THERE ARE PLENTY OF WAYS TO SPEND YOUR DAYS...
...BUT FOR US, THIS FEELS RIGHT.

# Rainbow
# Days

■  ■  ■  ■  ■  ■  ■

Everyone except Taizo got treated as extras,
but I amused myself making up characters
for the basketball team members.

## BASKETBALL TEAM
## SECOND-YEARS

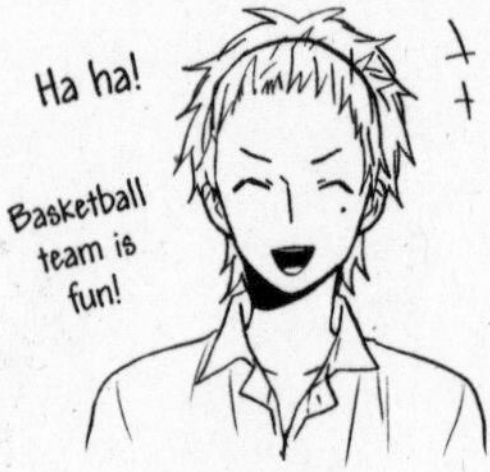
Ha ha!
Basketball team is fun!

**Taizo Sanada**

The Dad
Went to same junior high as Kei-chan
More focused on the team than romance right now

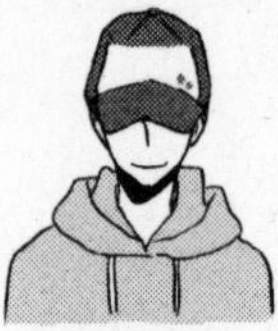

**Kakei**

The Man of Mystery
Face always covered up by cap

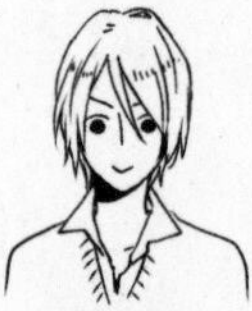

**Mochizuki**

The Hot One
Second-year ace
Half Russian

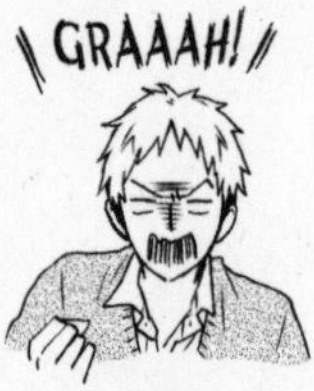
GRAAAH!

**Nezu**

The Warrior
From Kansai region
Passionate and loud

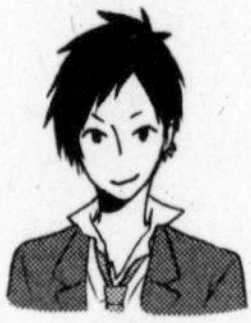

**Yuri**

The Fashion Plate
Has tongue piercing
Likes guitar

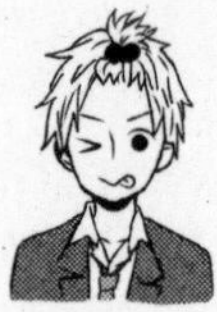

**Miyoshi**

The Shrimp
Feisty
Rock-paper-scissors champion

And there could be five others...?!

Must be hard to get out on the court with this many members!

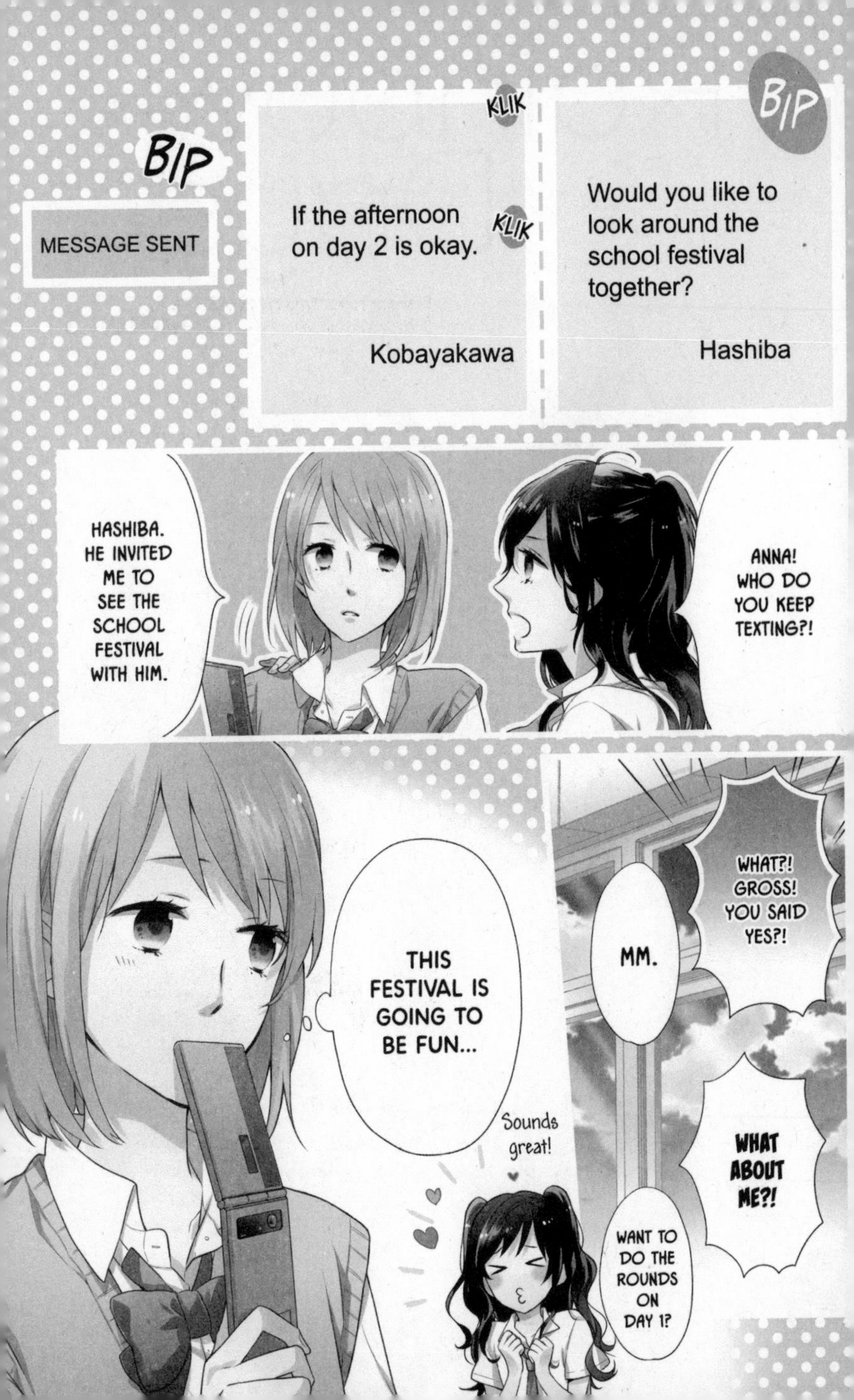
BIP
Would you like to look around the school festival together?
Hashiba
KLIK
If the afternoon on day 2 is okay.
KLIK
Kobayakawa
BIP
MESSAGE SENT
ANNA! WHO DO YOU KEEP TEXTING?!
HASHIBA. HE INVITED ME TO SEE THE SCHOOL FESTIVAL WITH HIM.
WHAT?! GROSS! YOU SAID YES?!
MM.
WHAT ABOUT ME?!
WANT TO DO THE ROUNDS ON DAY 1?
Sounds great!
THIS FESTIVAL IS GOING TO BE FUN...

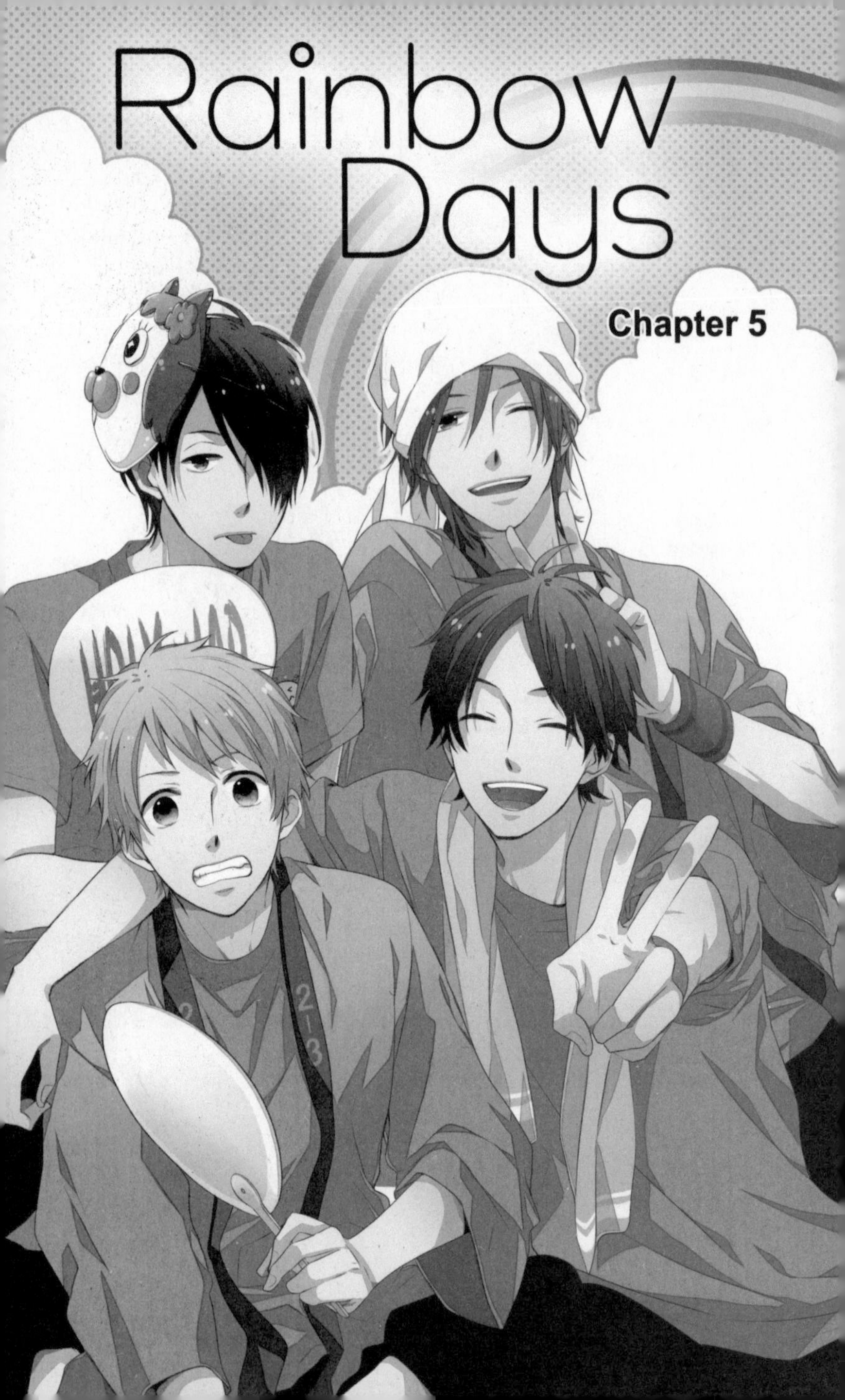
Rainbow Days
Chapter 5

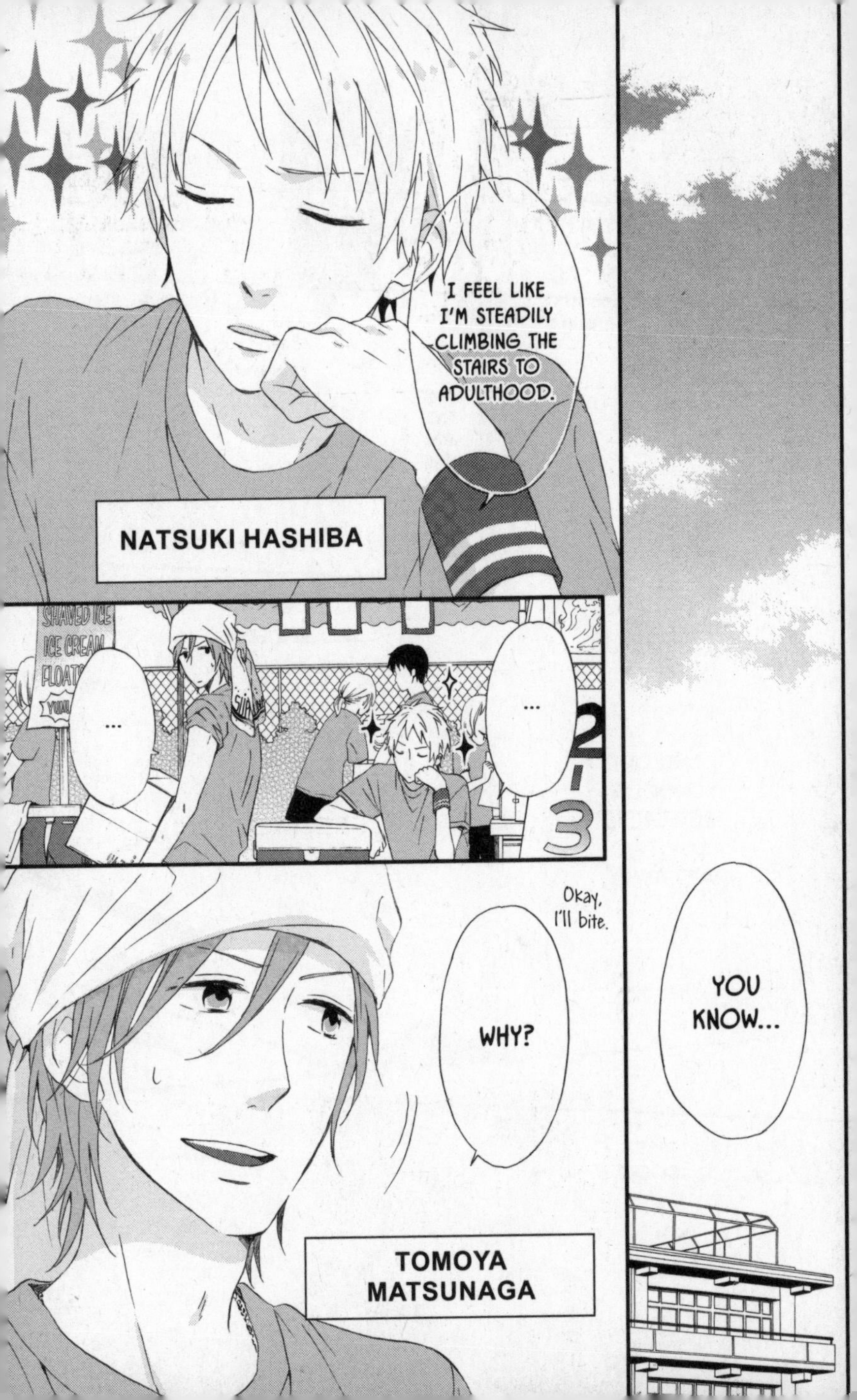

YOU KNOW...
I FEEL LIKE I'M STEADILY CLIMBING THE STAIRS TO ADULTHOOD.
NATSUKI HASHIBA
SHAVED ICE
ICE CREAM
...
...
2
3
Okay, I'll bite.
WHY?
TOMOYA MATSUNAGA

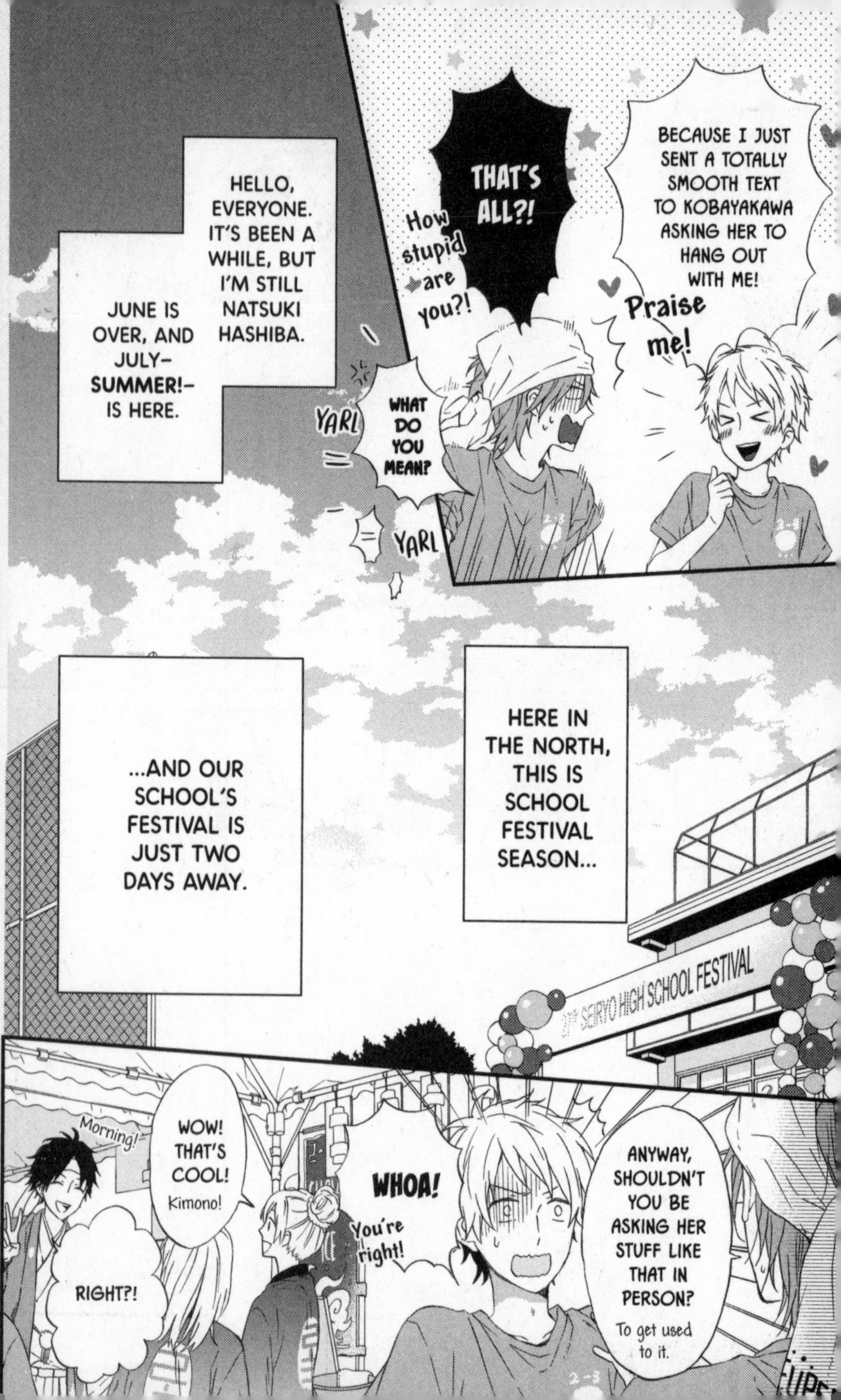
BECAUSE I JUST SENT A TOTALLY SMOOTH TEXT TO KOBAYAKAWA ASKING HER TO HANG OUT WITH ME!
Praise me!
THAT'S ALL?!
How stupid are you?!
YARL
WHAT DO YOU MEAN?
YARL
HELLO, EVERYONE. IT'S BEEN A WHILE, BUT I'M STILL NATSUKI HASHIBA.
JUNE IS OVER, AND JULY—SUMMER!—IS HERE.
HERE IN THE NORTH, THIS IS SCHOOL FESTIVAL SEASON...
...AND OUR SCHOOL'S FESTIVAL IS JUST TWO DAYS AWAY.
27th SEIRYO HIGH SCHOOL FESTIVAL
ANYWAY, SHOULDN'T YOU BE ASKING HER STUFF LIKE THAT IN PERSON?
To get used to it.
WHOA!
You're right!
WOW! THAT'S COOL!
Kimono!
Morning!
RIGHT?!

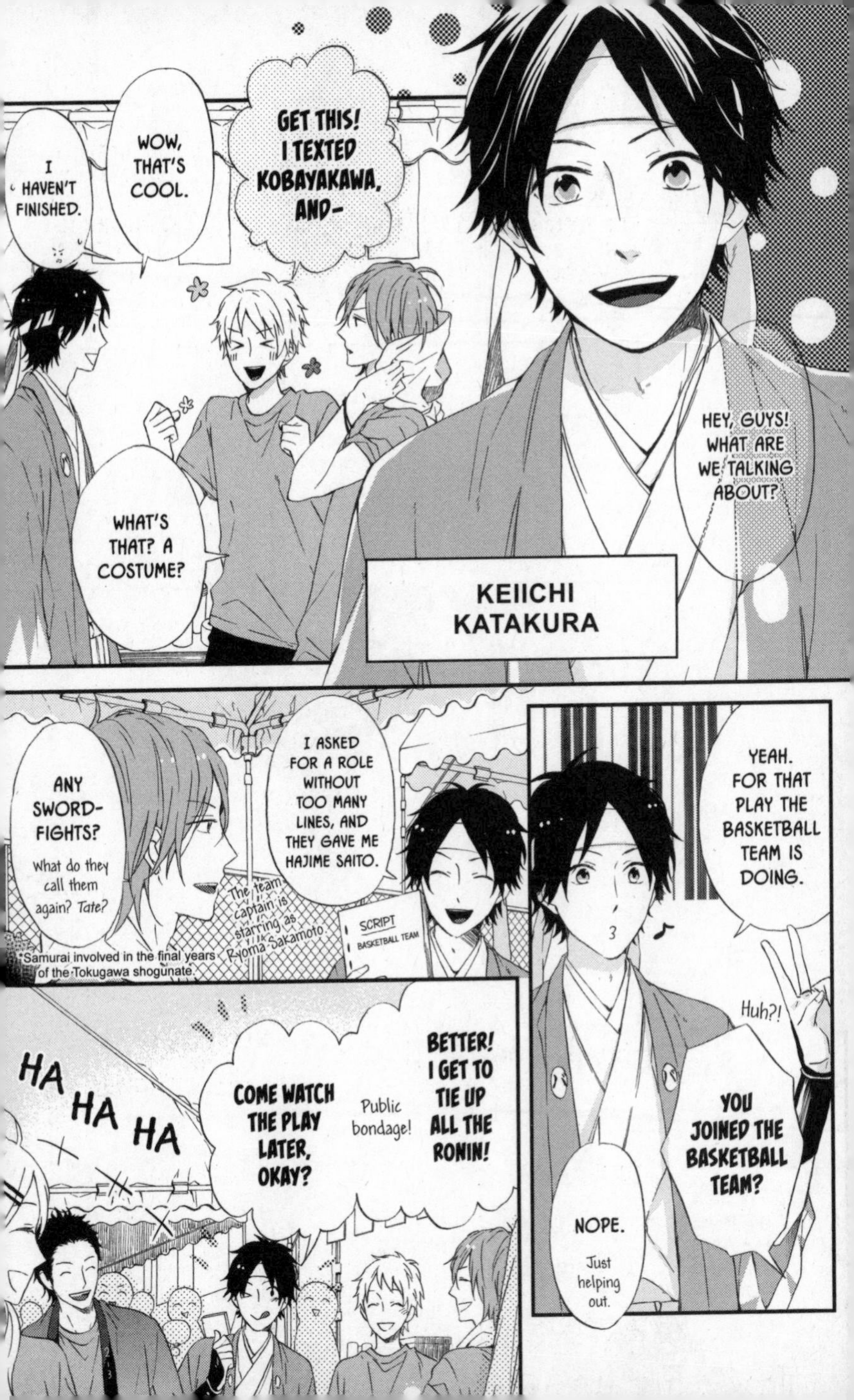
HEY, GUYS! WHAT ARE WE TALKING ABOUT?
KEIICHI KATAKURA
GET THIS! I TEXTED KOBAYAKAWA, AND-
WOW, THAT'S COOL.
I HAVEN'T FINISHED.
WHAT'S THAT? A COSTUME?
YEAH. FOR THAT PLAY THE BASKETBALL TEAM IS DOING.
Huh?!
YOU JOINED THE BASKETBALL TEAM?
NOPE.
Just helping out.
I ASKED FOR A ROLE WITHOUT TOO MANY LINES, AND THEY GAVE ME HAJIME SAITO.
ANY SWORD-FIGHTS?
What do they call them again? Tate?
The team captain is starring as Ryoma Sakamoto.
SCRIPT
BASKETBALL TEAM
*Samurai involved in the final years of the Tokugawa shogunate.
BETTER! I GET TO TIE UP ALL THE RONIN!
Public bondage!
COME WATCH THE PLAY LATER, OKAY?
HA HA HA

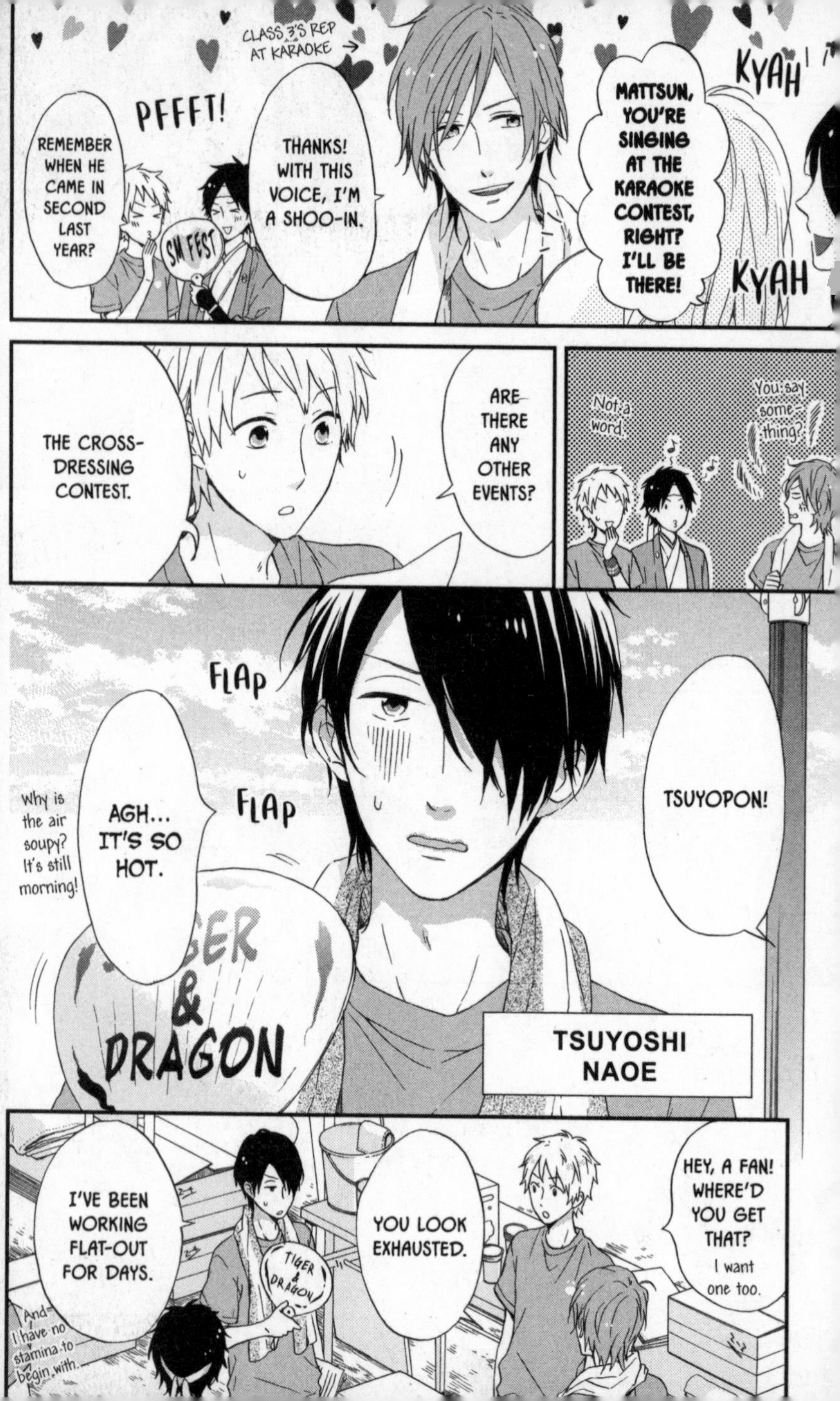
KYAH
KYAH
MATTSUN, YOU'RE SINGING AT THE KARAOKE CONTEST, RIGHT? I'LL BE THERE!
CLASS 3'S REP AT KARAOKE
THANKS! WITH THIS VOICE, I'M A SHOO-IN.
PFFFT!
REMEMBER WHEN HE CAME IN SECOND LAST YEAR?
SM FEST
You say some-thing?
Not a word.
ARE THERE ANY OTHER EVENTS?
THE CROSS-DRESSING CONTEST.
TSUYOPON!
TSUYOSHI NAOE
FLAP
FLAP
AGH... IT'S SO HOT.
Why is the air soupy? It's still morning!
& DRAGON
HEY, A FAN! WHERE'D YOU GET THAT?
I want one too.
YOU LOOK EXHAUSTED.
I'VE BEEN WORKING FLAT-OUT FOR DAYS.
TIGER & DRAGON
And I have no stamina to begin with.

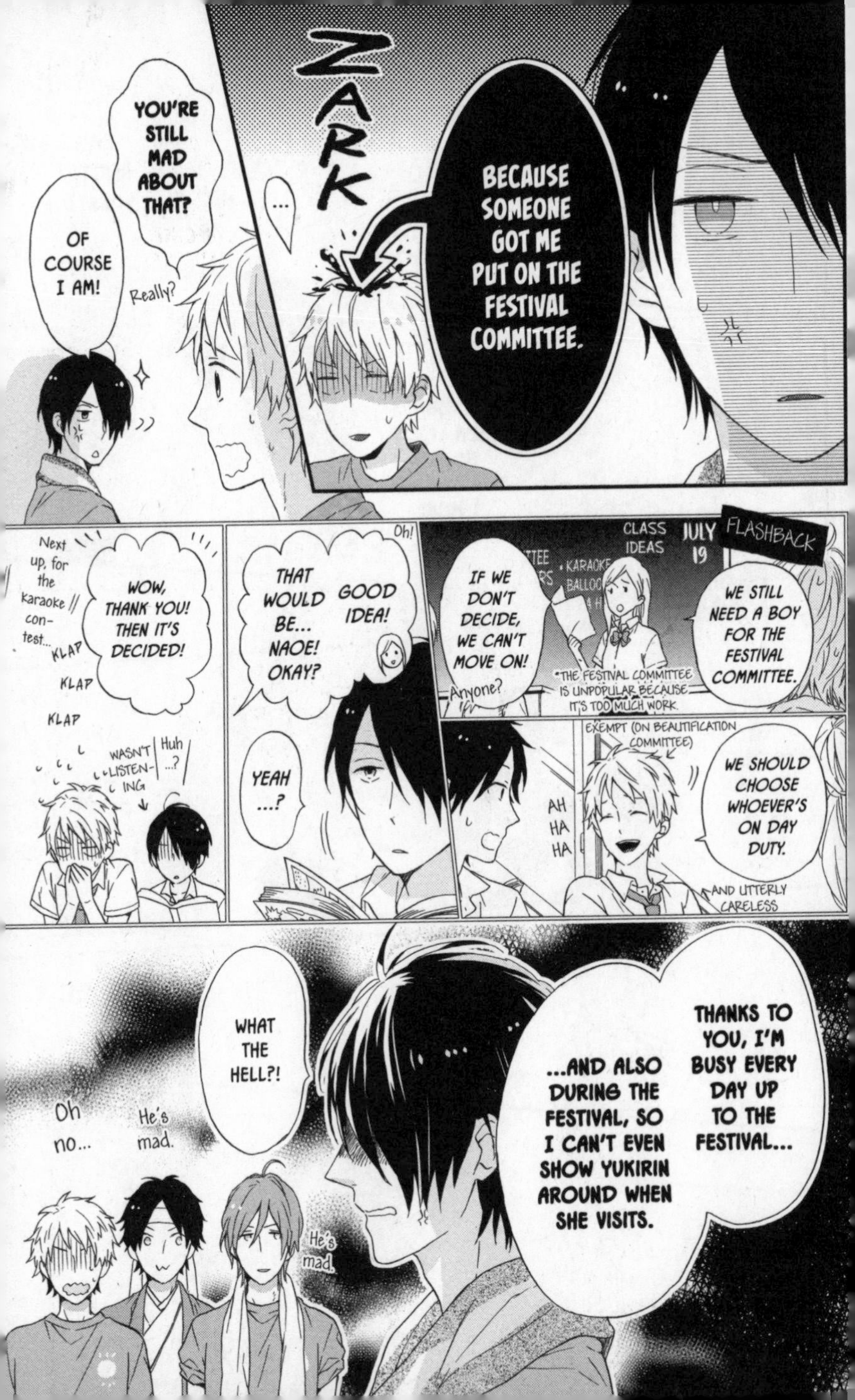
ZARK
BECAUSE SOMEONE GOT ME PUT ON THE FESTIVAL COMMITTEE.
...
YOU'RE STILL MAD ABOUT THAT?
Really?
OF COURSE I AM!
FLASHBACK
JULY 19
CLASS IDEAS
WE STILL NEED A BOY FOR THE FESTIVAL COMMITTEE.
IF WE DON'T DECIDE, WE CAN'T MOVE ON!
Anyone?
*THE FESTIVAL COMMITTEE IS UNPOPULAR BECAUSE IT'S TOO MUCH WORK.
WE SHOULD CHOOSE WHOEVER'S ON DAY DUTY.
EXEMPT (ON BEAUTIFICATION COMMITTEE)
AND UTTERLY CARELESS
AH HA HA
Oh!
GOOD IDEA!
THAT WOULD BE... NAOE! OKAY?
YEAH ...?
WOW, THANK YOU! THEN IT'S DECIDED!
Next up, for the karaoke contest...
KLAP
KLAP
KLAP
Huh ...?
WASN'T LISTENING
THANKS TO YOU, I'M BUSY EVERY DAY UP TO THE FESTIVAL...
...AND ALSO DURING THE FESTIVAL, SO I CAN'T EVEN SHOW YUKIRIN AROUND WHEN SHE VISITS.
WHAT THE HELL?!
He's mad.
He's mad.
Oh no...

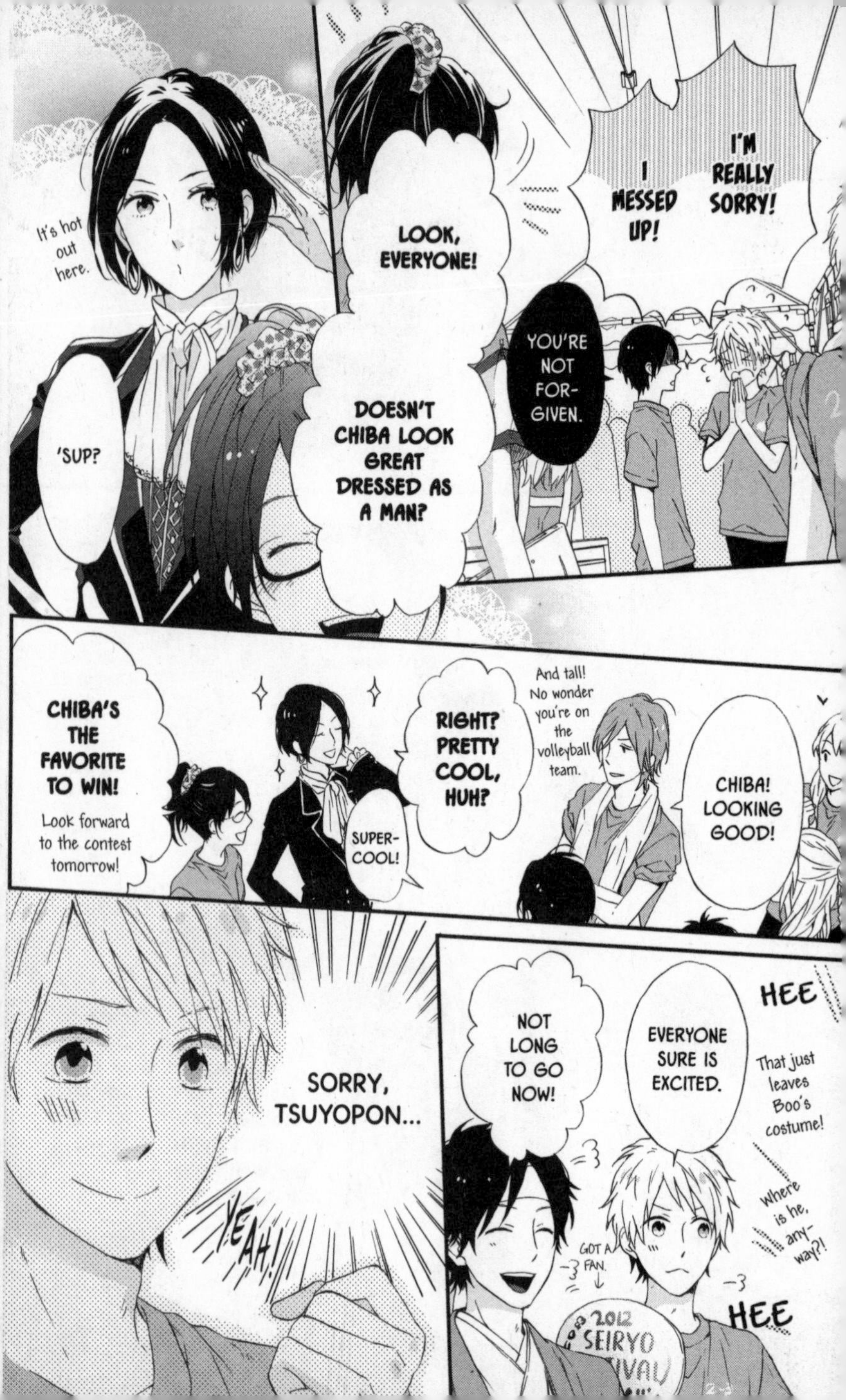

I'M REALLY SORRY!
I MESSED UP!
YOU'RE NOT FOR-GIVEN.
LOOK, EVERYONE!
DOESN'T CHIBA LOOK GREAT DRESSED AS A MAN?
It's hot out here.
'SUP?
CHIBA! LOOKING GOOD!
And tall! No wonder you're on the volleyball team.
RIGHT? PRETTY COOL, HUH?
SUPER-COOL!
CHIBA'S THE FAVORITE TO WIN!
Look forward to the contest tomorrow!
HEE
That just leaves Boo's costume!
EVERYONE SURE IS EXCITED.
NOT LONG TO GO NOW!
where is he, anyway?!
GOT A FAN.
2012 SEIRYO
HEE
SORRY, TSUYOPON...
YEAH!

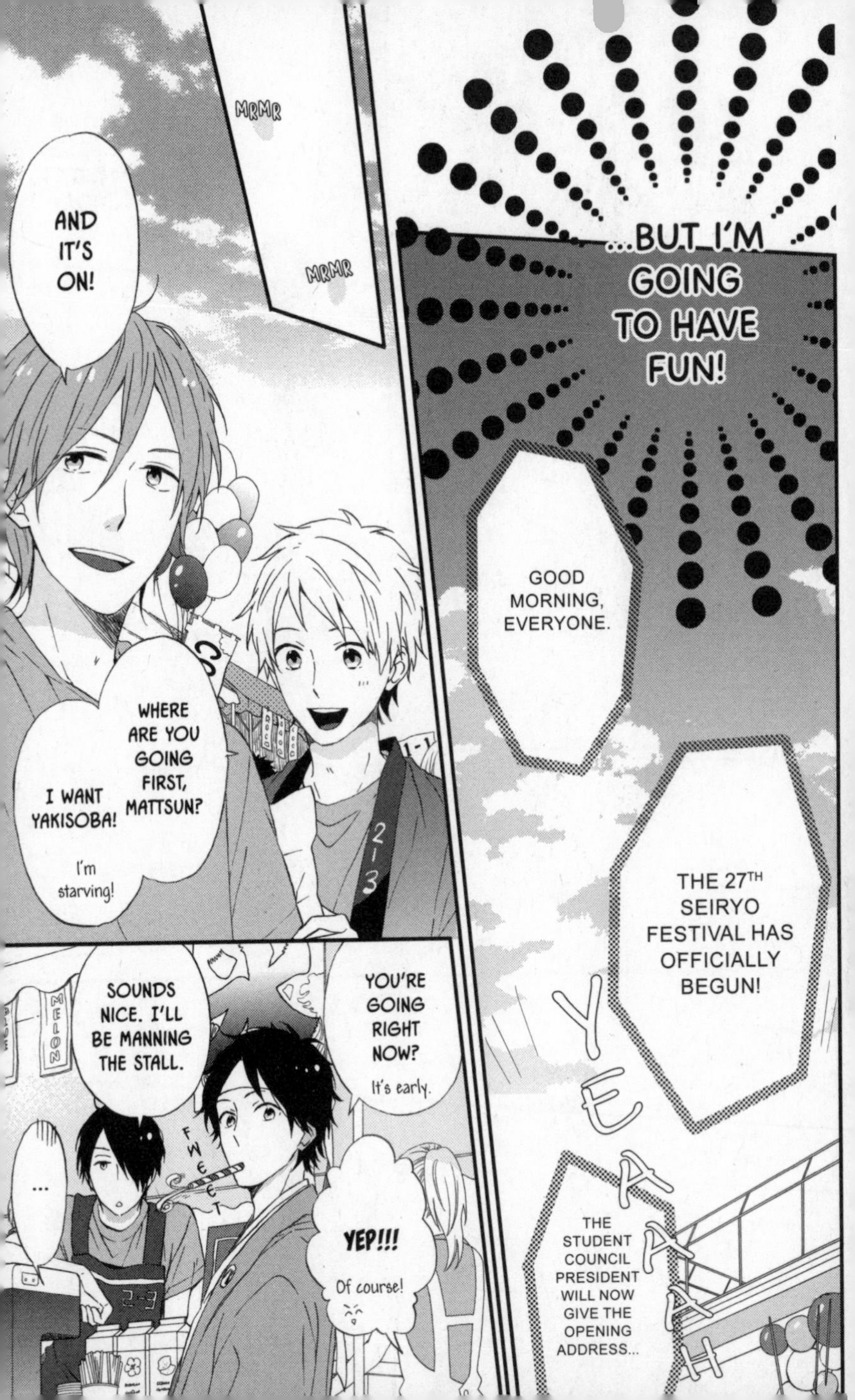
...BUT I'M GOING TO HAVE FUN!
GOOD MORNING, EVERYONE.
THE 27TH SEIRYO FESTIVAL HAS OFFICIALLY BEGUN!
YEAAAH
THE STUDENT COUNCIL PRESIDENT WILL NOW GIVE THE OPENING ADDRESS...
MRMR
MRMR
AND IT'S ON!
WHERE ARE YOU GOING FIRST, MATTSUN?
I WANT YAKISOBA!
I'm starving!
YOU'RE GOING RIGHT NOW?
It's early.
SOUNDS NICE. I'LL BE MANNING THE STALL.
FWEET
YEP!!!
Of course!
...

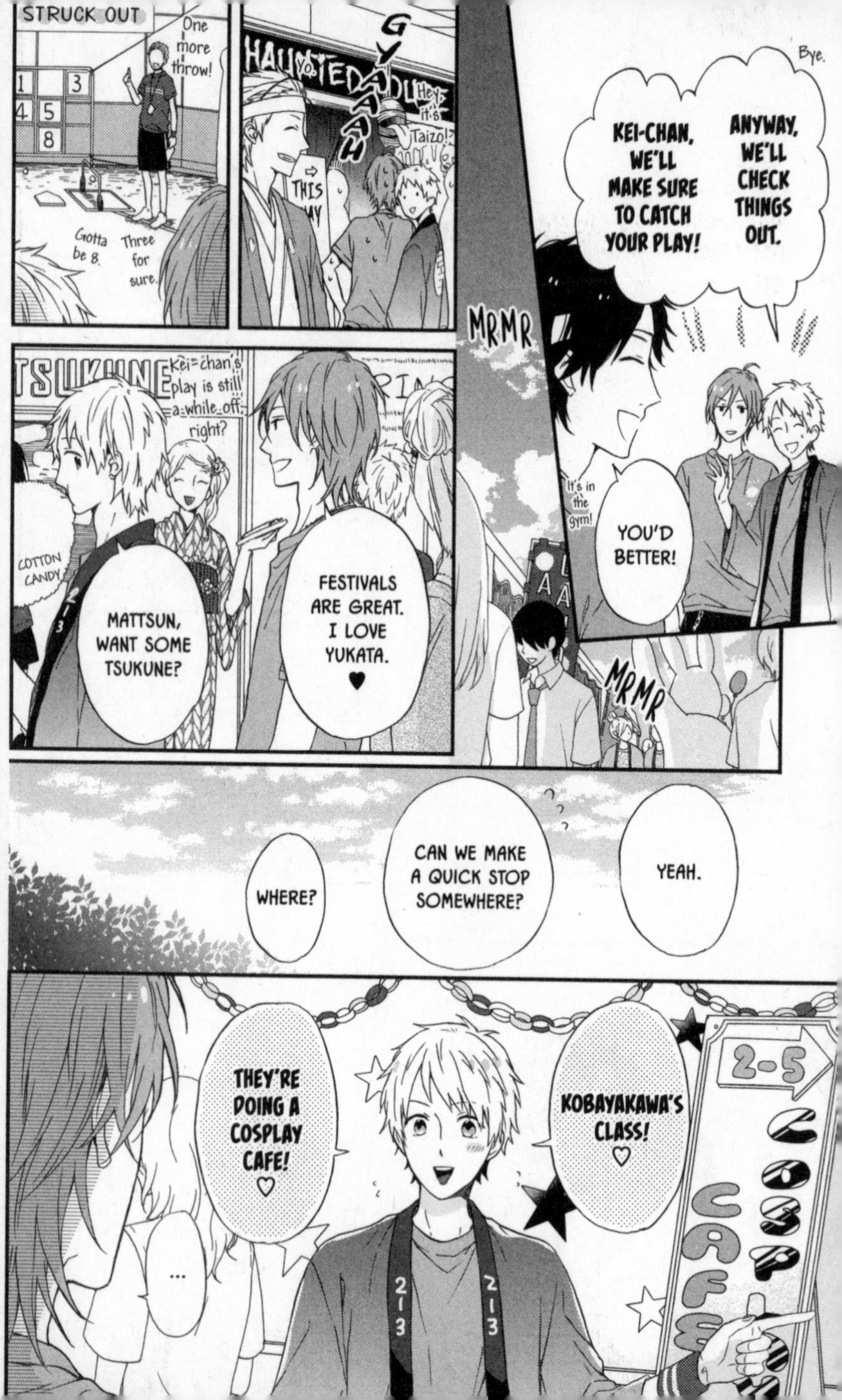
Bye.
ANYWAY, WE'LL CHECK THINGS OUT.
KEI-CHAN, WE'LL MAKE SURE TO CATCH YOUR PLAY!
MRMR
It's in the gym!
YOU'D BETTER!
MRMR
HAUNTED
GYAAAAH
Yo.
Hey, it's Taizo!
THIS WAY
STRUCK OUT
One more throw!
1 3
4 5
8
Three for sure.
Gotta be 8.
TSUKUNE
FESTIVALS ARE GREAT. I LOVE YUKATA. ♥
Kei=chan's play is still a while off, right?
MATTSUN, WANT SOME TSUKUNE?
COTTON CANDY
YEAH.
CAN WE MAKE A QUICK STOP SOMEWHERE?
WHERE?
2-5
COSPLAY CAFE
KOBAYAKAWA'S CLASS! ♡
THEY'RE DOING A COSPLAY CAFE! ♡
...

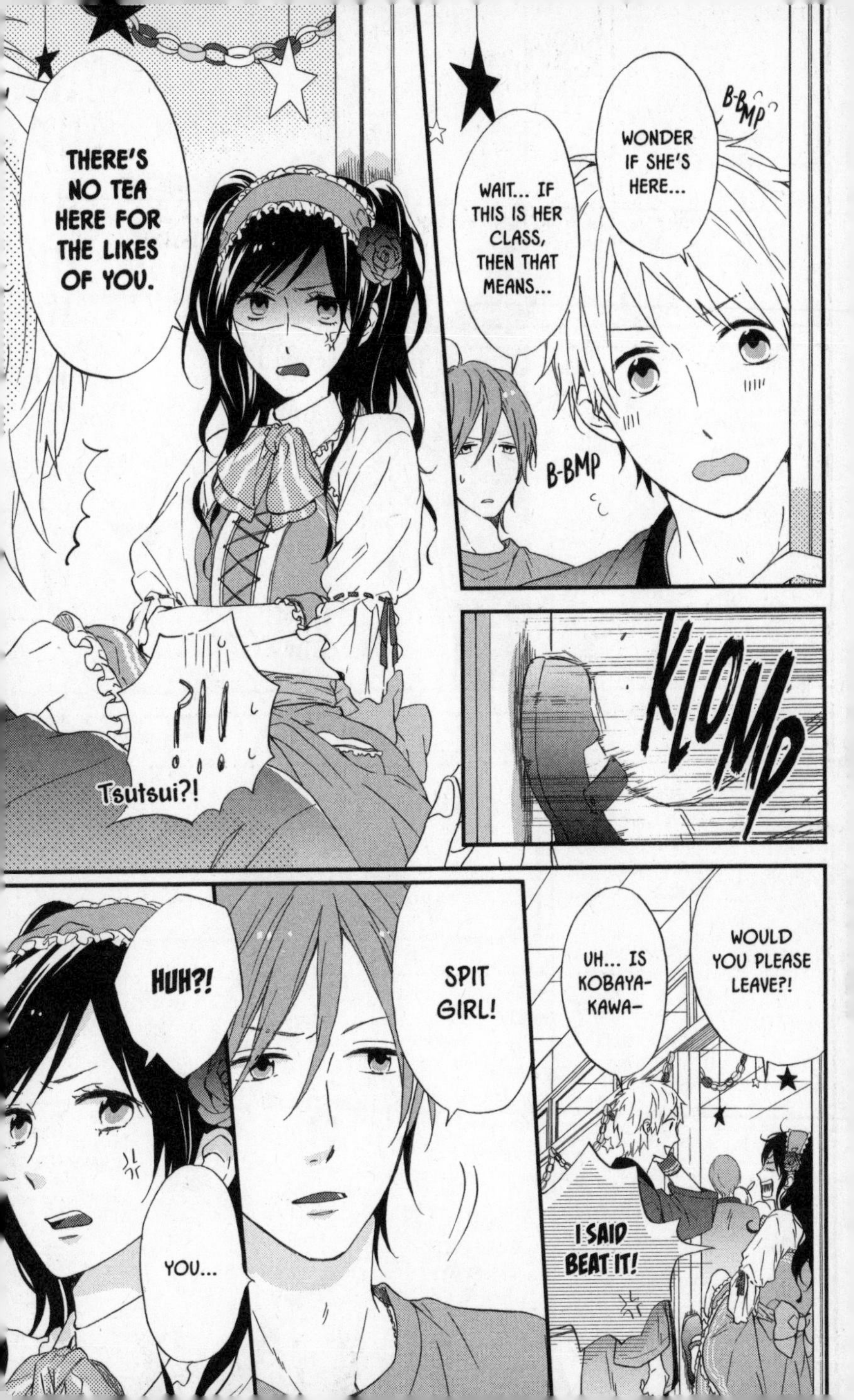
B-BMP
WONDER IF SHE'S HERE...
WAIT... IF THIS IS HER CLASS, THEN THAT MEANS...
B-BMP
KLOMP
THERE'S NO TEA HERE FOR THE LIKES OF YOU.
?!!
Tsutsui?!
WOULD YOU PLEASE LEAVE?!
UH... IS KOBAYA-KAWA-
I SAID BEAT IT!
SPIT GIRL!
HUH?!
YOU...

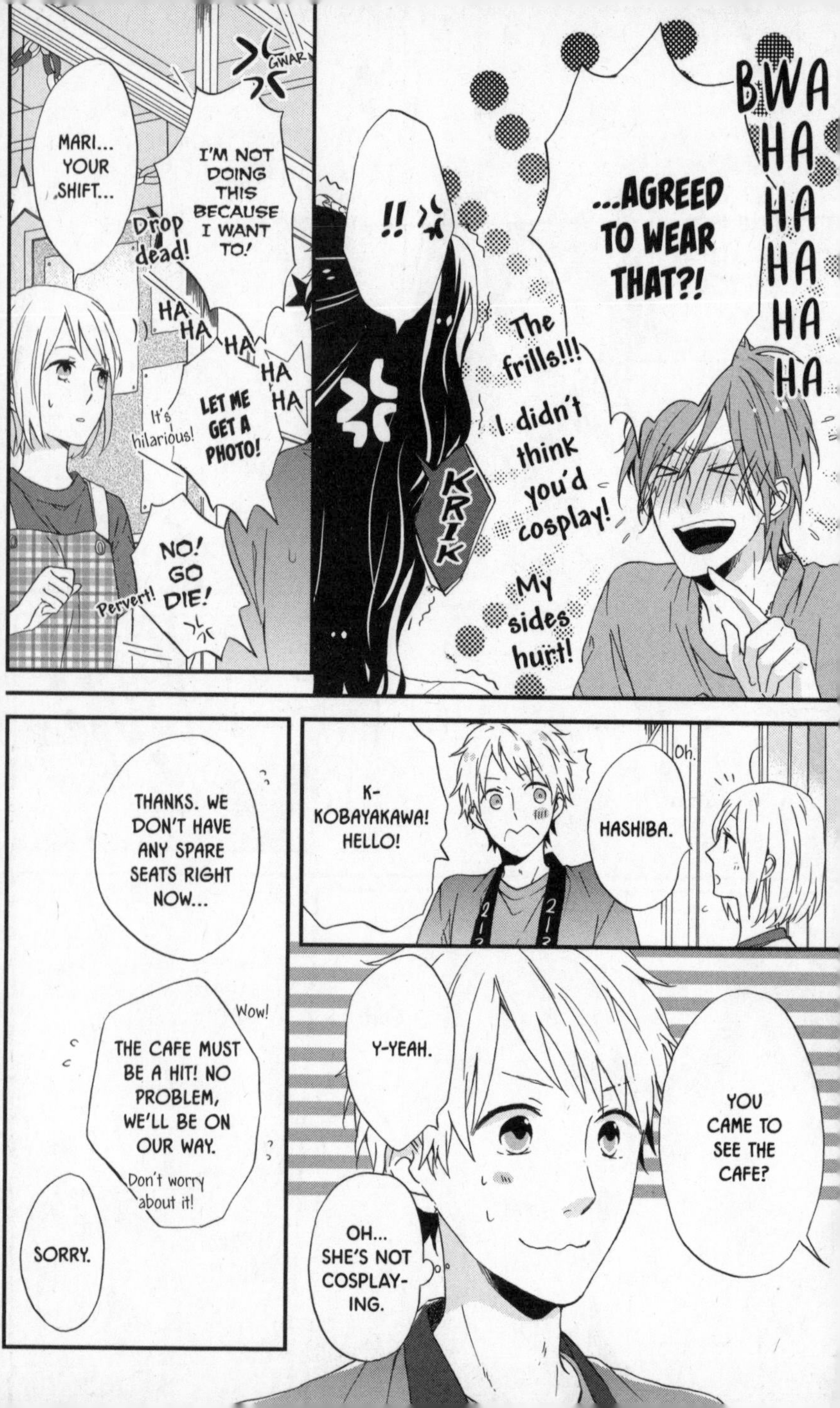
BWA HA HA HA HA HA HA
...AGREED TO WEAR THAT?!
!!
The frills!!!
I didn't think you'd cosplay!
My sides hurt!
KRIK
GWAR
I'M NOT DOING THIS BECAUSE I WANT TO!
Drop dead!
MARI... YOUR SHIFT...
HA HA HA HA HA
LET ME GET A PHOTO!
It's hilarious!
NO! GO DIE!
Pervert!
Oh.
HASHIBA.
K-KOBAYAKAWA! HELLO!
YOU CAME TO SEE THE CAFE?
Y-YEAH.
OH... SHE'S NOT COSPLAYING.
THANKS. WE DON'T HAVE ANY SPARE SEATS RIGHT NOW...
Wow!
THE CAFE MUST BE A HIT! NO PROBLEM, WE'LL BE ON OUR WAY.
Don't worry about it!
SORRY.

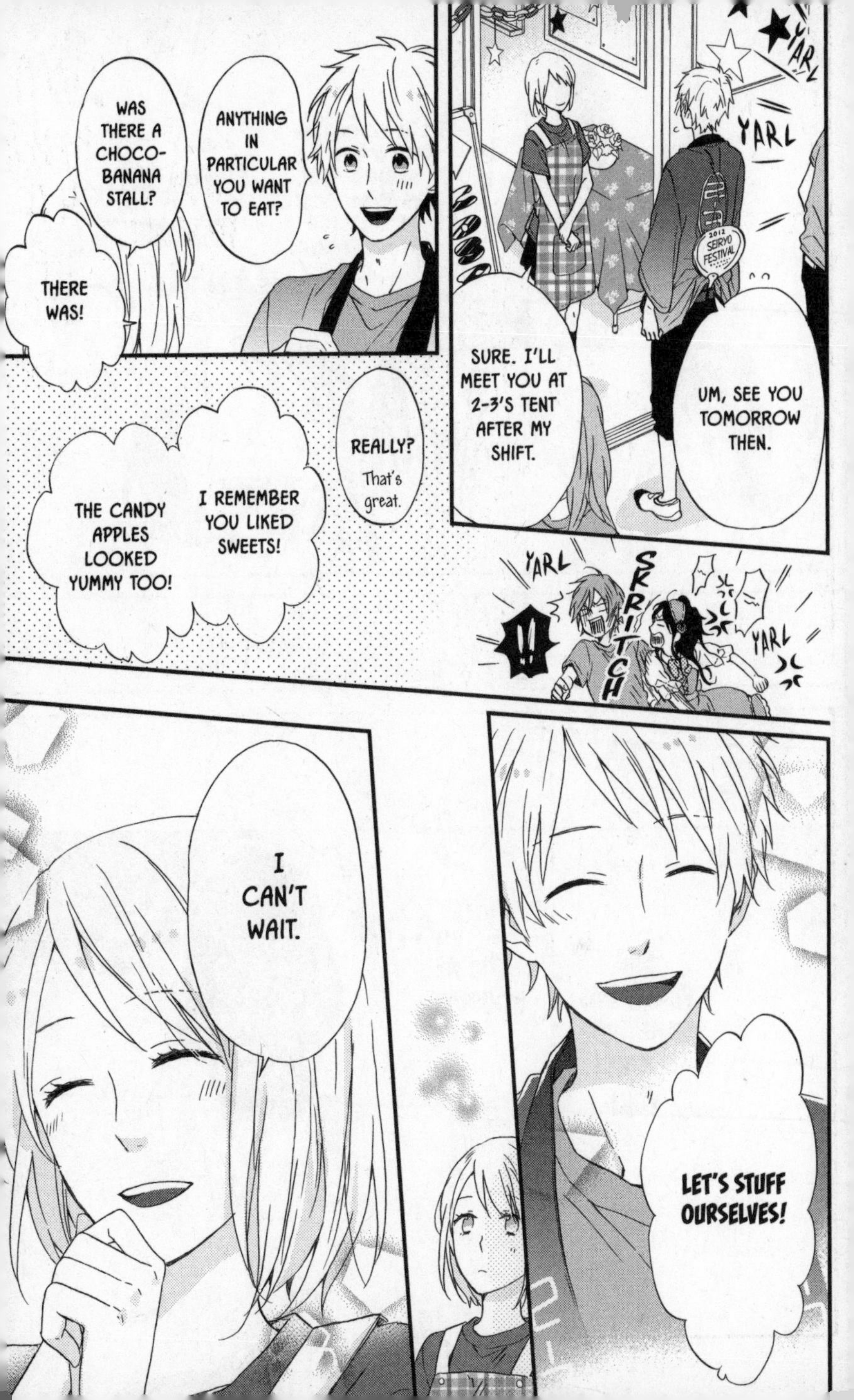
YARL
YARL
2012 SEIRYO FESTIVAL
UM, SEE YOU TOMORROW THEN.
SURE. I'LL MEET YOU AT 2-3'S TENT AFTER MY SHIFT.
ANYTHING IN PARTICULAR YOU WANT TO EAT?
WAS THERE A CHOCO-BANANA STALL?
THERE WAS!
REALLY? That's great.
I REMEMBER YOU LIKED SWEETS!
THE CANDY APPLES LOOKED YUMMY TOO!
YARL
SKRITCH
YARL
LET'S STUFF OURSELVES!
I CAN'T WAIT.

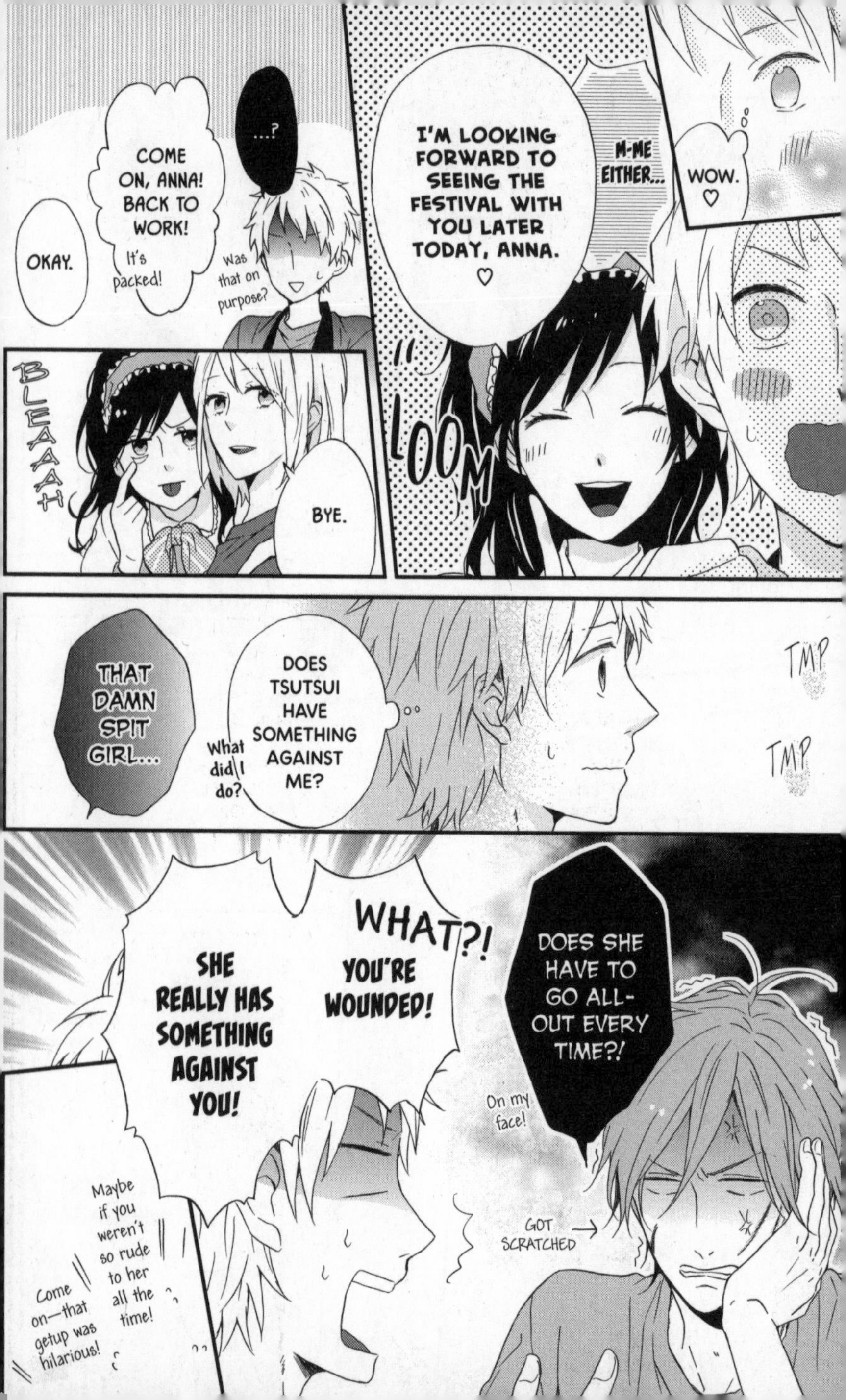
WOW. ♡
I'M LOOKING FORWARD TO SEEING THE FESTIVAL WITH YOU LATER TODAY, ANNA. ♡
M-ME EITHER...
LOOM
...?
Was that on purpose?
COME ON, ANNA! BACK TO WORK!
It's packed!
OKAY.
BYE.
BLEAAAAH
TMP
TMP
DOES TSUTSUI HAVE SOMETHING AGAINST ME?
What did I do?
THAT DAMN SPIT GIRL...
DOES SHE HAVE TO GO ALL-OUT EVERY TIME?!
On my face!
GOT SCRATCHED
WHAT?!
YOU'RE WOUNDED!
SHE REALLY HAS SOMETHING AGAINST YOU!
Maybe if you weren't so rude to her all the time!
Come on—that getup was hilarious!

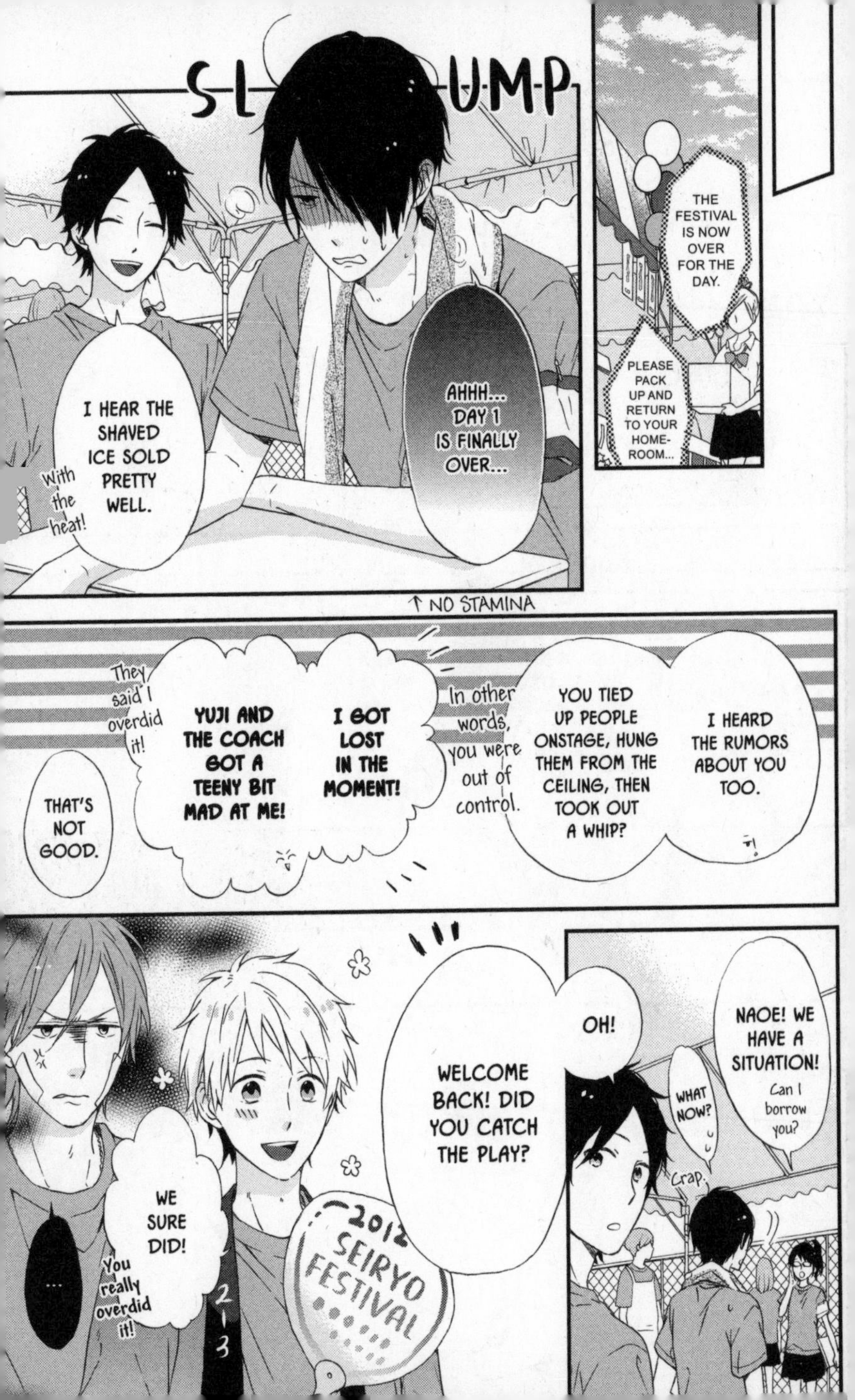
THE FESTIVAL IS NOW OVER FOR THE DAY.
PLEASE PACK UP AND RETURN TO YOUR HOME-ROOM...
S-L-U-M-P
AHHH... DAY 1 IS FINALLY OVER...
I HEAR THE SHAVED ICE SOLD PRETTY WELL.
With the heat!
↑ NO STAMINA
I HEARD THE RUMORS ABOUT YOU TOO.
YOU TIED UP PEOPLE ONSTAGE, HUNG THEM FROM THE CEILING, THEN TOOK OUT A WHIP?
In other words, you were out of control.
I GOT LOST IN THE MOMENT!
YUJI AND THE COACH GOT A TEENY BIT MAD AT ME!
They said I overdid it!
THAT'S NOT GOOD.
NAOE! WE HAVE A SITUATION!
Can I borrow you?
WHAT NOW?
Crap.
OH!
WELCOME BACK! DID YOU CATCH THE PLAY?
WE SURE DID!
You really overdid it!
...
2012 SEIRYO FESTIVAL

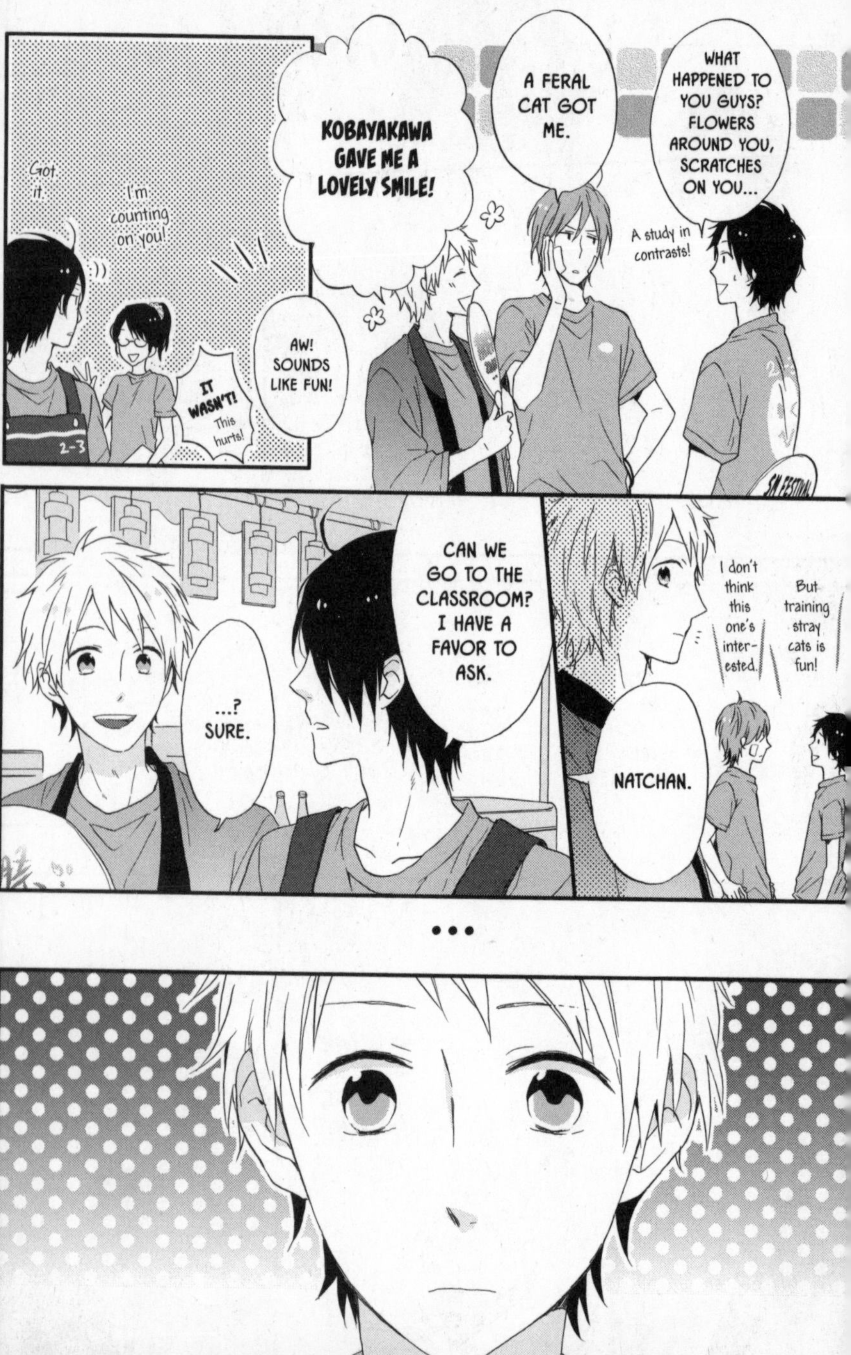
WHAT HAPPENED TO YOU GUYS? FLOWERS AROUND YOU, SCRATCHES ON YOU...
A study in contrasts!
A FERAL CAT GOT ME.
KOBAYAKAWA GAVE ME A LOVELY SMILE!
AW! SOUNDS LIKE FUN!
I'm counting on you!
Got it.
IT WASN'T! This hurts!
But training stray cats is fun!
I don't think this one's inter-ested.
NATCHAN.
CAN WE GO TO THE CLASSROOM? I HAVE A FAVOR TO ASK.
...? SURE.
•••

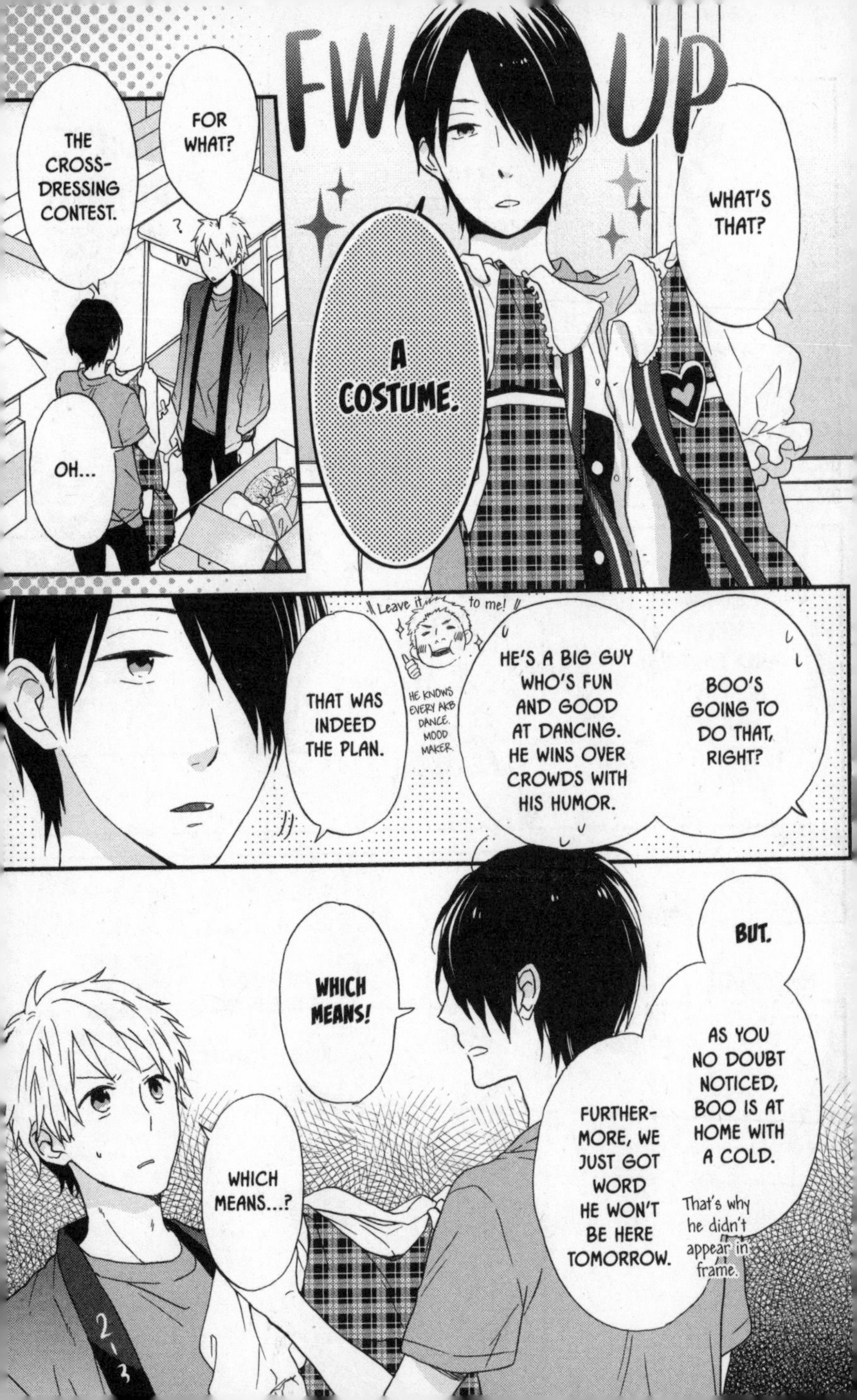
FW UP
WHAT'S THAT?
A COSTUME.
FOR WHAT?
THE CROSS-DRESSING CONTEST.
OH...
BOO'S GOING TO DO THAT, RIGHT?
HE'S A BIG GUY WHO'S FUN AND GOOD AT DANCING. HE WINS OVER CROWDS WITH HIS HUMOR.
Leave it to me!
HE KNOWS EVERY AKB DANCE. MOOD MAKER.
THAT WAS INDEED THE PLAN.
BUT.
AS YOU NO DOUBT NOTICED, BOO IS AT HOME WITH A COLD.
That's why he didn't appear in frame.
FURTHERMORE, WE JUST GOT WORD HE WON'T BE HERE TOMORROW.
WHICH MEANS!
WHICH MEANS...?

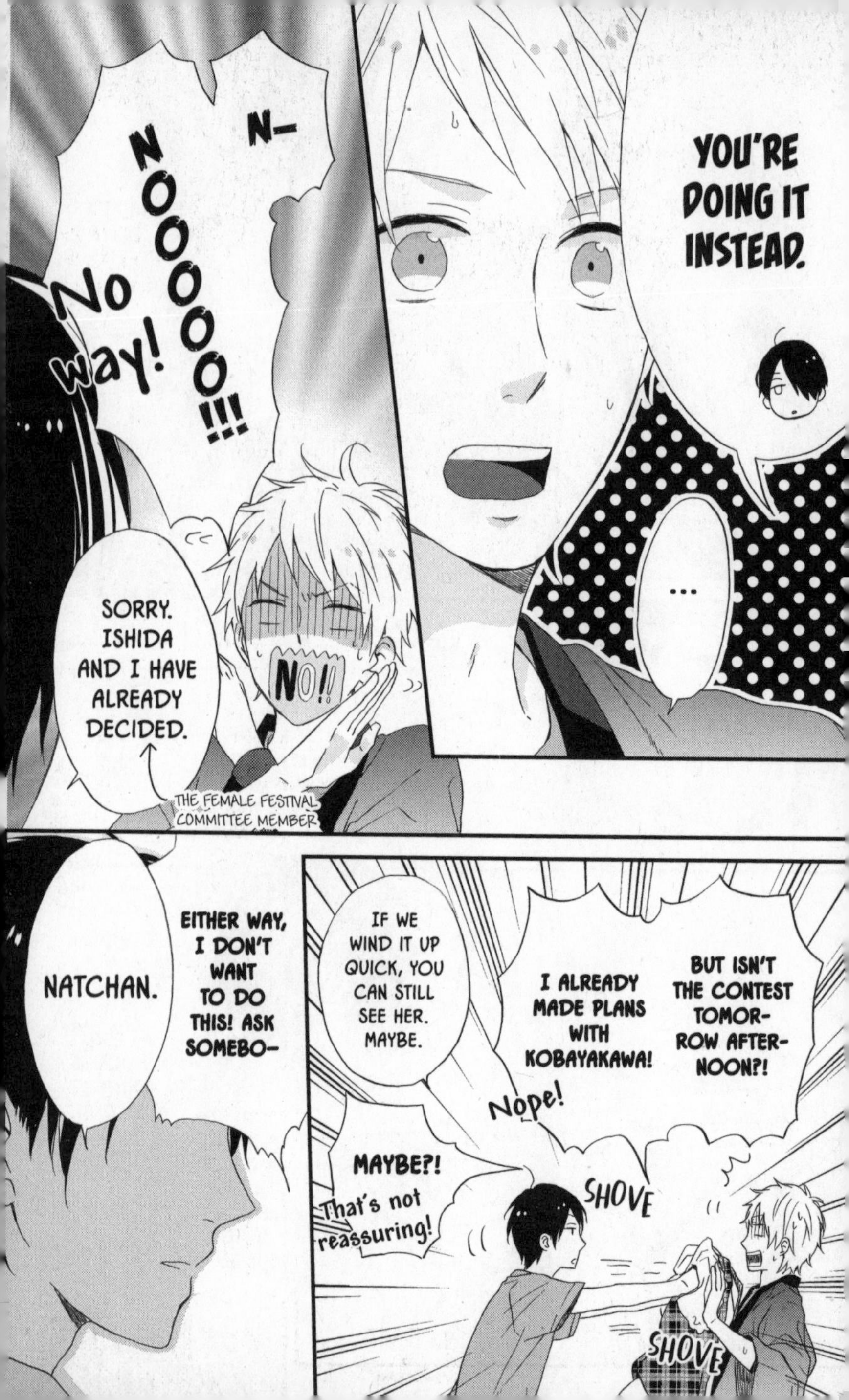
YOU'RE DOING IT INSTEAD.
...
N— NOOOOOO!!!
No way!
NO!!
SORRY. ISHIDA AND I HAVE ALREADY DECIDED.
THE FEMALE FESTIVAL COMMITTEE MEMBER
BUT ISN'T THE CONTEST TOMORROW AFTERNOON?!
I ALREADY MADE PLANS WITH KOBAYAKAWA!
Nope!
IF WE WIND IT UP QUICK, YOU CAN STILL SEE HER. MAYBE.
MAYBE?!
That's not reassuring!
SHOVE
SHOVE
EITHER WAY, I DON'T WANT TO DO THIS! ASK SOMEBO—
NATCHAN.

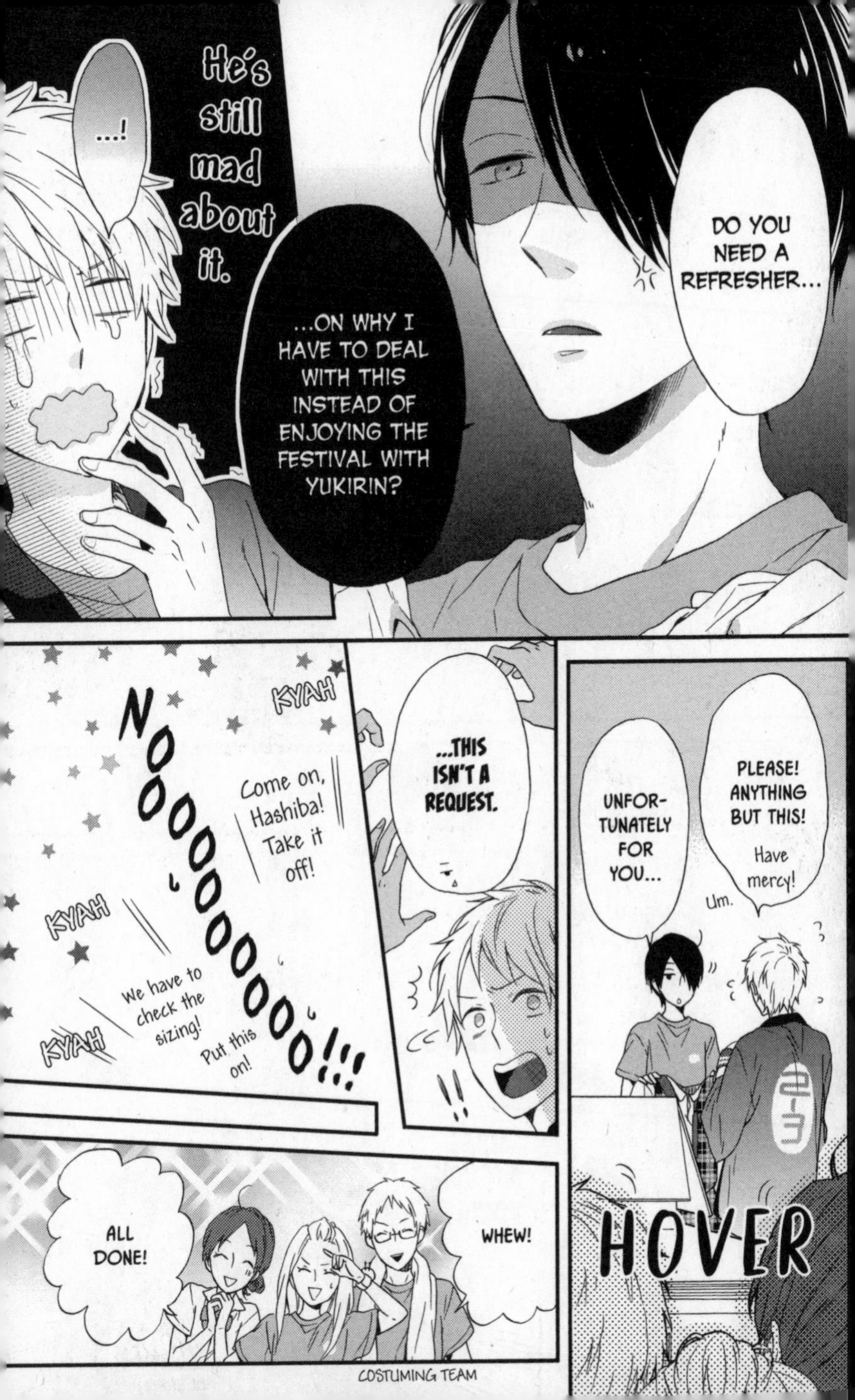
DO YOU NEED A REFRESHER...
...ON WHY I HAVE TO DEAL WITH THIS INSTEAD OF ENJOYING THE FESTIVAL WITH YUKIRIN?
...!
He's still mad about it.
PLEASE! ANYTHING BUT THIS!
Have mercy!
Um.
UNFORTUNATELY FOR YOU...
HOVER
...THIS ISN'T A REQUEST.
KYAH
NOOOOOOOOOOOOO!!!
Come on, Hashiba! Take it off!
KYAH
We have to check the sizing!
KYAH
Put this on!
WHEW!
ALL DONE!
COSTUMING TEAM

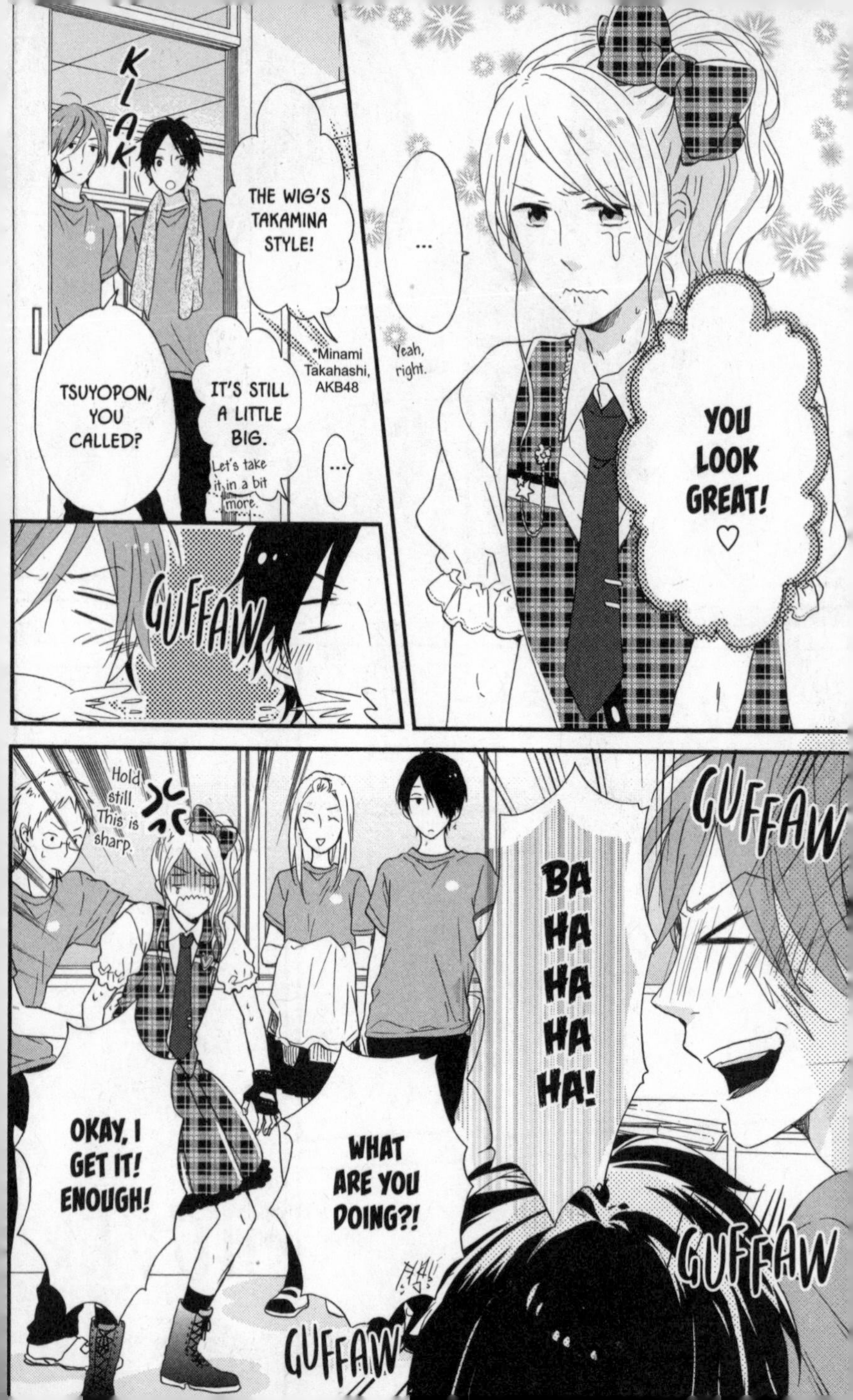
YOU LOOK GREAT! ♡
...
Yeah, right.
KLAK
THE WIG'S TAKAMINA STYLE!
*Minami Takahashi, AKB48
IT'S STILL A LITTLE BIG.
Let's take it in a bit more.
...
TSUYOPON, YOU CALLED?
GUFFAW
GUFFAW
BAHAHAHAHAHA!
GUFFAW
WHAT ARE YOU DOING?!
Hold still. This is sharp.
OKAY, I GET IT! ENOUGH!
GUFFAW

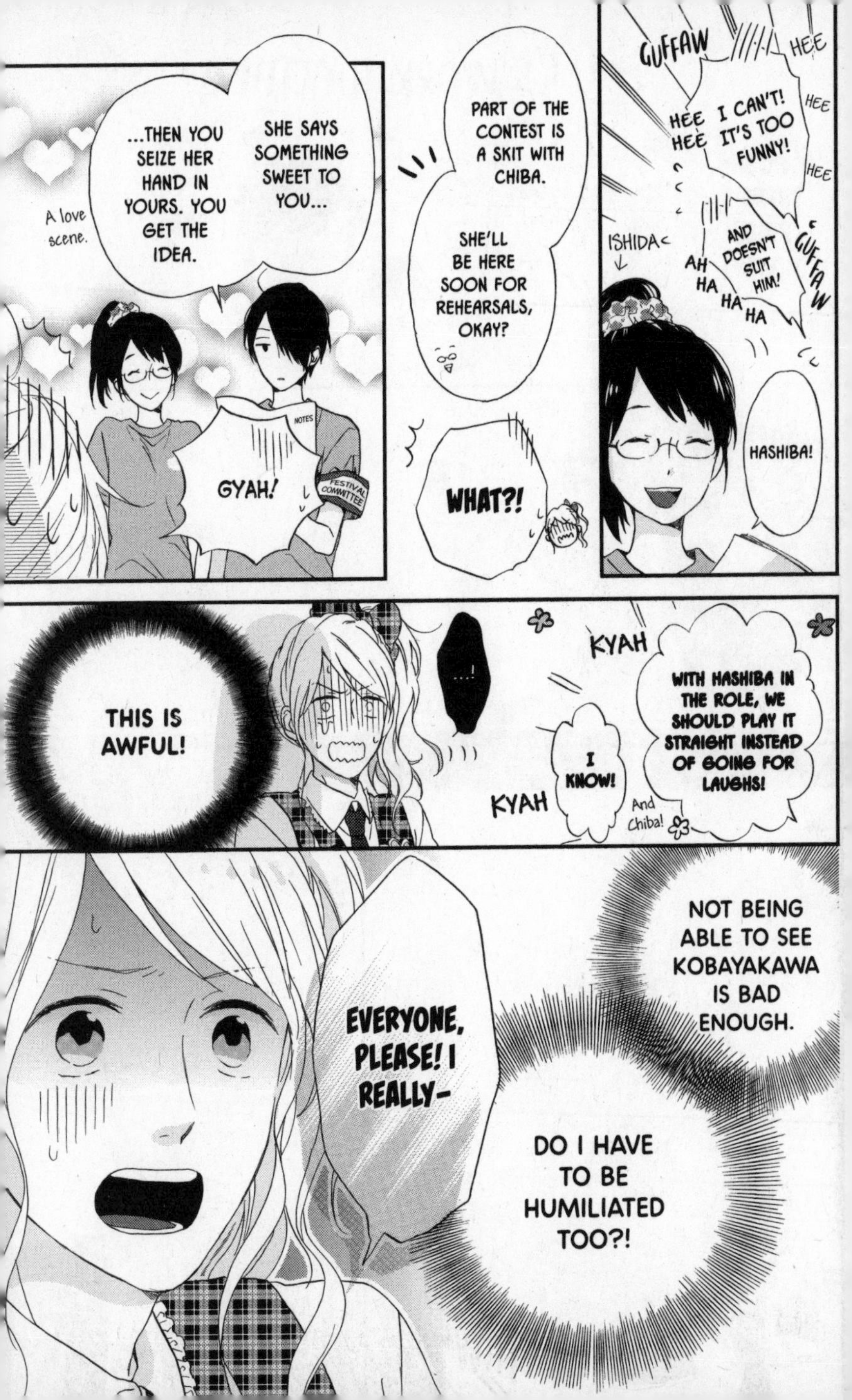
GUFFAW
HEE
HEE
HEE
HEE HEE
I CAN'T! IT'S TOO FUNNY!
AND DOESN'T SUIT HIM!
GUFFAW
AH HA HA HA
ISHIDA
HASHIBA!
PART OF THE CONTEST IS A SKIT WITH CHIBA.
SHE'LL BE HERE SOON FOR REHEARSALS, OKAY?
WHAT?!
SHE SAYS SOMETHING SWEET TO YOU...
...THEN YOU SEIZE HER HAND IN YOURS. YOU GET THE IDEA.
A love scene.
NOTES
FESTIVAL COMMITTEE
GYAH!
KYAH
WITH HASHIBA IN THE ROLE, WE SHOULD PLAY IT STRAIGHT INSTEAD OF GOING FOR LAUGHS!
I KNOW!
And Chiba!
KYAH
...!
THIS IS AWFUL!
NOT BEING ABLE TO SEE KOBAYAKAWA IS BAD ENOUGH.
DO I HAVE TO BE HUMILIATED TOO?!
EVERYONE, PLEASE! I REALLY-

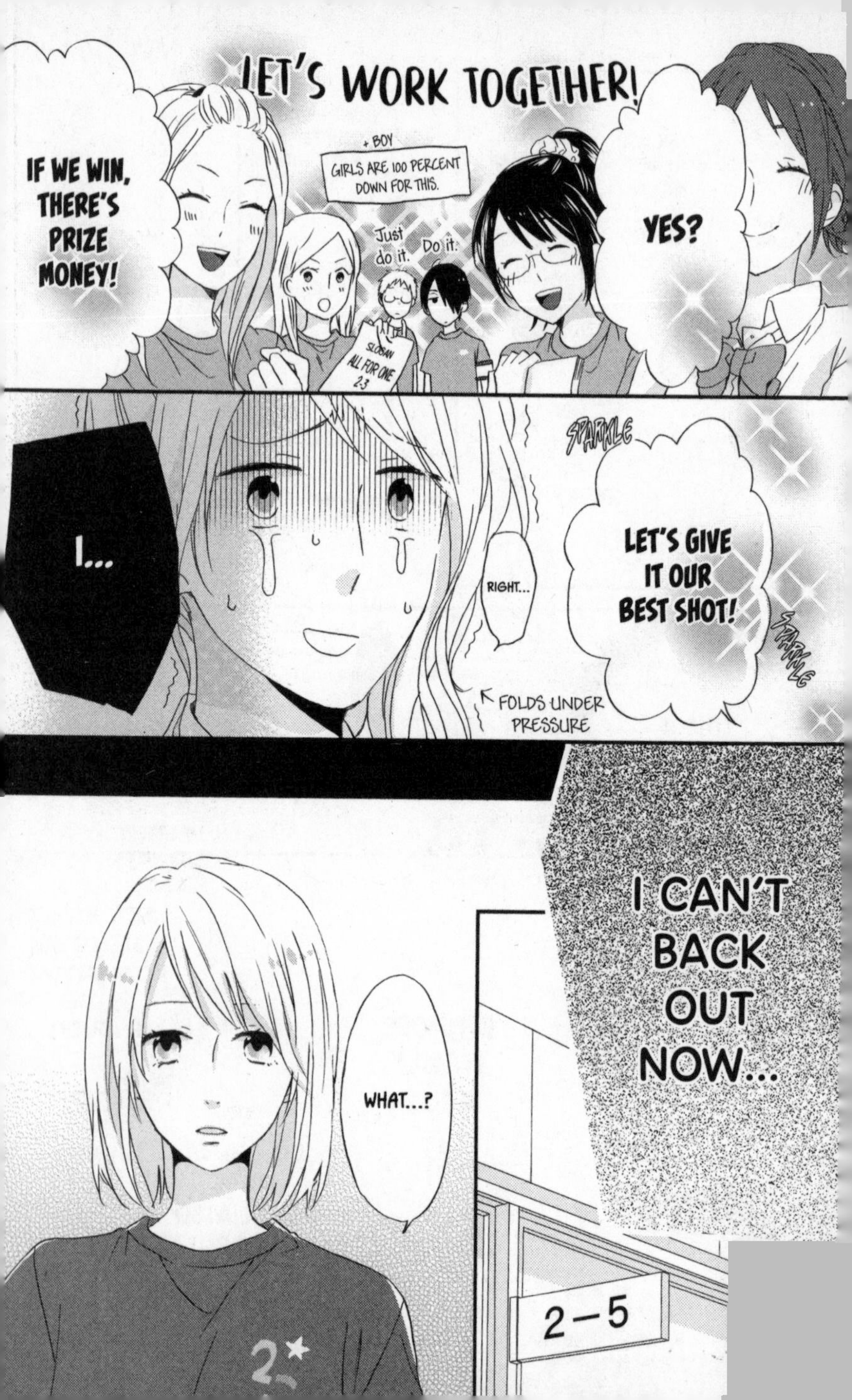
LET'S WORK TOGETHER!
YES?
+ BOY
GIRLS ARE 100 PERCENT DOWN FOR THIS.
Do it.
Just do it.
IF WE WIN, THERE'S PRIZE MONEY!
SLOGAN ALL FOR ONE 2-3
SPARKLE
LET'S GIVE IT OUR BEST SHOT!
SPARKLE
RIGHT...
FOLDS UNDER PRESSURE
I...
I CAN'T BACK OUT NOW...
2-5
WHAT...?

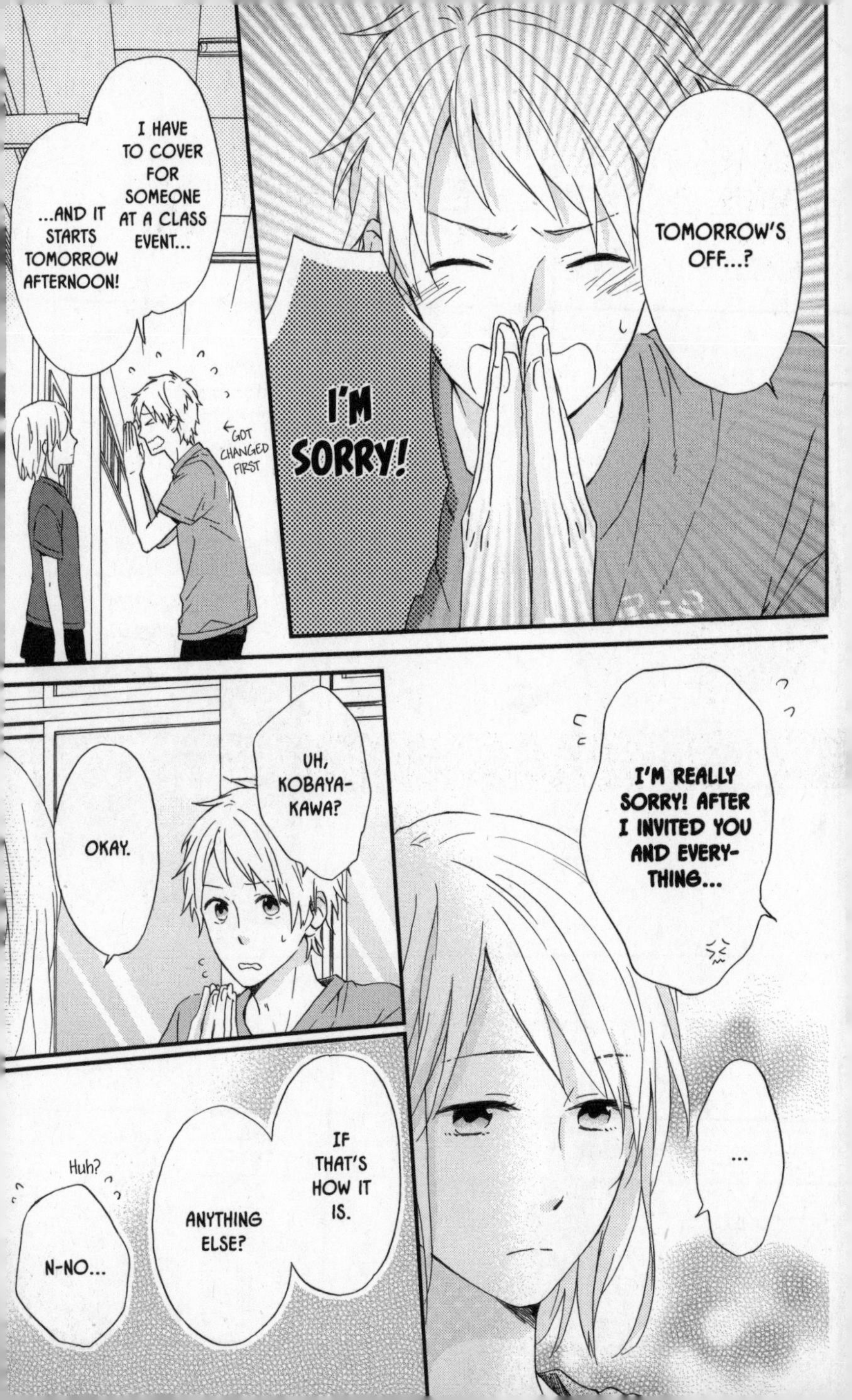
TOMORROW'S OFF...?
I'M SORRY!
I HAVE TO COVER FOR SOMEONE AT A CLASS EVENT...
...AND IT STARTS TOMORROW AFTERNOON!
GOT CHANGED FIRST
I'M REALLY SORRY! AFTER I INVITED YOU AND EVERY-THING...
...
UH, KOBAYA-KAWA?
OKAY.
IF THAT'S HOW IT IS.
ANYTHING ELSE?
Huh?
N-NO...

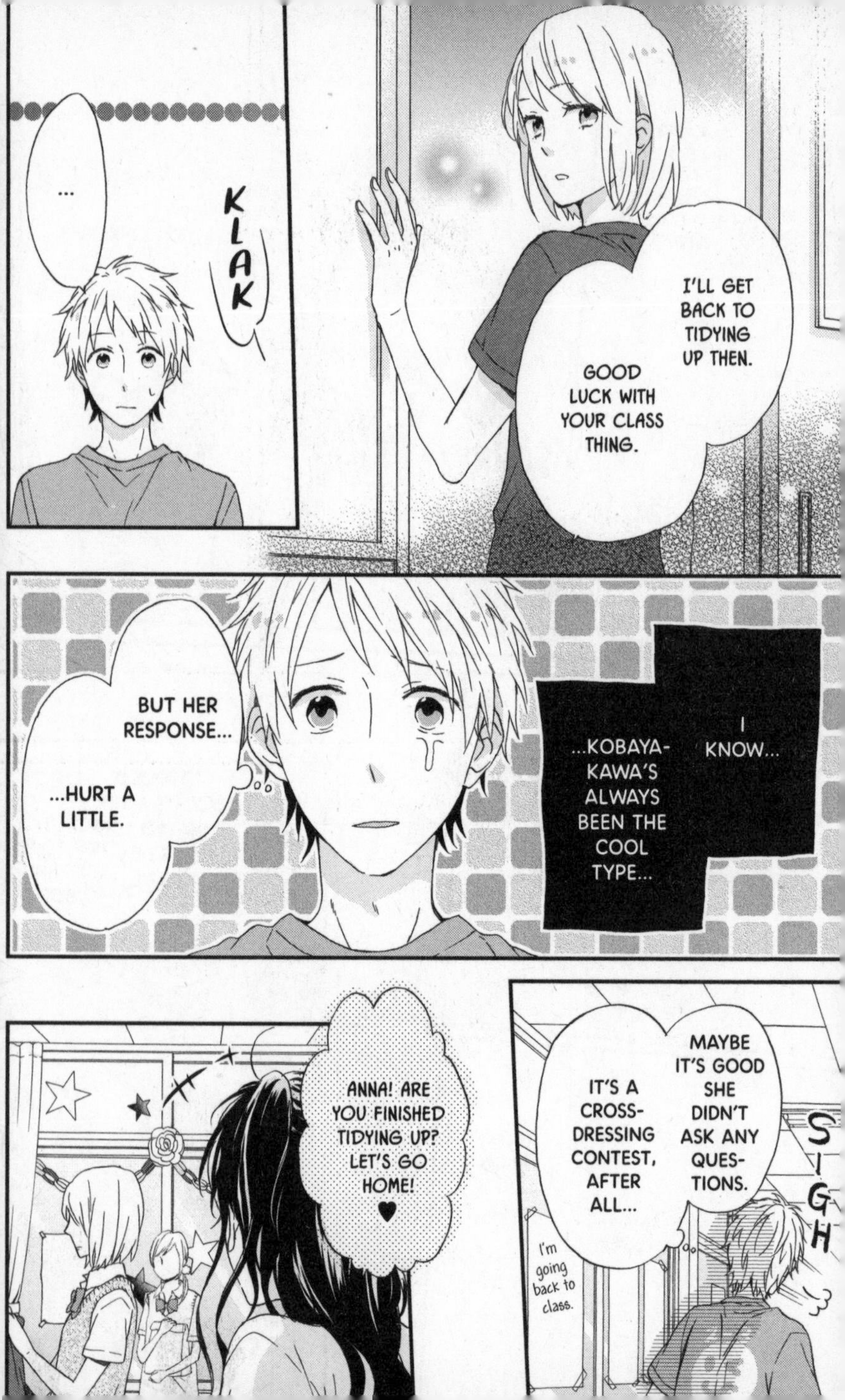
I'LL GET BACK TO TIDYING UP THEN.
GOOD LUCK WITH YOUR CLASS THING.
KLAK
...
I KNOW...
...KOBAYAKAWA'S ALWAYS BEEN THE COOL TYPE...
BUT HER RESPONSE...
...HURT A LITTLE.
SIGH
MAYBE IT'S GOOD SHE DIDN'T ASK ANY QUESTIONS.
IT'S A CROSS-DRESSING CONTEST, AFTER ALL...
I'm going back to class.
ANNA! ARE YOU FINISHED TIDYING UP? LET'S GO HOME! ♥

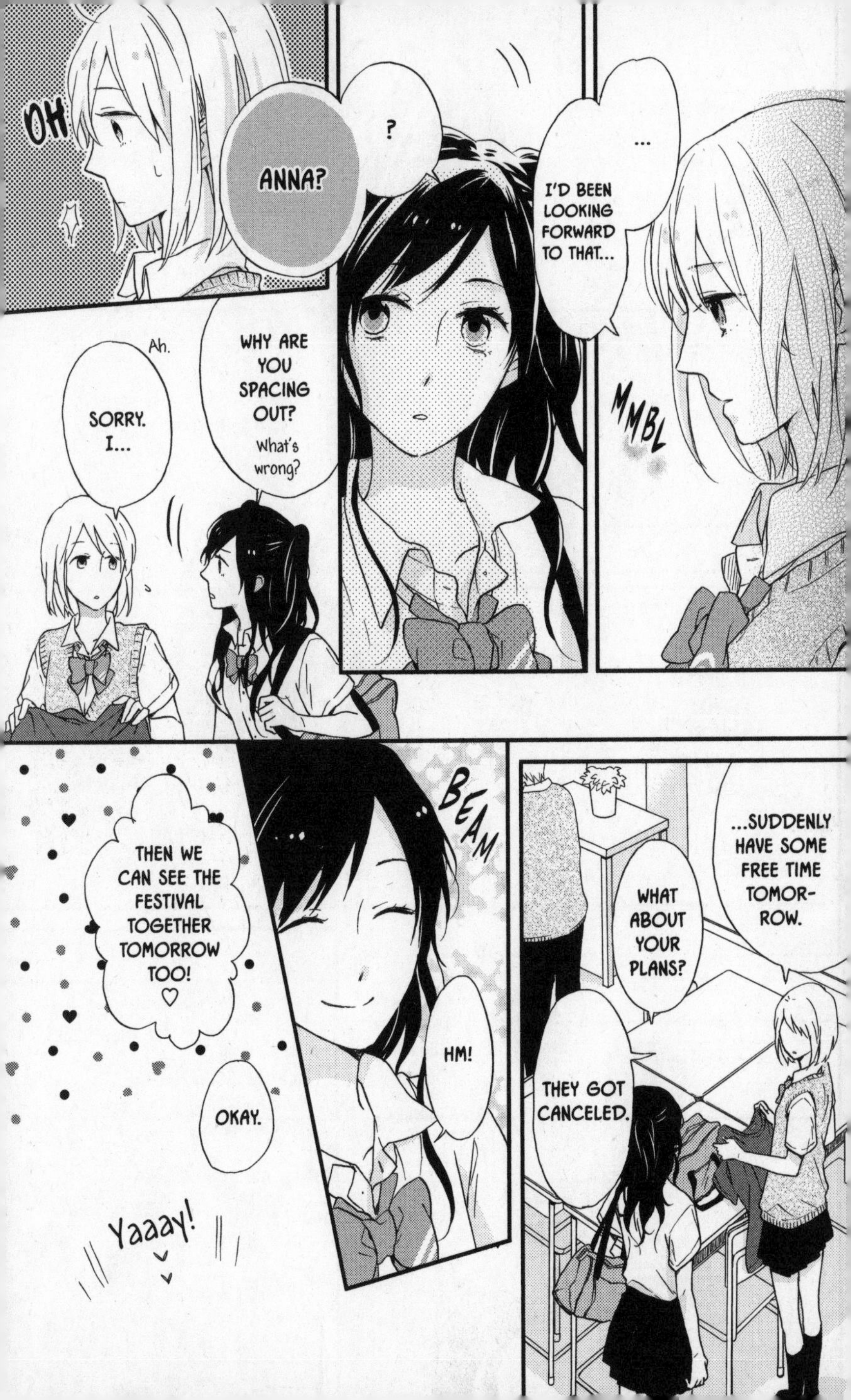
...
I'D BEEN LOOKING FORWARD TO THAT...
MMBL
?
OH
ANNA?
WHY ARE YOU SPACING OUT?
What's wrong?
Ah.
SORRY. I...
...SUDDENLY HAVE SOME FREE TIME TOMOR-ROW.
WHAT ABOUT YOUR PLANS?
THEY GOT CANCELED.
BEAM
HM!
THEN WE CAN SEE THE FESTIVAL TOGETHER TOMORROW TOO! ♡
OKAY.
Yaaay!

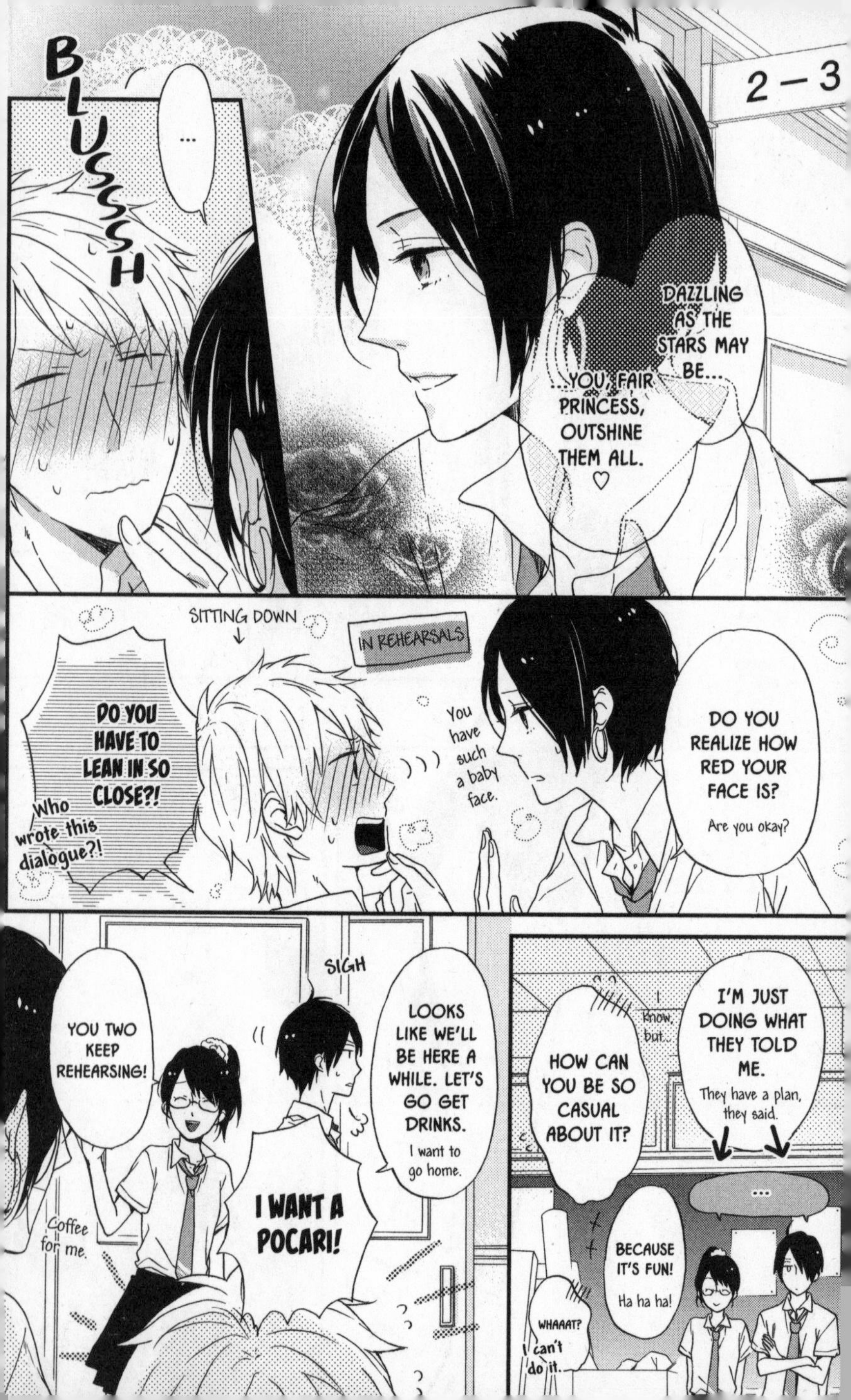
2-3
DAZZLING AS THE STARS MAY BE... ...YOU, FAIR PRINCESS, OUTSHINE THEM ALL. ♡
BLUSSSH
...
DO YOU REALIZE HOW RED YOUR FACE IS?
Are you okay?
You have such a baby face.
IN REHEARSALS
SITTING DOWN
DO YOU HAVE TO LEAN IN SO CLOSE?!
Who wrote this dialogue?!
I'M JUST DOING WHAT THEY TOLD ME.
They have a plan, they said.
I know, but...
HOW CAN YOU BE SO CASUAL ABOUT IT?
...
BECAUSE IT'S FUN!
Ha ha ha!
WHAAAT?
I can't do it.
SIGH
LOOKS LIKE WE'LL BE HERE A WHILE. LET'S GO GET DRINKS.
I want to go home.
YOU TWO KEEP REHEARSING!
I WANT A POCARI!
Coffee for me.

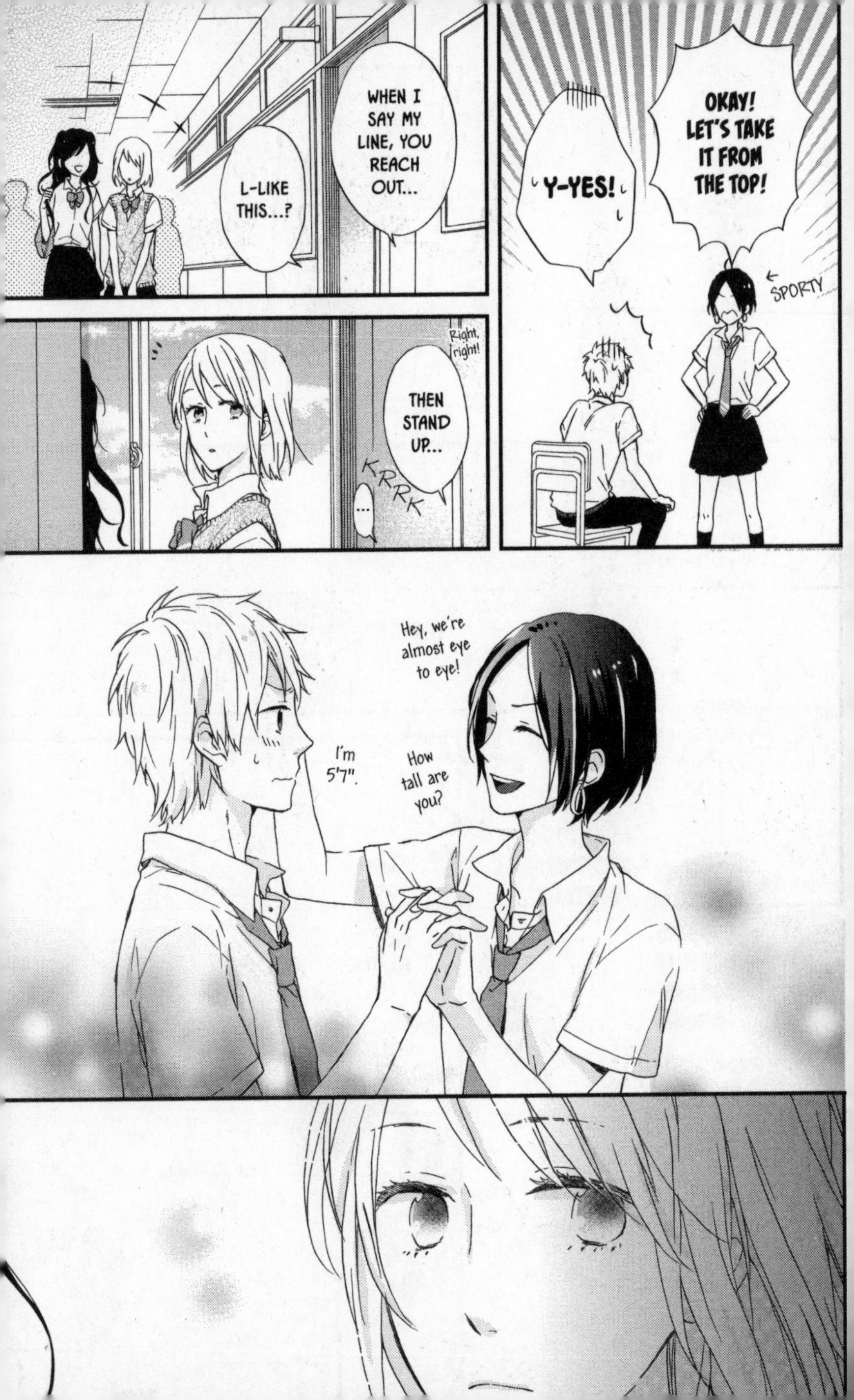
OKAY! LET'S TAKE IT FROM THE TOP!
Y-YES!
SPORTY
WHEN I SAY MY LINE, YOU REACH OUT...
L-LIKE THIS...?
Right, right!
THEN STAND UP...
KRRK
...
Hey, we're almost eye to eye!
How tall are you?
I'm 5'7".

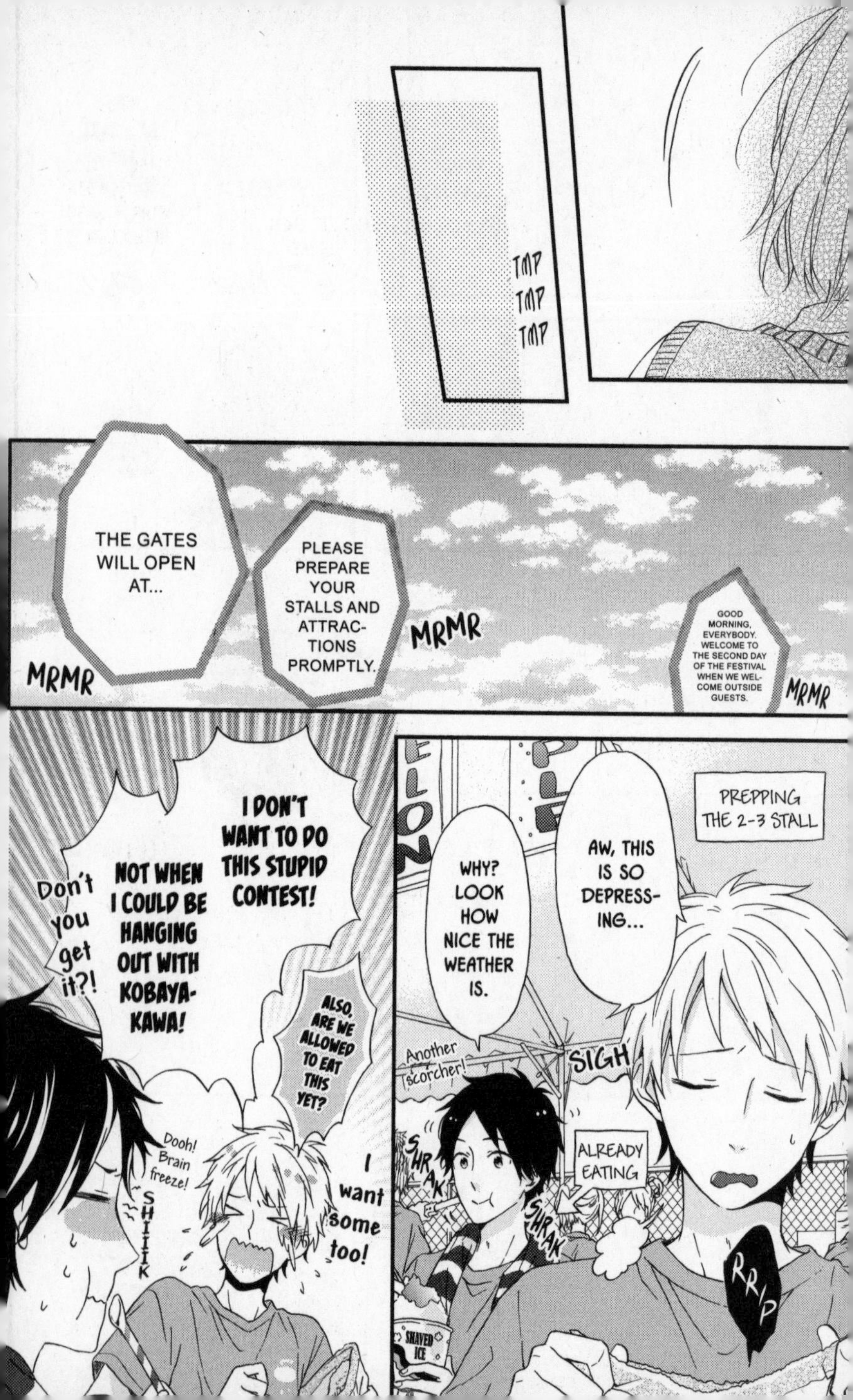
TMP
TMP
TMP
GOOD MORNING, EVERYBODY. WELCOME TO THE SECOND DAY OF THE FESTIVAL WHEN WE WEL- COME OUTSIDE GUESTS.
MRMR
PLEASE PREPARE YOUR STALLS AND ATTRAC- TIONS PROMPTLY.
MRMR
THE GATES WILL OPEN AT...
MRMR
PREPPING THE 2-3 STALL
AW, THIS IS SO DEPRESS- ING...
WHY? LOOK HOW NICE THE WEATHER IS.
SIGH
Another scorcher!
ALREADY EATING
SHRAK
SHRAK
RRIP
SHAVED ICE
I DON'T WANT TO DO THIS STUPID CONTEST!
NOT WHEN I COULD BE HANGING OUT WITH KOBAYA- KAWA!
Don't you get it?!
ALSO, ARE WE ALLOWED TO EAT THIS YET?
I want some too!
Dooh! Brain freeze!
SHIIIK

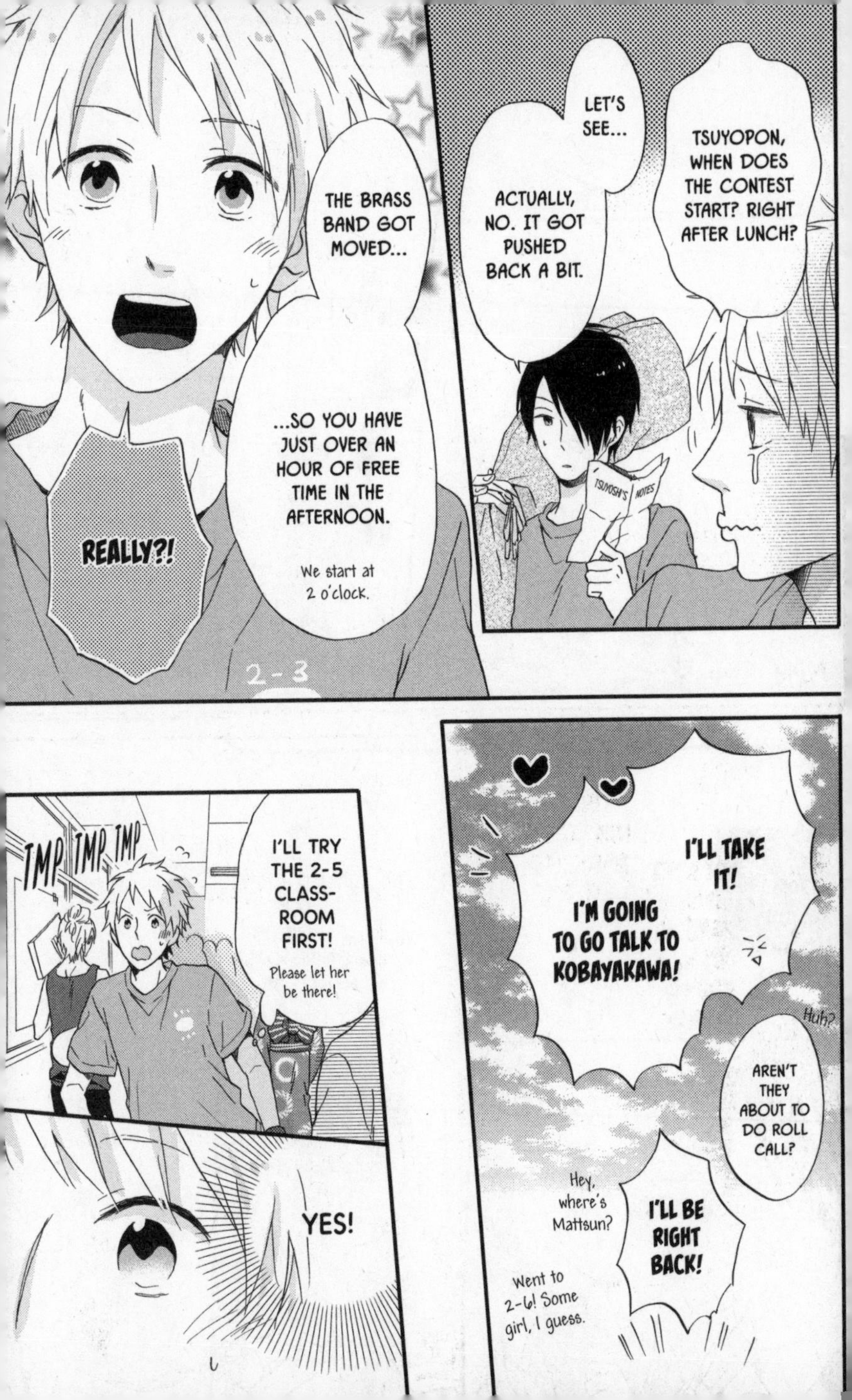
TSUYOPON, WHEN DOES THE CONTEST START? RIGHT AFTER LUNCH?
LET'S SEE...
ACTUALLY, NO. IT GOT PUSHED BACK A BIT.
TSUYOSH'S NOTES
THE BRASS BAND GOT MOVED...
...SO YOU HAVE JUST OVER AN HOUR OF FREE TIME IN THE AFTERNOON.
We start at 2 o'clock.
REALLY?!
2-3
I'LL TAKE IT!
I'M GOING TO GO TALK TO KOBAYAKAWA!
Huh?
AREN'T THEY ABOUT TO DO ROLL CALL?
I'LL BE RIGHT BACK!
Hey, where's Mattsun?
Went to 2-6! Some girl, I guess.
I'LL TRY THE 2-5 CLASS-ROOM FIRST!
Please let her be there!
TMP TMP TMP
YES!

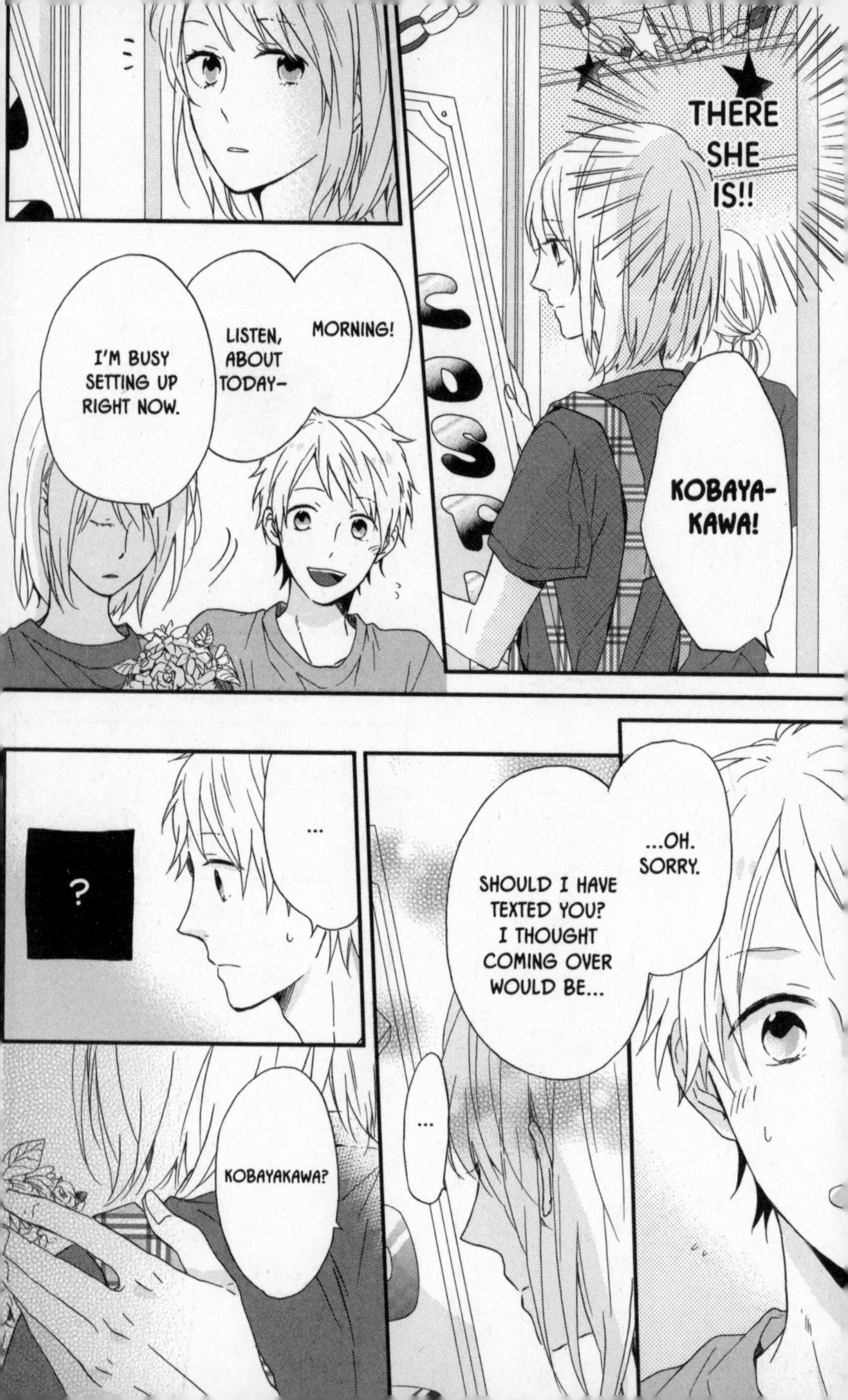
THERE SHE IS!!
KOBAYA-KAWA!
MORNING!
LISTEN, ABOUT TODAY—
I'M BUSY SETTING UP RIGHT NOW.
...OH. SORRY.
SHOULD I HAVE TEXTED YOU? I THOUGHT COMING OVER WOULD BE...
...
...
?
KOBAYAKAWA?

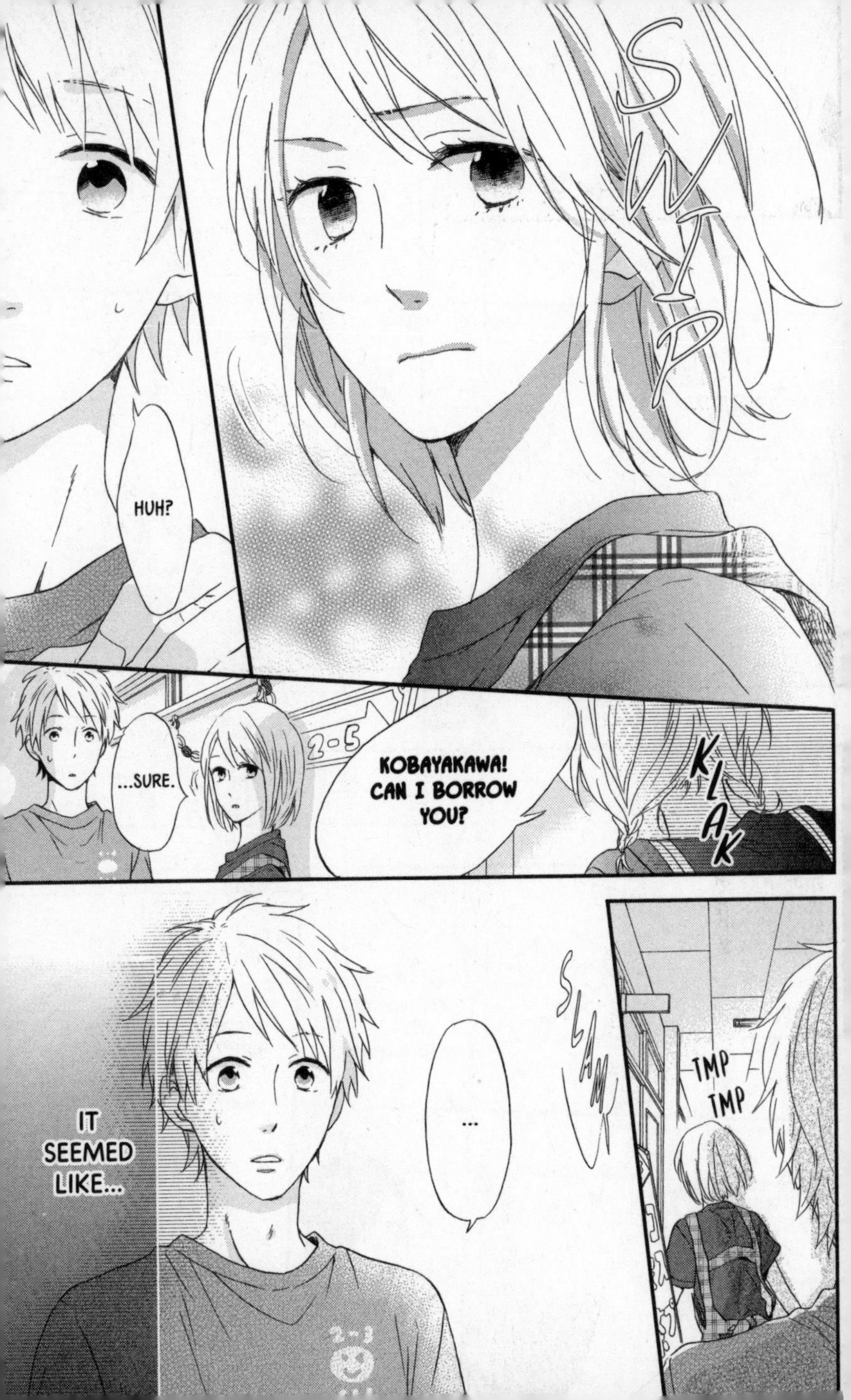
SWIP
HUH?
KLAK
KOBAYAKAWA! CAN I BORROW YOU?
...SURE.
TMP TMP
SLAM
...
IT SEEMED LIKE...

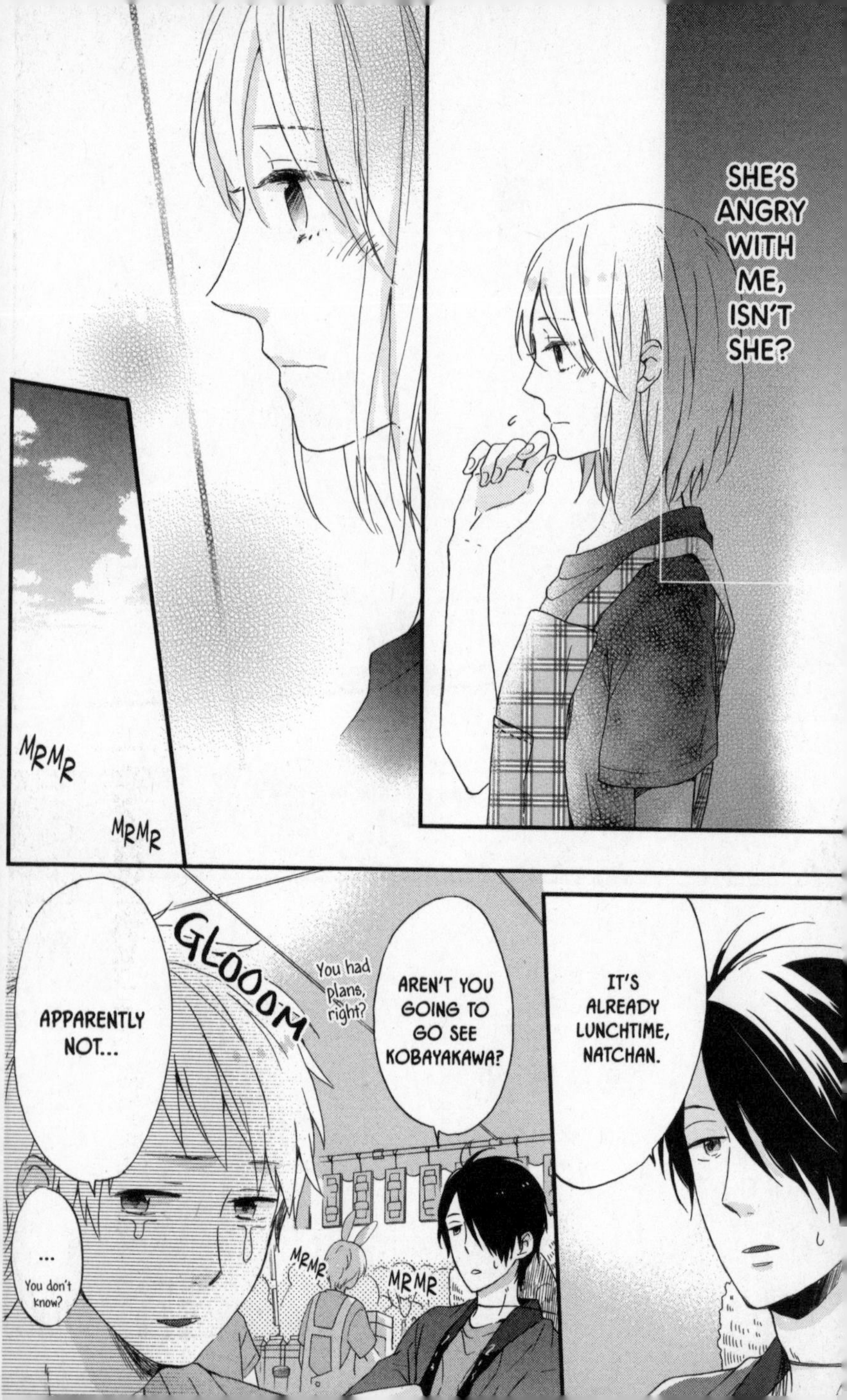
SHE'S ANGRY WITH ME, ISN'T SHE?
MRMR
MRMR
IT'S ALREADY LUNCHTIME, NATCHAN.
AREN'T YOU GOING TO GO SEE KOBAYAKAWA?
You had plans, right?
GLOOOM
APPARENTLY NOT...
MRMR
MRMR
... You don't know?

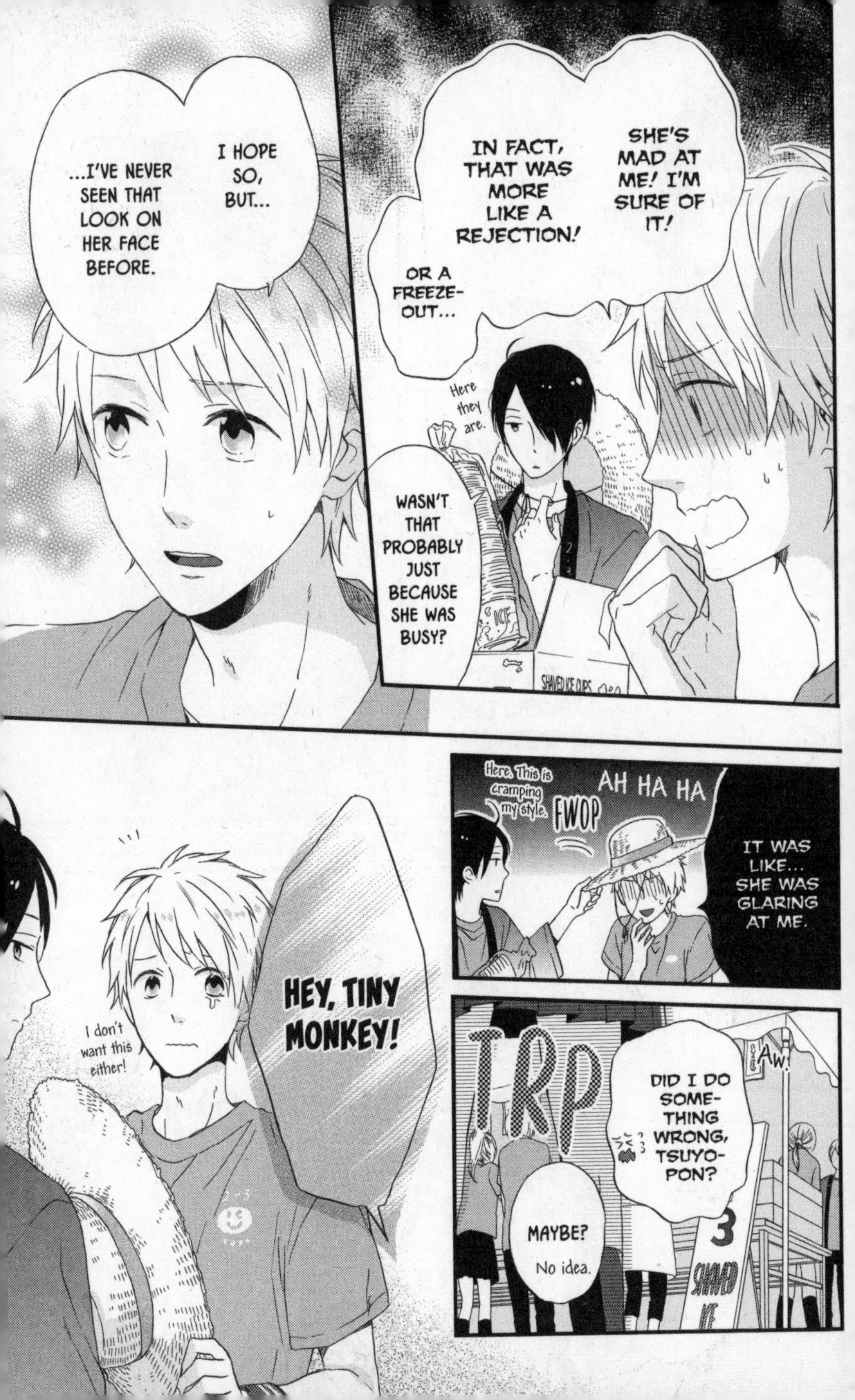
SHE'S MAD AT ME! I'M SURE OF IT!
IN FACT, THAT WAS MORE LIKE A REJECTION!
OR A FREEZE-OUT...
Here they are.
WASN'T THAT PROBABLY JUST BECAUSE SHE WAS BUSY?
ICE
SHAVED ICE CUPS
I HOPE SO, BUT...
...I'VE NEVER SEEN THAT LOOK ON HER FACE BEFORE.
IT WAS LIKE... SHE WAS GLARING AT ME.
AH HA HA
FWOP
Here. This is cramping my style.
AW!
DID I DO SOMETHING WRONG, TSUYO-PON?
TRP
MAYBE?
No idea.
3
SHAVED ICE
HEY, TINY MONKEY!
I don't want this either!

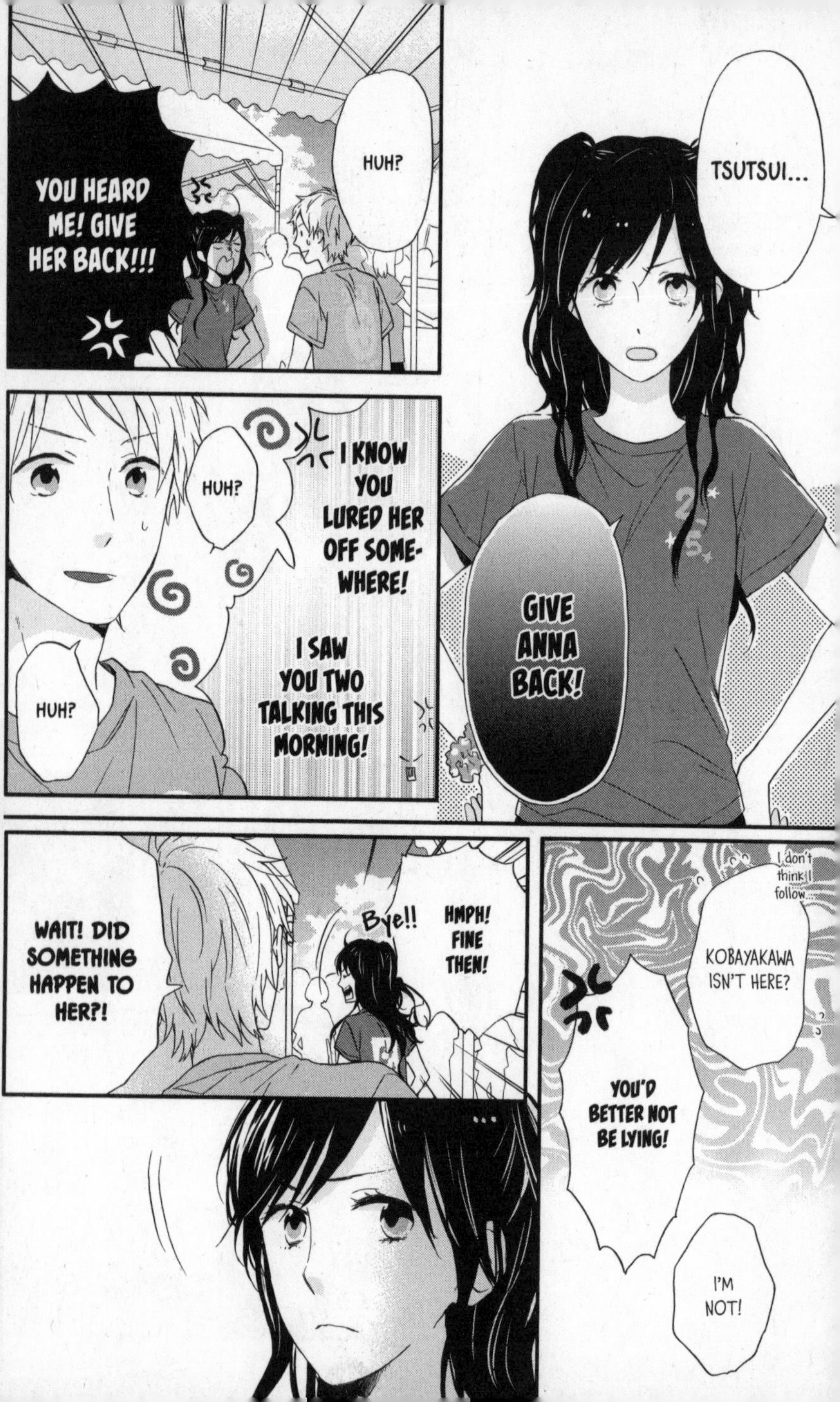
TSUTSUI...
GIVE ANNA BACK!
HUH?
YOU HEARD ME! GIVE HER BACK!!!
I KNOW YOU LURED HER OFF SOME-WHERE!
HUH?
I SAW YOU TWO TALKING THIS MORNING!
HUH?
I don't think I follow...
KOBAYAKAWA ISN'T HERE?
YOU'D BETTER NOT BE LYING!
I'M NOT!
HMPH! FINE THEN!
Bye!!
WAIT! DID SOMETHING HAPPEN TO HER?!

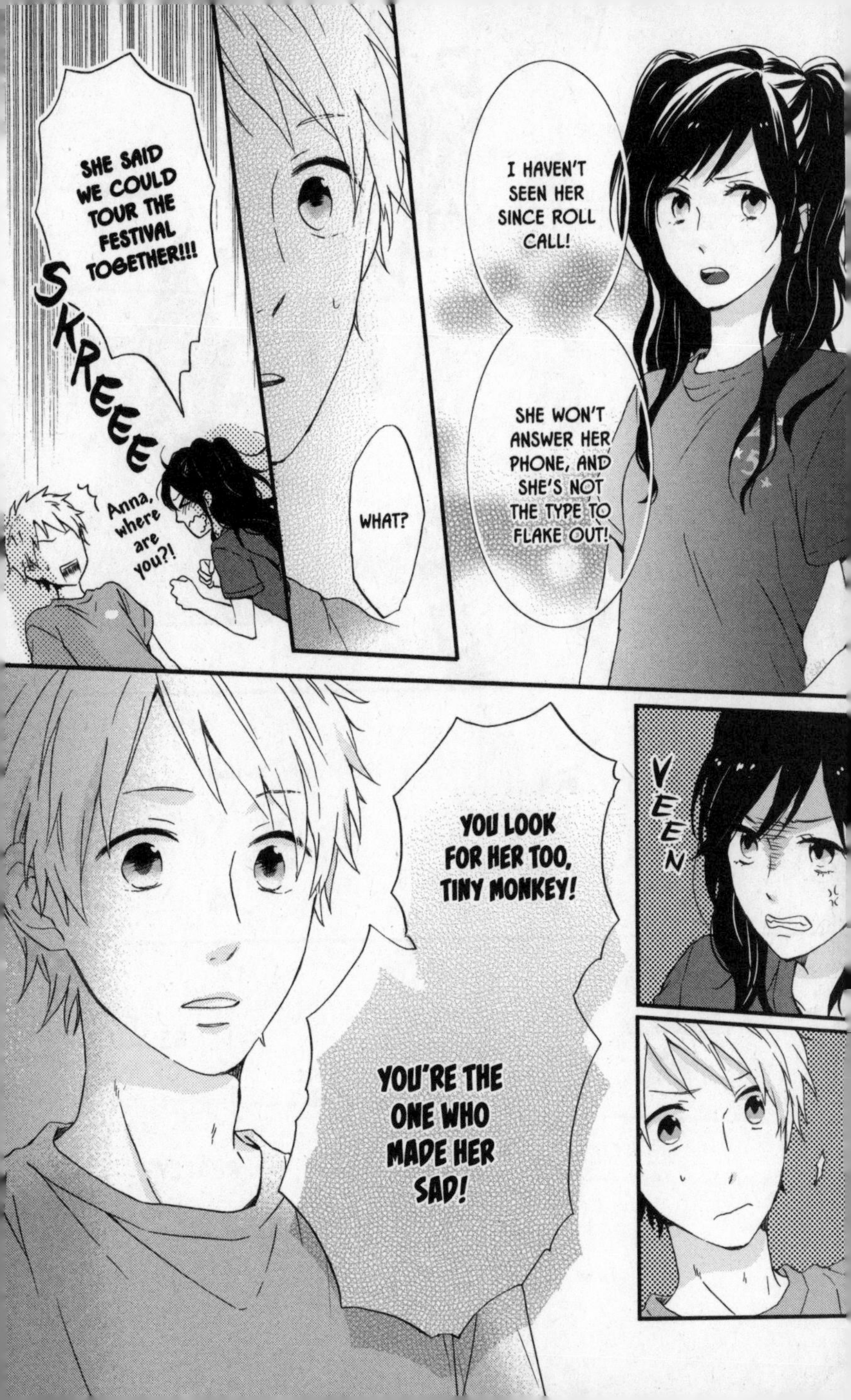
I HAVEN'T SEEN HER SINCE ROLL CALL!
SHE WON'T ANSWER HER PHONE, AND SHE'S NOT THE TYPE TO FLAKE OUT!
WHAT?
SHE SAID WE COULD TOUR THE FESTIVAL TOGETHER!!!
SKREEE
Anna, where are you?!
VEEN
YOU LOOK FOR HER TOO, TINY MONKEY!
YOU'RE THE ONE WHO MADE HER SAD!

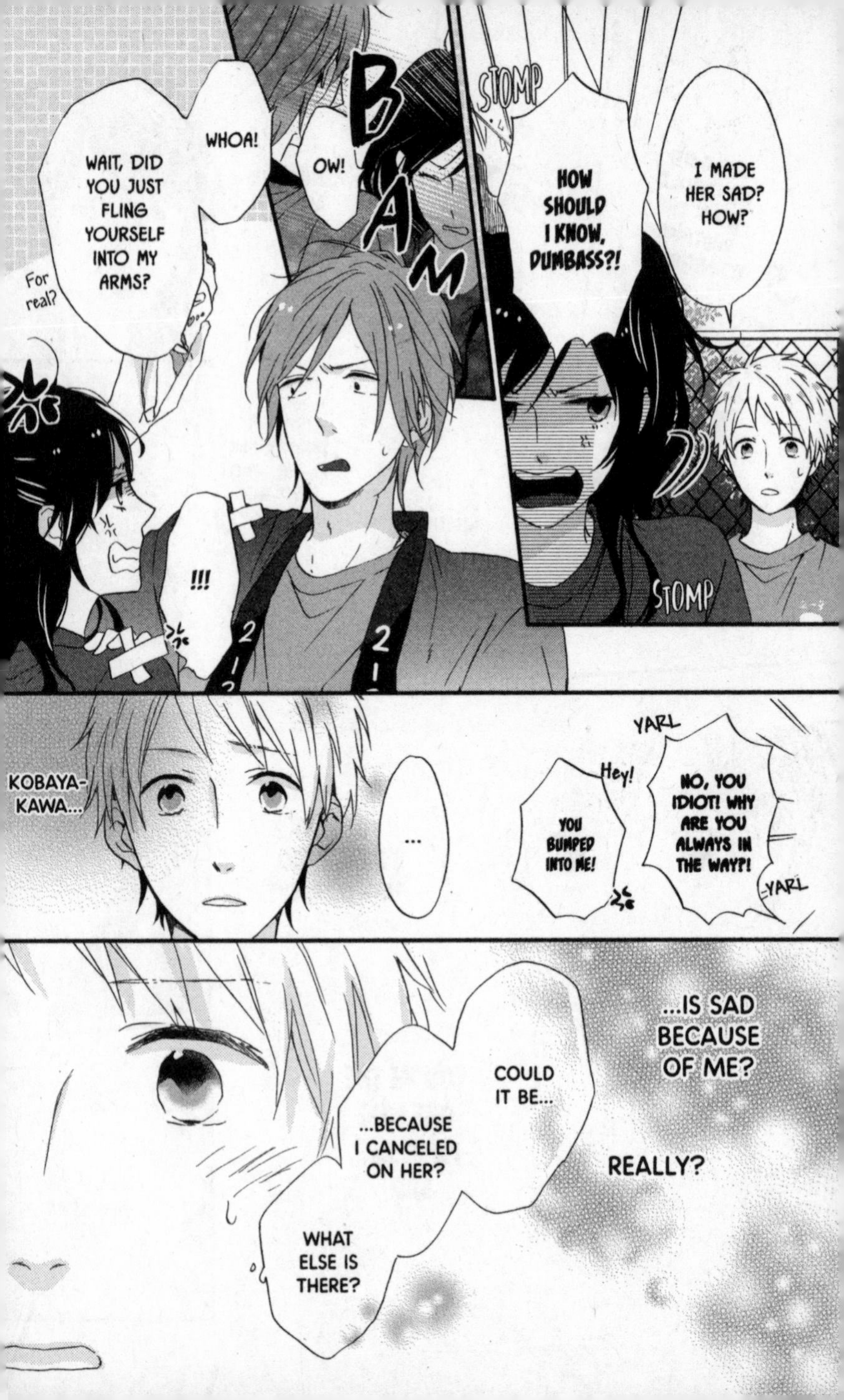
I MADE HER SAD? HOW?
STOMP
HOW SHOULD I KNOW, DUMBASS?!
STOMP
BAM
OW!
WHOA!
WAIT, DID YOU JUST FLING YOURSELF INTO MY ARMS?
For real?
!!!
YARL
NO, YOU IDIOT! WHY ARE YOU ALWAYS IN THE WAY?!
Hey!
YOU BUMPED INTO ME!
YARL
...
KOBAYA-KAWA...
...IS SAD BECAUSE OF ME?
REALLY?
COULD IT BE...
...BECAUSE I CANCELED ON HER?
WHAT ELSE IS THERE?

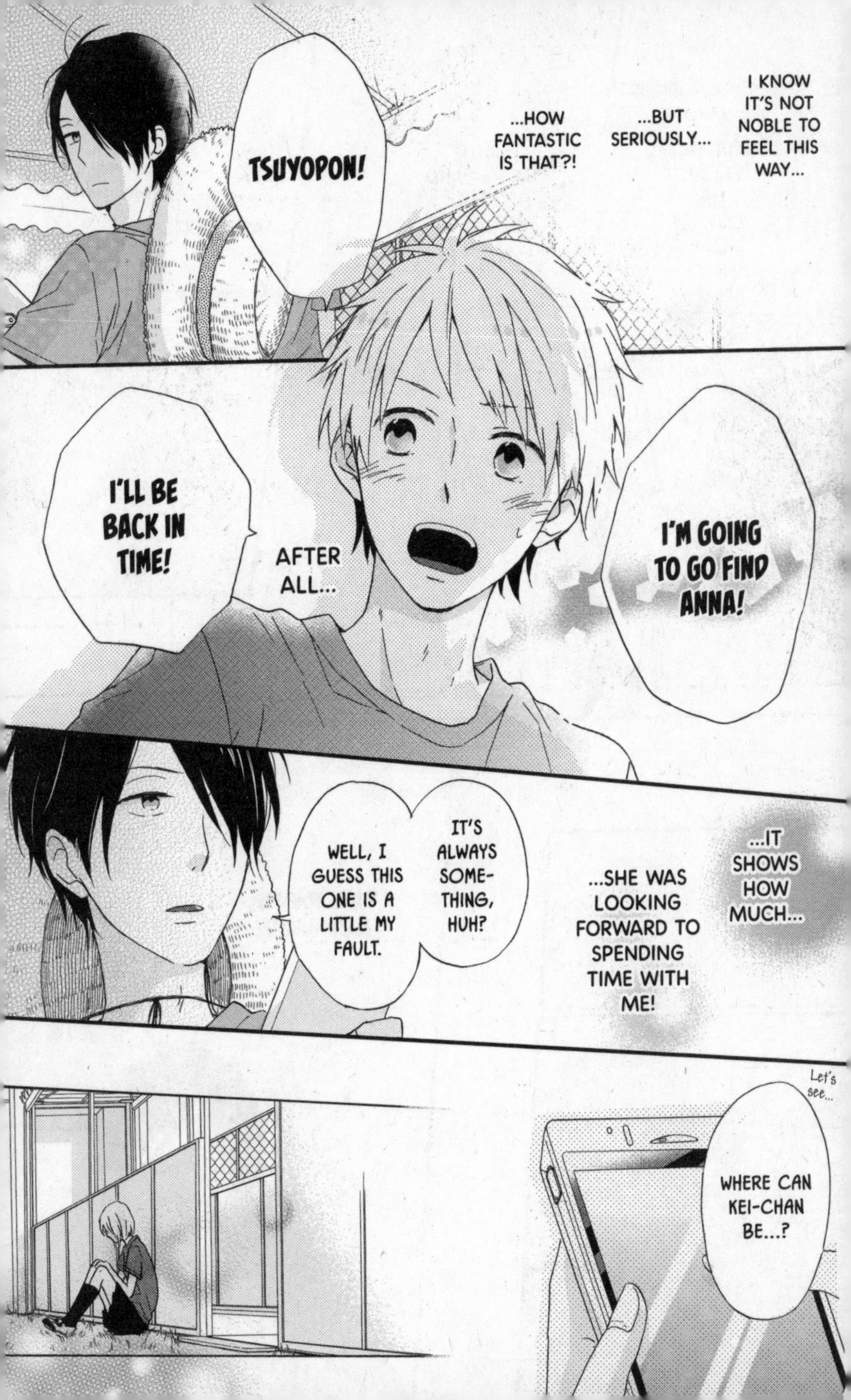
I KNOW IT'S NOT NOBLE TO FEEL THIS WAY...
...BUT SERIOUSLY...
...HOW FANTASTIC IS THAT?!
TSUYOPON!
I'M GOING TO GO FIND ANNA!
AFTER ALL...
I'LL BE BACK IN TIME!
...IT SHOWS HOW MUCH...
...SHE WAS LOOKING FORWARD TO SPENDING TIME WITH ME!
IT'S ALWAYS SOMETHING, HUH?
WELL, I GUESS THIS ONE IS A LITTLE MY FAULT.
Let's see...
WHERE CAN KEI-CHAN BE...?

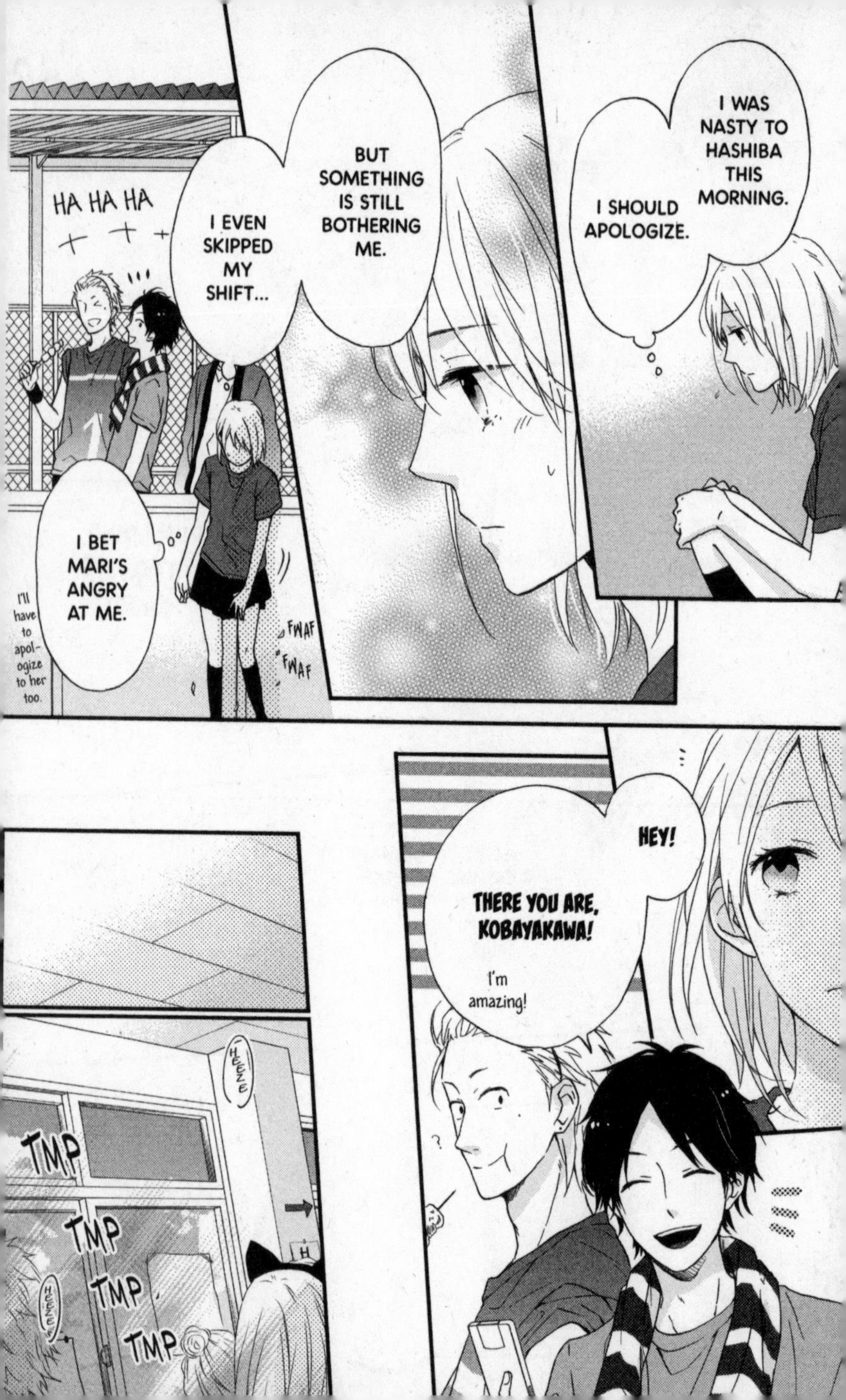
I WAS NASTY TO HASHIBA THIS MORNING.
I SHOULD APOLOGIZE.
BUT SOMETHING IS STILL BOTHERING ME.
I EVEN SKIPPED MY SHIFT...
HA HA HA
I BET MARI'S ANGRY AT ME.
I'll have to apol-ogize to her too.
FWAF
FWAF
HEY!
THERE YOU ARE, KOBAYAKAWA!
I'm amazing!
HEEZE
TMP
TMP
TMP
TMP
HEEZE

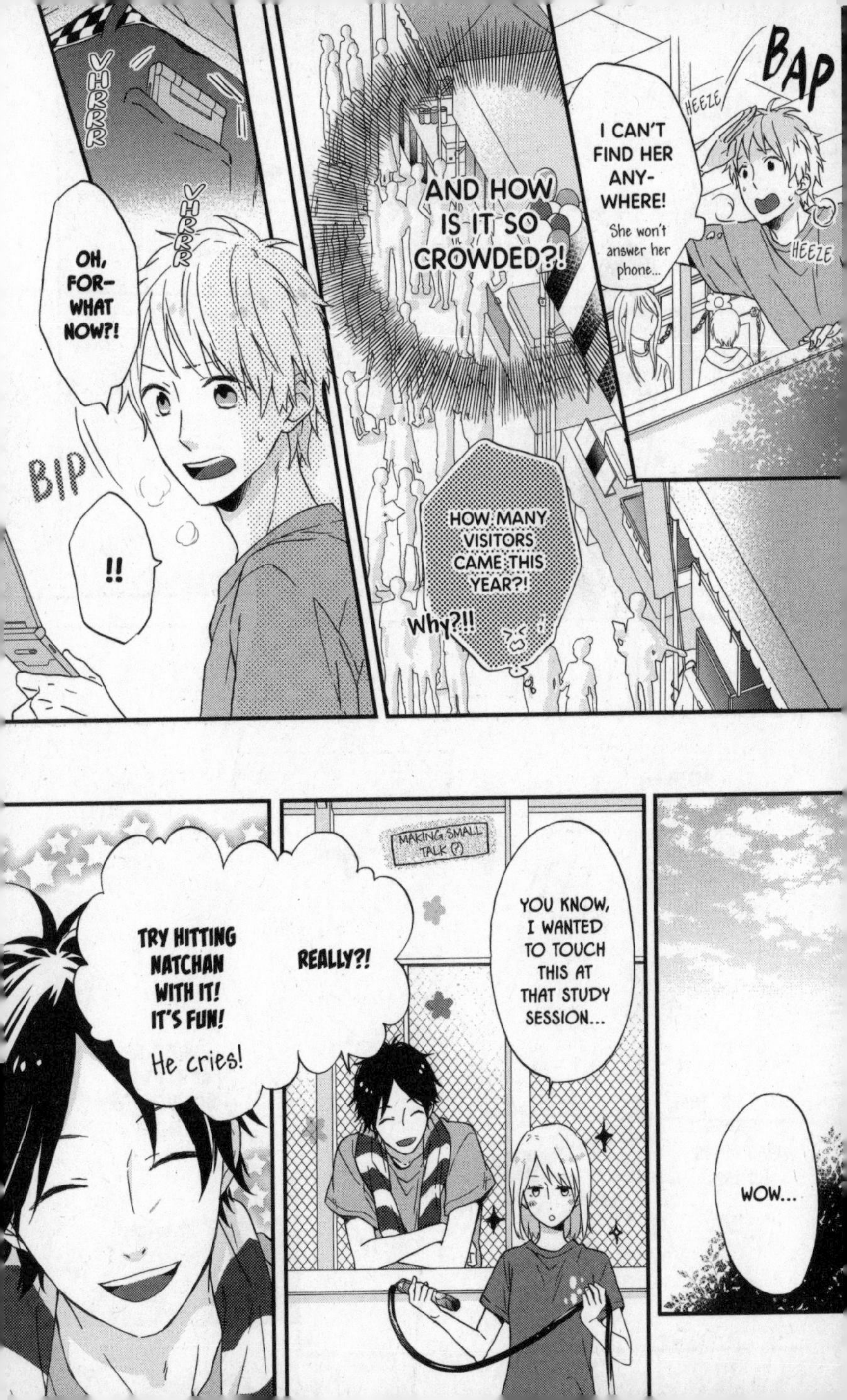
BAP
HEEZE
I CAN'T FIND HER ANYWHERE!
She won't answer her phone...
HEEZE
AND HOW IS IT SO CROWDED?!
HOW MANY VISITORS CAME THIS YEAR?!
Why?!!
VHRRR
VHRRR
OH, FOR-WHAT NOW?!
BIP
!!
WOW...
YOU KNOW, I WANTED TO TOUCH THIS AT THAT STUDY SESSION...
MAKING SMALL TALK (?)
TRY HITTING NATCHAN WITH IT! IT'S FUN!
REALLY?!
He cries!

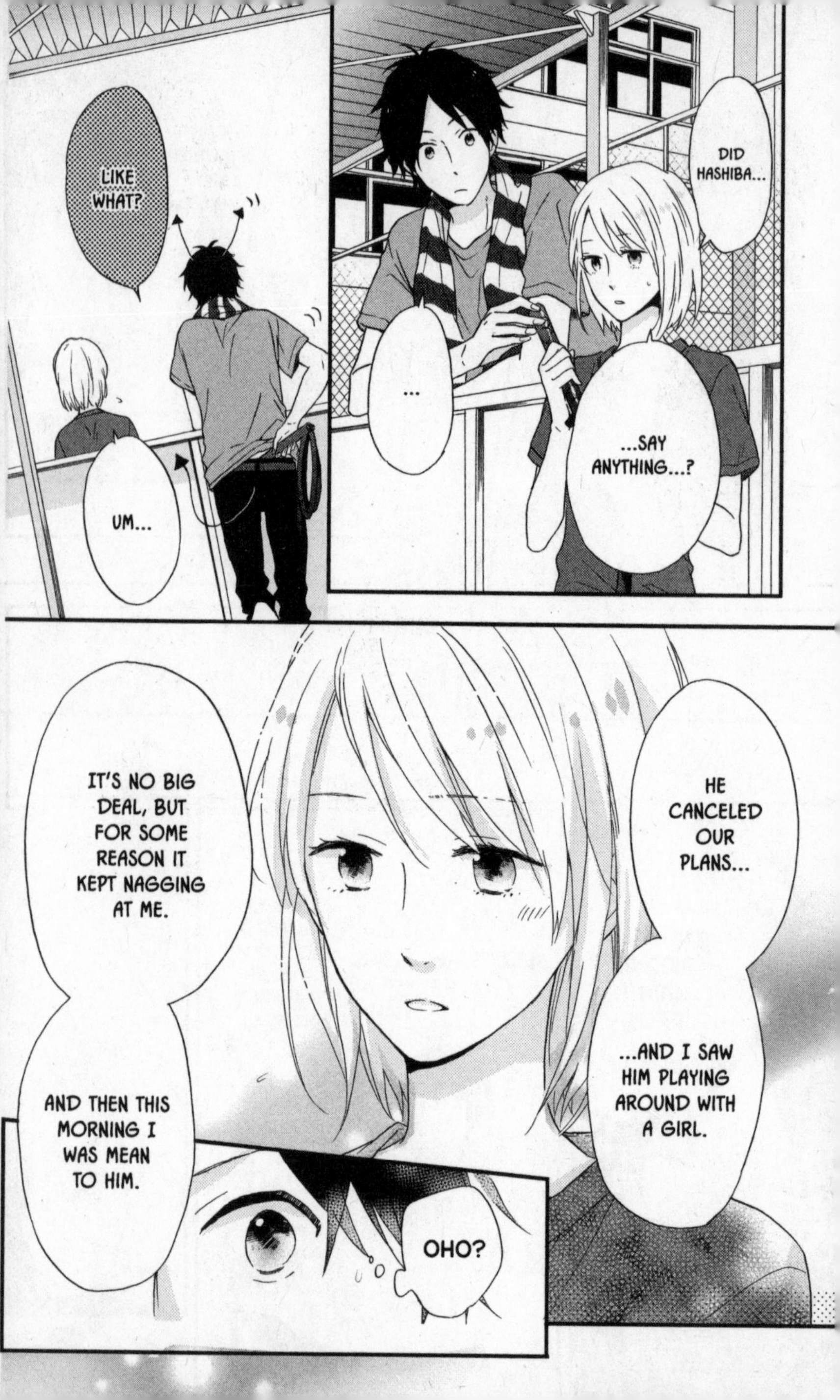
DID HASHIBA...
...SAY ANYTHING...?
...
LIKE WHAT?
UM...
HE CANCELED OUR PLANS...
...AND I SAW HIM PLAYING AROUND WITH A GIRL.
IT'S NO BIG DEAL, BUT FOR SOME REASON IT KEPT NAGGING AT ME.
AND THEN THIS MORNING I WAS MEAN TO HIM.
OHO?

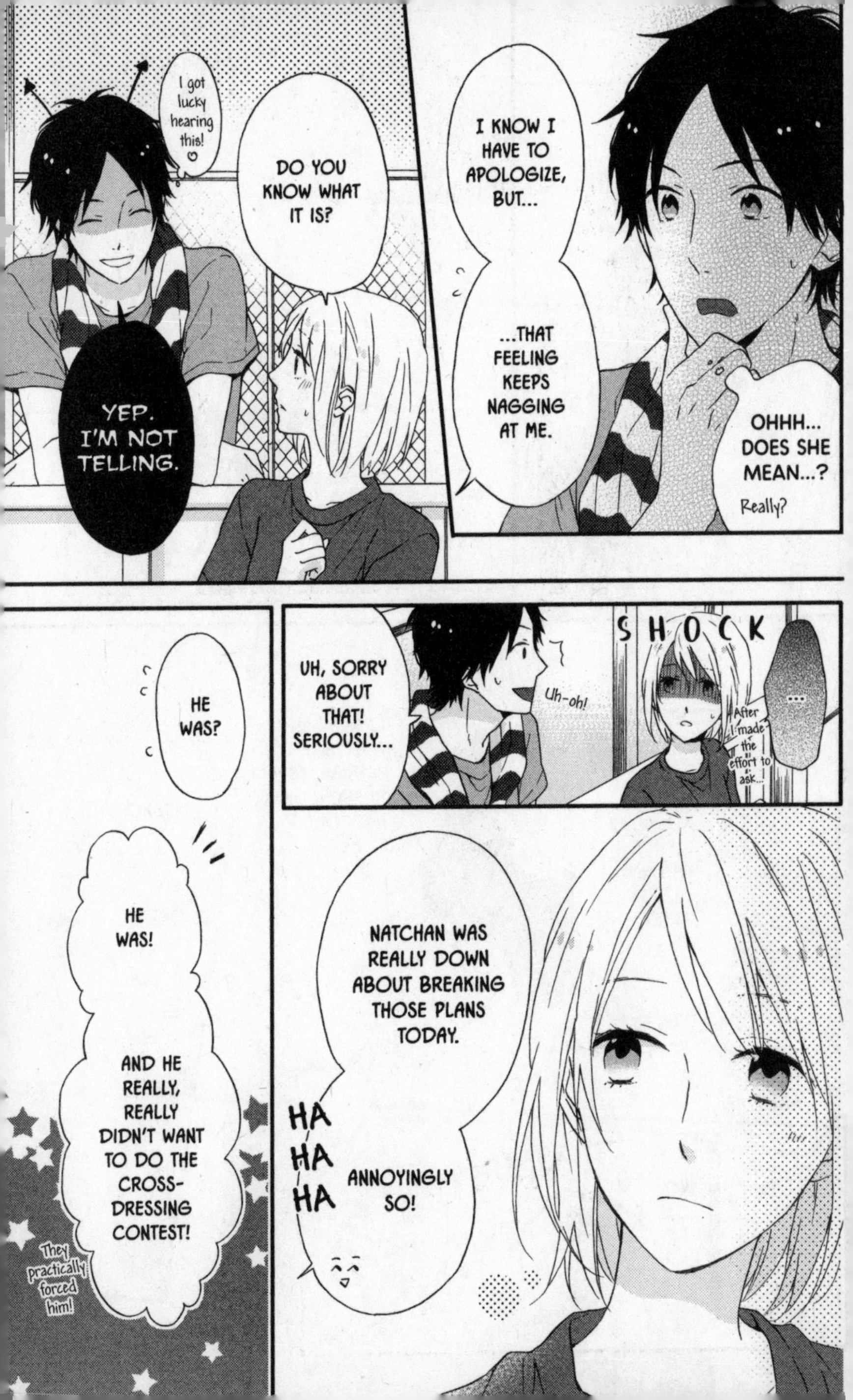
I KNOW I HAVE TO APOLOGIZE, BUT...
...THAT FEELING KEEPS NAGGING AT ME.
OHHH... DOES SHE MEAN...?
Really?
DO YOU KNOW WHAT IT IS?
I got lucky hearing this!
YEP. I'M NOT TELLING.
...
After I made the effort to ask...
SHOCK
Uh-oh!
UH, SORRY ABOUT THAT! SERIOUSLY...
NATCHAN WAS REALLY DOWN ABOUT BREAKING THOSE PLANS TODAY.
ANNOYINGLY SO!
HA HA HA
HE WAS?
HE WAS!
AND HE REALLY, REALLY DIDN'T WANT TO DO THE CROSS-DRESSING CONTEST!
They practically forced him!

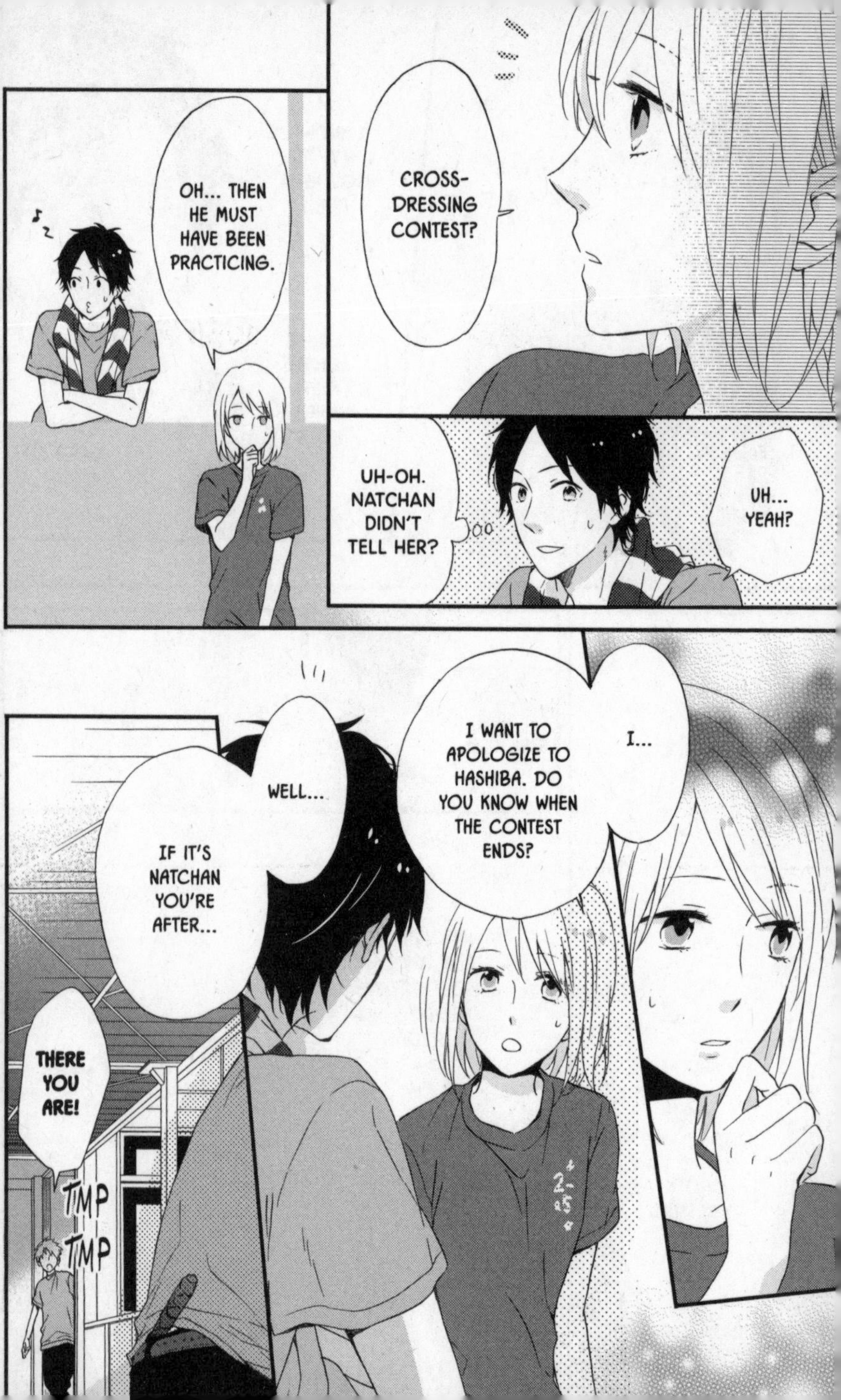
CROSS-DRESSING CONTEST?
UH... YEAH?
UH-OH. NATCHAN DIDN'T TELL HER?
OH... THEN HE MUST HAVE BEEN PRACTICING.
I...
I WANT TO APOLOGIZE TO HASHIBA. DO YOU KNOW WHEN THE CONTEST ENDS?
WELL...
IF IT'S NATCHAN YOU'RE AFTER...
THERE YOU ARE!
TMP TMP

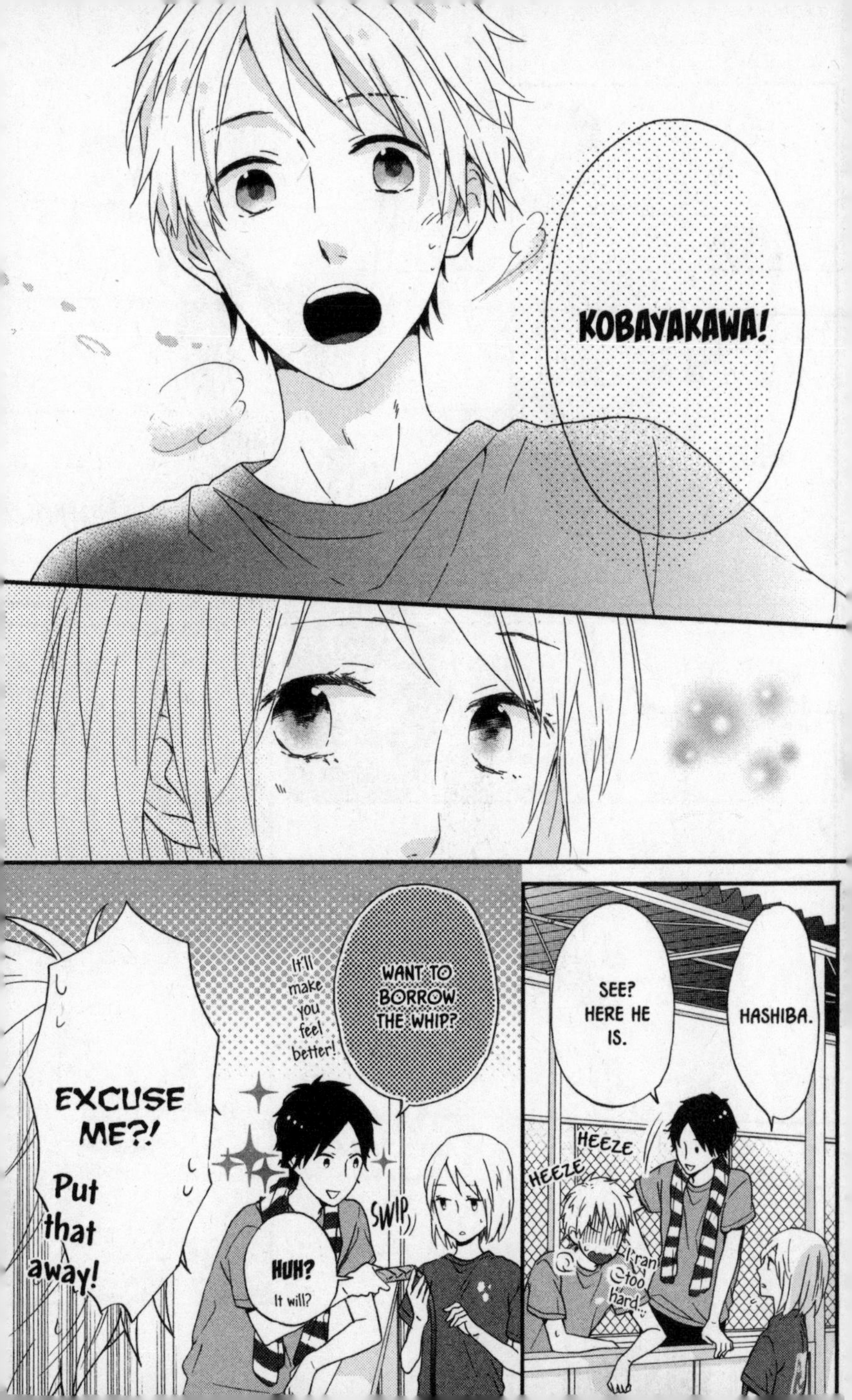
KOBAYAKAWA!
HASHIBA.
SEE? HERE HE IS.
HEEZE
HEEZE
I ran too hard...
WANT TO BORROW THE WHIP?
It'll make you feel better!
EXCUSE ME?!
Put that away!
SWIP
HUH?
It will?

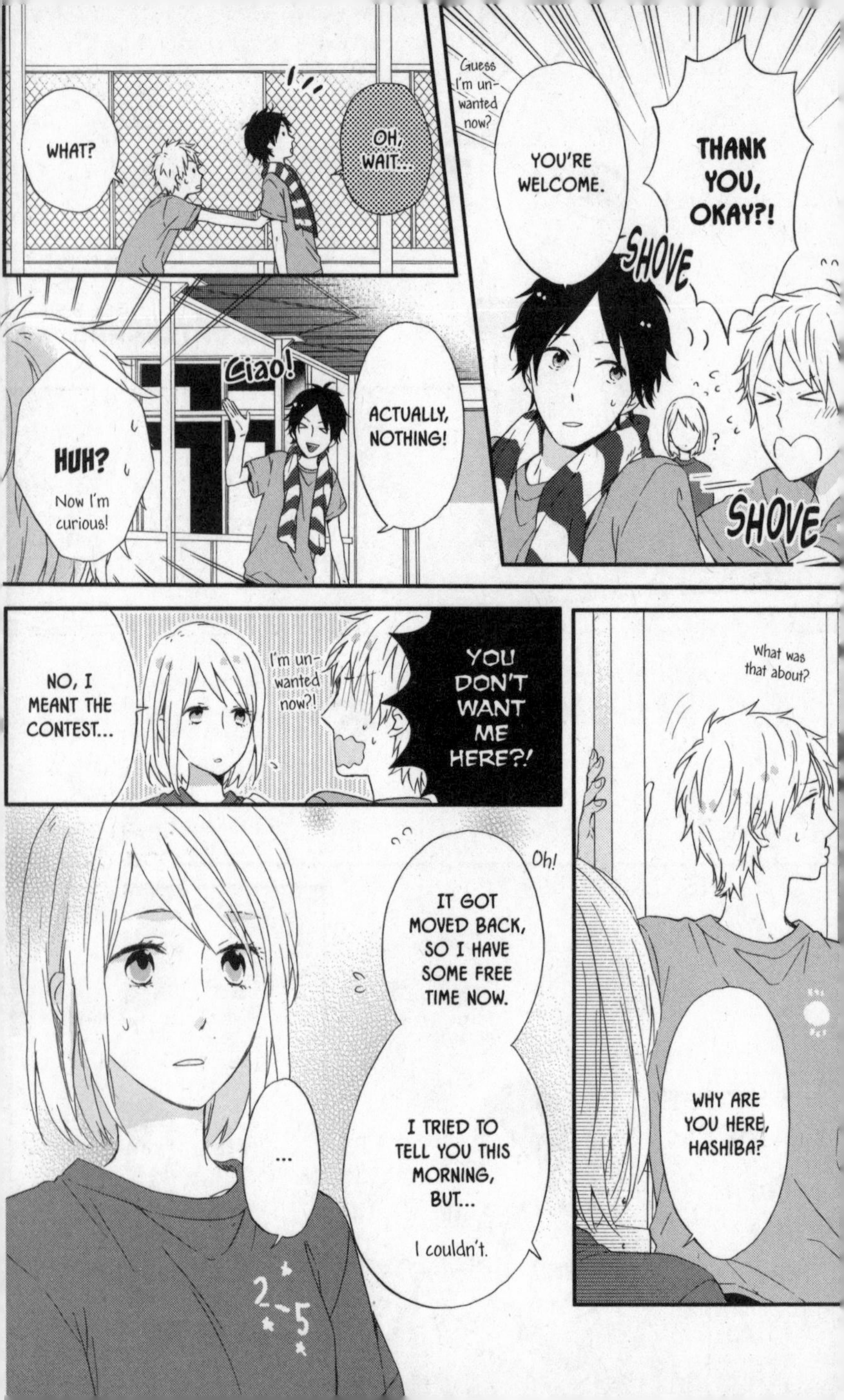
THANK YOU, OKAY?!
SHOVE
YOU'RE WELCOME.
Guess I'm un-wanted now?
SHOVE
OH, WAIT...
WHAT?
ACTUALLY, NOTHING!
Ciao!
HUH?
Now I'm curious!
What was that about?
Oh!
WHY ARE YOU HERE, HASHIBA?
YOU DON'T WANT ME HERE?!
I'm un-wanted now?!
NO, I MEANT THE CONTEST...
IT GOT MOVED BACK, SO I HAVE SOME FREE TIME NOW.
I TRIED TO TELL YOU THIS MORNING, BUT...
I couldn't.
...
2-5

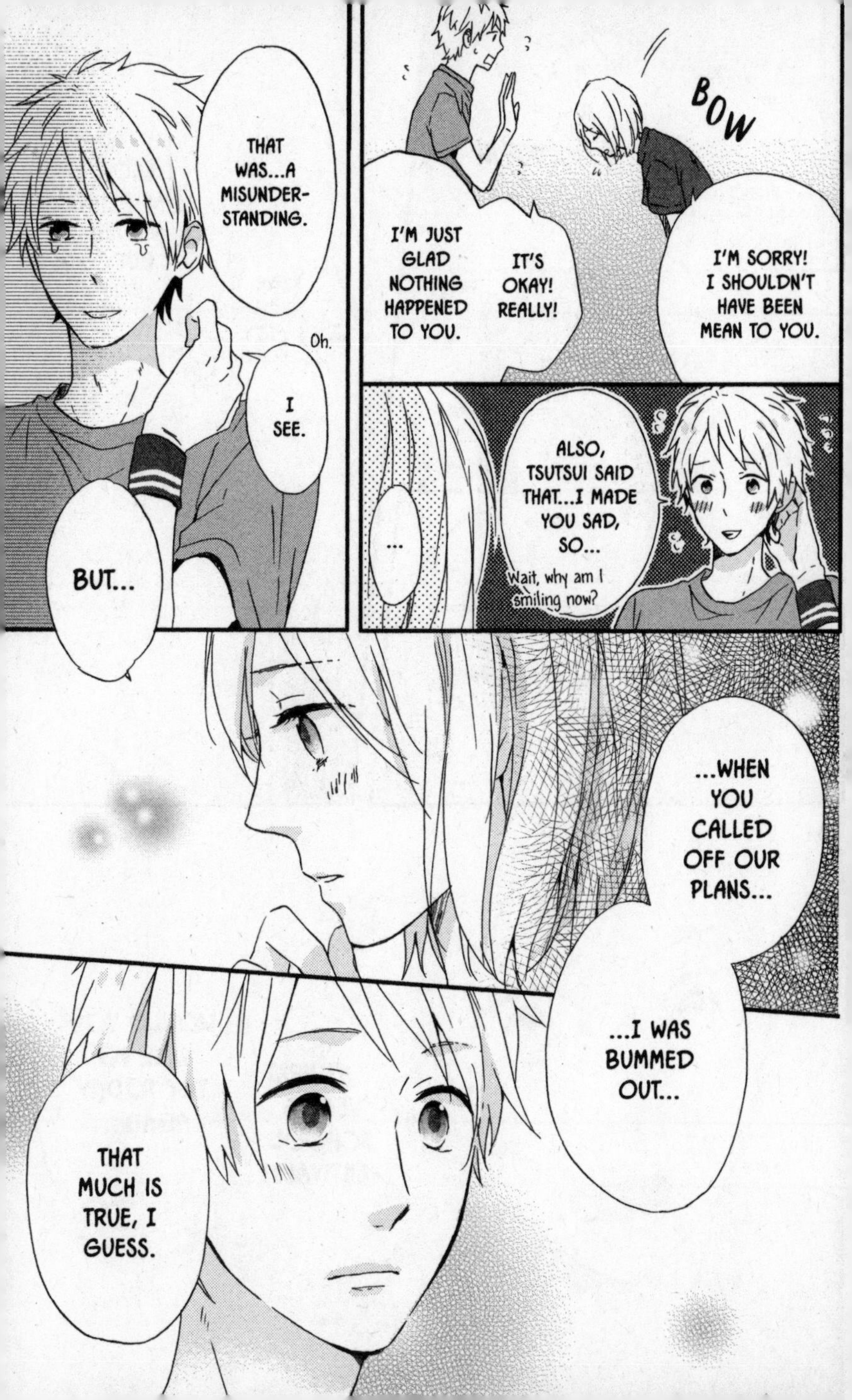
BOW
I'M SORRY! I SHOULDN'T HAVE BEEN MEAN TO YOU.
IT'S OKAY! REALLY!
I'M JUST GLAD NOTHING HAPPENED TO YOU.
ALSO, TSUTSUI SAID THAT...I MADE YOU SAD, SO...
Wait, why am I smiling now?
...
THAT WAS...A MISUNDER-STANDING.
Oh.
I SEE.
BUT...
...WHEN YOU CALLED OFF OUR PLANS...
...I WAS BUMMED OUT...
THAT MUCH IS TRUE, I GUESS.

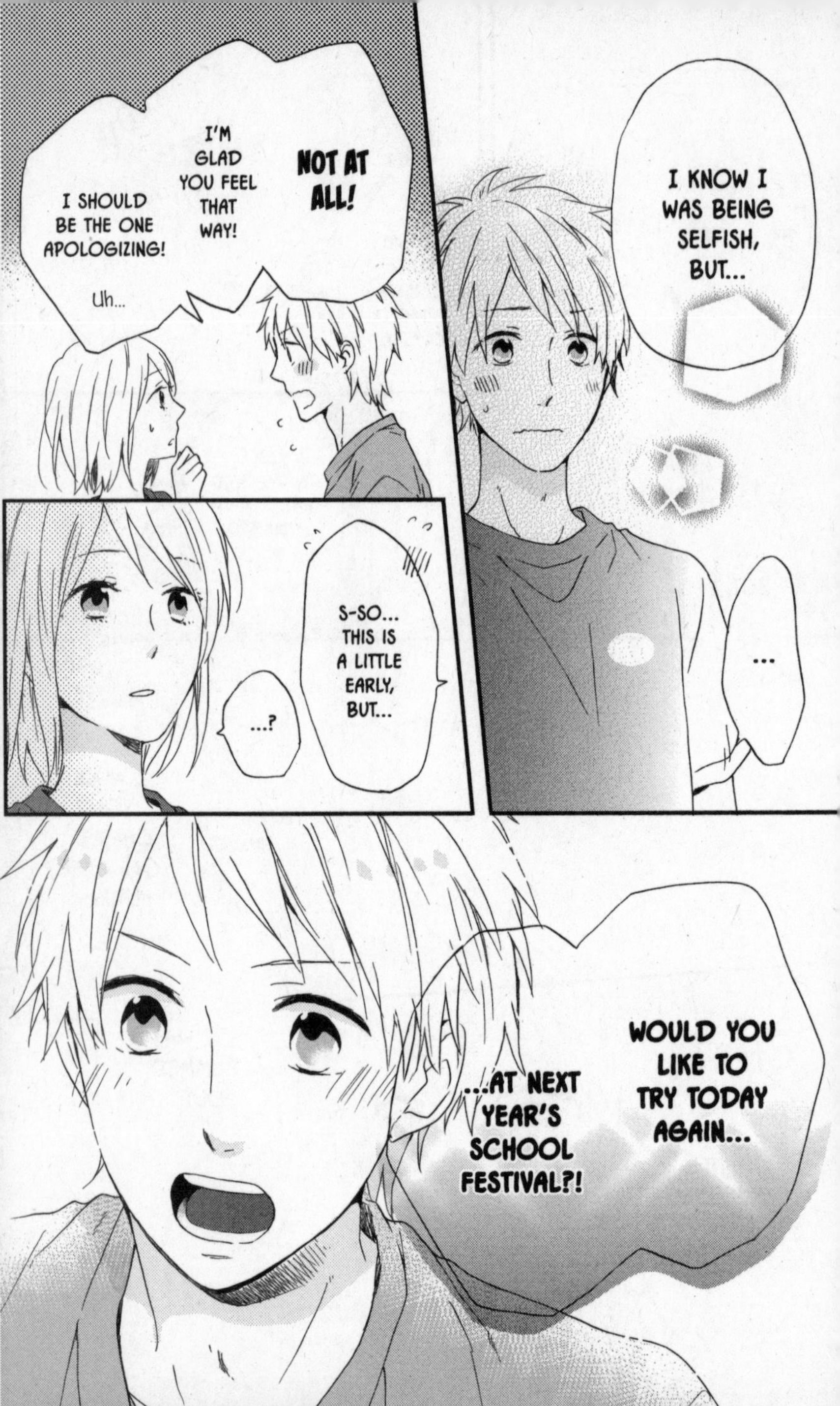
I KNOW I WAS BEING SELFISH, BUT...
...
NOT AT ALL!
I'M GLAD YOU FEEL THAT WAY!
I SHOULD BE THE ONE APOLOGIZING!
Uh...
S-SO... THIS IS A LITTLE EARLY, BUT...
...?
WOULD YOU LIKE TO TRY TODAY AGAIN...
...AT NEXT YEAR'S SCHOOL FESTIVAL?!

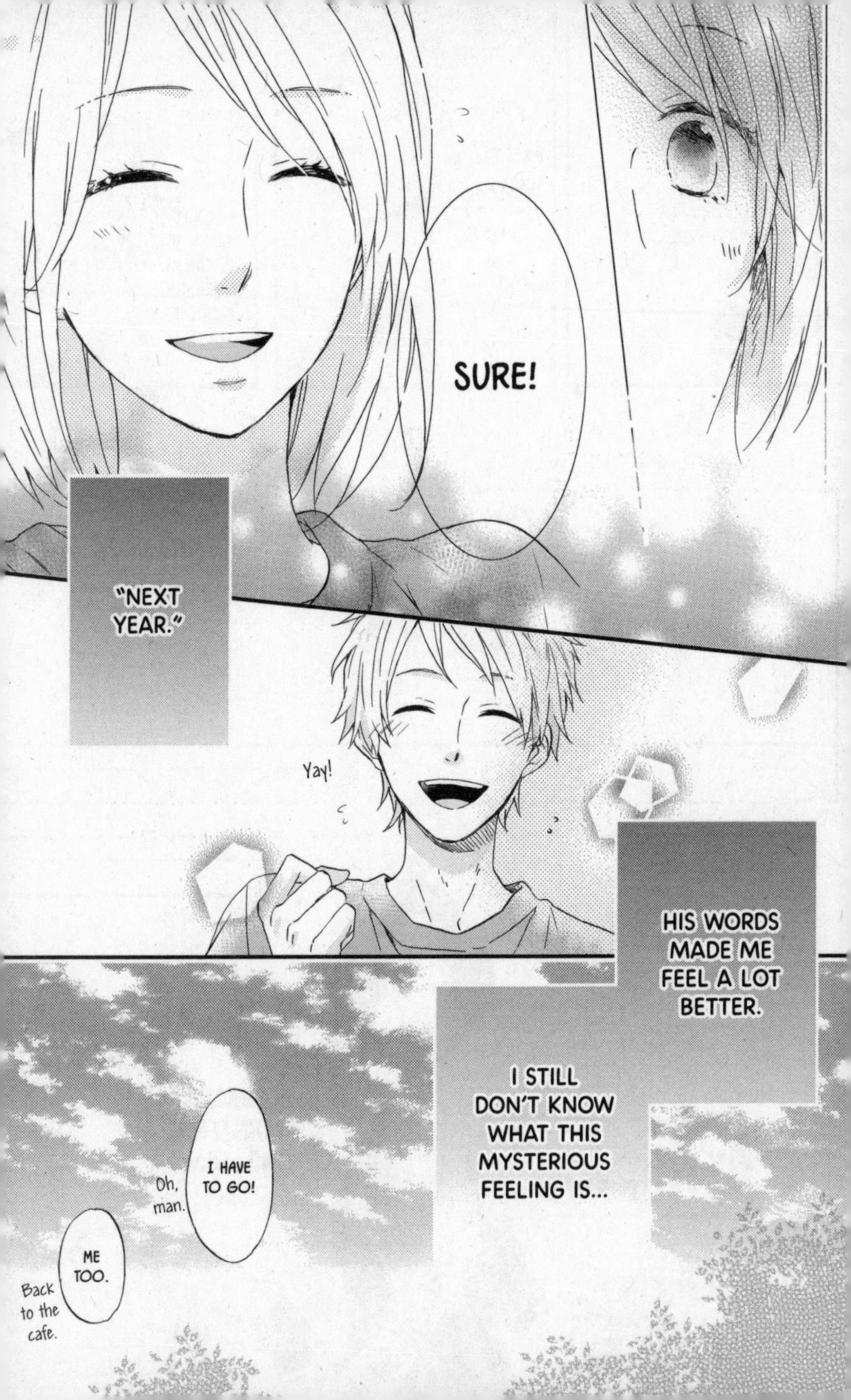
SURE!
"NEXT YEAR."
Yay!
HIS WORDS MADE ME FEEL A LOT BETTER.
I STILL DON'T KNOW WHAT THIS MYSTERIOUS FEELING IS...
I HAVE TO GO!
Oh, man.
ME TOO.
Back to the cafe.

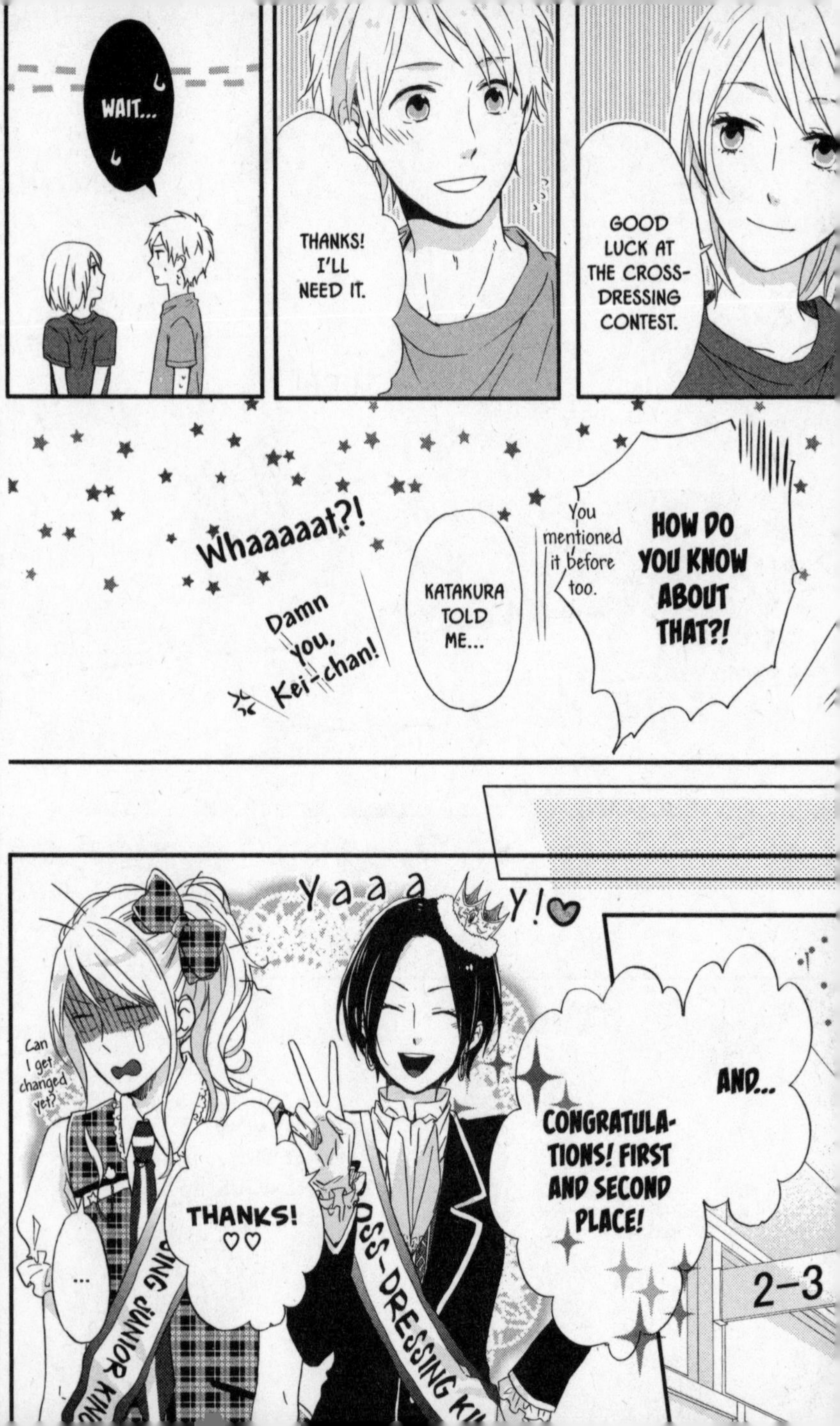
GOOD LUCK AT THE CROSS-DRESSING CONTEST.
THANKS! I'LL NEED IT.
WAIT...
HOW DO YOU KNOW ABOUT THAT?!
You mentioned it before too.
KATAKURA TOLD ME...
Whaaaaat?!
Damn you, Kei-chan!
AND...
CONGRATULATIONS! FIRST AND SECOND PLACE!
2-3
Yaaaay!♡
THANKS! ♡♡
Can I get changed yet?
...

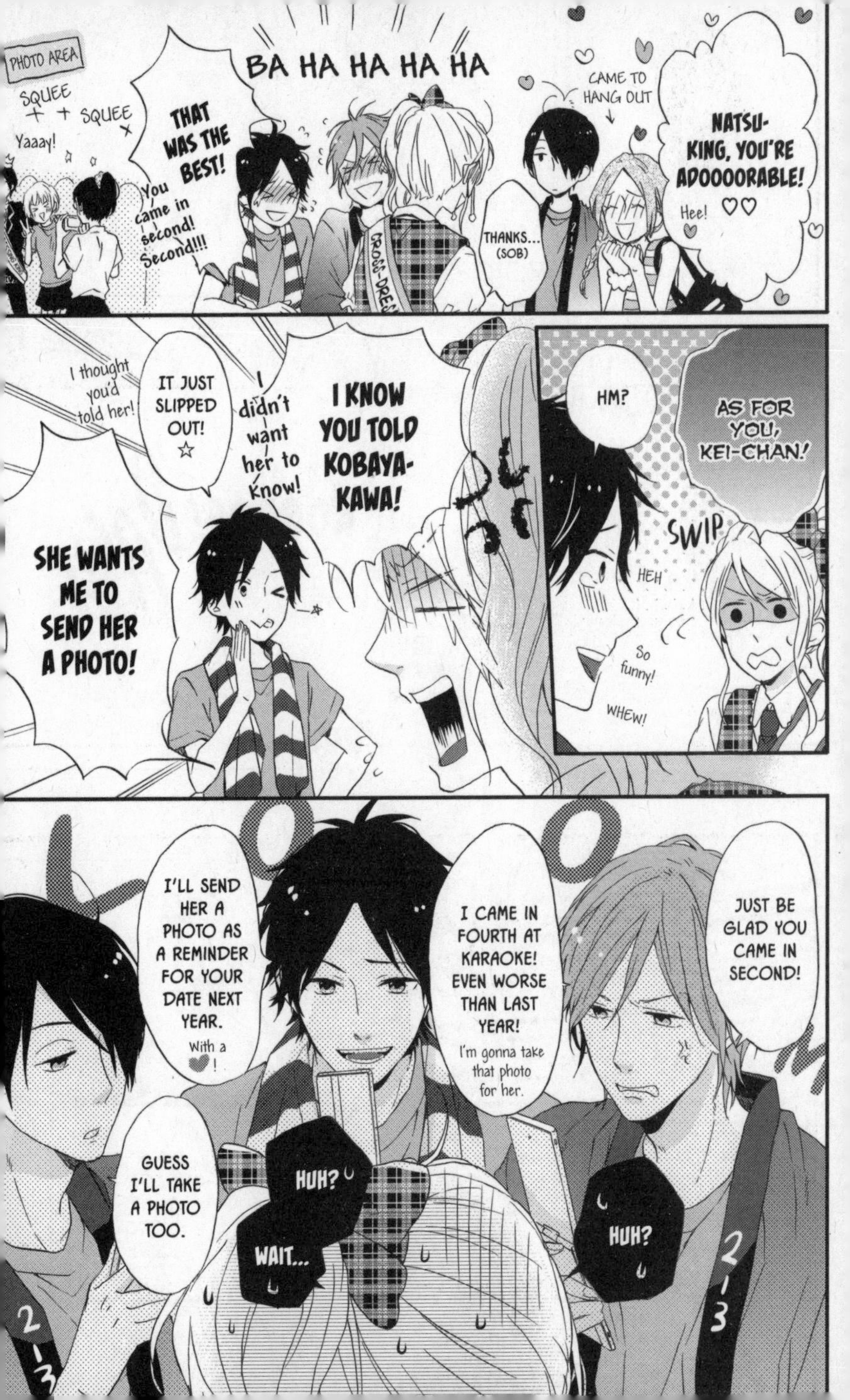
NATSU-KING, YOU'RE ADOOOORABLE! ♡♡
Hee!
CAME TO HANG OUT
THANKS... (SOB)
BA HA HA HA HA
THAT WAS THE BEST!
You came in second! Second!!!
SQUEE SQUEE
Yaaay!
PHOTO AREA
AS FOR YOU, KEI-CHAN!
HM?
SWIP
HEH
So funny!
WHEW!
I KNOW YOU TOLD KOBAYAKAWA!
I didn't want her to know!
IT JUST SLIPPED OUT! ☆
I thought you'd told her!
SHE WANTS ME TO SEND HER A PHOTO!
JUST BE GLAD YOU CAME IN SECOND!
I CAME IN FOURTH AT KARAOKE! EVEN WORSE THAN LAST YEAR!
I'm gonna take that photo for her.
I'LL SEND HER A PHOTO AS A REMINDER FOR YOUR DATE NEXT YEAR.
With a ♥!
HUH?
HUH?
WAIT...
GUESS I'LL TAKE A PHOTO TOO.

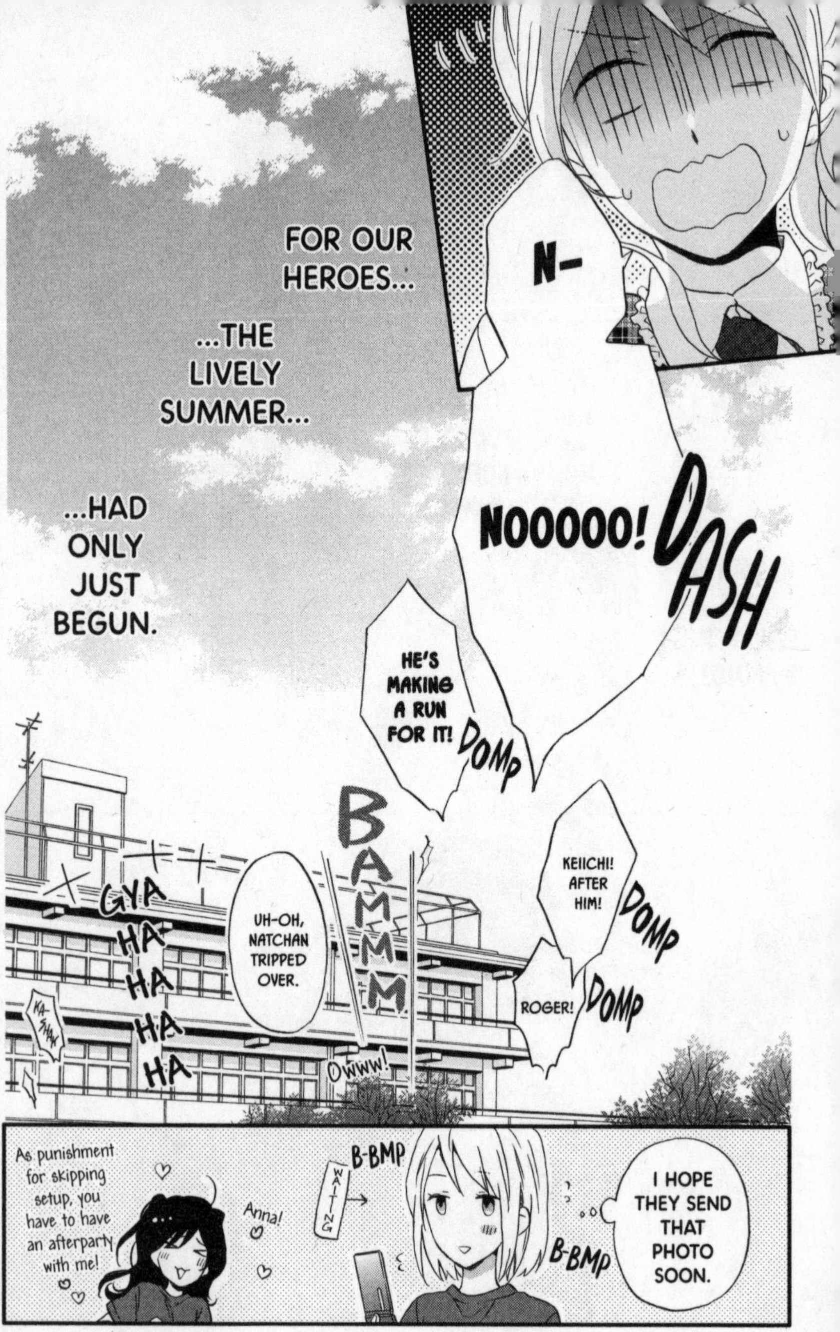
N-
FOR OUR HEROES...
...THE LIVELY SUMMER...
...HAD ONLY JUST BEGUN.
NOOOOO!
DASH
HE'S MAKING A RUN FOR IT!
DOMP
KEIICHI! AFTER HIM!
DOMP
ROGER!
DOMP
BAMMM
UH-OH, NATCHAN TRIPPED OVER.
OWWW!
GYA HA HA HA HA
KA-SHAK
I HOPE THEY SEND THAT PHOTO SOON.
B-BMP
B-BMP
WAITING
Anna!
As punishment for skipping setup, you have to have an afterparty with me!

Rainbow
Days
■  ■  ■  ■  ■  ■  ■

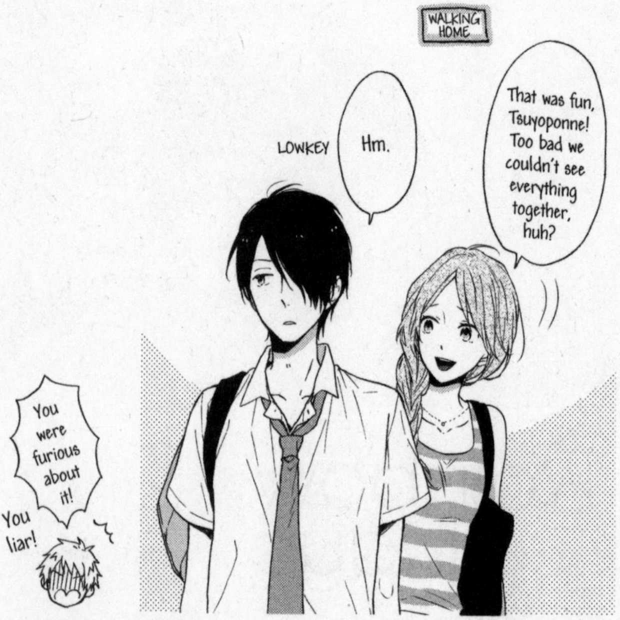
WALKING HOME
That was fun, Tsuyoponne! Too bad we couldn't see everything together, huh?
Hm.
LOWKEY
You were furious about it!
You liar!

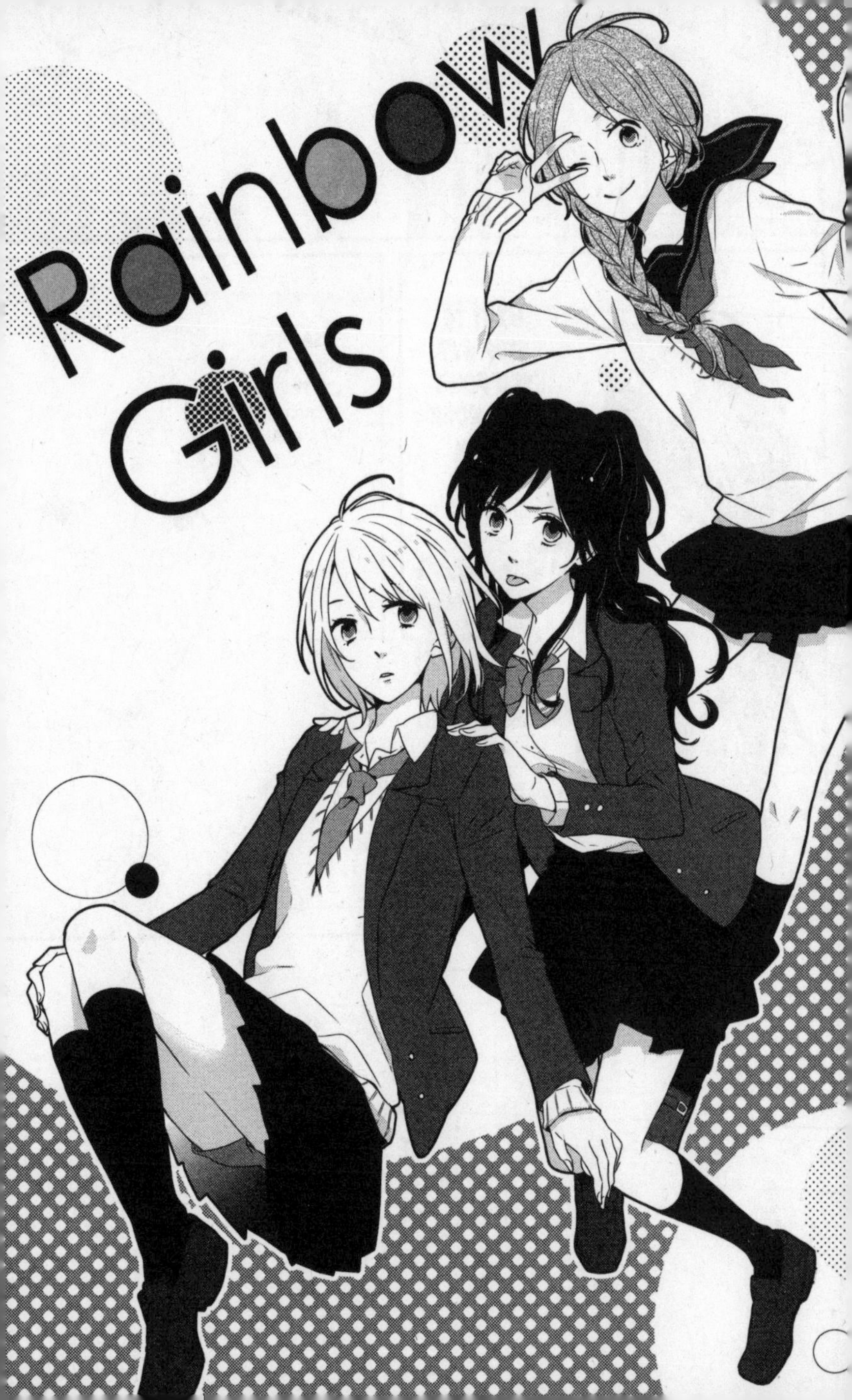
Rainbow
Girls

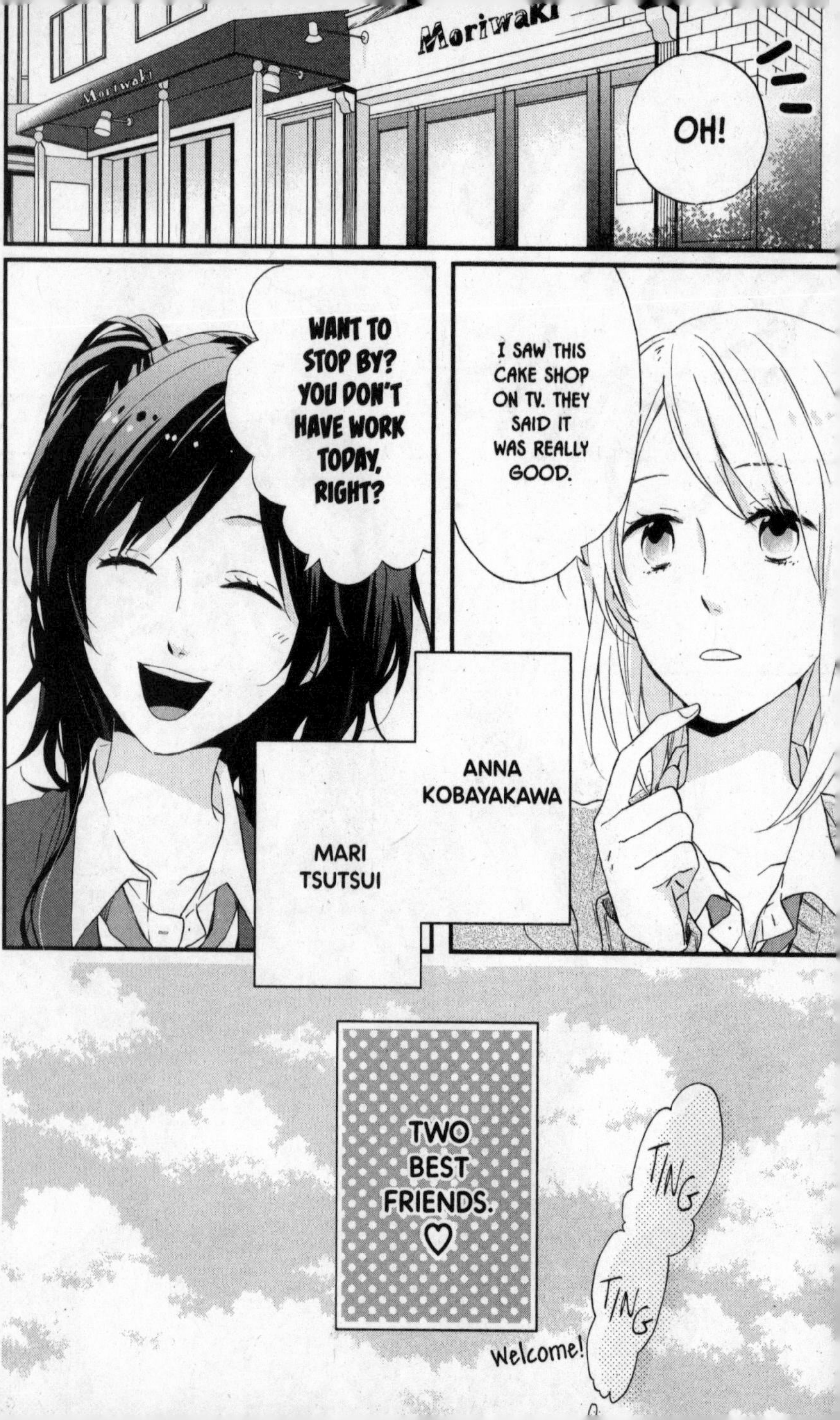
Moriwaki
Moriwaki
OH!
I SAW THIS CAKE SHOP ON TV. THEY SAID IT WAS REALLY GOOD.
ANNA KOBAYAKAWA
WANT TO STOP BY? YOU DON'T HAVE WORK TODAY, RIGHT?
MARI TSUTSUI
TWO BEST FRIENDS. ♡
TING
TING
Welcome!

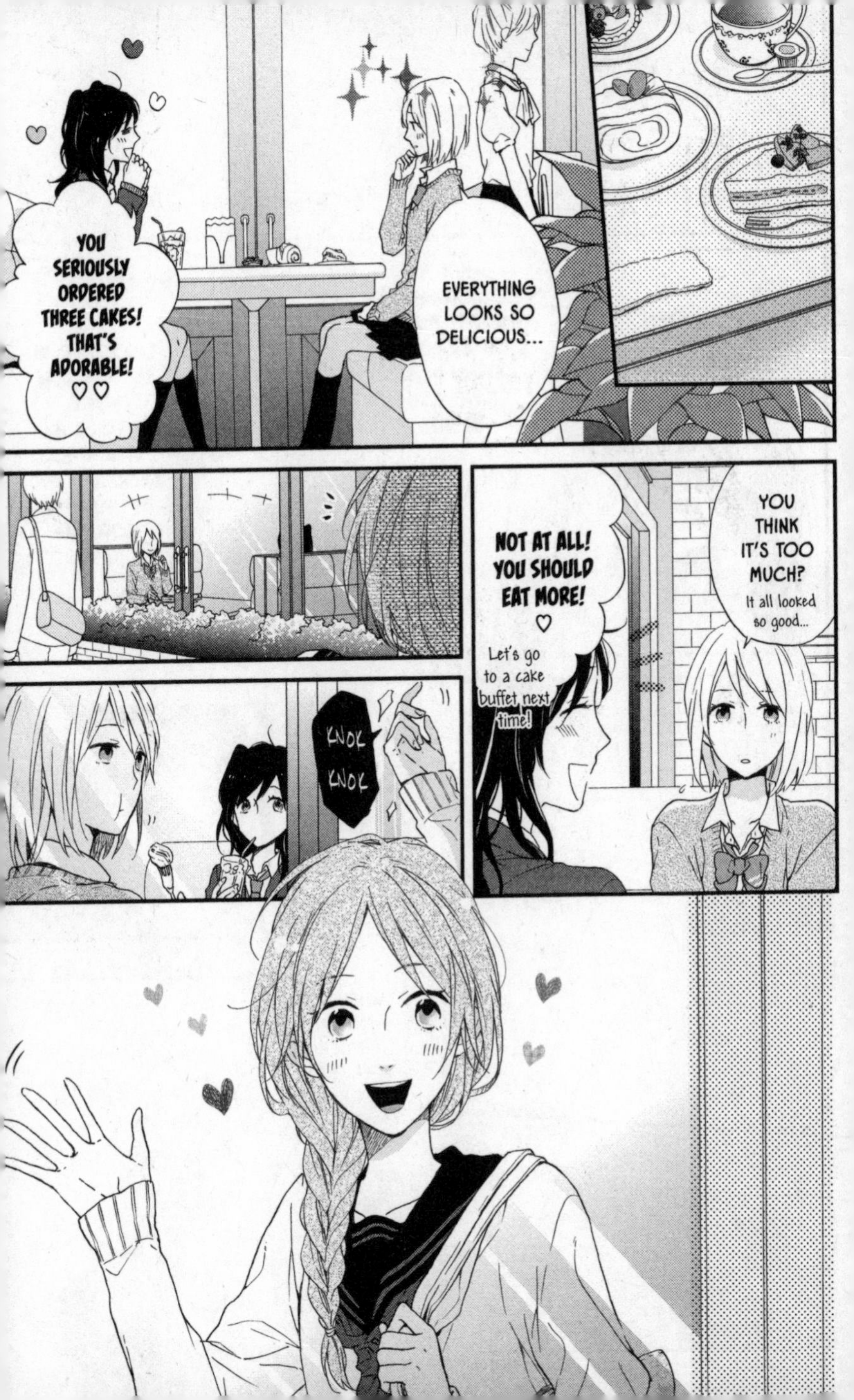
EVERYTHING LOOKS SO DELICIOUS...
YOU SERIOUSLY ORDERED THREE CAKES! THAT'S ADORABLE! ♡♡
YOU THINK IT'S TOO MUCH?
It all looked so good...
NOT AT ALL! YOU SHOULD EAT MORE! ♡
Let's go to a cake buffet next time!
KNOK KNOK

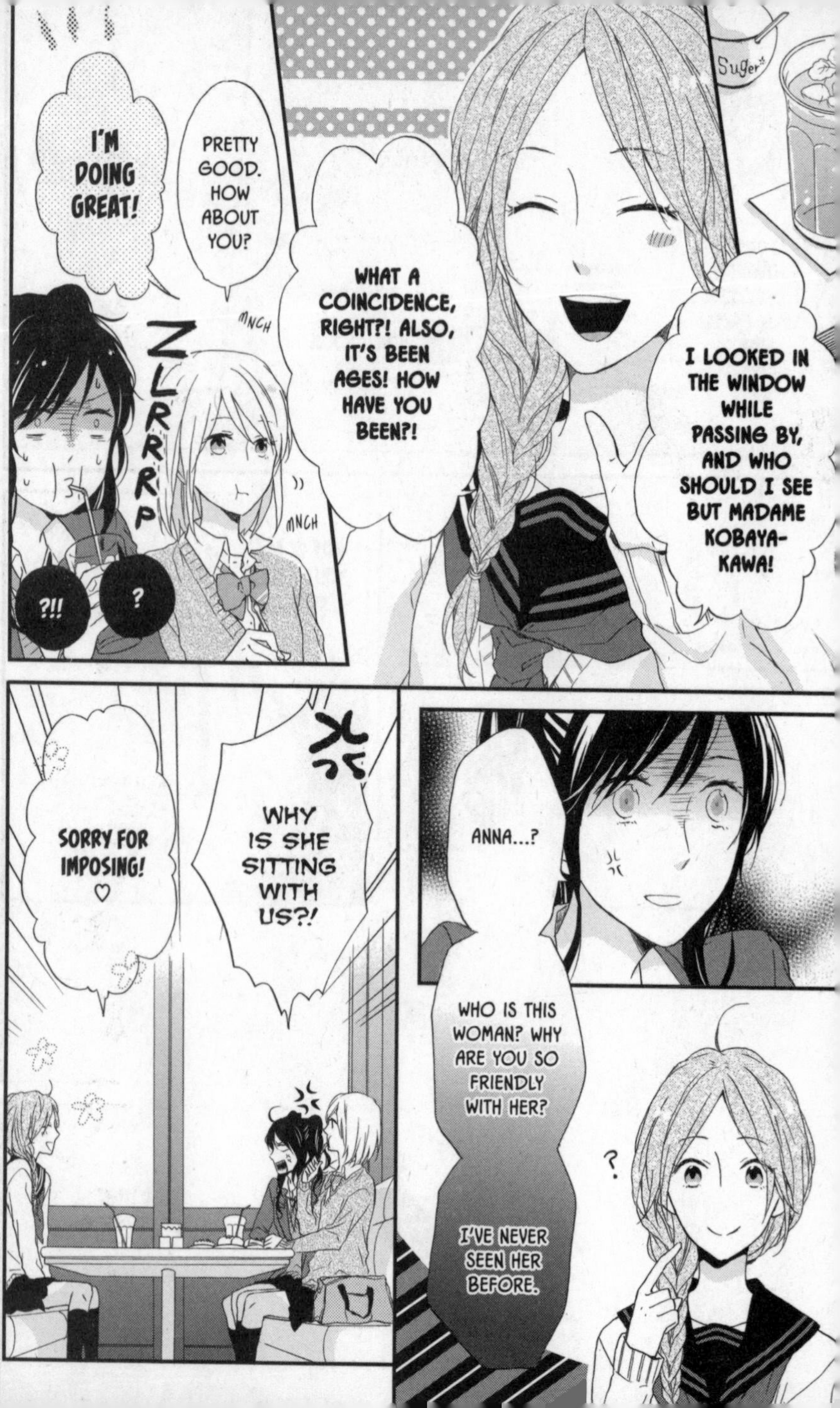
I LOOKED IN THE WINDOW WHILE PASSING BY, AND WHO SHOULD I SEE BUT MADAME KOBAYA-KAWA!
WHAT A COINCIDENCE, RIGHT?! ALSO, IT'S BEEN AGES! HOW HAVE YOU BEEN?!
PRETTY GOOD. HOW ABOUT YOU?
I'M DOING GREAT!
MNCH
ZLRRRP
MNCH
?
?!!
ANNA...?
WHO IS THIS WOMAN? WHY ARE YOU SO FRIENDLY WITH HER?
I'VE NEVER SEEN HER BEFORE.
?
WHY IS SHE SITTING WITH US?!
SORRY FOR IMPOSING! ♡

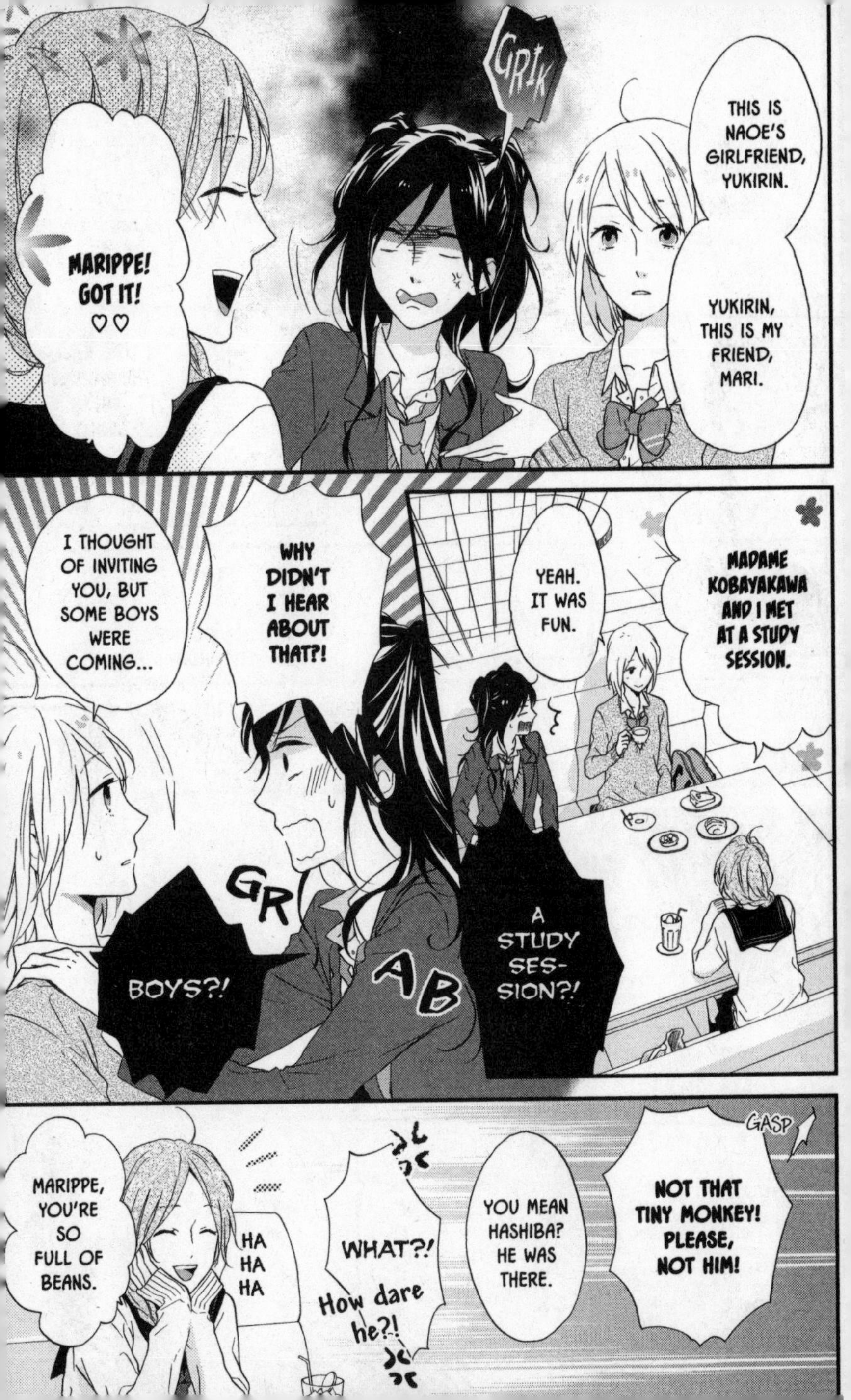
GRIK
THIS IS NAOE'S GIRLFRIEND, YUKIRIN.
YUKIRIN, THIS IS MY FRIEND, MARI.
MARIPPE! GOT IT! ♡♡
MADAME KOBAYAKAWA AND I MET AT A STUDY SESSION.
YEAH. IT WAS FUN.
A STUDY SES-SION?!
WHY DIDN'T I HEAR ABOUT THAT?!
I THOUGHT OF INVITING YOU, BUT SOME BOYS WERE COMING...
GR AB
BOYS?!
GASP
NOT THAT TINY MONKEY! PLEASE, NOT HIM!
YOU MEAN HASHIBA? HE WAS THERE.
WHAT?!
How dare he?!
HA HA HA
MARIPPE, YOU'RE SO FULL OF BEANS.

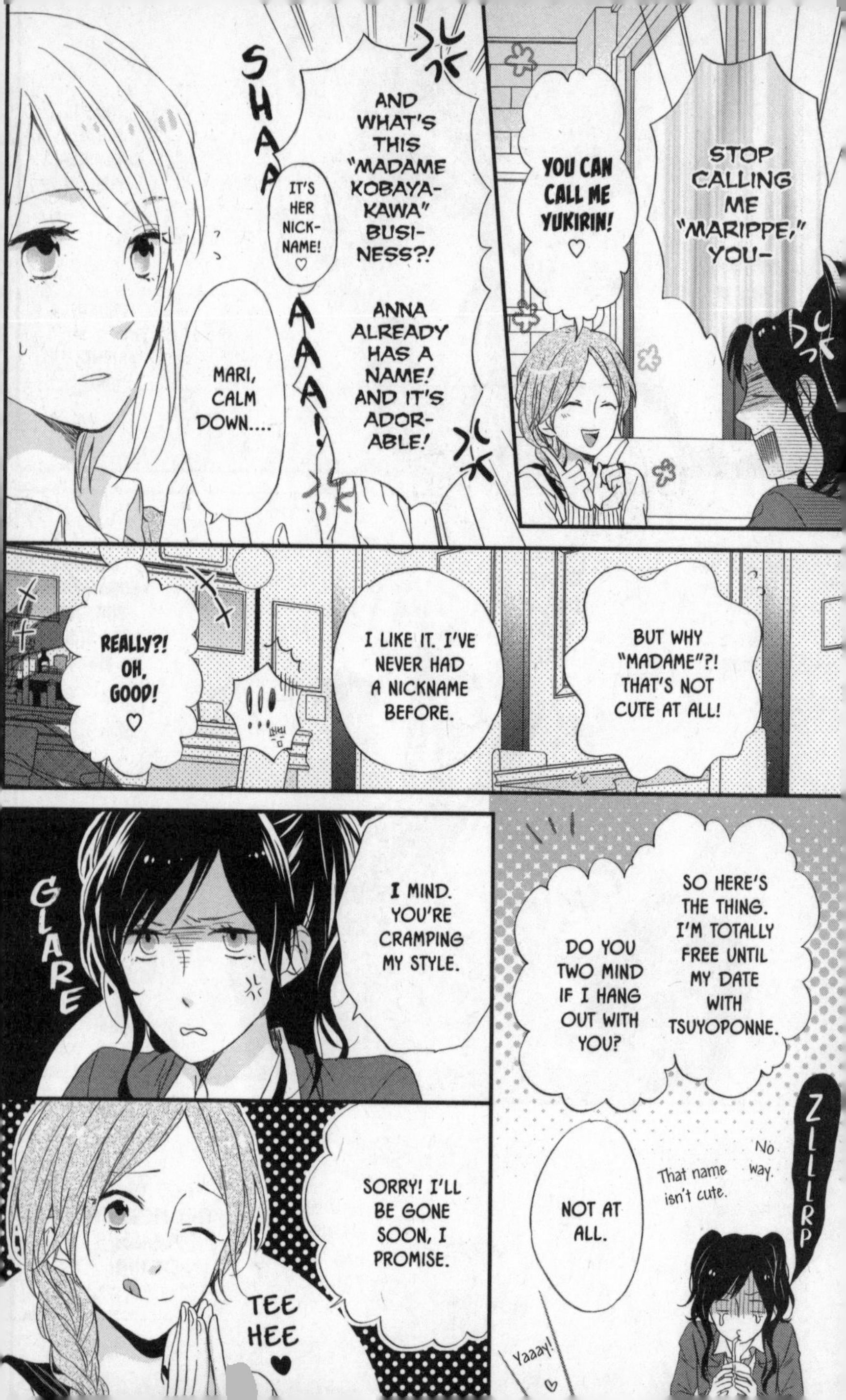
STOP CALLING ME "MARIPPE," YOU-
YOU CAN CALL ME YUKIRIN! ♡
AND WHAT'S THIS "MADAME KOBAYA-KAWA" BUSI-NESS?!
IT'S HER NICK-NAME! ♡
SHAAAAA!
ANNA ALREADY HAS A NAME! AND IT'S ADOR-ABLE!
MARI, CALM DOWN....
BUT WHY "MADAME"?! THAT'S NOT CUTE AT ALL!
I LIKE IT. I'VE NEVER HAD A NICKNAME BEFORE.
!!!
REALLY?! OH, GOOD! ♡
SO HERE'S THE THING. I'M TOTALLY FREE UNTIL MY DATE WITH TSUYOPONNE.
DO YOU TWO MIND IF I HANG OUT WITH YOU?
NOT AT ALL.
No way.
That name isn't cute.
ZLLLRP
Yaaay! ♡
I MIND. YOU'RE CRAMPING MY STYLE.
GLARE
SORRY! I'LL BE GONE SOON, I PROMISE.
TEE HEE ♥

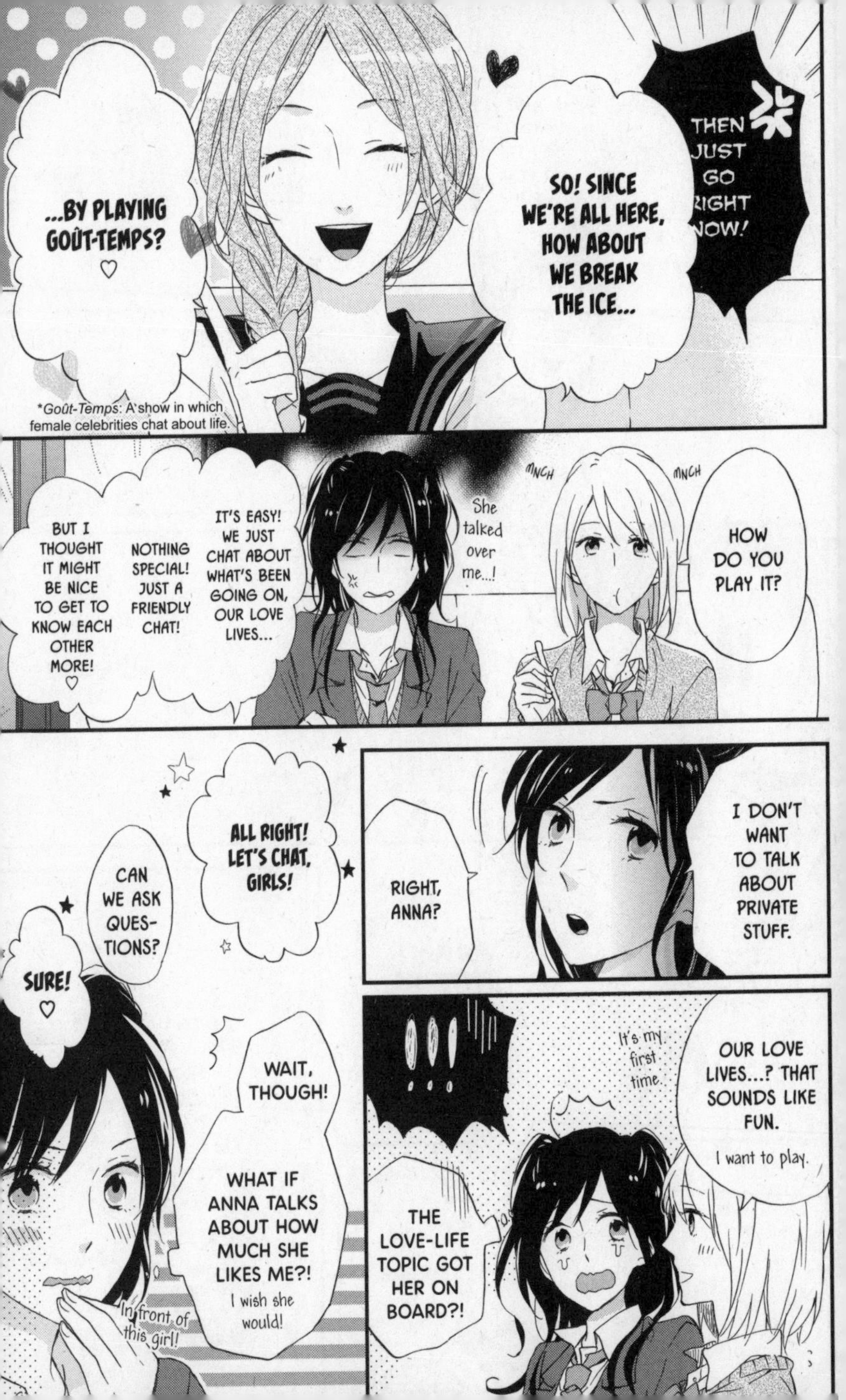
THEN JUST GO RIGHT NOW!
SO! SINCE WE'RE ALL HERE, HOW ABOUT WE BREAK THE ICE...
...BY PLAYING GOÛT-TEMPS? ♡
*Goût-Temps: A show in which female celebrities chat about life.
HOW DO YOU PLAY IT?
MNCH
MNCH
She talked over me...!
IT'S EASY! WE JUST CHAT ABOUT WHAT'S BEEN GOING ON, OUR LOVE LIVES...
NOTHING SPECIAL! JUST A FRIENDLY CHAT!
BUT I THOUGHT IT MIGHT BE NICE TO GET TO KNOW EACH OTHER MORE! ♡
I DON'T WANT TO TALK ABOUT PRIVATE STUFF.
RIGHT, ANNA?
ALL RIGHT! LET'S CHAT, GIRLS!
CAN WE ASK QUES-TIONS?
SURE! ♡
OUR LOVE LIVES...? THAT SOUNDS LIKE FUN.
I want to play.
It's my first time.
THE LOVE-LIFE TOPIC GOT HER ON BOARD?!
WAIT, THOUGH!
WHAT IF ANNA TALKS ABOUT HOW MUCH SHE LIKES ME?!
I wish she would!
In front of this girl!

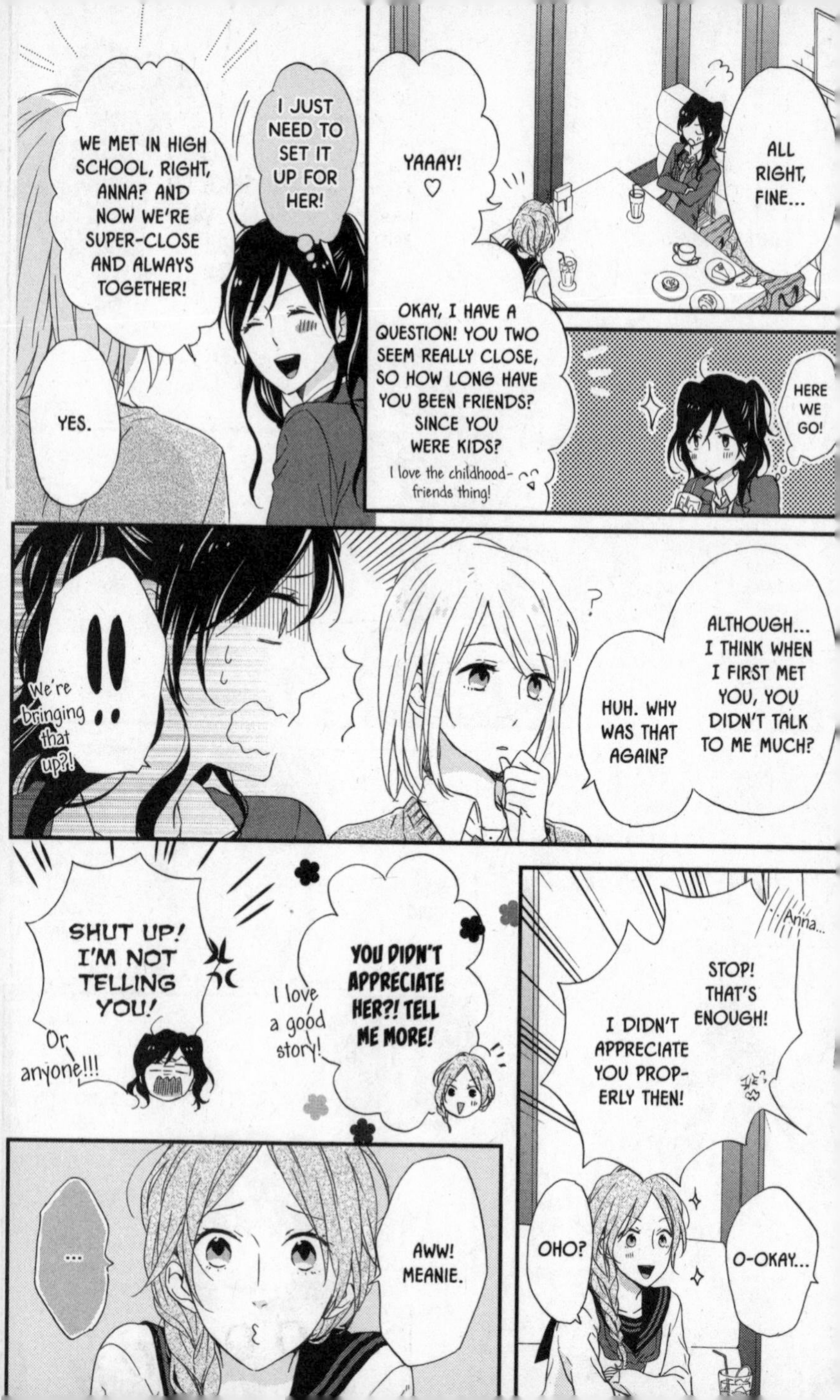
ALL RIGHT, FINE...
YAAAY! ♡
OKAY, I HAVE A QUESTION! YOU TWO SEEM REALLY CLOSE, SO HOW LONG HAVE YOU BEEN FRIENDS? SINCE YOU WERE KIDS?
I love the childhood-friends thing!
HERE WE GO!
I JUST NEED TO SET IT UP FOR HER!
WE MET IN HIGH SCHOOL, RIGHT, ANNA? AND NOW WE'RE SUPER-CLOSE AND ALWAYS TOGETHER!
YES.
ALTHOUGH... I THINK WHEN I FIRST MET YOU, YOU DIDN'T TALK TO ME MUCH?
HUH. WHY WAS THAT AGAIN?
!!
We're bringing that up?!
Anna...
STOP! THAT'S ENOUGH!
I DIDN'T APPRECIATE YOU PROPERLY THEN!
O-OKAY...
OHO?
YOU DIDN'T APPRECIATE HER?! TELL ME MORE!
I love a good story!
SHUT UP! I'M NOT TELLING YOU!
Or anyone!!!
AWW! MEANIE.
...

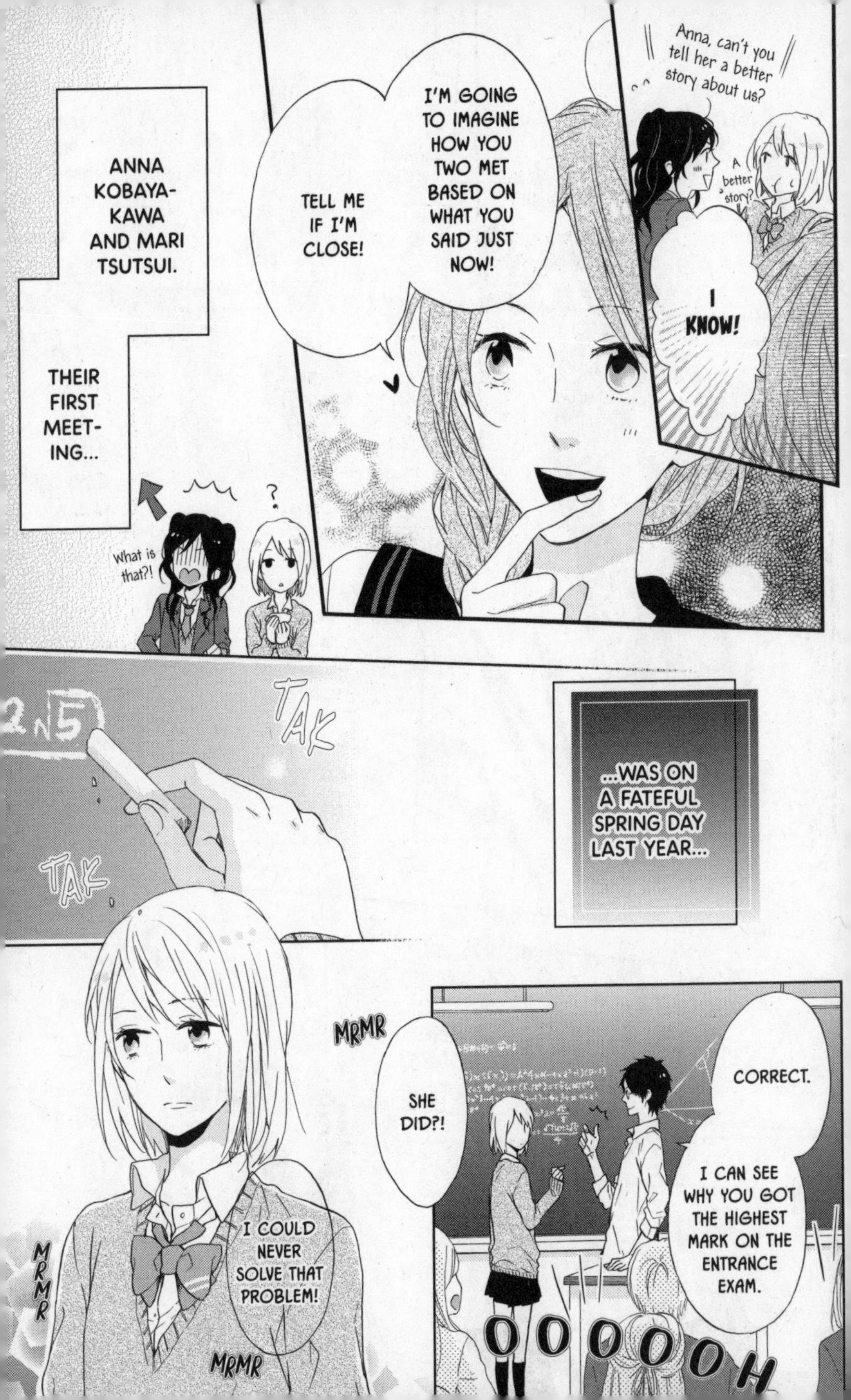
Anna, can't you tell her a better story about us?
A better story?
I KNOW!
I'M GOING TO IMAGINE HOW YOU TWO MET BASED ON WHAT YOU SAID JUST NOW!
TELL ME IF I'M CLOSE!
ANNA KOBAYA-KAWA AND MARI TSUTSUI.
THEIR FIRST MEET-ING...
?
What is that?!
...WAS ON A FATEFUL SPRING DAY LAST YEAR...
TAK
TAK
CORRECT.
I CAN SEE WHY YOU GOT THE HIGHEST MARK ON THE ENTRANCE EXAM.
SHE DID?!
MRMR
OOOOOH
I COULD NEVER SOLVE THAT PROBLEM!
MRMR
MRMR

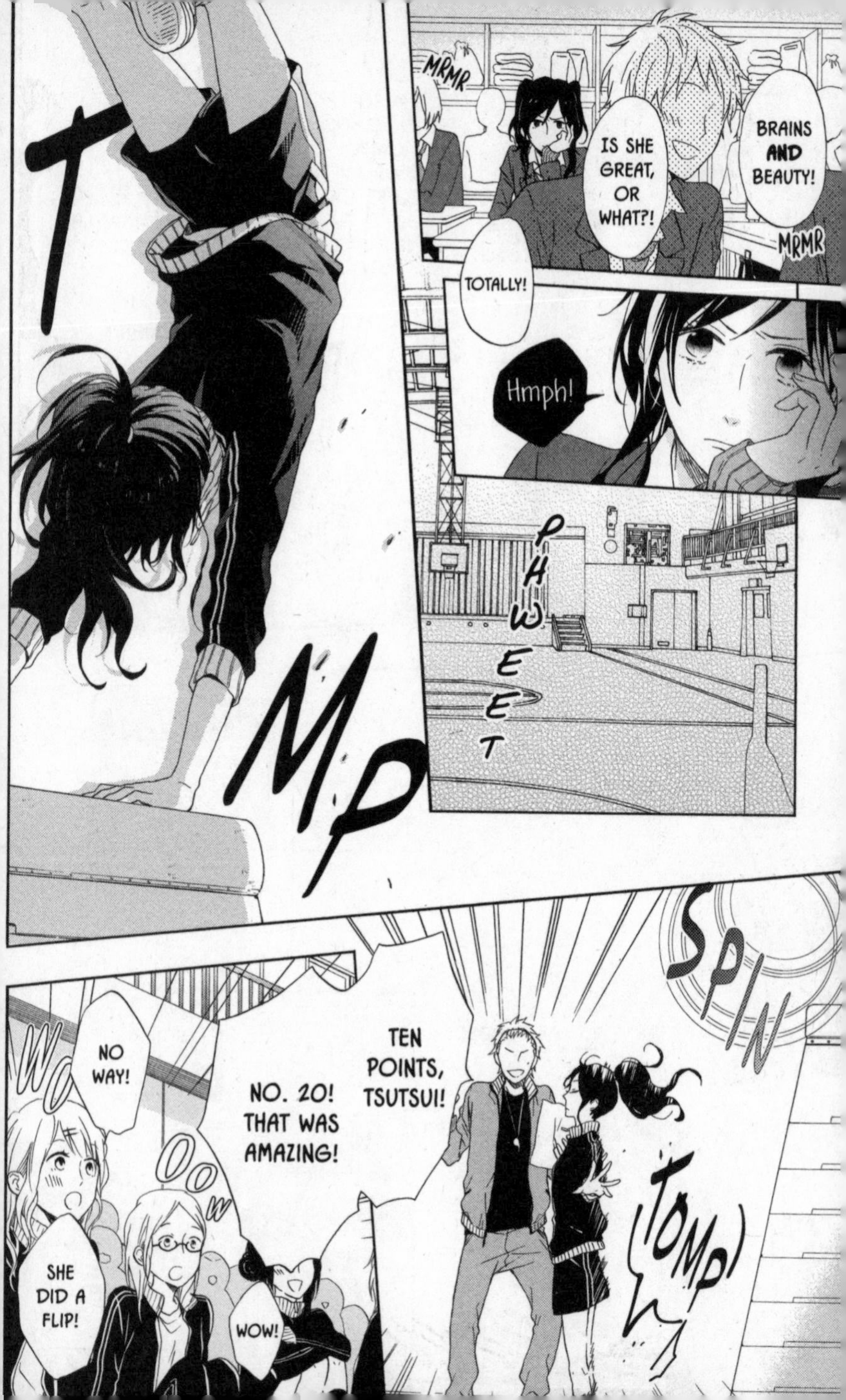
BRAINS AND BEAUTY!
IS SHE GREAT, OR WHAT?!
MRMR
MRMR
TOTALLY!
Hmph!
PHWEEET
MP
SPIN
TEN POINTS, TSUTSUI!
TOMP
NO. 20! THAT WAS AMAZING!
NO WAY!
WOOOW
SHE DID A FLIP!
WOW!

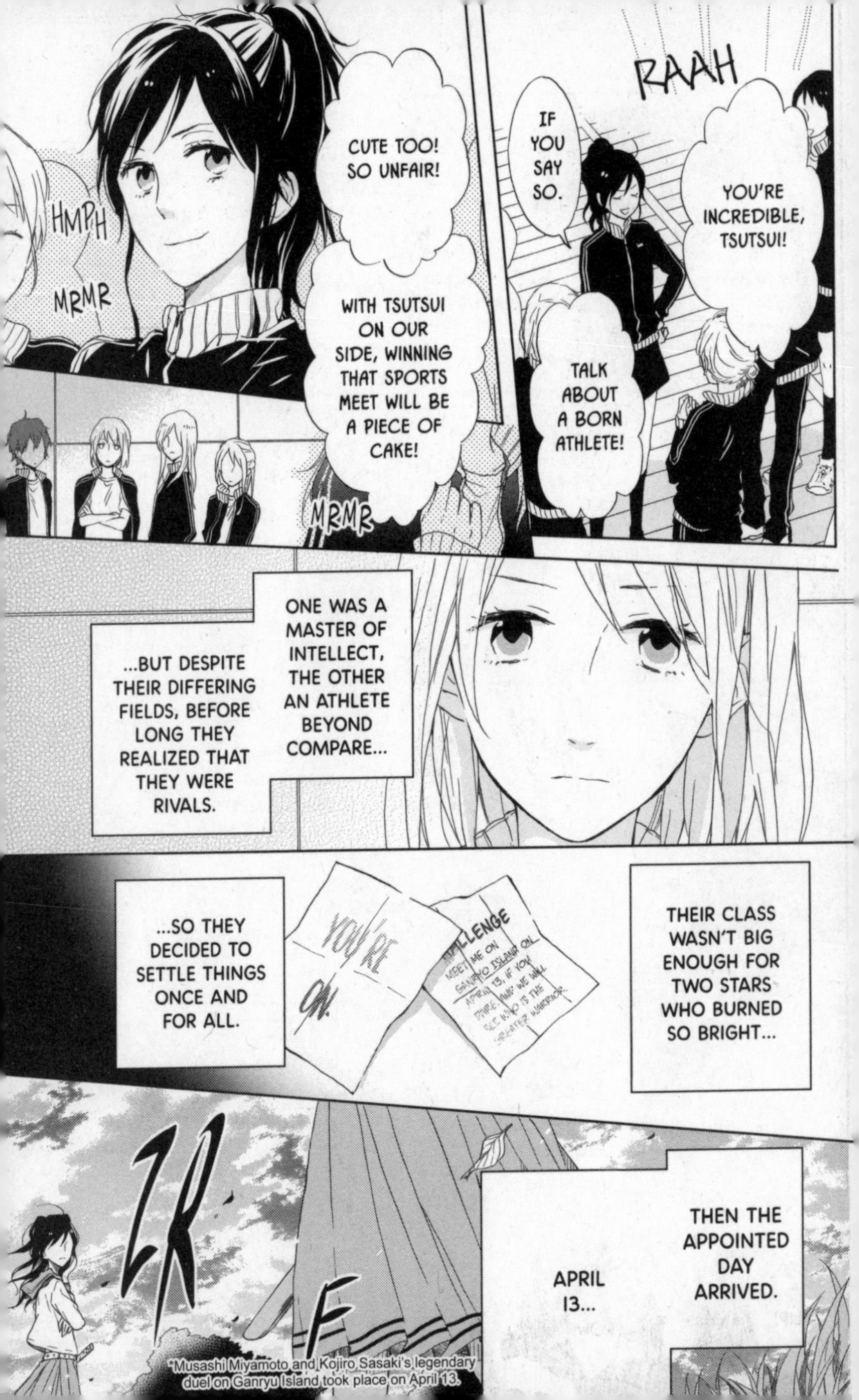
RAAH
YOU'RE INCREDIBLE, TSUTSUI!
IF YOU SAY SO.
TALK ABOUT A BORN ATHLETE!
CUTE TOO! SO UNFAIR!
HMPH
MRMR
WITH TSUTSUI ON OUR SIDE, WINNING THAT SPORTS MEET WILL BE A PIECE OF CAKE!
MRMR
ONE WAS A MASTER OF INTELLECT, THE OTHER AN ATHLETE BEYOND COMPARE...
...BUT DESPITE THEIR DIFFERING FIELDS, BEFORE LONG THEY REALIZED THAT THEY WERE RIVALS.
THEIR CLASS WASN'T BIG ENOUGH FOR TWO STARS WHO BURNED SO BRIGHT...
YOU'RE ON.
...SO THEY DECIDED TO SETTLE THINGS ONCE AND FOR ALL.
THEN THE APPOINTED DAY ARRIVED.
APRIL 13...
ZR
F
*Musashi Miyamoto and Kojiro Sasaki's legendary duel on Ganryu Island took place on April 13.

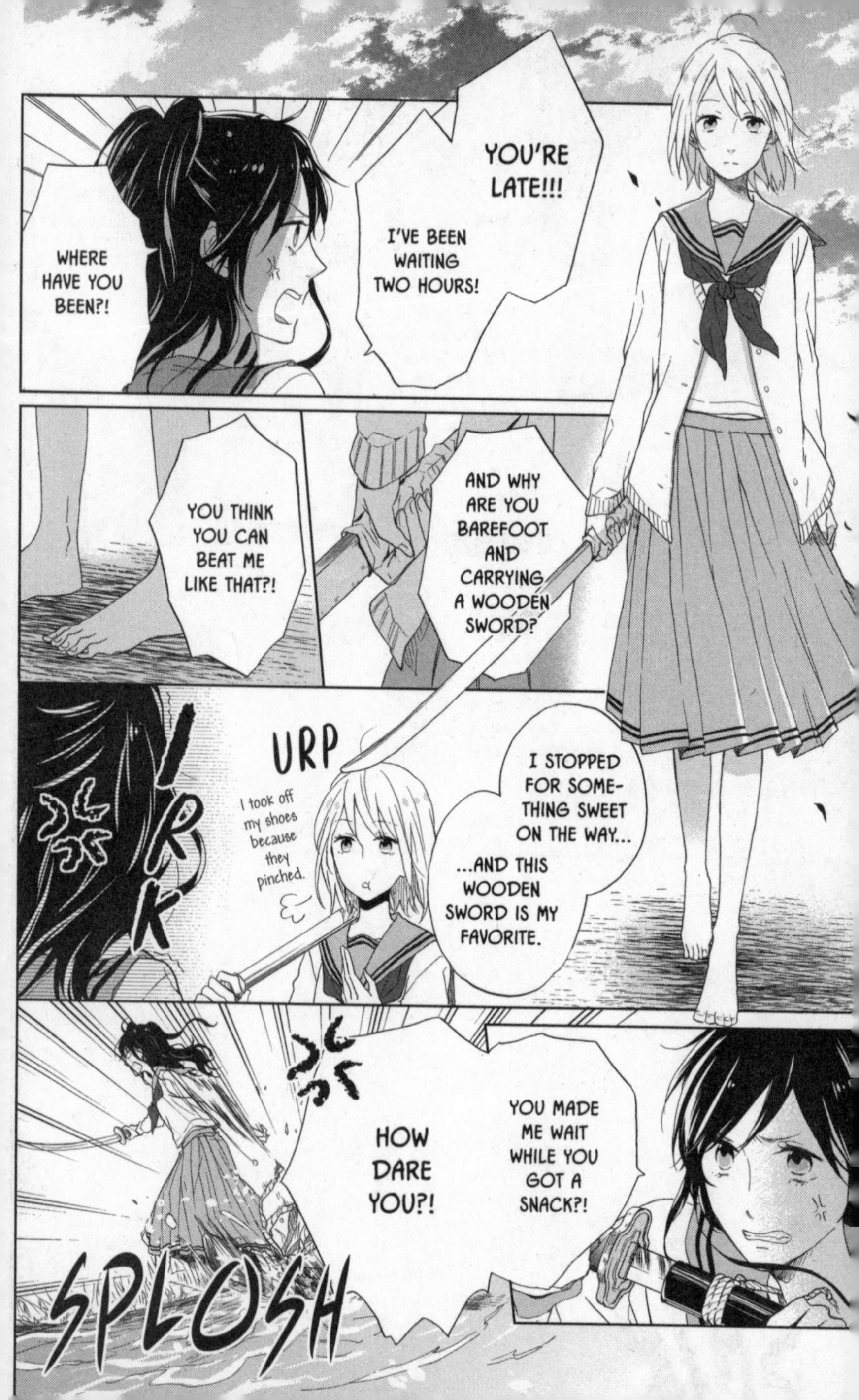
YOU'RE LATE!!!
I'VE BEEN WAITING TWO HOURS!
WHERE HAVE YOU BEEN?!
AND WHY ARE YOU BAREFOOT AND CARRYING A WOODEN SWORD?
YOU THINK YOU CAN BEAT ME LIKE THAT?!
I STOPPED FOR SOME-THING SWEET ON THE WAY...
...AND THIS WOODEN SWORD IS MY FAVORITE.
URP
I took off my shoes because they pinched.
IRK
YOU MADE ME WAIT WHILE YOU GOT A SNACK?!
HOW DARE YOU?!
SPLOSH

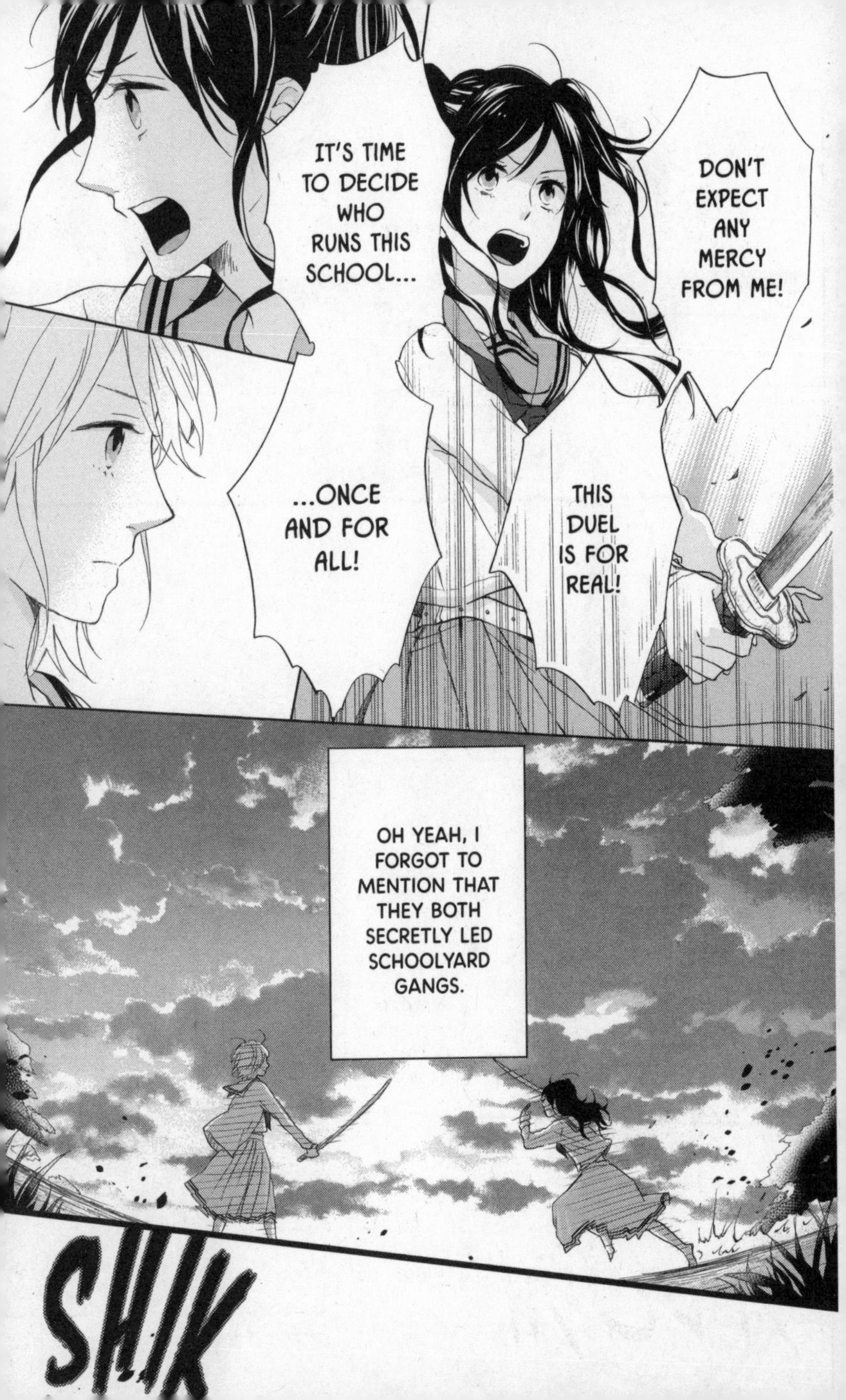
DON'T EXPECT ANY MERCY FROM ME!
THIS DUEL IS FOR REAL!
IT'S TIME TO DECIDE WHO RUNS THIS SCHOOL...
...ONCE AND FOR ALL!
OH YEAH, I FORGOT TO MENTION THAT THEY BOTH SECRETLY LED SCHOOLYARD GANGS.
SHIK

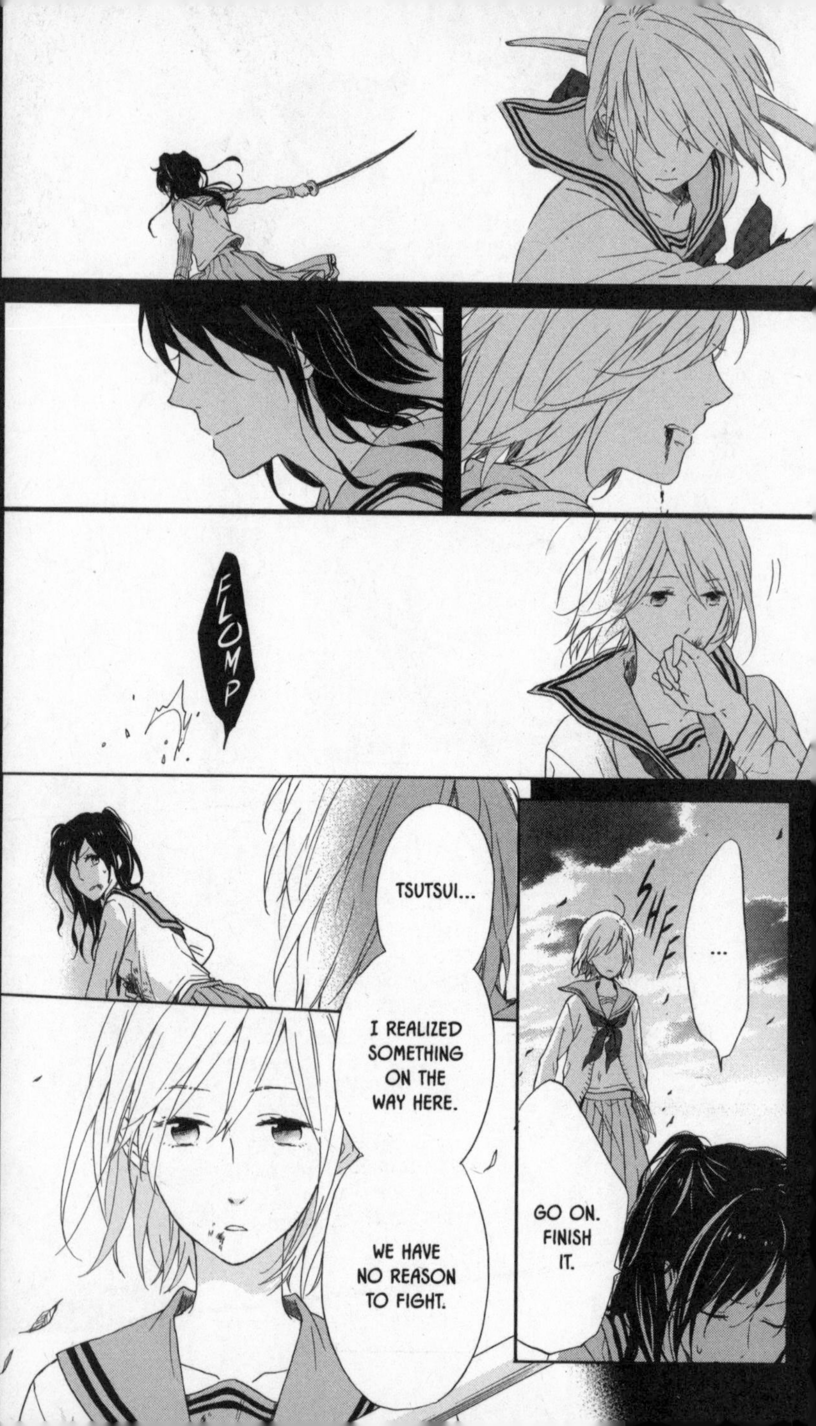
FLOMP
SHFF
...
GO ON. FINISH IT.
TSUTSUI...
I REALIZED SOMETHING ON THE WAY HERE.
WE HAVE NO REASON TO FIGHT.

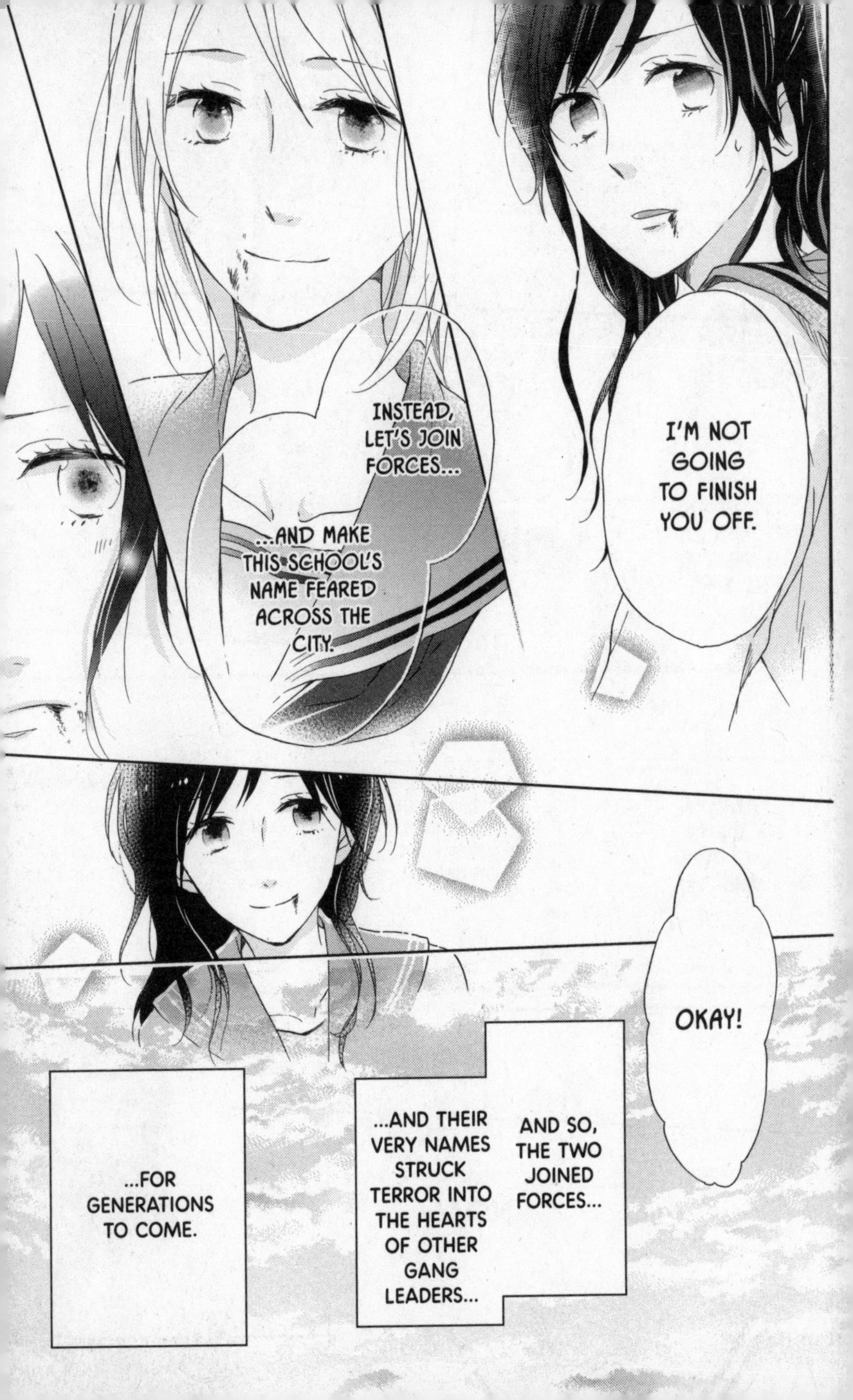
I'M NOT GOING TO FINISH YOU OFF.
INSTEAD, LET'S JOIN FORCES...
...AND MAKE THIS SCHOOL'S NAME FEARED ACROSS THE CITY.
OKAY!
AND SO, THE TWO JOINED FORCES...
...AND THEIR VERY NAMES STRUCK TERROR INTO THE HEARTS OF OTHER GANG LEADERS...
...FOR GENERATIONS TO COME.

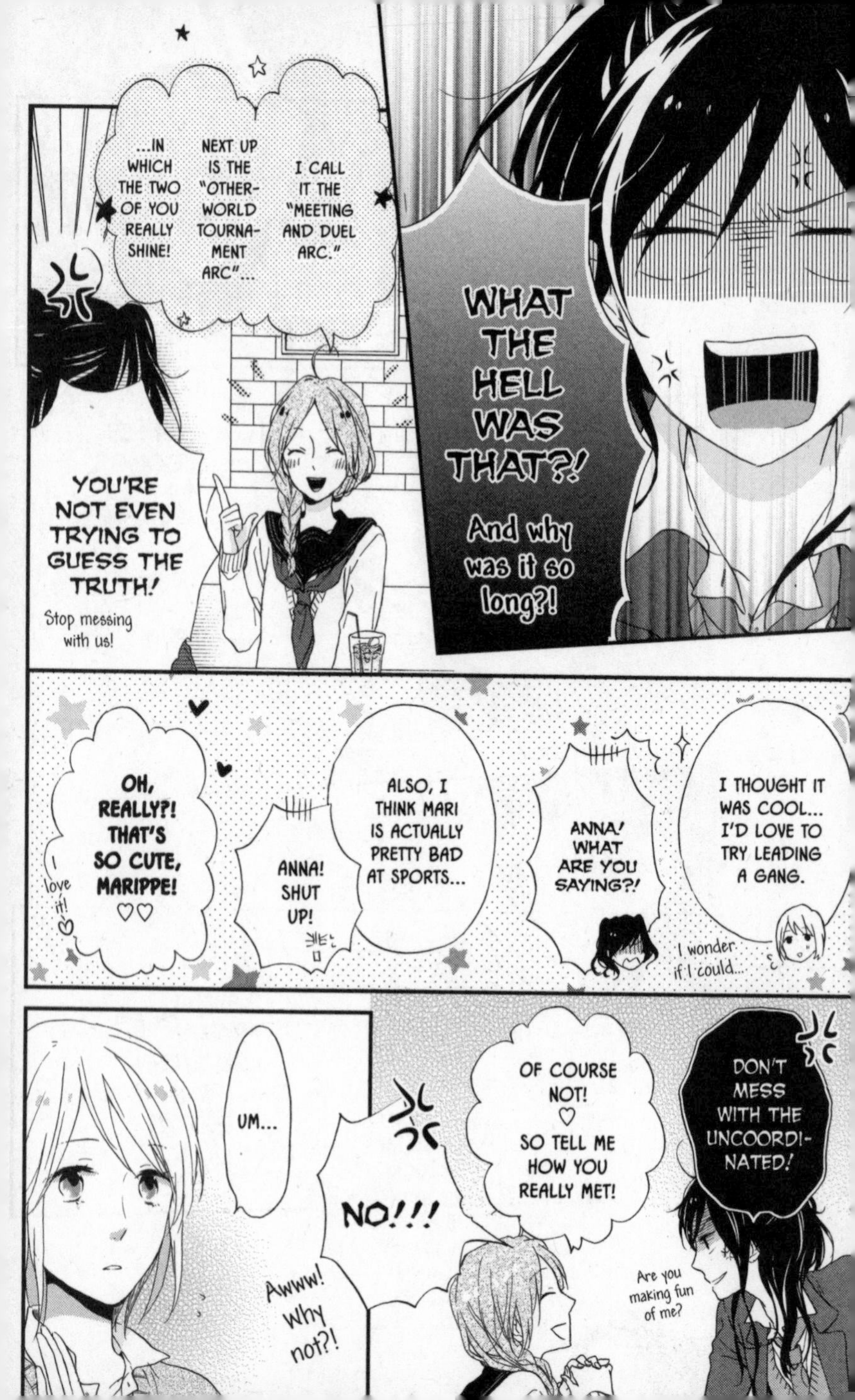
WHAT THE HELL WAS THAT?!
And why was it so long?!
I CALL IT THE "MEETING AND DUEL ARC."
NEXT UP IS THE "OTHER-WORLD TOURNAMENT ARC"...
...IN WHICH THE TWO OF YOU REALLY SHINE!
YOU'RE NOT EVEN TRYING TO GUESS THE TRUTH!
Stop messing with us!
I THOUGHT IT WAS COOL... I'D LOVE TO TRY LEADING A GANG.
I wonder if I could...
ANNA! WHAT ARE YOU SAYING?!
ALSO, I THINK MARI IS ACTUALLY PRETTY BAD AT SPORTS...
ANNA! SHUT UP!
OH, REALLY?! THAT'S SO CUTE, MARIPPE! ♡♡
I love it! ♡
DON'T MESS WITH THE UNCOORDINATED!
Are you making fun of me?
OF COURSE NOT! ♡ SO TELL ME HOW YOU REALLY MET!
NO!!!
Awww! Why not?!
UM...

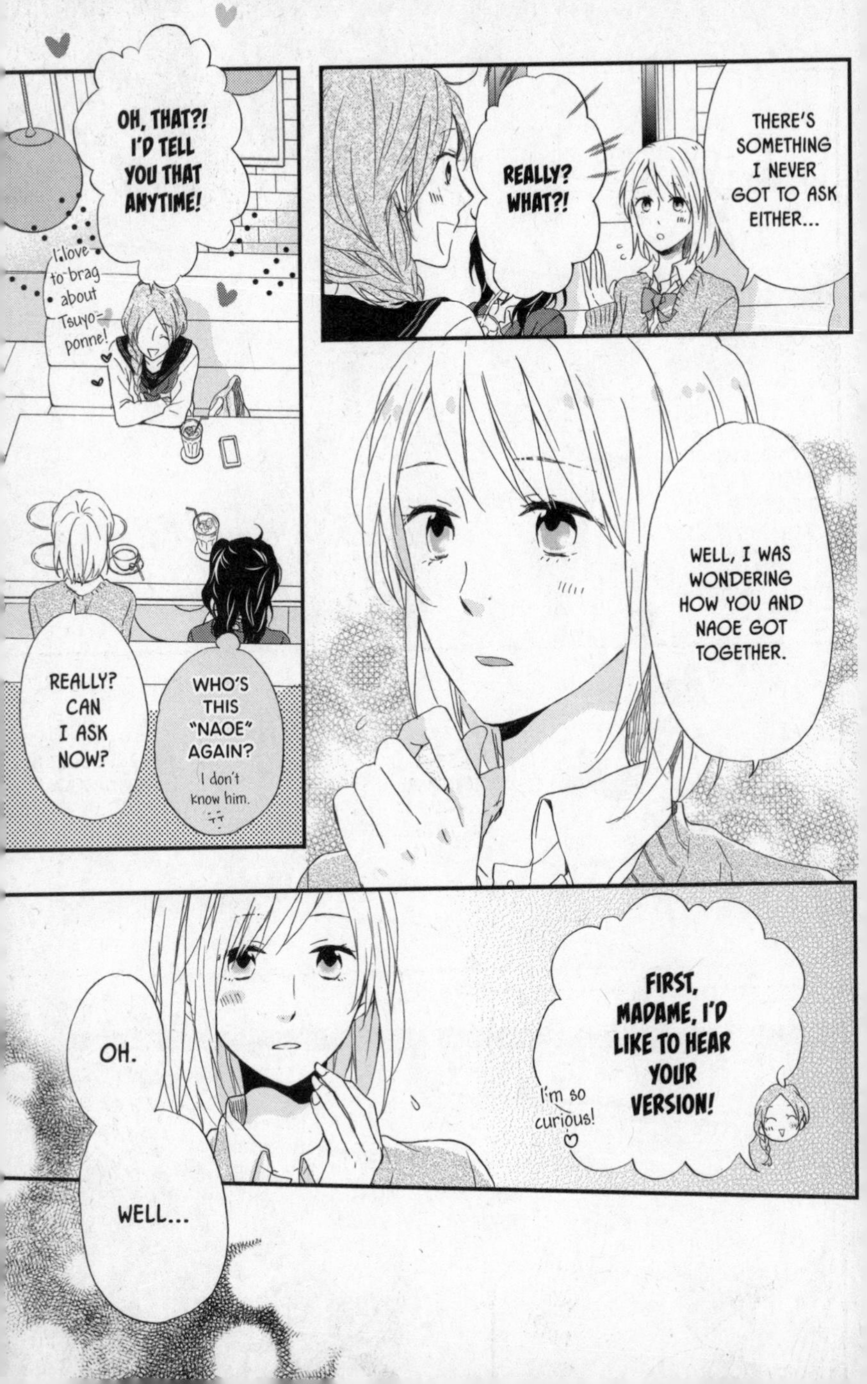
THERE'S SOMETHING I NEVER GOT TO ASK EITHER...
REALLY? WHAT?!
WELL, I WAS WONDERING HOW YOU AND NAOE GOT TOGETHER.
OH, THAT?! I'D TELL YOU THAT ANYTIME!
I love to brag about Tsuyo-ponne!
WHO'S THIS "NAOE" AGAIN?
I don't know him.
REALLY? CAN I ASK NOW?
FIRST, MADAME, I'D LIKE TO HEAR YOUR VERSION!
I'm so curious!
OH.
WELL...

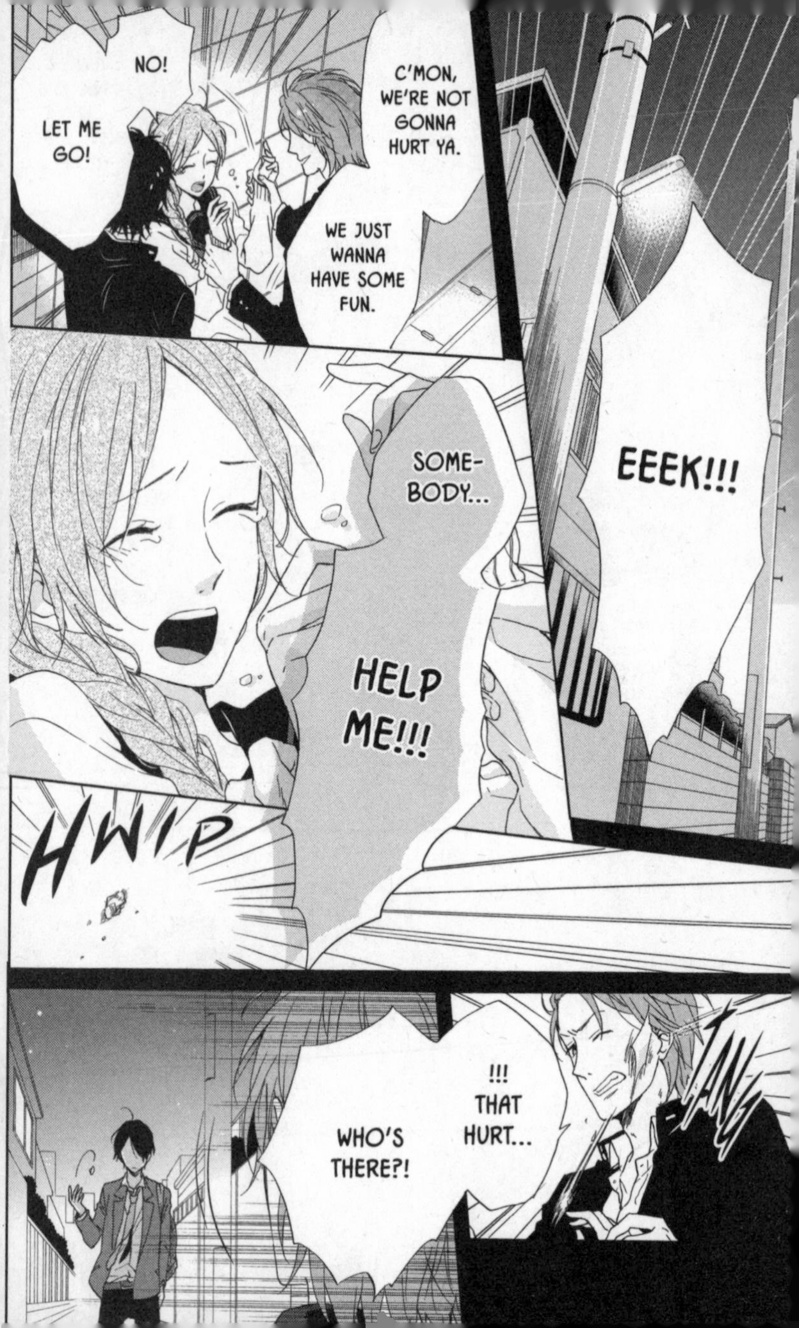
EEEK!!!
C'MON, WE'RE NOT GONNA HURT YA.
WE JUST WANNA HAVE SOME FUN.
NO!
LET ME GO!
SOME-BODY...
HELP ME!!!
HWIP
!!! THAT HURT...
WHO'S THERE?!

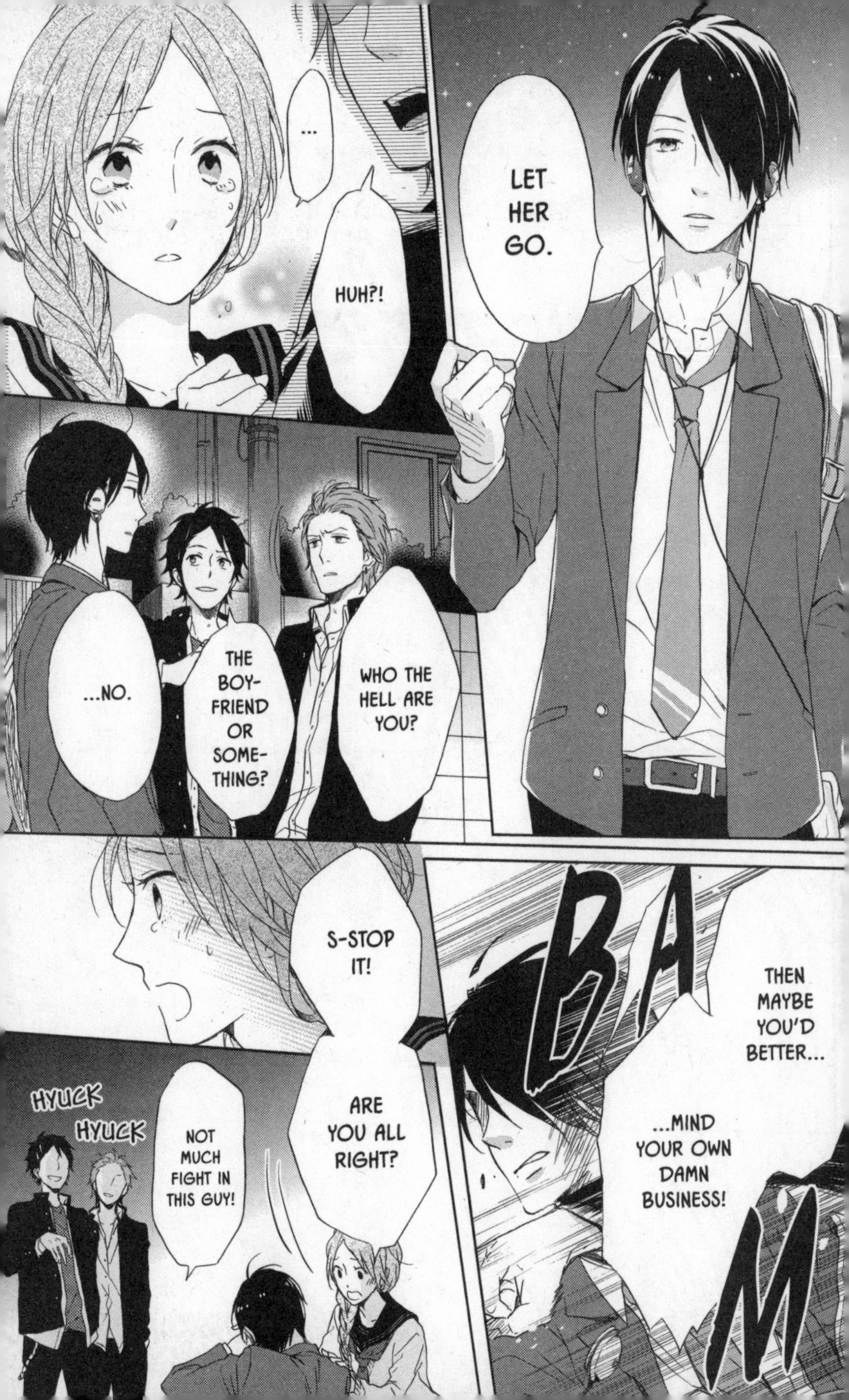
LET HER GO.
...
HUH?!
WHO THE HELL ARE YOU?
THE BOY-FRIEND OR SOME-THING?
...NO.
BAM
THEN MAYBE YOU'D BETTER...
...MIND YOUR OWN DAMN BUSINESS!
S-STOP IT!
ARE YOU ALL RIGHT?
NOT MUCH FIGHT IN THIS GUY!
HYUCK HYUCK

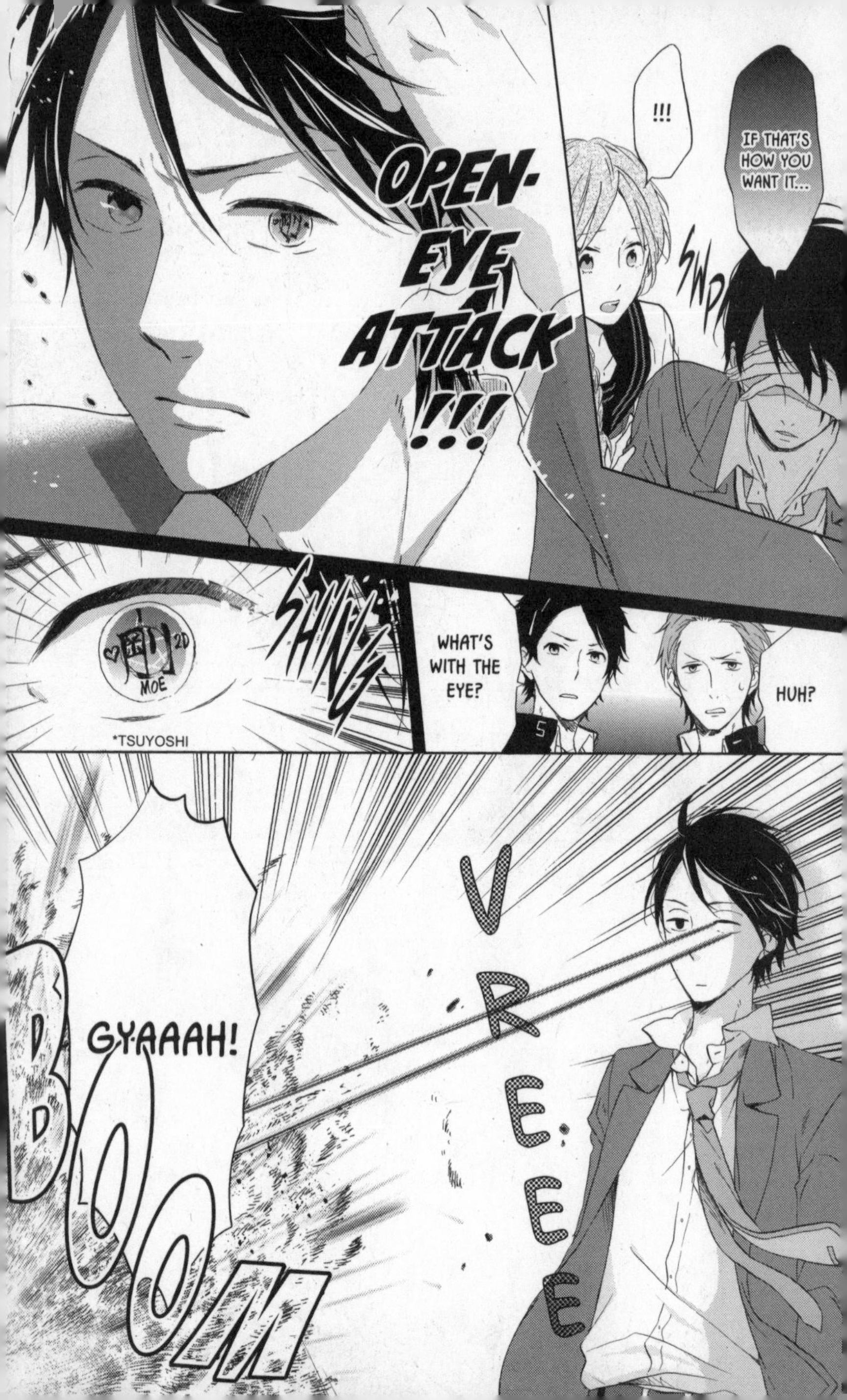
!!!
IF THAT'S HOW YOU WANT IT...
SWP
OPEN-EYE ATTACK!!!
WHAT'S WITH THE EYE?
HUH?
SHING
2D
MOE
*TSUYOSHI
VREEE
GYAAAH!
BOOM
DD

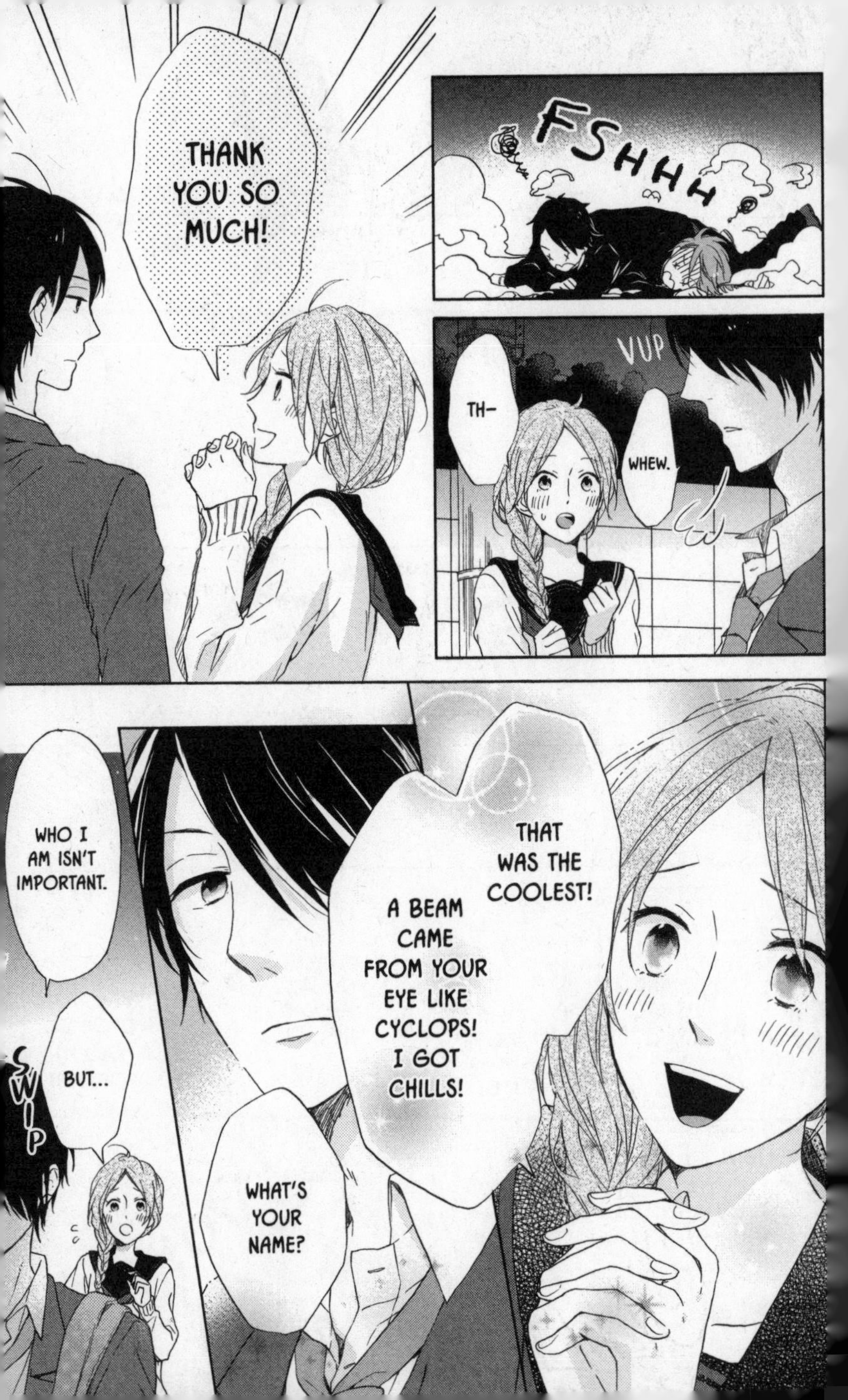
FSHHH
VUP
TH-
WHEW.
THANK YOU SO MUCH!
THAT WAS THE COOLEST!
A BEAM CAME FROM YOUR EYE LIKE CYCLOPS! I GOT CHILLS!
WHO I AM ISN'T IMPORTANT.
BUT...
SWIP
WHAT'S YOUR NAME?

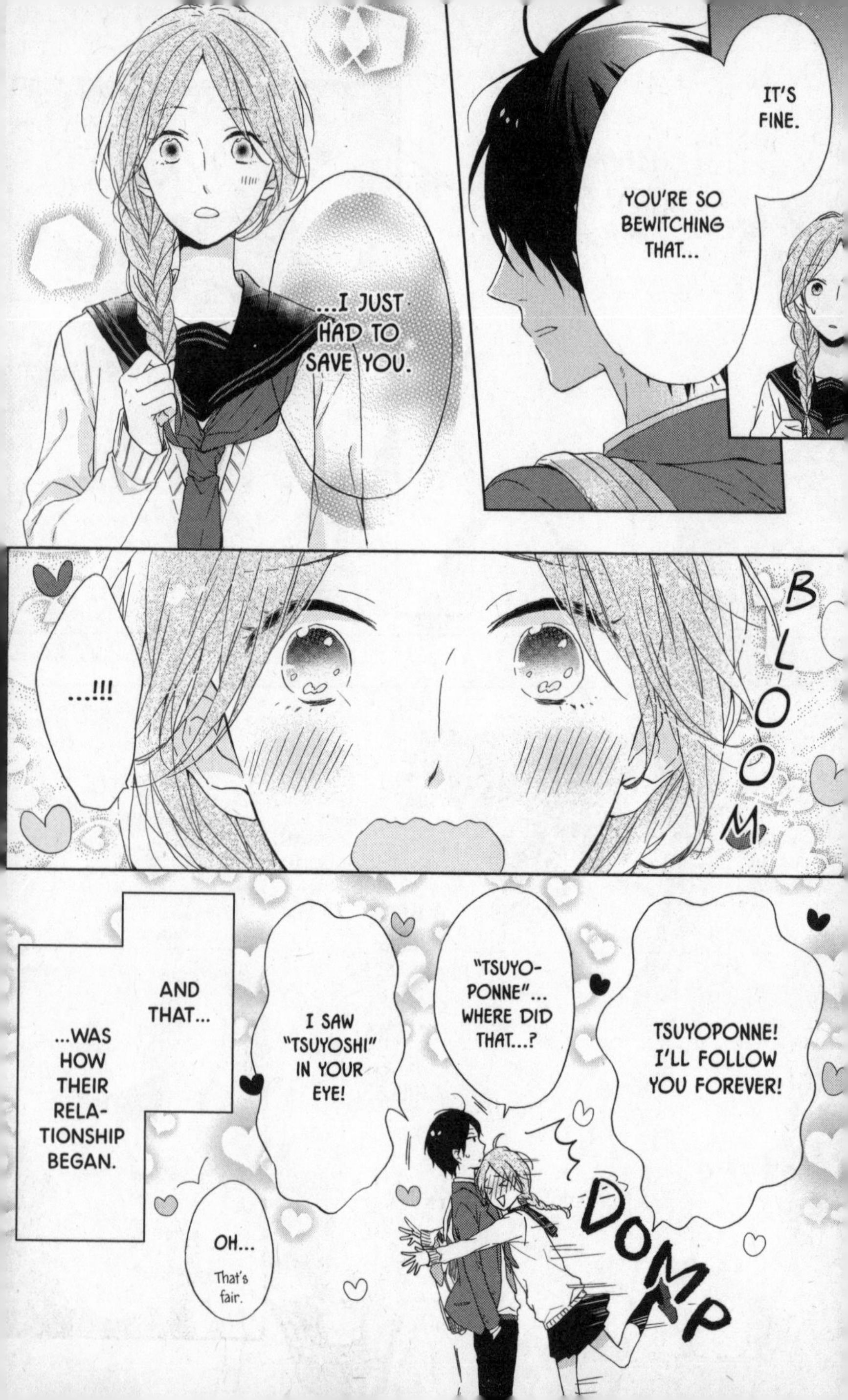
IT'S FINE.
YOU'RE SO BEWITCHING THAT...
...I JUST HAD TO SAVE YOU.
BLOOM
...!!!
TSUYOPONNE! I'LL FOLLOW YOU FOREVER!
DOMP
"TSUYO-PONNE"... WHERE DID THAT...?
I SAW "TSUYOSHI" IN YOUR EYE!
OH...
That's fair.
AND THAT...
...WAS HOW THEIR RELA-TIONSHIP BEGAN.

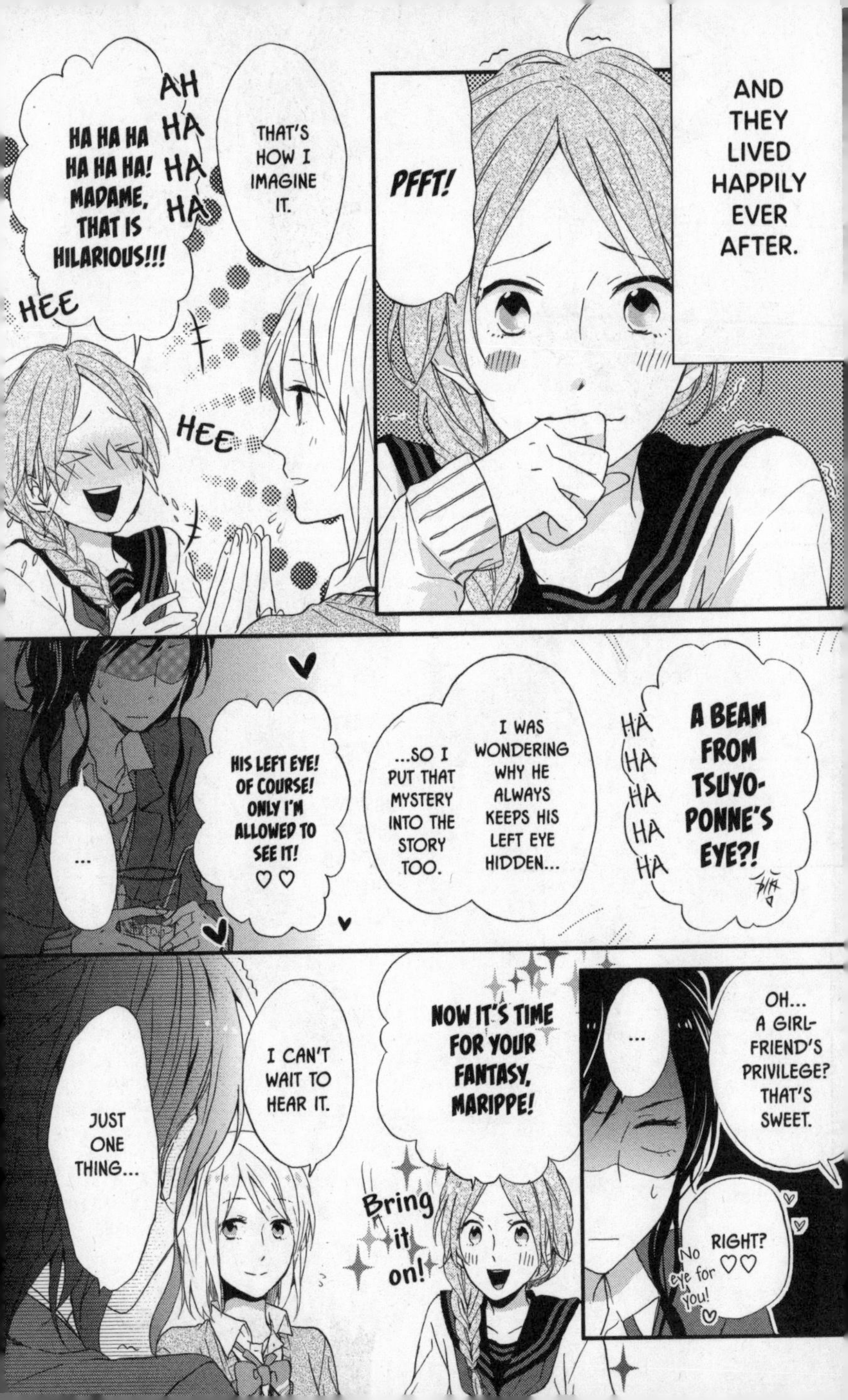
AND THEY LIVED HAPPILY EVER AFTER.
PFFT!
THAT'S HOW I IMAGINE IT.
AH HA HA HA
HA HA HA HA HA HA! MADAME, THAT IS HILARIOUS!!!
HEE
HEE
HA HA HA HA HA
A BEAM FROM TSUYO-PONNE'S EYE?!
I WAS WONDERING WHY HE ALWAYS KEEPS HIS LEFT EYE HIDDEN...
...SO I PUT THAT MYSTERY INTO THE STORY TOO.
HIS LEFT EYE! OF COURSE! ONLY I'M ALLOWED TO SEE IT! ♡♡
...
OH... A GIRL-FRIEND'S PRIVILEGE? THAT'S SWEET.
...
RIGHT? ♡♡
No eye for you!
NOW IT'S TIME FOR YOUR FANTASY, MARIPPE!
Bring it on!
I CAN'T WAIT TO HEAR IT.
JUST ONE THING...

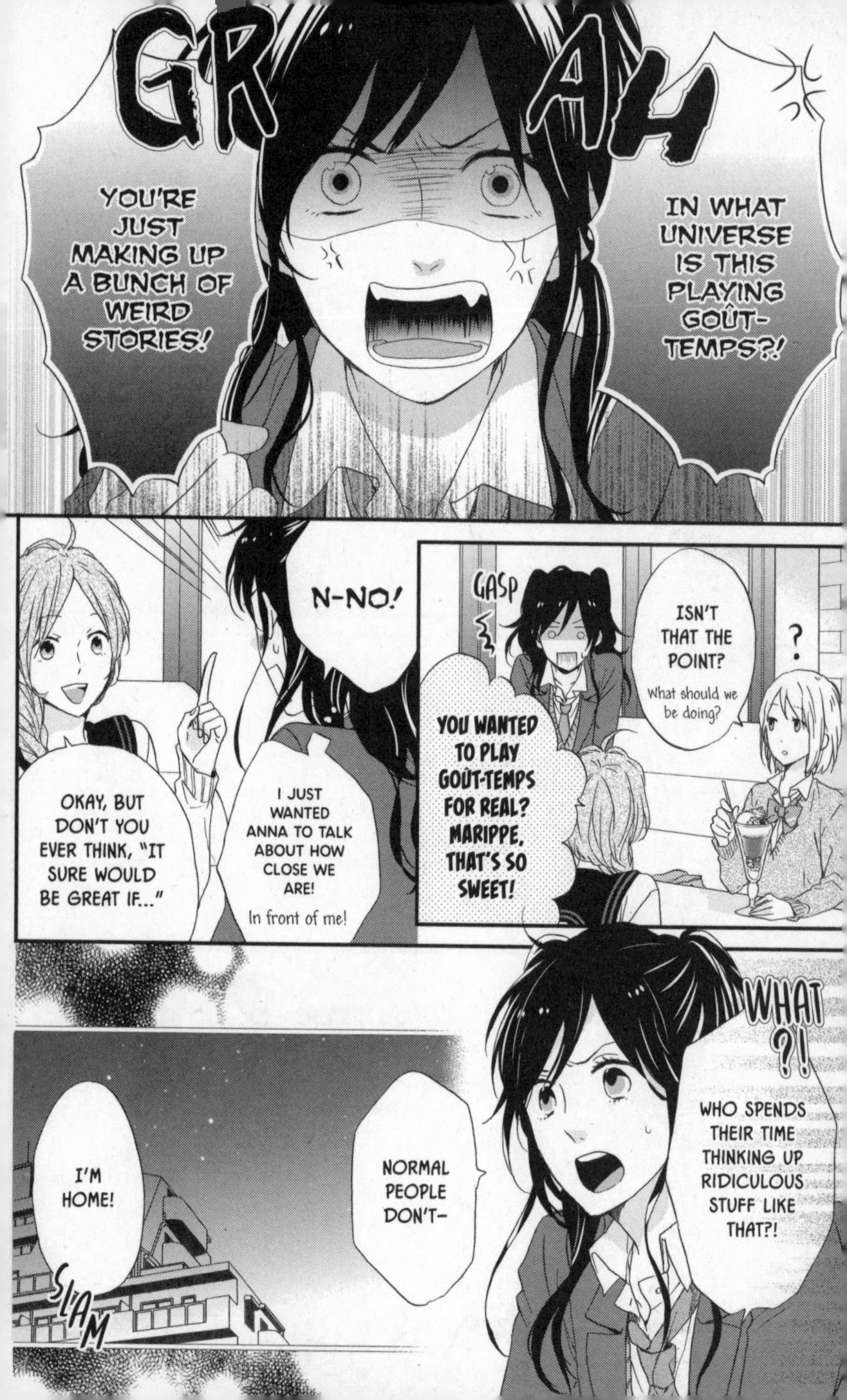

GRAH
IN WHAT UNIVERSE IS THIS PLAYING GOÛT-TEMPS?!
YOU'RE JUST MAKING UP A BUNCH OF WEIRD STORIES!
ISN'T THAT THE POINT?
What should we be doing?
?
GASP
YOU WANTED TO PLAY GOÛT-TEMPS FOR REAL? MARIPPE, THAT'S SO SWEET!
N-NO!
I JUST WANTED ANNA TO TALK ABOUT HOW CLOSE WE ARE!
In front of me!
OKAY, BUT DON'T YOU EVER THINK, "IT SURE WOULD BE GREAT IF..."
WHAT?!
WHO SPENDS THEIR TIME THINKING UP RIDICULOUS STUFF LIKE THAT?!
NORMAL PEOPLE DON'T-
I'M HOME!
SLAM

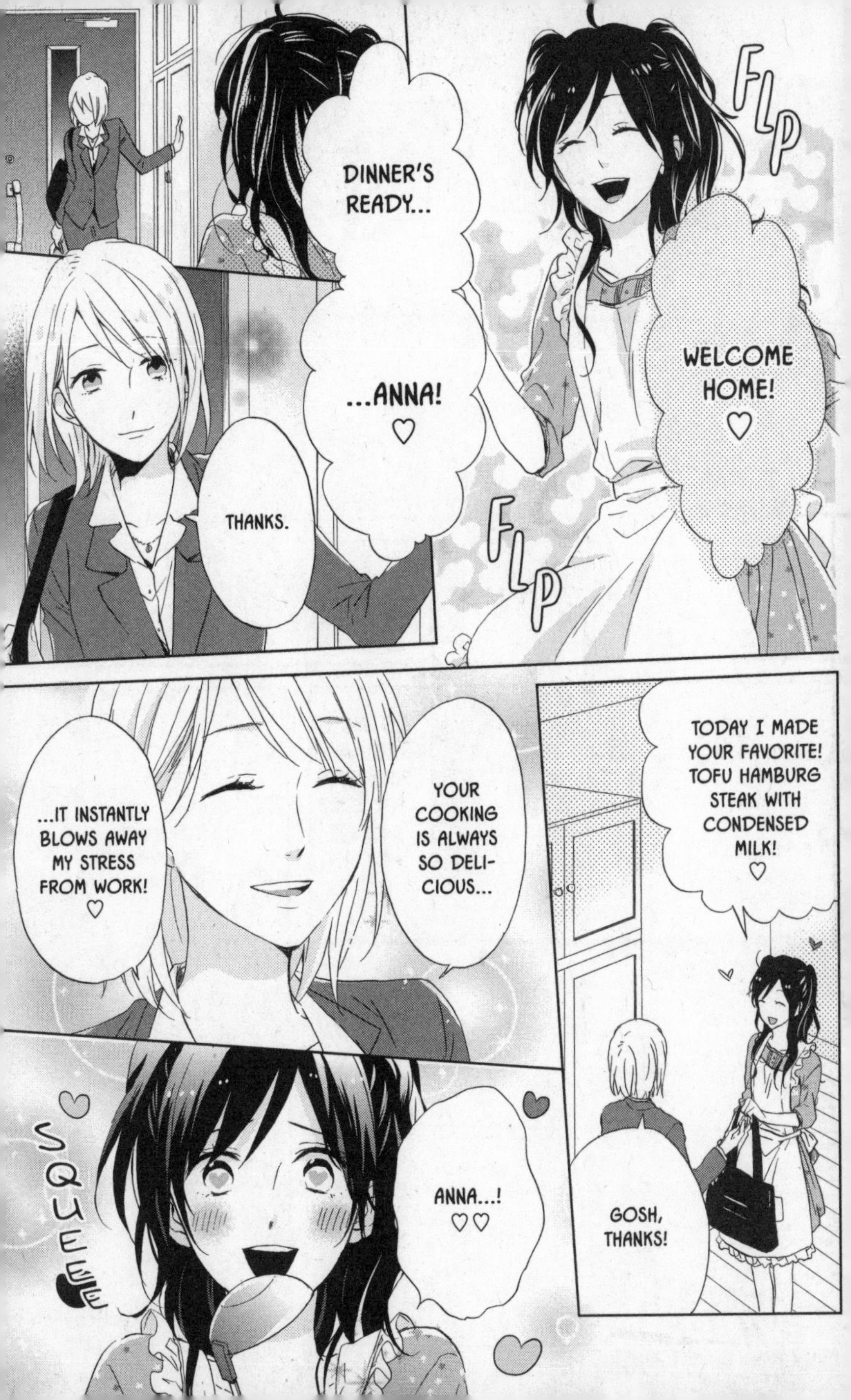
FLP
WELCOME HOME! ♡
FLP
DINNER'S READY... ...ANNA! ♡
THANKS.
TODAY I MADE YOUR FAVORITE! TOFU HAMBURG STEAK WITH CONDENSED MILK! ♡
GOSH, THANKS!
YOUR COOKING IS ALWAYS SO DELI-CIOUS...
...IT INSTANTLY BLOWS AWAY MY STRESS FROM WORK! ♡
ANNA...! ♡♡
SQUEEEE

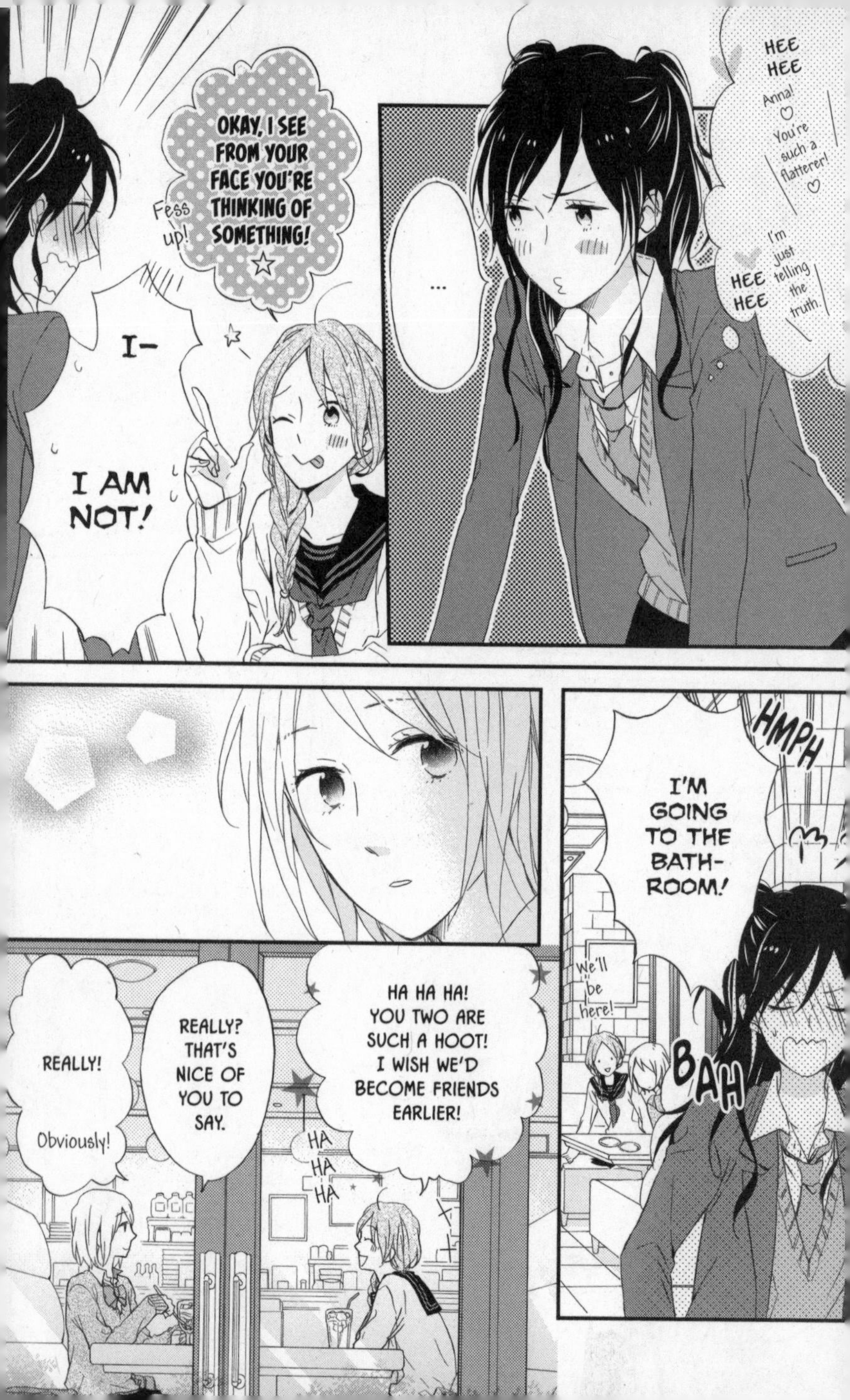
HEE HEE
Anna! ♡ You're such a flatterer! ♡
HEE HEE
I'm just telling the truth.
...
OKAY, I SEE FROM YOUR FACE YOU'RE THINKING OF SOMETHING! ☆
Fess up!
I–
I AM NOT!
HMPH
I'M GOING TO THE BATH-ROOM!
We'll be here!
BAH
HA HA HA! YOU TWO ARE SUCH A HOOT! I WISH WE'D BECOME FRIENDS EARLIER!
HA HA HA
REALLY? THAT'S NICE OF YOU TO SAY.
REALLY!
Obviously!

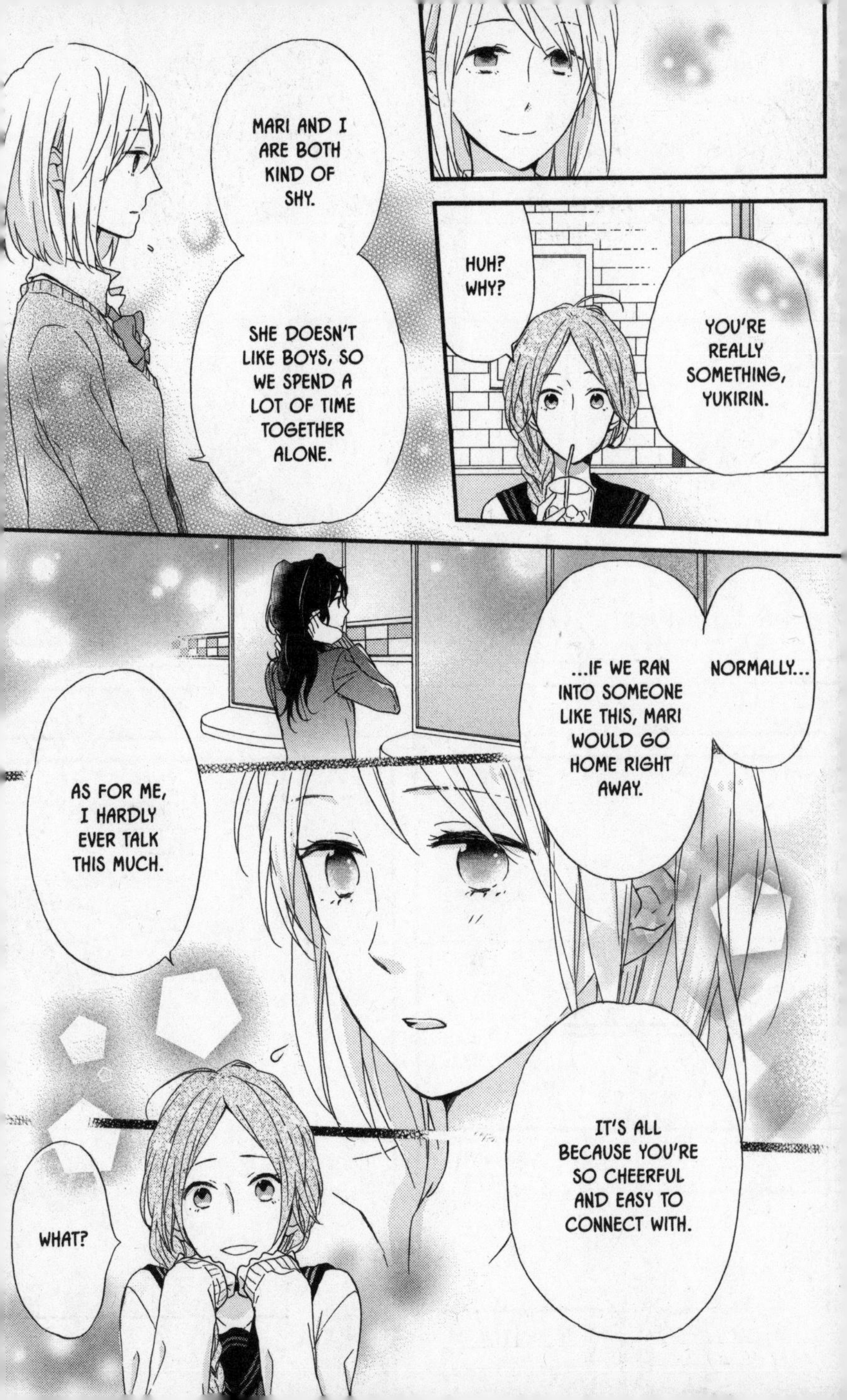
YOU'RE REALLY SOMETHING, YUKIRIN.
HUH? WHY?
MARI AND I ARE BOTH KIND OF SHY.
SHE DOESN'T LIKE BOYS, SO WE SPEND A LOT OF TIME TOGETHER ALONE.
NORMALLY...
...IF WE RAN INTO SOMEONE LIKE THIS, MARI WOULD GO HOME RIGHT AWAY.
AS FOR ME, I HARDLY EVER TALK THIS MUCH.
IT'S ALL BECAUSE YOU'RE SO CHEERFUL AND EASY TO CONNECT WITH.
WHAT?

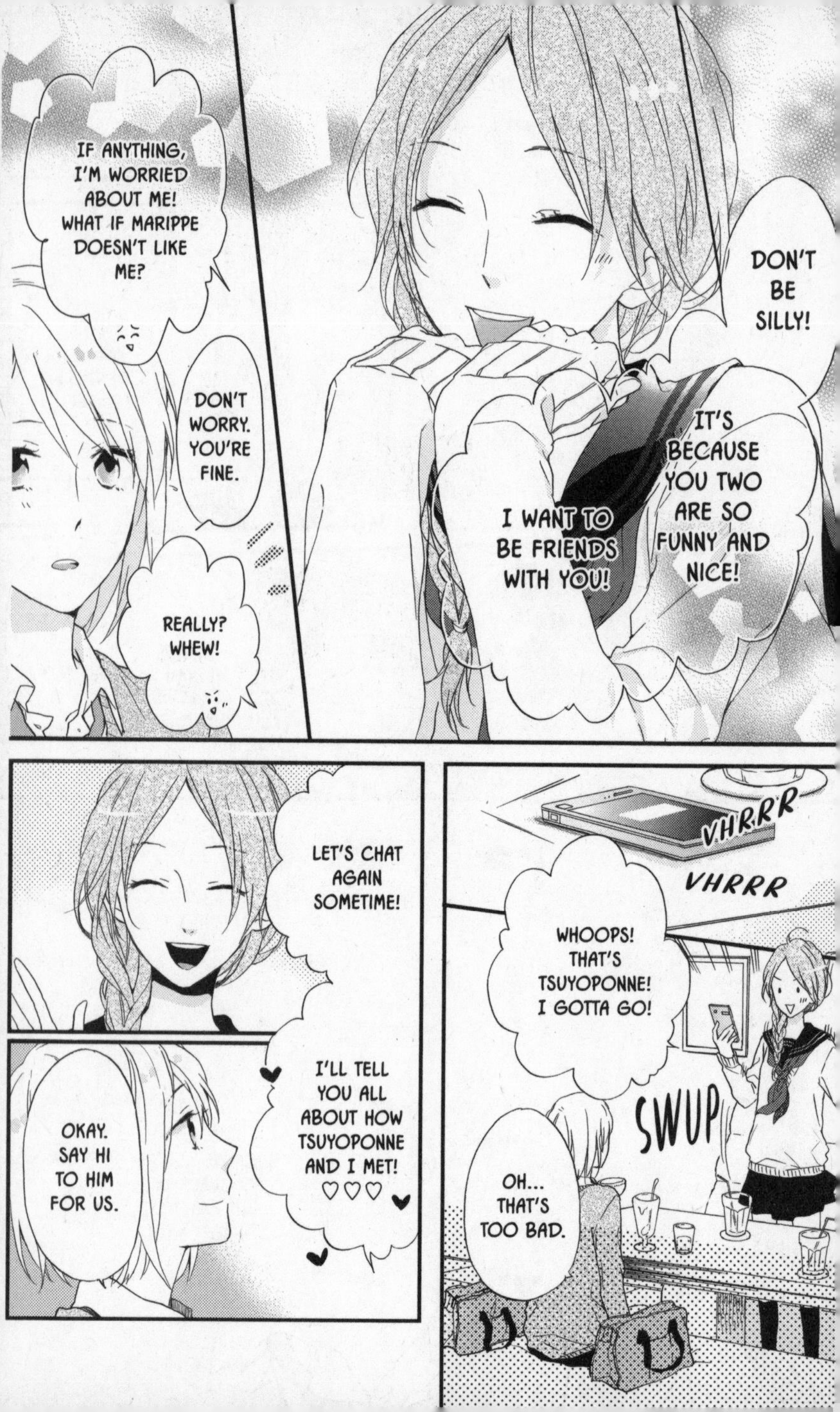
DON'T BE SILLY!
IT'S BECAUSE YOU TWO ARE SO FUNNY AND NICE!
I WANT TO BE FRIENDS WITH YOU!
IF ANYTHING, I'M WORRIED ABOUT ME! WHAT IF MARIPPE DOESN'T LIKE ME?
DON'T WORRY. YOU'RE FINE.
REALLY? WHEW!
VHRRR
VHRRR
WHOOPS! THAT'S TSUYOPONNE! I GOTTA GO!
SWUP
OH... THAT'S TOO BAD.
LET'S CHAT AGAIN SOMETIME!
I'LL TELL YOU ALL ABOUT HOW TSUYOPONNE AND I MET! ♡♡♡
OKAY. SAY HI TO HIM FOR US.

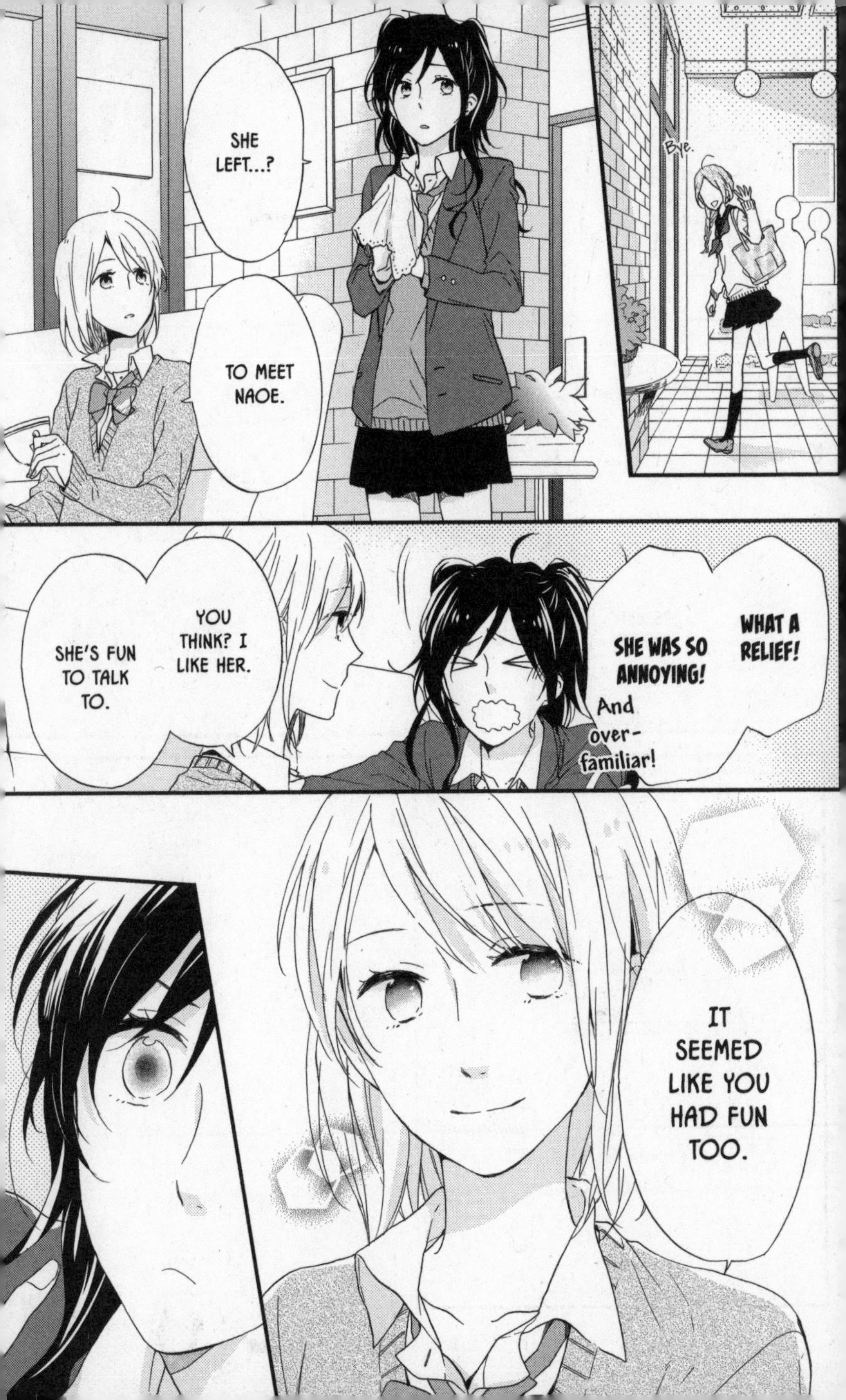

Bye.
SHE LEFT...?
TO MEET NAOE.
WHAT A RELIEF! SHE WAS SO ANNOYING!
And over-familiar!
YOU THINK? I LIKE HER. SHE'S FUN TO TALK TO.
IT SEEMED LIKE YOU HAD FUN TOO.

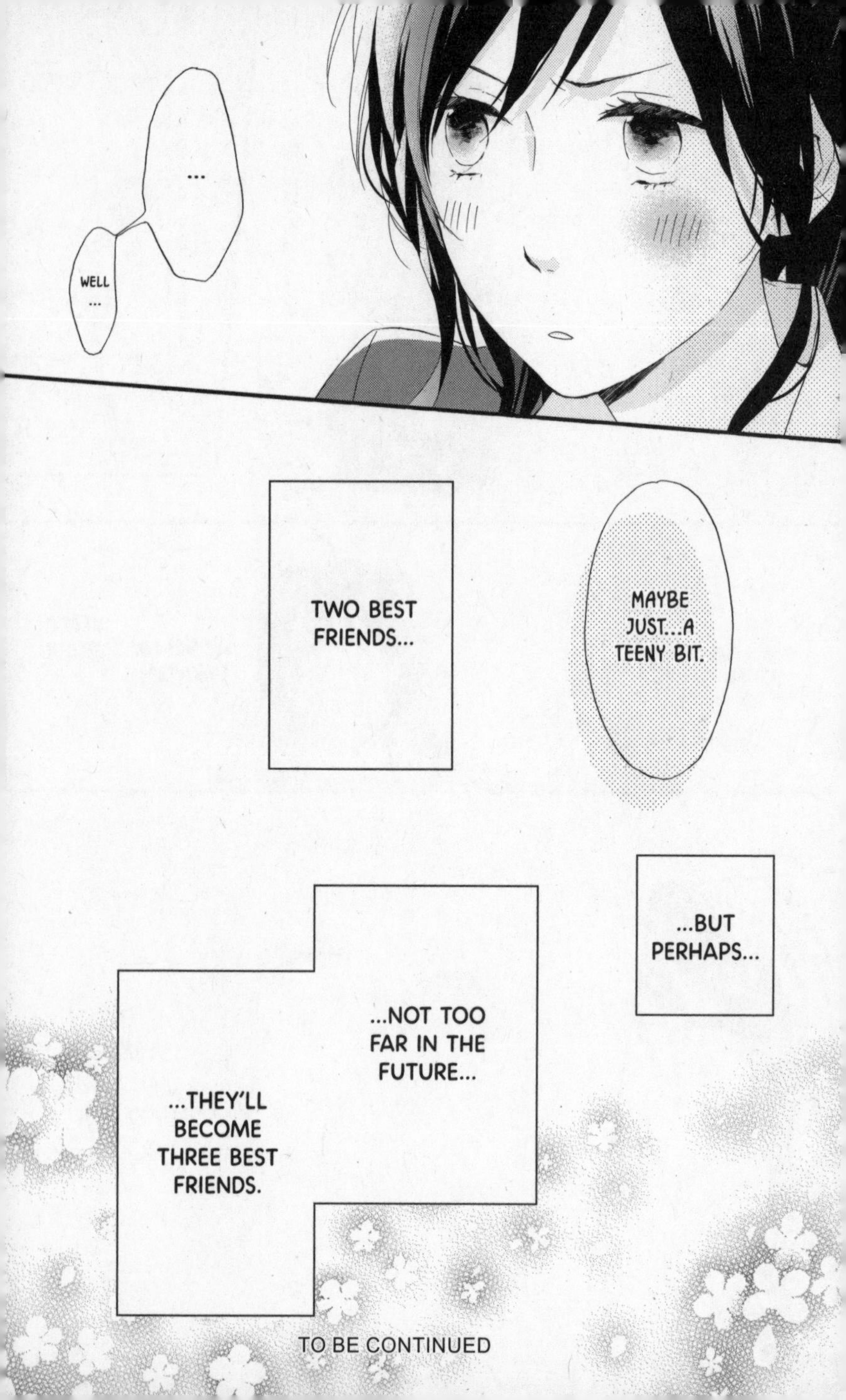
...
WELL ...
MAYBE JUST...A TEENY BIT.
TWO BEST FRIENDS...
...BUT PERHAPS...
...NOT TOO FAR IN THE FUTURE...
...THEY'LL BECOME THREE BEST FRIENDS.
TO BE CONTINUED

Rainbow
Days

■ ■ ■ ■ ■ ■ ■

## NATSUKI HASHIBA

Height: 5'7"
Weight: 119 lb
Birthday: August 7
Blood Type: A
Family: Mother, two older sisters
Image Color: Yellow

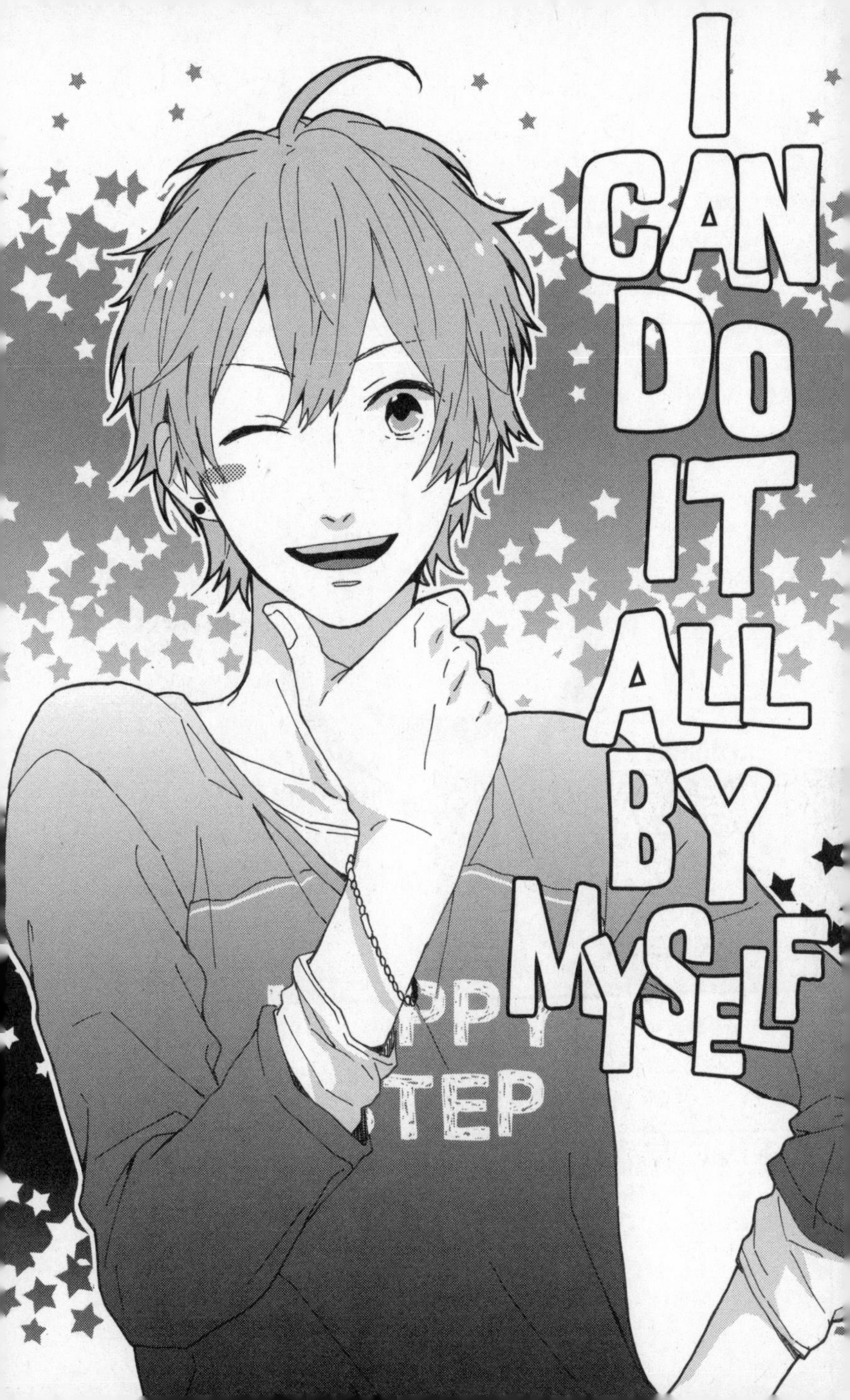
I CAN DO IT ALL BY MYSELF
PPY
TEP

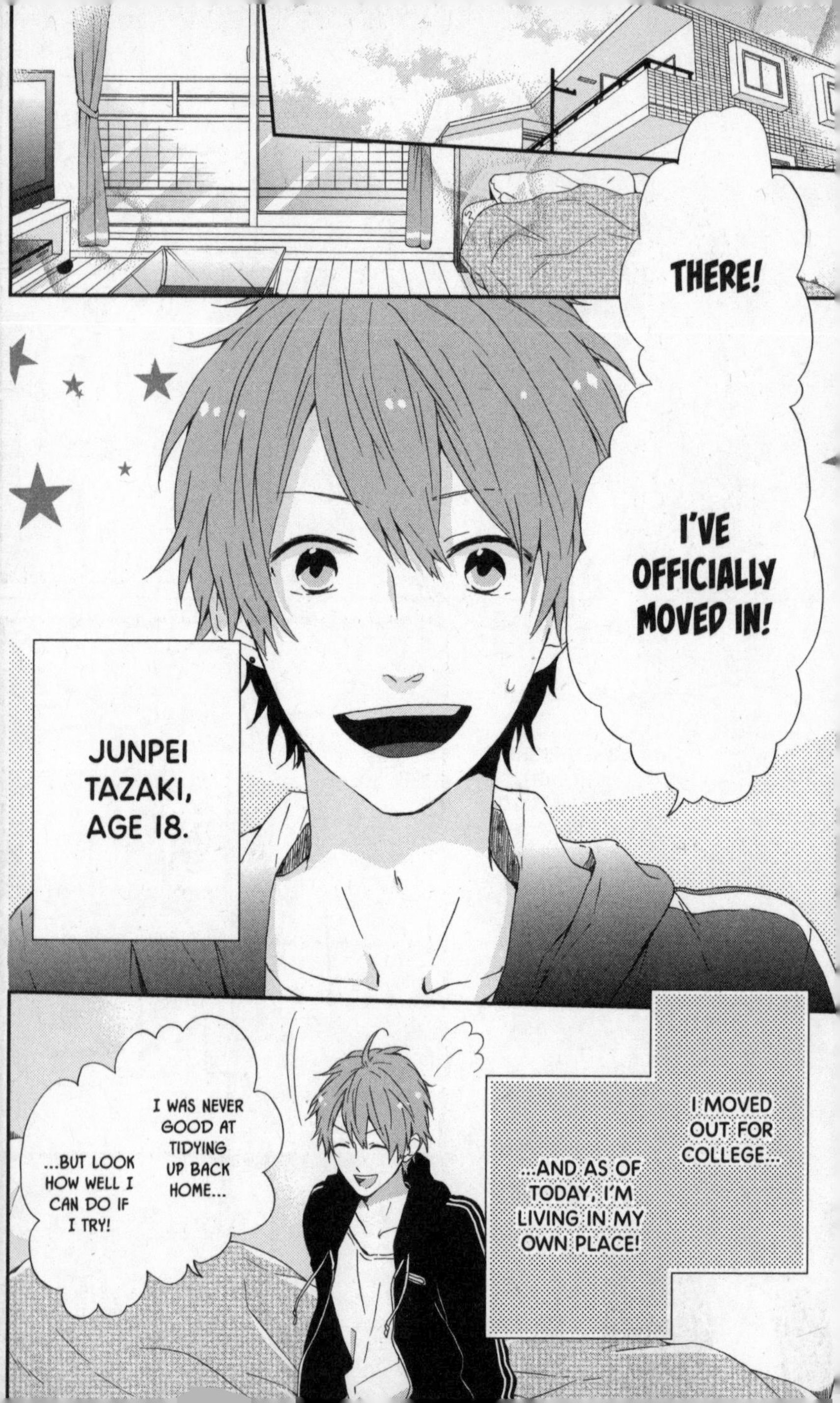
THERE!
I'VE OFFICIALLY MOVED IN!
JUNPEI TAZAKI, AGE 18.
I MOVED OUT FOR COLLEGE...
...AND AS OF TODAY, I'M LIVING IN MY OWN PLACE!
I WAS NEVER GOOD AT TIDYING UP BACK HOME...
...BUT LOOK HOW WELL I CAN DO IF I TRY!

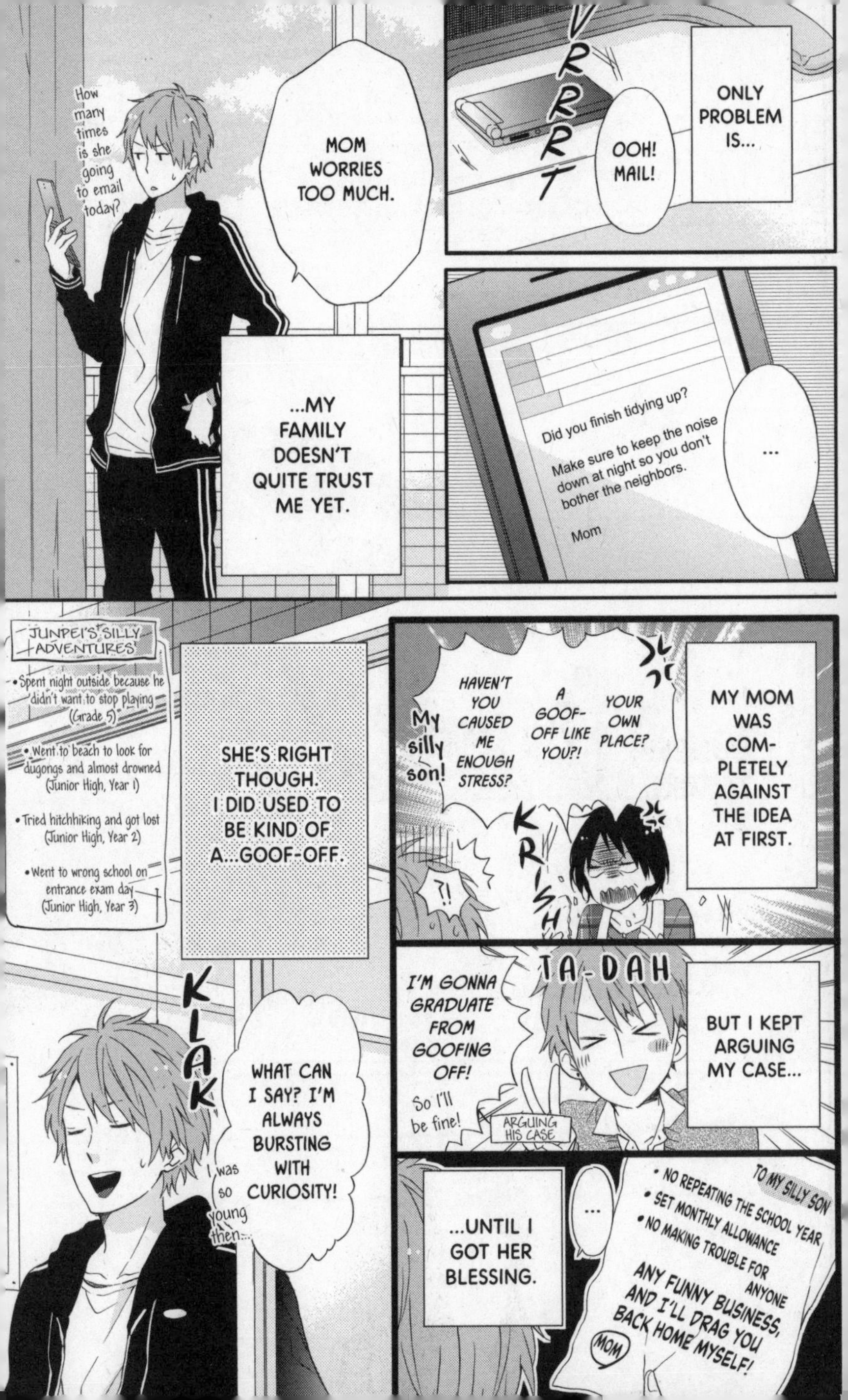
ONLY PROBLEM IS...
OOH! MAIL!
VRRRT
Did you finish tidying up?
Make sure to keep the noise down at night so you don't bother the neighbors.
Mom
...
MOM WORRIES TOO MUCH.
...MY FAMILY DOESN'T QUITE TRUST ME YET.
How many times is she going to email today?
MY MOM WAS COMPLETELY AGAINST THE IDEA AT FIRST.
YOUR OWN PLACE?
A GOOF-OFF LIKE YOU?!
HAVEN'T YOU CAUSED ME ENOUGH STRESS?
My silly son!
KRISH
?!
BUT I KEPT ARGUING MY CASE...
TA-DAH
I'M GONNA GRADUATE FROM GOOFING OFF!
So I'll be fine!
ARGUING HIS CASE
TO MY SILLY SON
• NO REPEATING THE SCHOOL YEAR
• SET MONTHLY ALLOWANCE
• NO MAKING TROUBLE FOR ANYONE
ANY FUNNY BUSINESS, AND I'LL DRAG YOU BACK HOME MYSELF!
MOM
...
...UNTIL I GOT HER BLESSING.
SHE'S RIGHT THOUGH. I DID USED TO BE KIND OF A...GOOF-OFF.
JUNPEI'S SILLY ADVENTURES
• Spent night outside because he didn't want to stop playing (Grade 5)
• Went to beach to look for dugongs and almost drowned (Junior High, Year 1)
• Tried hitchhiking and got lost (Junior High, Year 2)
• Went to wrong school on entrance exam day (Junior High, Year 3)
KLAK
WHAT CAN I SAY? I'M ALWAYS BURSTING WITH CURIOSITY!
I was so young then...

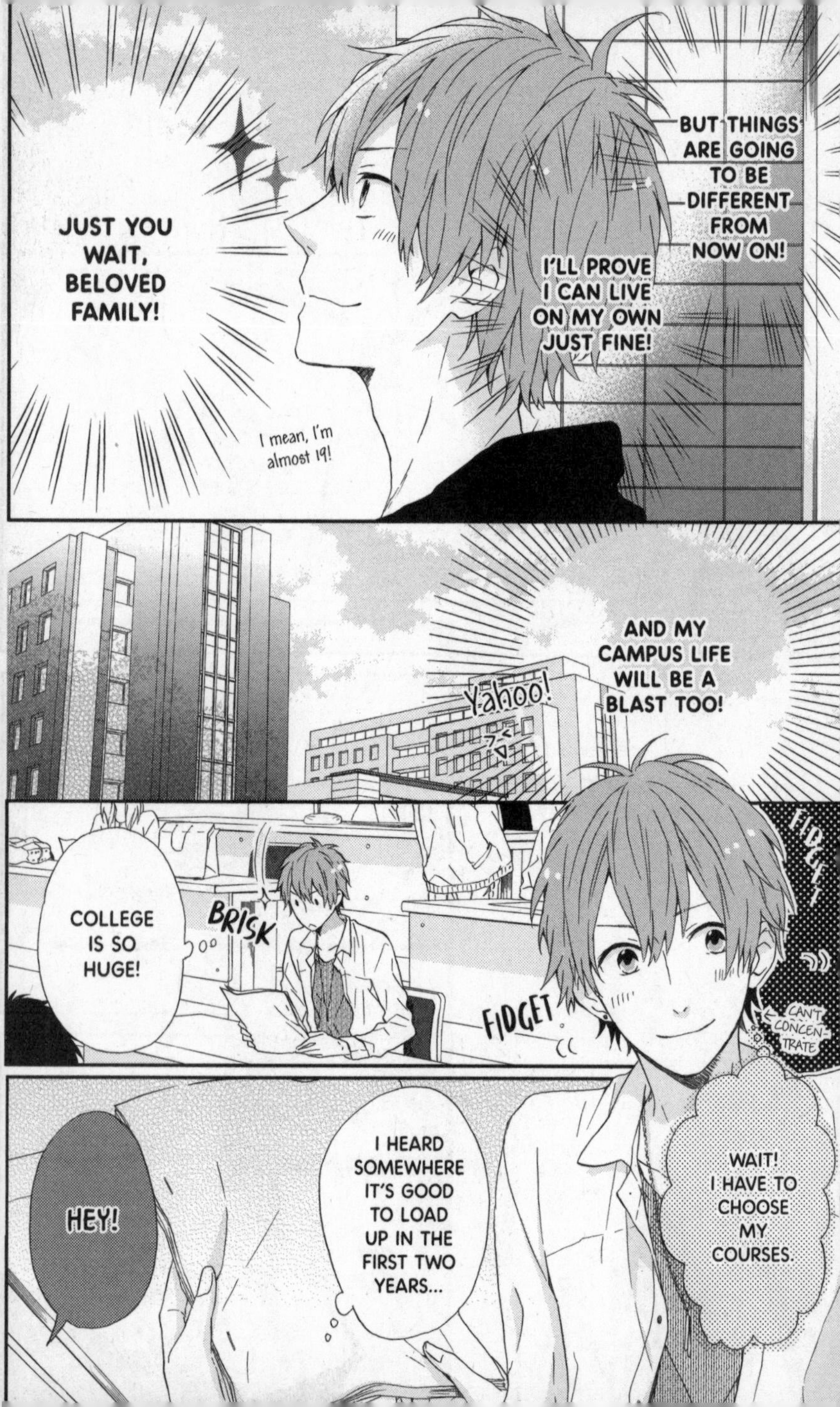
BUT THINGS ARE GOING TO BE DIFFERENT FROM NOW ON!
I'LL PROVE I CAN LIVE ON MY OWN JUST FINE!
JUST YOU WAIT, BELOVED FAMILY!
I mean, I'm almost 19!
AND MY CAMPUS LIFE WILL BE A BLAST TOO!
Yahoo!
FIDGET
CAN'T CONCENTRATE
FIDGET
BRISK
COLLEGE IS SO HUGE!
WAIT! I HAVE TO CHOOSE MY COURSES.
I HEARD SOMEWHERE IT'S GOOD TO LOAD UP IN THE FIRST TWO YEARS...
HEY!

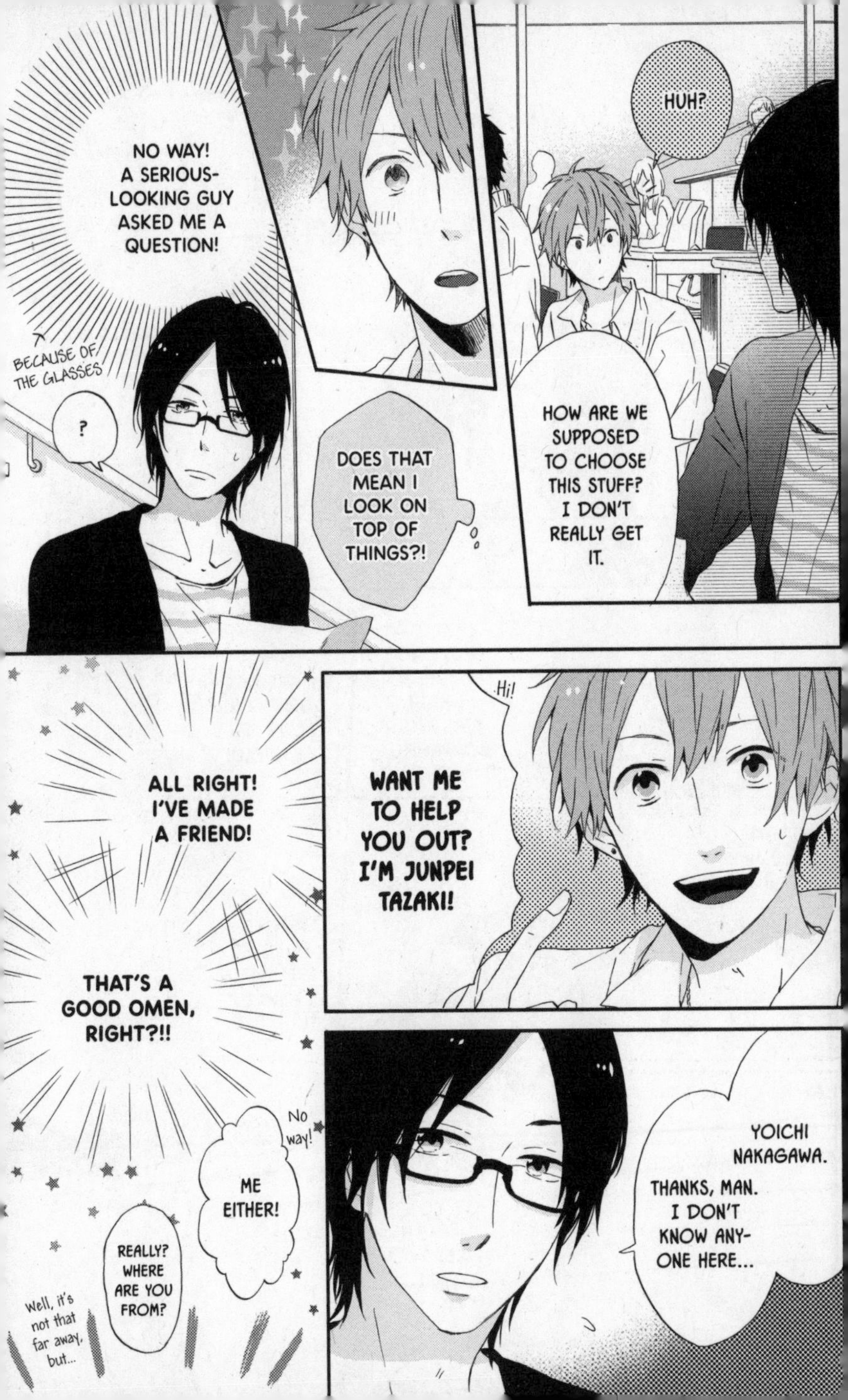
HUH?
HOW ARE WE SUPPOSED TO CHOOSE THIS STUFF? I DON'T REALLY GET IT.
NO WAY! A SERIOUS-LOOKING GUY ASKED ME A QUESTION!
DOES THAT MEAN I LOOK ON TOP OF THINGS?!
?
BECAUSE OF THE GLASSES
Hi!
WANT ME TO HELP YOU OUT? I'M JUNPEI TAZAKI!
YOICHI NAKAGAWA.
THANKS, MAN. I DON'T KNOW ANY-ONE HERE...
ALL RIGHT! I'VE MADE A FRIEND!
THAT'S A GOOD OMEN, RIGHT?!!
No way!
ME EITHER!
REALLY? WHERE ARE YOU FROM?
Well, it's not that far away, but...

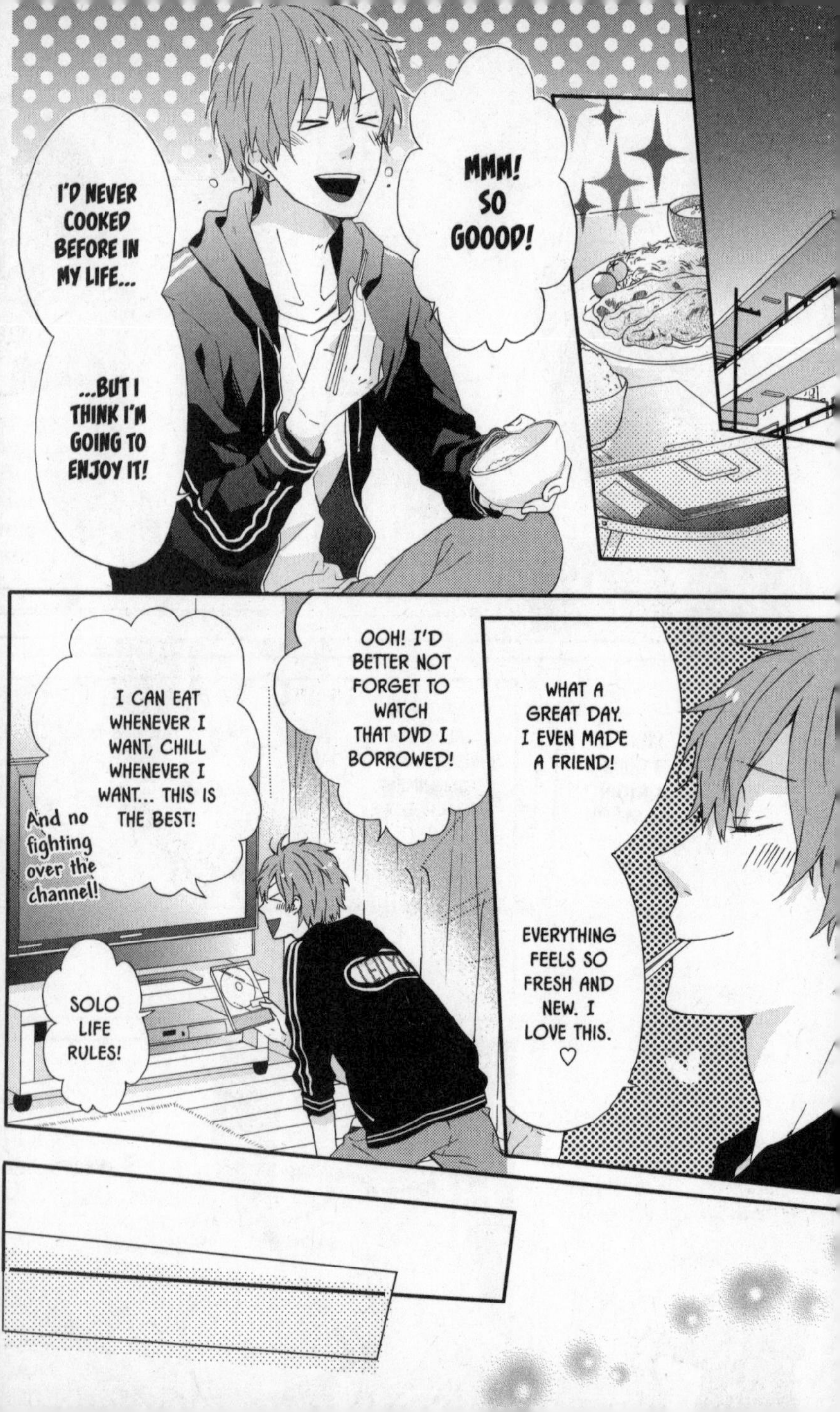
MMM! SO GOOOD!
I'D NEVER COOKED BEFORE IN MY LIFE...
...BUT I THINK I'M GOING TO ENJOY IT!
WHAT A GREAT DAY. I EVEN MADE A FRIEND!
EVERYTHING FEELS SO FRESH AND NEW. I LOVE THIS. ♡
OOH! I'D BETTER NOT FORGET TO WATCH THAT DVD I BORROWED!
I CAN EAT WHENEVER I WANT, CHILL WHENEVER I WANT... THIS IS THE BEST!
And no fighting over the channel!
SOLO LIFE RULES!

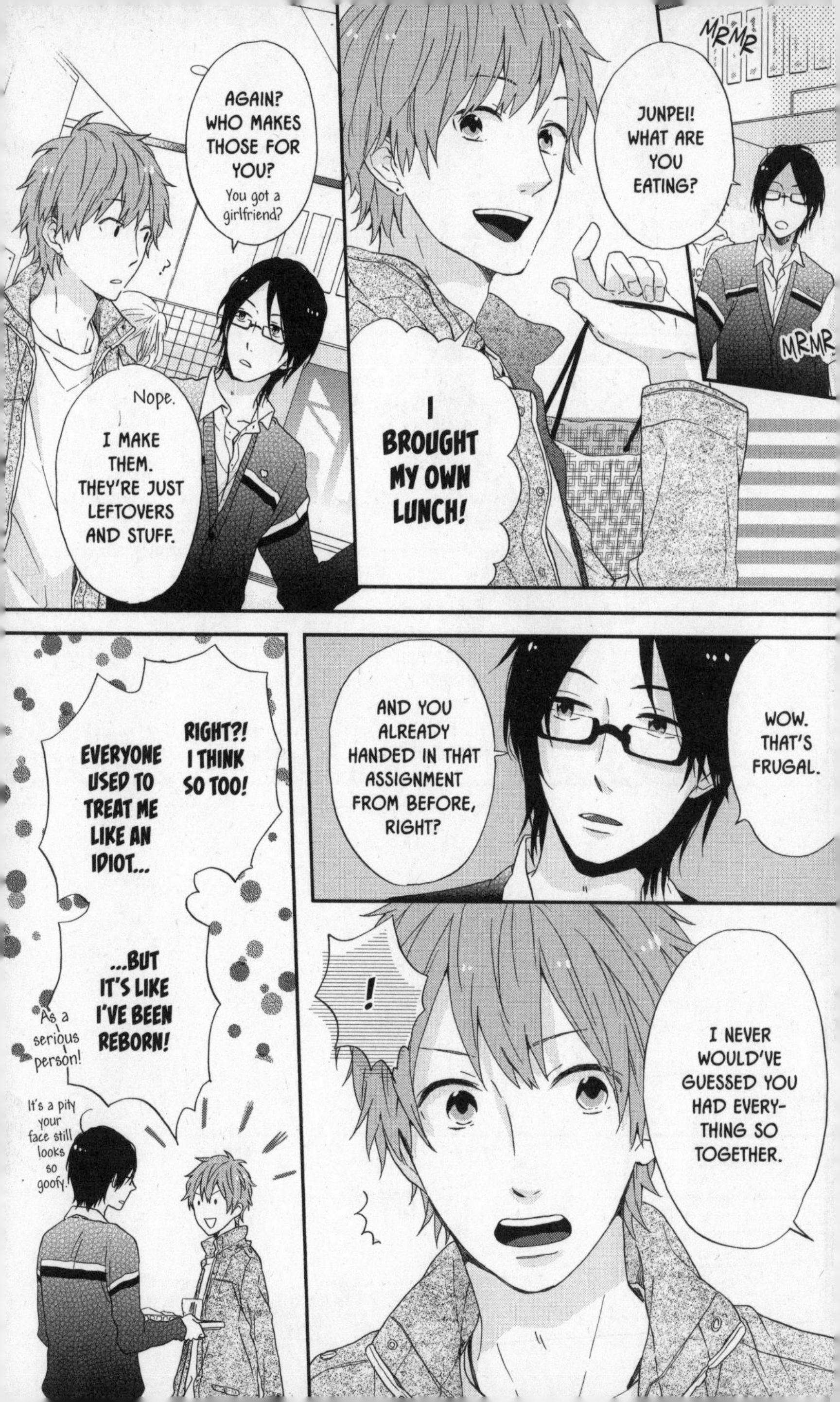
MRMR
JUNPEI! WHAT ARE YOU EATING?
MRMR
I BROUGHT MY OWN LUNCH!
AGAIN? WHO MAKES THOSE FOR YOU? You got a girlfriend?
?
Nope. I MAKE THEM. THEY'RE JUST LEFTOVERS AND STUFF.
WOW. THAT'S FRUGAL.
AND YOU ALREADY HANDED IN THAT ASSIGNMENT FROM BEFORE, RIGHT?
RIGHT?! I THINK SO TOO!
EVERYONE USED TO TREAT ME LIKE AN IDIOT...
...BUT IT'S LIKE I'VE BEEN REBORN!
As a serious person!
It's a pity your face still looks so goofy.
I NEVER WOULD'VE GUESSED YOU HAD EVERY-THING SO TOGETHER.
!

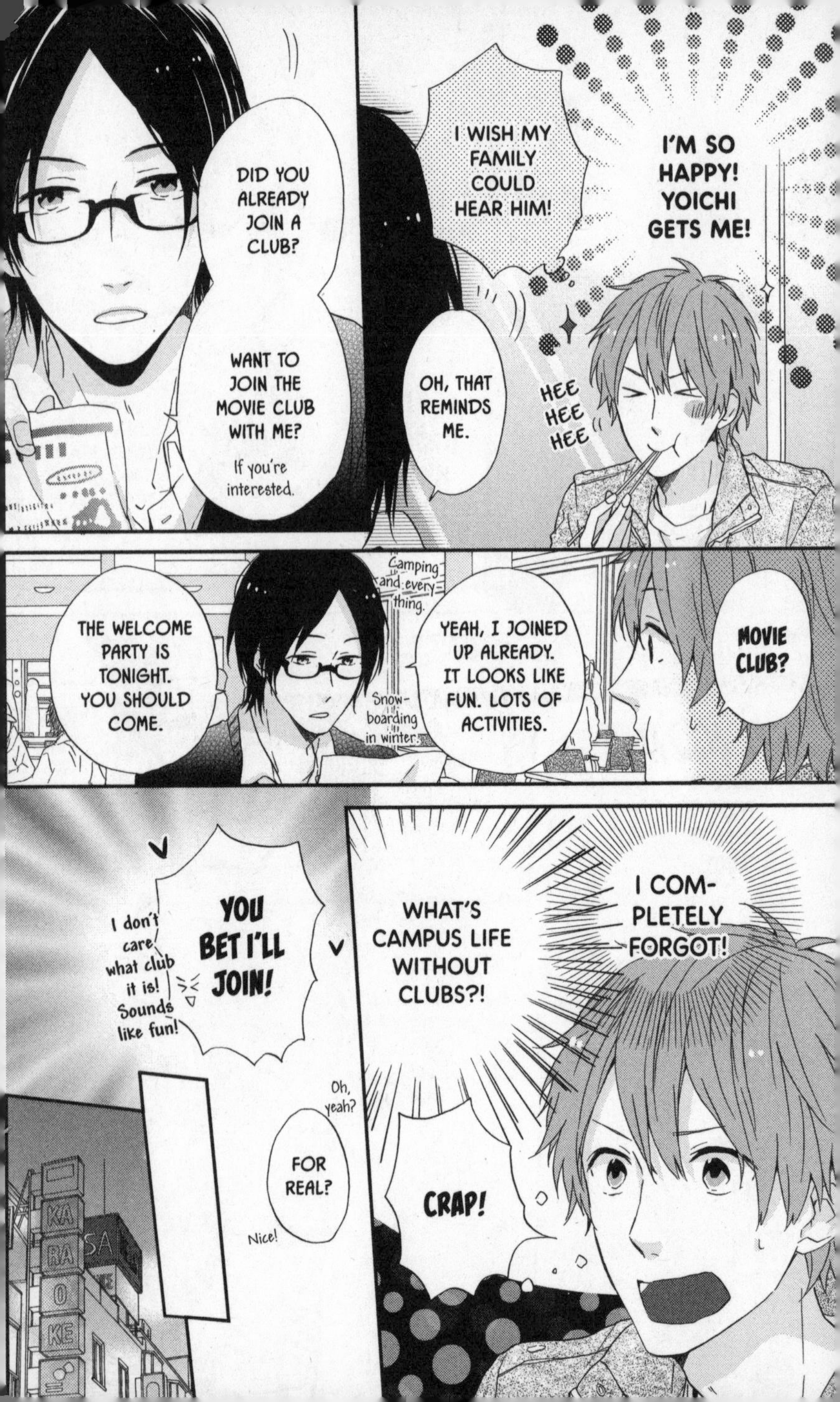
I'M SO HAPPY! YOICHI GETS ME!
I WISH MY FAMILY COULD HEAR HIM!
HEE HEE HEE
OH, THAT REMINDS ME.
DID YOU ALREADY JOIN A CLUB?
WANT TO JOIN THE MOVIE CLUB WITH ME?
If you're interested.
MOVIE CLUB?
YEAH, I JOINED UP ALREADY. IT LOOKS LIKE FUN. LOTS OF ACTIVITIES.
Camping and every-thing.
Snow-boarding in winter.
THE WELCOME PARTY IS TONIGHT. YOU SHOULD COME.
I COM-PLETELY FORGOT!
WHAT'S CAMPUS LIFE WITHOUT CLUBS?!
CRAP!
YOU BET I'LL JOIN!
I don't care what club it is! Sounds like fun!
FOR REAL?
Oh, yeah?
Nice!
KARAOKE

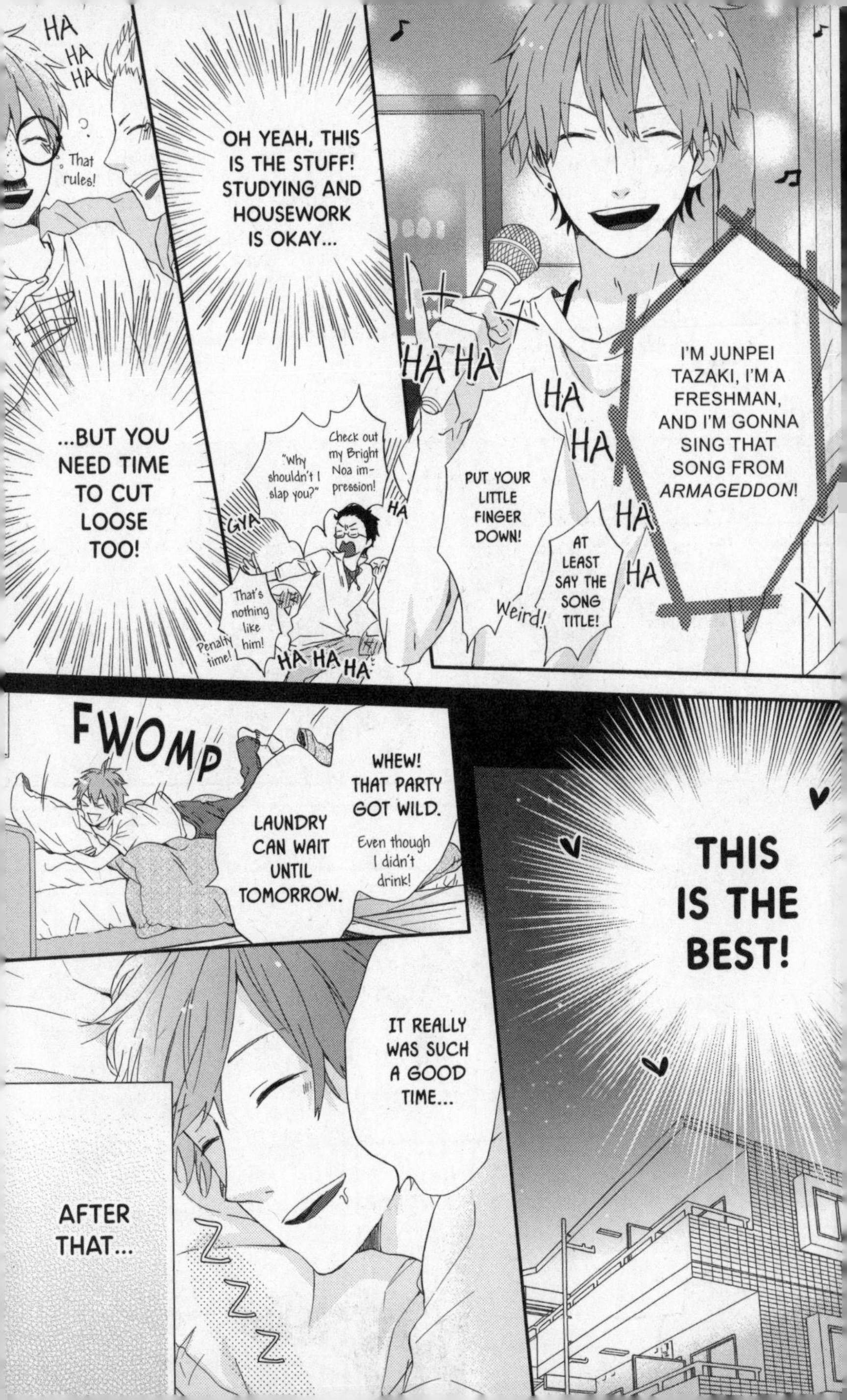
I'M JUNPEI TAZAKI, I'M A FRESHMAN, AND I'M GONNA SING THAT SONG FROM *ARMAGEDDON*!
HA HA HA HA HA HA
AT LEAST SAY THE SONG TITLE!
PUT YOUR LITTLE FINGER DOWN!
Weird!
OH YEAH, THIS IS THE STUFF! STUDYING AND HOUSEWORK IS OKAY...
HA HA HA
That rules!
...BUT YOU NEED TIME TO CUT LOOSE TOO!
Check out my Bright Noa impression!
"Why shouldn't I slap you?"
HA
GYA
That's nothing like him!
Penalty time!
HA HA HA
THIS IS THE BEST!
WHEW! THAT PARTY GOT WILD.
Even though I didn't drink!
LAUNDRY CAN WAIT UNTIL TOMORROW.
FWOMP
IT REALLY WAS SUCH A GOOD TIME...
Z Z Z
AFTER THAT...

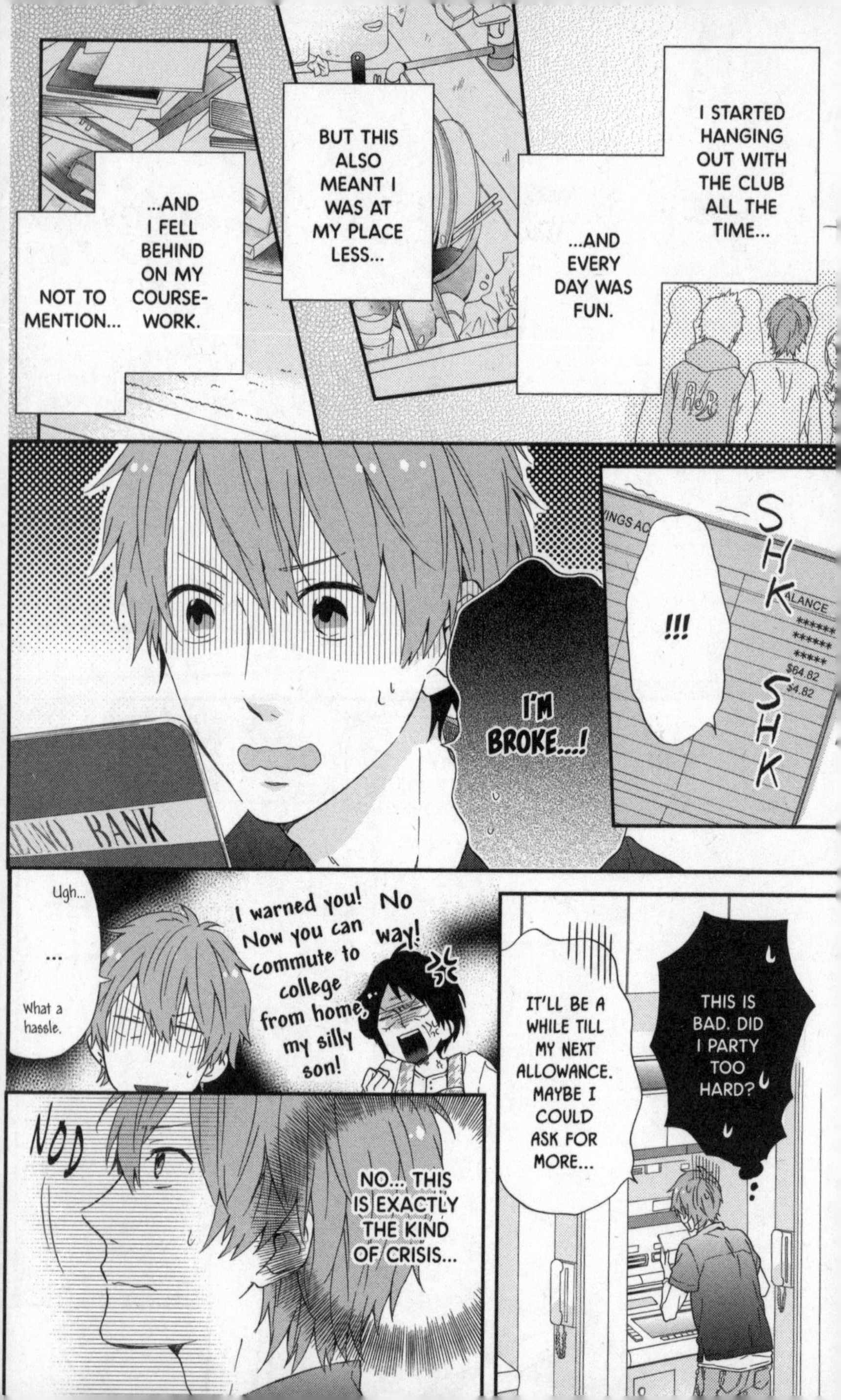

I STARTED HANGING OUT WITH THE CLUB ALL THE TIME...
...AND EVERY DAY WAS FUN.
BUT THIS ALSO MEANT I WAS AT MY PLACE LESS...
...AND I FELL BEHIND ON MY COURSE-WORK.
NOT TO MENTION...
SHK
SHK
!!!
BALANCE
$64.82
$4.82
I'M BROKE...!
BANK
THIS IS BAD. DID I PARTY TOO HARD?
IT'LL BE A WHILE TILL MY NEXT ALLOWANCE. MAYBE I COULD ASK FOR MORE...
No way!
I warned you! Now you can commute to college from home, my silly son!
Ugh...
...
What a hassle.
NOD
NO... THIS IS EXACTLY THE KIND OF CRISIS...

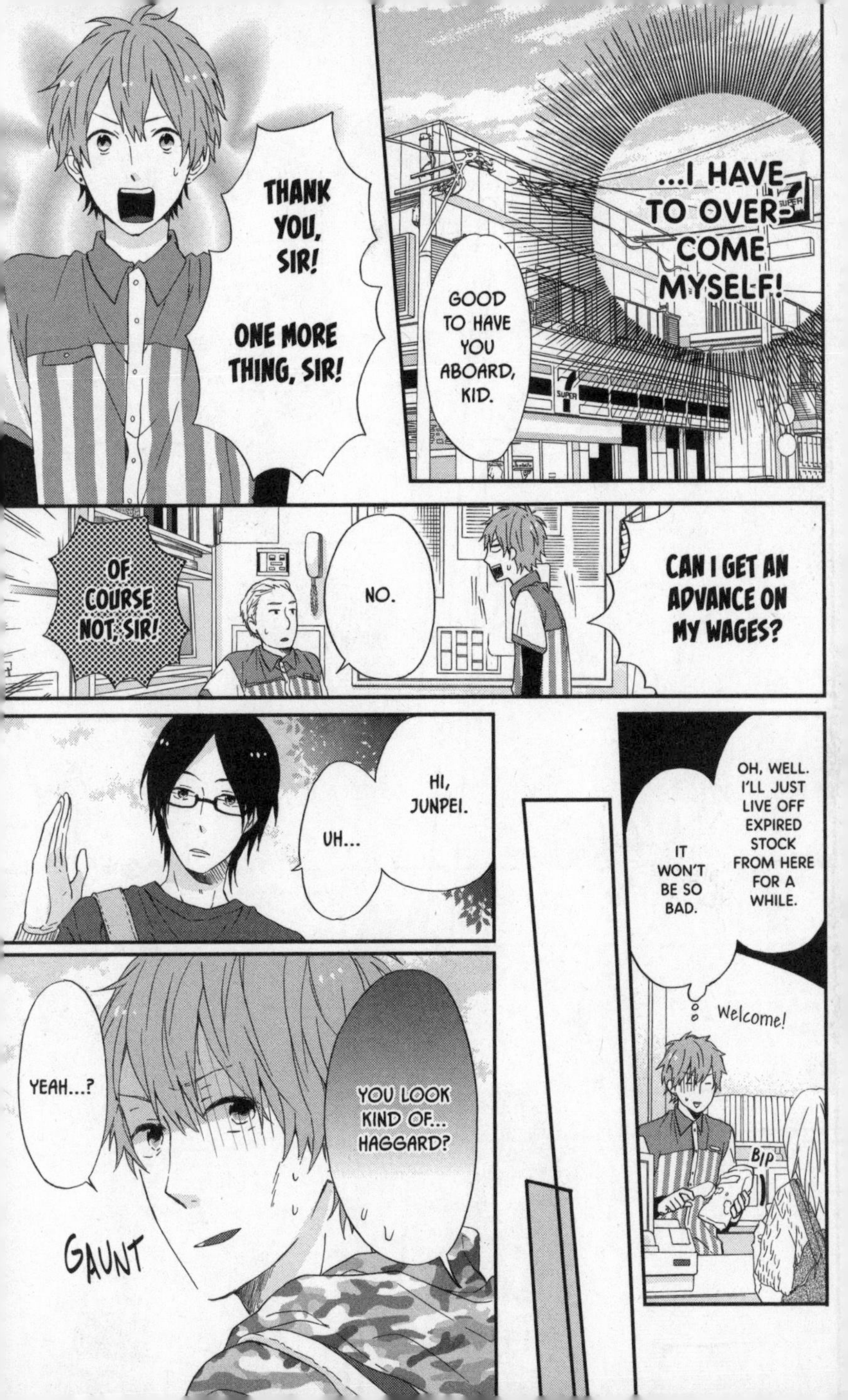
...I HAVE TO OVERCOME MYSELF!
GOOD TO HAVE YOU ABOARD, KID.
THANK YOU, SIR!
ONE MORE THING, SIR!
CAN I GET AN ADVANCE ON MY WAGES?
NO.
OF COURSE NOT, SIR!
OH, WELL. I'LL JUST LIVE OFF EXPIRED STOCK FROM HERE FOR A WHILE.
IT WON'T BE SO BAD.
Welcome!
BIP
HI, JUNPEI.
UH...
YOU LOOK KIND OF... HAGGARD?
YEAH...?
GAUNT

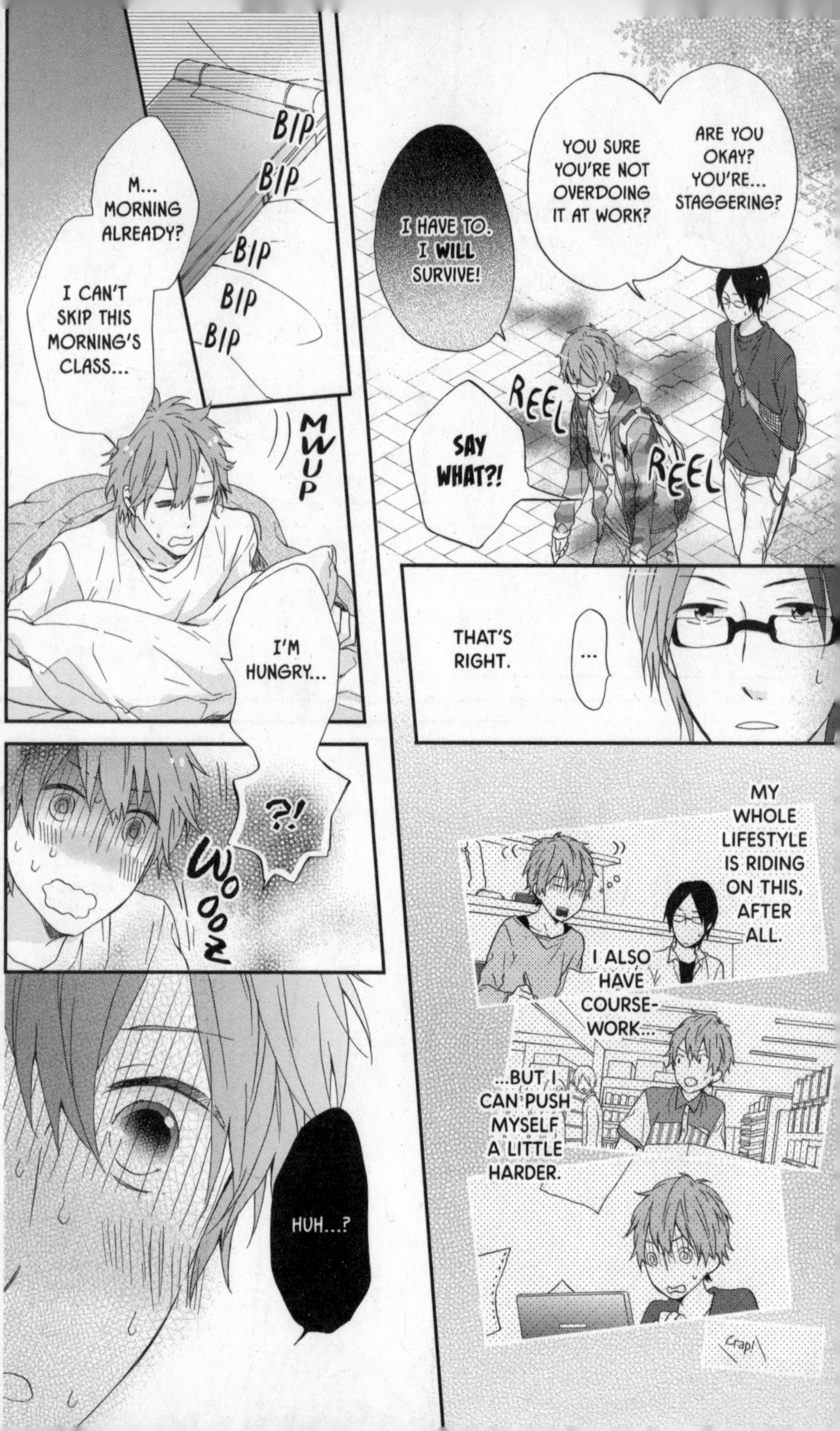
ARE YOU OKAY? YOU'RE... STAGGERING?
YOU SURE YOU'RE NOT OVERDOING IT AT WORK?
I HAVE TO. I WILL SURVIVE!
REEL
SAY WHAT?!
REEL
...
THAT'S RIGHT.
MY WHOLE LIFESTYLE IS RIDING ON THIS, AFTER ALL.
I ALSO HAVE COURSE-WORK...
...BUT I CAN PUSH MYSELF A LITTLE HARDER.
Crap!
BIP BIP
BIP BIP BIP
M... MORNING ALREADY?
I CAN'T SKIP THIS MORNING'S CLASS...
MWUP
I'M HUNGRY...
?!
WOOOZ
HUH...?

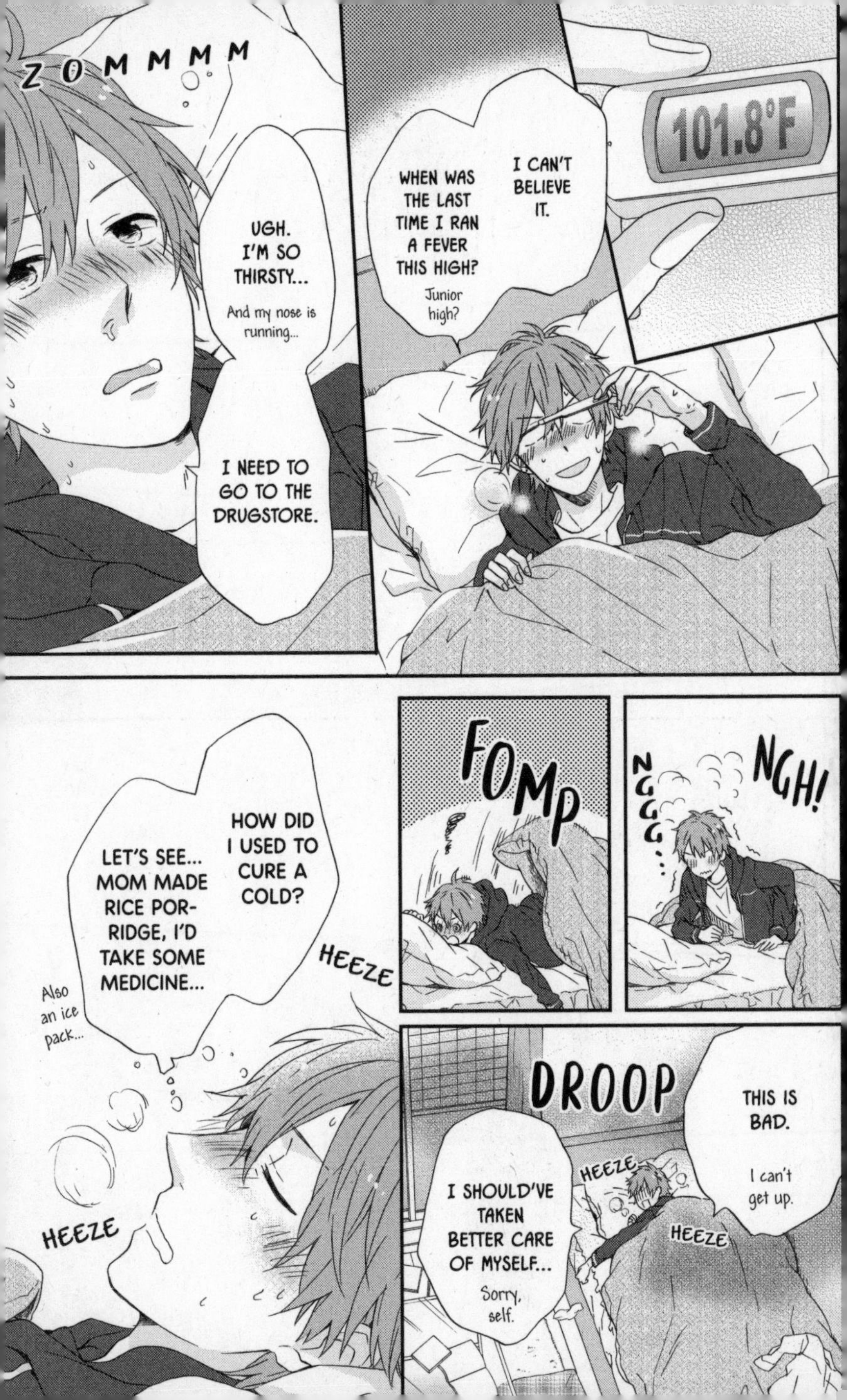
101.8°F
I CAN'T BELIEVE IT.
WHEN WAS THE LAST TIME I RAN A FEVER THIS HIGH?
Junior high?
ZOMMMMM
UGH. I'M SO THIRSTY...
And my nose is running...
I NEED TO GO TO THE DRUGSTORE.
NGH!
NGGG...
FOMP
DROOP
THIS IS BAD.
I can't get up.
HEEZE
HEEZE
I SHOULD'VE TAKEN BETTER CARE OF MYSELF...
Sorry, self.
HOW DID I USED TO CURE A COLD?
LET'S SEE... MOM MADE RICE POR-RIDGE, I'D TAKE SOME MEDICINE...
Also an ice pack...
HEEZE
HEEZE

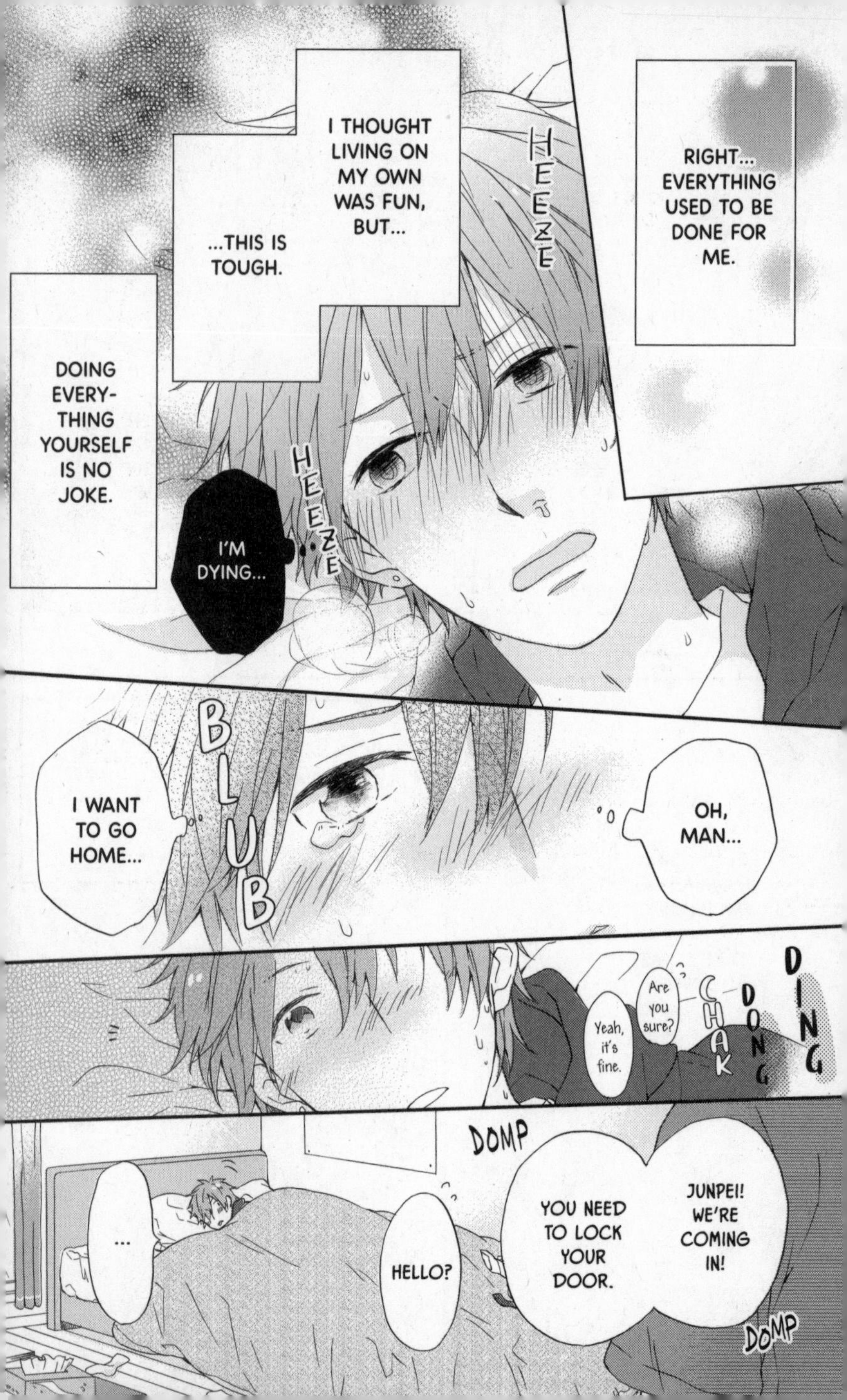
RIGHT... EVERYTHING USED TO BE DONE FOR ME.
I THOUGHT LIVING ON MY OWN WAS FUN, BUT...
HEEZE
...THIS IS TOUGH.
HEEZE
I'M DYING...
DOING EVERY-THING YOURSELF IS NO JOKE.
OH, MAN...
BLUB
I WANT TO GO HOME...
DING
DONG
CHAK
Are you sure?
Yeah, it's fine.
JUNPEI! WE'RE COMING IN!
DOMP
YOU NEED TO LOCK YOUR DOOR.
DOMP
HELLO?
...

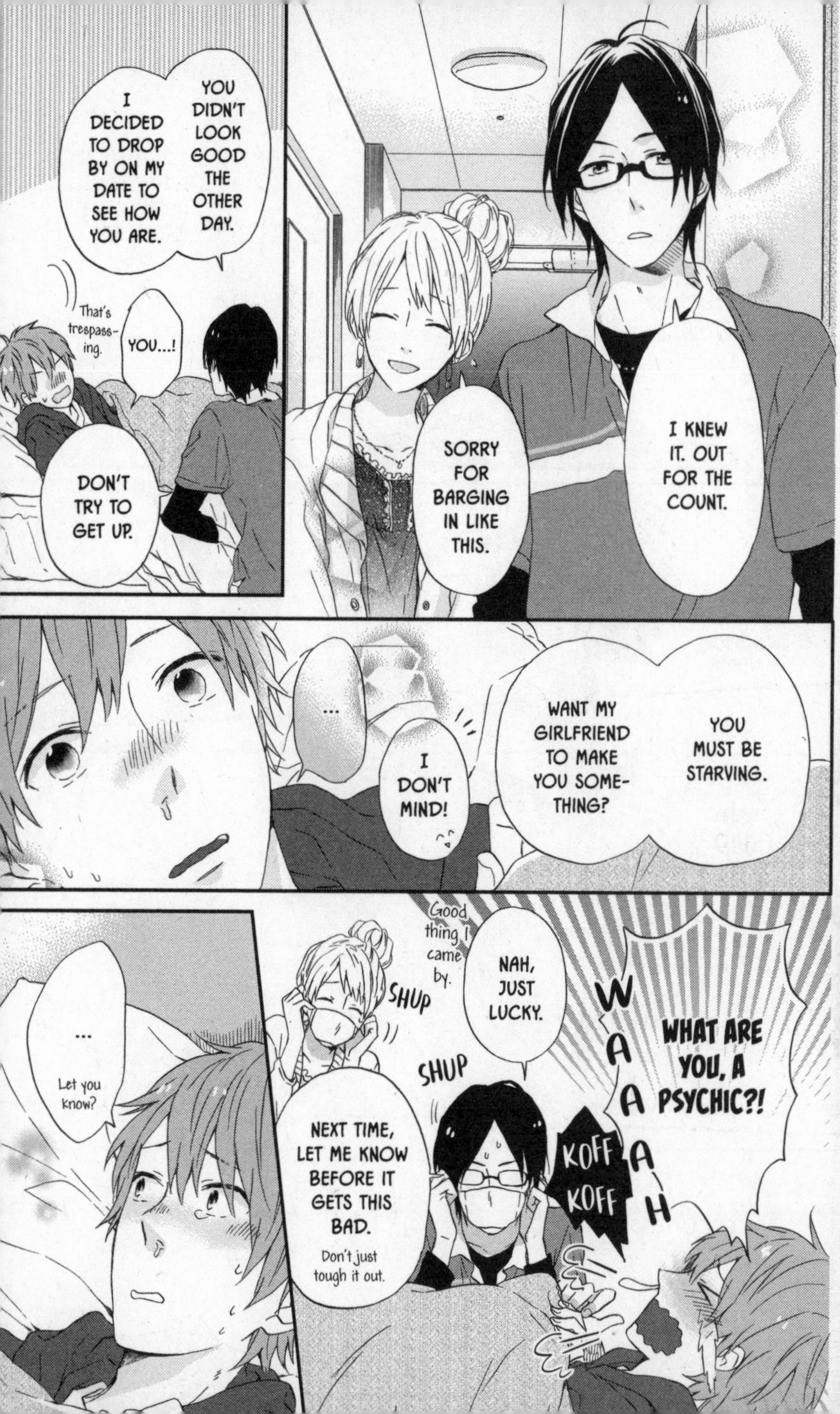
I KNEW IT. OUT FOR THE COUNT.
SORRY FOR BARGING IN LIKE THIS.
YOU DIDN'T LOOK GOOD THE OTHER DAY.
I DECIDED TO DROP BY ON MY DATE TO SEE HOW YOU ARE.
YOU...!
That's trespass-ing.
DON'T TRY TO GET UP.
YOU MUST BE STARVING.
WANT MY GIRLFRIEND TO MAKE YOU SOME-THING?
I DON'T MIND!
...
WHAT ARE YOU, A PSYCHIC?!
WAAAH
KOFF KOFF
NAH, JUST LUCKY.
Good thing I came by.
SHUP
SHUP
NEXT TIME, LET ME KNOW BEFORE IT GETS THIS BAD.
Don't just tough it out.
...
Let you know?

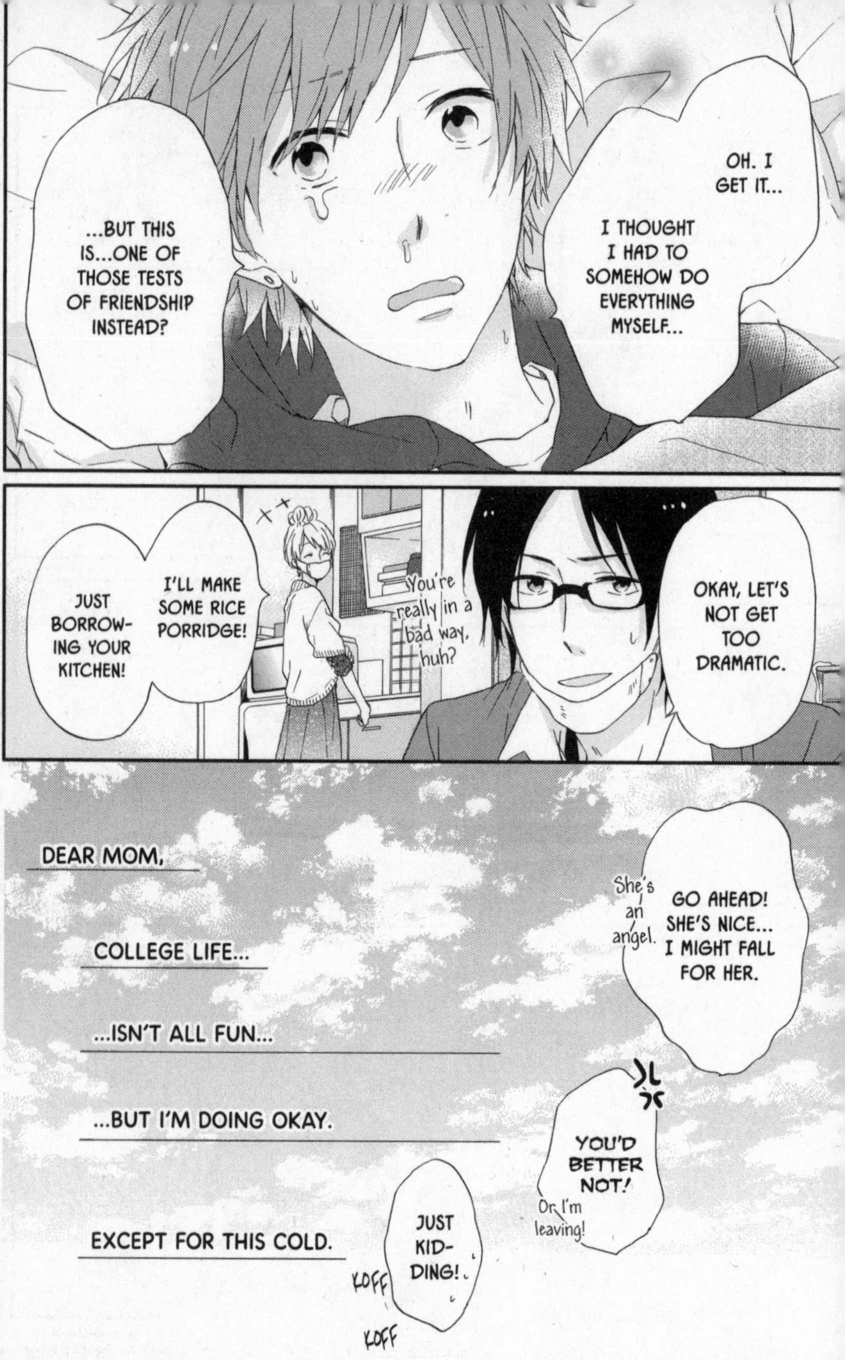
OH. I GET IT...
I THOUGHT I HAD TO SOMEHOW DO EVERYTHING MYSELF...
...BUT THIS IS...ONE OF THOSE TESTS OF FRIENDSHIP INSTEAD?
OKAY, LET'S NOT GET TOO DRAMATIC.
You're really in a bad way, huh?
I'LL MAKE SOME RICE PORRIDGE!
JUST BORROWING YOUR KITCHEN!
GO AHEAD! SHE'S NICE... I MIGHT FALL FOR HER.
She's an angel.
YOU'D BETTER NOT!
Or I'm leaving!
JUST KIDDING!
KOFF
KOFF
DEAR MOM,
COLLEGE LIFE...
...ISN'T ALL FUN...
...BUT I'M DOING OKAY.
EXCEPT FOR THIS COLD.

THE END

# • AFTERWORD •

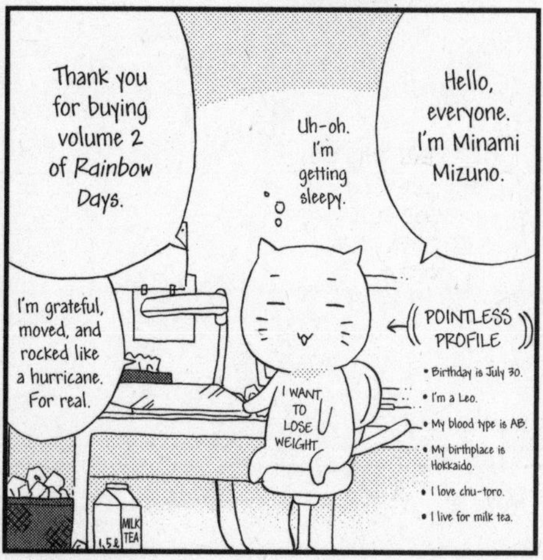
Hello, everyone. I'm Minami Mizuno.
(( POINTLESS PROFILE ))
• Birthday is July 30.
• I'm a Leo.
• My blood type is AB.
• My birthplace is Hokkaido.
• I love chu-toro.
• I live for milk tea.
Uh-oh. I'm getting sleepy.
Thank you for buying volume 2 of *Rainbow Days*.
I'm grateful, moved, and rocked like a hurricane. For real.
I WANT TO LOSE WEIGHT
MILK TEA
1.5ℓ

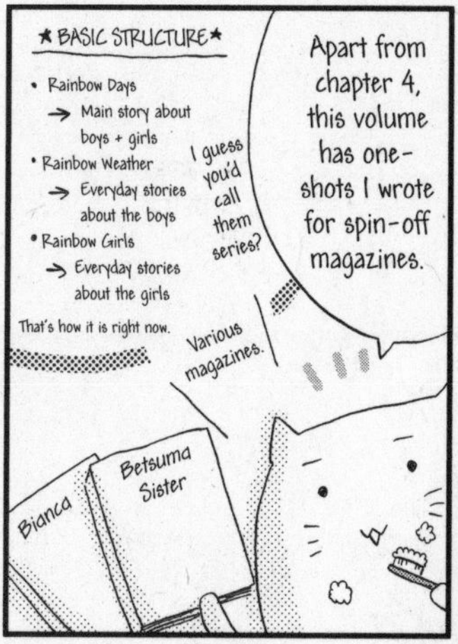
Apart from chapter 4, this volume has one-shots I wrote for spin-off magazines.
I guess you'd call them series?
★ BASIC STRUCTURE ★
• Rainbow Days → Main story about boys + girls
• Rainbow Weather → Everyday stories about the boys
• Rainbow Girls → Everyday stories about the girls
That's how it is right now.
Various magazines.
Betsuma Sister
Bianca

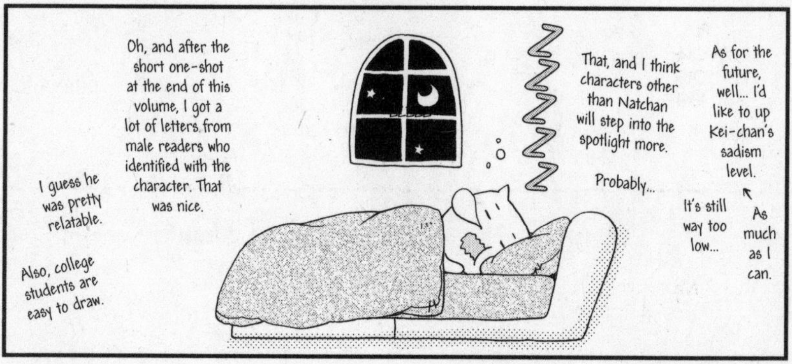
As for the future, well... I'd like to up Kei-chan's sadism level.
As much as I can.
It's still way too low...
That, and I think characters other than Natchan will step into the spotlight more.
Probably...
Oh, and after the short one-shot at the end of this volume, I got a lot of letters from male readers who identified with the character. That was nice.
I guess he was pretty relatable.
Also, college students are easy to draw.

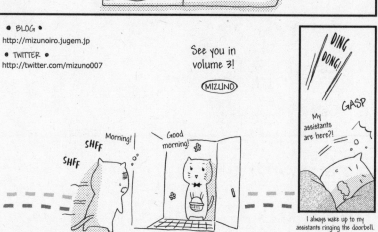

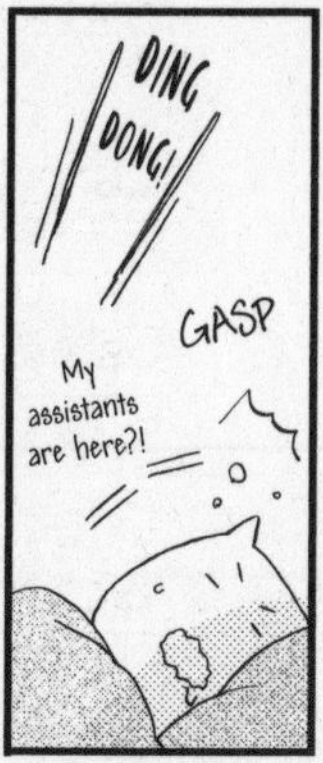
DING DONG!
GASP
My assistants are here?!

I always wake up to my assistants ringing the doorbell.

See you in volume 3!

MIZUNO

• BLOG •
http://mizunoiro.jugem.jp

• TWITTER •
http://twitter.com/mizuno007

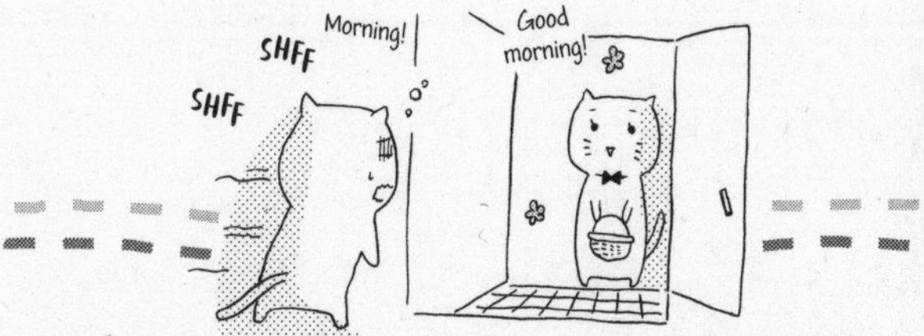
Good morning!
Morning!
SHFF
SHFF

# Special Thanks

Hiromi Okawa-sama
Cozmi-sama
Nanami Koyama-sama
Rui Hase-sama
Erina Matsunaga-sama
Ame Morizuki-sama

kgr-sama
nao-sama
sanarin-sama
Riku-sama

Ayaka T.-sama

My family

Editor: Yabu-sama
Designer: Kawatani-sama

Everyone involved in publishing this book


And everyone who read all the way to the end


Thank you very much!  ヾ(*´∀`*)ﾉ'

When it comes to snacks to go with drinks,
I'm 100 percent in the savory camp. Barley or
sweet potato shochu plus shiokara is an unbeatable
combination. People say I sound like an old man, but
it's really delicious! Incidentally, I can't drink beer.

**Minami Mizuno**

**Minami Mizuno** was born on July 30 in Sapporo, Japan.
She debuted with *Tama ni wa Konna Watashi to Anata*
(We Get like This Sometimes, You and I) in 2006.
*Rainbow Days* was nominated for the 40th Kodansha Manga Award
in 2016, and her subsequent work, *We Don't Know Love Yet*,
was nominated for the 66th Shogakukan Manga Award in 2020.

# Rainbow Days

## Volume 2
### Shojo Beat Edition

Story and Art by
**Minami Mizuno**

TRANSLATION + ADAPTATION **Max Greenway**
TOUCH-UP ART + LETTERING **Inori Fukuda Trant**
DESIGN **Shawn Carrico**
EDITOR **Nancy Thistlethwaite**

NIJIIRO DAYS © 2011 by Minami Mizuno
All rights reserved.
First published in Japan in 2011 by SHUEISHA Inc., Tokyo.
English translation rights arranged by SHUEISHA Inc.

Printed in Canada

Published by VIZ Media, LLC
P.O. Box 77010
San Francisco, CA 94107

10 9 8 7 6 5 4 3 2 1
First printing, February 2023

**PARENTAL ADVISORY**
RAINBOW DAYS is rated T+ for Older Teen
and is recommended for ages 16 and up. This
volume may contain suggestive situations.

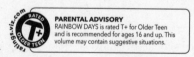

viz.com          shojobeat.com

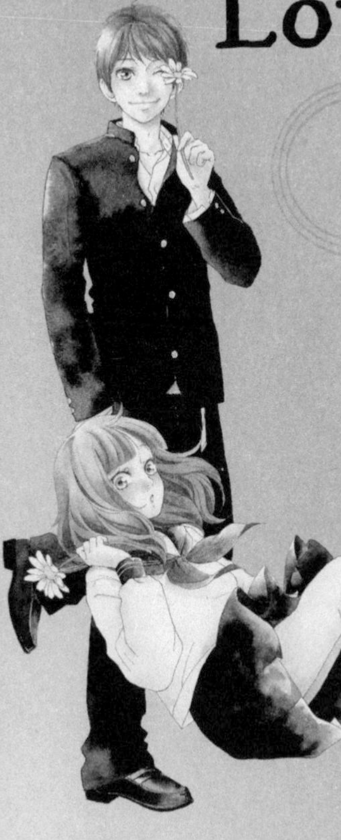
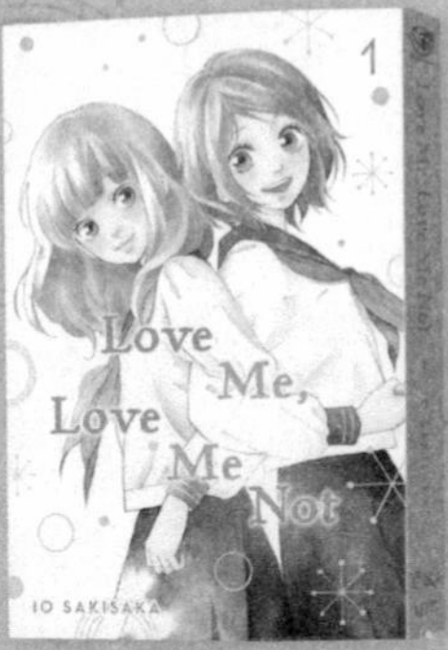
1
Love Me, Love Me Not
IO SAKISAKA
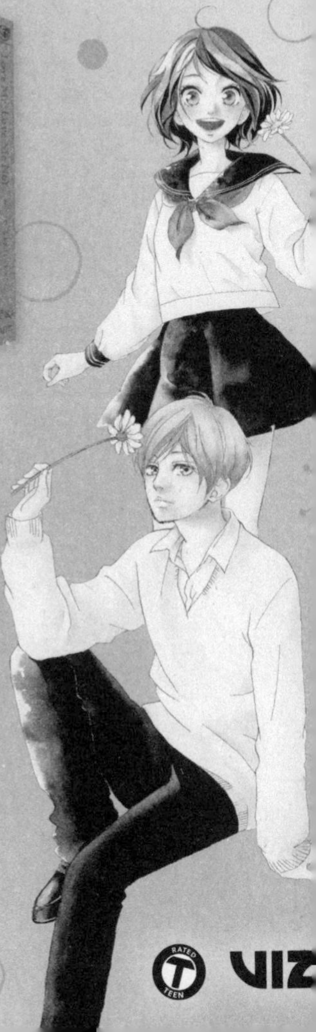

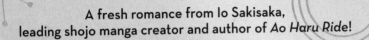

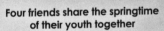

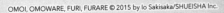

# Stop!

## You may be reading the wrong way.

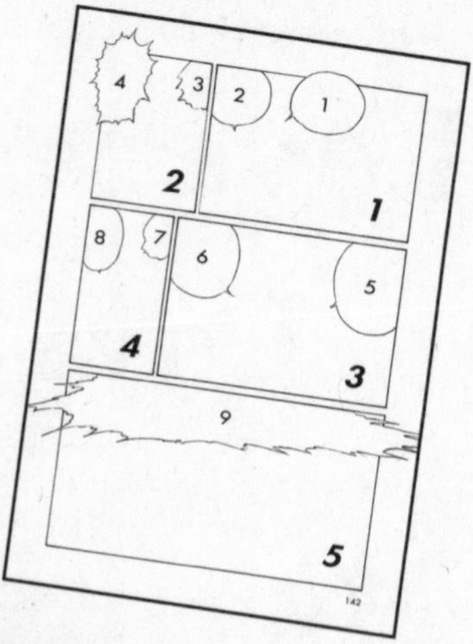
1
2
3
4
5
6
7
8
9
1
2
3
4
5
142

In keeping with the original Japanese comic format, this book reads from right to left—so action, sound effects, and word balloons are completely reversed to preserve the orientation of the original artwork. Check out the diagram shown here to get the hang of things, and then turn to the other side of the book to get started!

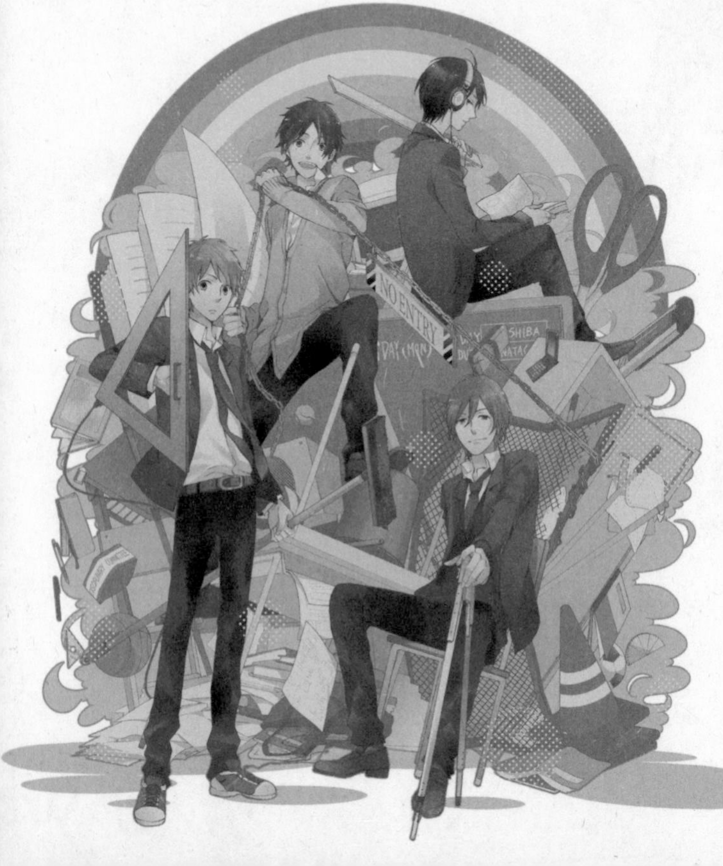
NO ENTRY